the Authentic I-Ching

A NEW TRANSLATION WITH COMMENTARY

BY

HENRY WEI, B.A., WESTERN AND CHINESE LITERATURE,

LINGNAN UNIVERSITY, CANTON

M.A., PH.D., INTERNATIONAL LAW AND HISTORY,

UNIVERSITY OF CHICAGO

Introduction by Prof. Jay G. Williams,
Chairman, Dept. of Religion, Hamilton College

NEWCASTLE PUBLISHING CO., INC.

NORTH HOLLYWOOD, CALIFORNIA

1987

D1082455

Edited by Hank Stine
Cover/Book design by Riley K. Smith

FIRST EDITION

A NEWCASTLE BOOK
First Printing, January 1987
9 8 7 6 5 4 3 2
Printed in the United States of America

CONTENTS

CONTENTS

To the memory of my brother, Wei Tat (1901– 1977), author of An Exposition of the I-Ching *and translator of the entire* Ch'eng Wei Shih Lun (Doctrine of Mere-Consciousness), *by Hsuan Tsang, a Buddhist luminary of the T'ang dynasty.*

INTRODUCTION

SINCE THE LATE nineteenth century many scholars have tried their hand at translating and commenting upon the *I-Ching*. James Legge, who rendered so many classical Chinese works into English, produced a version of the *I-Ching* which was to be standard for decades. More recently, Richard Wilhelm's German translation has been rendered into English by Cary F. Baynes and has become particularly popular. John Blofeld has also offered his very interesting version of the *I-Ching* in English. With these and many other works before us the question must be: Do we need yet one more translation and commentary?

Henry Wei, well-known for his wonderful translation of the *Tao Teh Ching*, proves to us that we do. In fact, until his translation has been read, the reader of English will not realize how much, in other versions, has been missed. Somehow Wei is able to preserve the severe terseness of the text without lapsing into sheer enigma. He makes each Chinese word, so pregnant with metaphorical significance, sing for us.

Moreover, he adds to the translation a commentary full of insights from the Chinese Masters. This work, more than any other on the *I-Ching*, engages us in conversation with the great commentators like Wang Pi and Chu Hsi. For an understanding of the history of Chinese thought this is particularly important, since so many intellectual developments arose from a subtle rereading of the classic texts. Chinese philosophy often revovles around shades of meaning evoked by a particular Chinese character, subtleties not easily appreciated by the ordinary American reader. Wei not only introduces some of these disputes but makes them intelligible to us.

It may be that initially readers will be somewhat put off by one feature of this volume. That is, the author has a strong tendency to repeat and defend classic historical attributions rather than rely upon more critical modern scholarship. I was, myself, at first critical of his attempts to justify the historicity of such shadowy figures as Fu Hsi. Further consideration, however, has led me to a more positive assessment of his traditional account. At the very least one must say that to understand the "feel" of the book as it was known in traditional China, one must begin with a sense of the work's enormous antiquity. Traditional attribution of the Wings to Confucius himself also provides an important link to the great Master and his tradition.

Skeptical scholarship, of course, always finds it easy to raise question-marks about such traditional attributions. "I doubt it" is not only a facile remark; it is also fashionable. To the nonbeliever, it doesn't make any difference anyway. It is by no means clear, however, that such skepticism is fully warranted or that it actually helps very much. What it does do is destroy the "feel" of the work by making it appear more a forgery and less an authentic piece of literature.

That seems to me to be unfortunate, for the I-Ching surely does not deserve such designation. Therefore, I have come around to the traditional approach of the author. After all, if the trigrams were not discovered by Fu Hsi, they may well have been uncovered by someone else with the same name! What is important is not the name Fu Hsi but the sense that the work finds its origins in the mists of greatest antiquity. The I-Ching, in presenting a chorus of voices from antiquity, illustrates, perhaps better than any other book, the great unity of humankind.

Together, human beings of every age stand before the great mystery, the mystery of existence itself. Together we wrestle with all those gross and subtle transformations which make life so disquieting and gratifying. The I-Ching demonstrates that although many things in the world have changed dramatically—we moderns love to pride ourselves about that—in fact the essential transformations of life remain forever the same. Those trigrams discovered by some Neolithic Fu Hsi are as revelatory in our day as they were in his.

It was Rudyard Kipling who expressed so eloquently our prejudice that "East is East and West is West and ne'er the twain shall meet." The *I-Ching* proves how false this is. Modern Americans seem to have little or nothing in common with traditional Chinese Confucians. Who could imagine the formally robed Mandarin and the blue-jeaned Westerner having much to share at all? Nevertheless, *I-Ching* speaks very clearly to each, revealing that, at the root of the self, there appears one common nature. As Confucius once said:

> In our natures we approximate one another; habits put
> us further and further apart. (*Sayings* XII.2)

The *I-Ching* calls us to return from our divisive habits to our common nature, and in so doing affirms once more the mystery and the glory of our humanity. If this volume helps us to do that—and I know that it does—it has more than fulfilled its task.

THE I-CHING AND DIVINATION

The one aspect of the *I-Ching* that most often brings readers to peruse its pages is its reputed power as an oracle. But can the *I-Ching* predict? Can it be legitimately used to foretell the future? Is not the *I-Ching* after all only an antiquated curiosity which once permeated the whole of Chinese intellectual life, but which the world can now see through and eliminate?

To answer this question we must begin by looking more carefully at the nature of the *I-Ching*'s prognostications. Unlike many other oracles (including the election projection computer), the *I-Ching* seldom gives a yes-or-no answer to a given question, nor does it predict specific results. Rather what it offers is a symbolic picture of a situation or set of situations which the inquirer is called upon to interpret for him or herself. In other words, the "answer" of the *I-Ching* marks the initiation of a dialectic, a curious conversation between the inquirer and the symbols. In this dialectic the inquirer is forced to consider many aspects of the problem, aspects which may or may not have been thought of before.

Thus, the *I-Ching* is like a mirror which allows the inquirer to see the situation and the self more clearly and reflectively. As in the Rorshach test used by psychologists, the results of the inquiry reveal more about the person asking the question than about the future per se. That is, the *I-Ching* is a device for self-knowledge.

So then why is it necessary to engage in all those complicated manipulations to get the "right" answer? If the *I-Ching* is only a mirror, wouldn't it be just as profitable merely to open the book "at random" and look at the first hexagram that appears? Isn't all the rest—the parting of the yarrow stalks and the painfully slow construction of the hexagram—irrelevant?

A partial answer to this question is that self-reflection is itself a painfully slow and difficult process. Preparation for self-aware-ness ought not to be hurried or abrupt. The process prescribed for consulting the *I-Ching* promotes a quiet seriousness appropriate for genuine inquiry. Only those people who don't much care about the question asked would feel satisfied by a random open-ing of the book. The length of the process prompted by the num-ber of manipulations necessary to identify even one line of the hexagram gives time for the human mind to focus upon the ques-tion raised and to explore, albeit subconsciously, its dimensions. This is why the parting of yarrow stalks is superior to the alterna-tive and very popular method of casting coins.

Having said all this, however, an important problem for the Western mind still remains, for the *I-Ching* still asserts that the results of this lengthy process are not random or arbitrary. If procedures have been followed correctly, the hexagram(s) arrived at are regarded as somehow also correct. What looks to be a ran-dom process is not. The results reflect the true situation.

Before we address this problem directly, it may be best to take a backward glance at our own intellectual history, for it is this his-tory which defines the problem for us. There was a time, not so many centuries ago, when scientists emphasized almost exclu-sively final causes and, at the same time, eschewed any belief in randomness. For Aristoteleans there are no random events be-cause all motion is explicable in terms of the Unmoved Mover, that great, divine magnet who draws all things to Him(It)self.

Modern science began with a revolt against such teleology. Efficient causation replaced final causation as the primary explicative paradigm. Final causes were bracketed as inappropriate for scientific investigation. Gradually the brackets were replaced by deletions. Science no longer asked "why?" Neither should anyone else.

Along with this scientific dismissal of the final cause came the development of a mind-body dualism by the famous French philosopher, René Descartes. Descartes asserted the existence of two kinds of substance: thinking substance and extended substance. The former is what I know when I am self-conscious. (*Je pense, donc je suis.*) The latter is the macrocosmic world of space and time. For Descartes these two worlds, so radically different in nature, were only connected by animal spirits through the pineal gland.

Although many have attacked Descartes' specific philosophic proposals, nevertheless he set the Western philosophic agenda from that time to this. Philosophers have worried ever since about how the mind and the world can possibly be related. The result has been a world-view in which the world can only affect the mind through the body *and* vice versa. Moreover, final causes—purposes—may be attributed to mind, but not to the macrocosm. The world, itself, is random, purposeless, valueless.

There is, however, something peculiar about this view of reality. In the first place, the world and consciousness are obviously not dual opposites, for the world *as we know it* is the contents of consciousness. The world is what we are conscious of. If there were no world, consciousness would "collapse." If there were no consciousness, the world would "collapse." Moreover, insofar as we are aware of ourselves, we are a part of that world which Descartes says we stand over against. I exist in the world; I am *of* the world.

Second, the world of which I am is a construct. As David Hume and Immanuel Kant and a host of other philosophers have demonstrated, what we call the world is a result of the interaction of our "minds"—whatever they may be—and an unknown "somewhat" which produces in us sensations of color and sound, etc., structured in a spatial-temporal matrix. This structured cosmos is surrounded, as it were, by mystery. How that unconscious mind upon which consciousness floats relates to that unknown world which is the source of our sensations is an enigma.

Because we do not know, however, does not mean that there is no connection. Indeed, it would seem more reasonable to believe that the unknown mystery called by Jungians the unconscious is part and parcel of that unknown mystery which is the source of the world. After all, consciousness, as known, is a part of the sensed world.

All of this is a complicated way of saying that we do not really know what interconnections exist within the universe. The fact that my ordinary way of affecting the world is through bodily action does not mean that this is the only way. Our own Western philosophical prejudices should not blind us to new (or ancient) possibilities, particularly when those prejudices are so obviously suspect.

When we part yarrow stalks or cast coins or shuffle cards, we do not know why our bodies act exactly as they do. As a consequence we call the results random. The word random, however, is an admission of our lack of knowledge, not necessarily a description of the way things really are. In sexual intercourse many sperm are released. We do not know why the egg usually allows only one sperm to penetrate, thus causing a particular conception. Therefore, we call the result random. If it is random, however, then every person is merely a result of chance, a mere fluke. Meaning evaporates from human life.

The question is ultimately not whether the results of the *I-Ching* are random and hence meaningless, but whether *all* events are random. Because all events are in one way or another interrelated, if any event is random, then all events participate in randomness; and if randomness indicates meaninglessness, then all existence is meaningless.

The *I-Ching* takes a radically different approach, for it assumes that the individual is a part of the universe. Therefore, whatever meanings and purposes are found on a microcosmic level have their counterparts and analogies on the macrocosmic level too. Meaning is not a human invention, it pervades the universe.

Just as certain external signs—skin color, pulse, vigor—tell us much about internal health, so external signs may tell us also of the macrocosm. Parting yarrow stalks is like taking the pulse of the universe. A careful reading can tell much about what is going on in the unknowable world.

Such a position, however, cannot be arrived at abstractly; it is learned through experience. Faith in the prognostic abilities of the *I* comes not from theorizing but from faithful use. My own experience—which flies in the face of all my common sense—is that the *I-Ching* consistently speaks directly to questions asked. The number of obvious "hits" simply far exceeds any probability based upon the assumption of randomness. Such a conclusion, however, cannot be demonstrated *ex cathedra*. The only way to experience the uncanny wisdom of the *I-Ching* is to use it.

Jay G. Williams
Chairman, Dept. of Religion,
Hamilton College

October 1986

PREFACE

THE PURPOSE OF this work is to present a better translation of the *I-Ching*, or *Book of Changes*, and a more cogent commentary on its teachings, so as to bring out its intrinsic merits. There is no claim that this purpose has been successfully fulfilled, but great definite efforts have been made to do so.

How I began to take a keen interest in the study of the *I-Ching* was the offspring of unforeseen and encouraging circumstances. It happened that in the 1960's there occurred in the United States a rising tide of interest in Eastern philosophy and metaphysics. As a result, the *I-Ching* and the *Tao Teh Ching*, two ancient and time-honored classics noted for their mystic and mysterious nature, enjoyed a wide appeal and aroused considerable curiosity. This rather unexpected turn of events was a great and pleasant surprise to me and could not but induce me, after studying international relations for many years, to revive my interest in a literature and philosophy which were my subjects of study while at college in China. Naturally, my major attention had been devoted to the two classics.

Until 1965, there were but two English translations of the *I-Ching*: one by the English scholar and Sinologue, James Legge, published in 1882; the other by Cary Baynes, a tranlsation of the German version by scholar and Sinologue Richard Wilhelm, which first appeared in 1950.

In 1965, an English scholar, John Blofeld, also put out a translation of the *I-Ching*, but one greatly limited in scope. In the introduction to his translation, Blofeld levied a scathing criticism of Baynes' translation, citing a number of instances from her work to substantiate his criticism.[1] This led me to the reading of Baynes' translation. Before long, I became convinced that Blofeld's criticism was well founded.

One thing led to another: later, I also waded through Legge's translation and commentary. I admired his scholarship, but soon realized that his attitude toward the *I-Ching* was highly critical and negative, and his translation somewhat involved and consequently difficult to grasp, especially for beginners. The following examples may be taken as typical specimens of his translation, which usually contain explanatory phrases inside brackets:

> Pi indicates that (under the conditions which it sup-poses) there is good fortune. But let (the principal party intended in it) re-examine himself, (as if by divination, whether his virtue be great, unintermitting, and firm.

> Kan gives the intimation of ease and development. When (the time of) movement (which it indicates) comes, (the subject of the hexagram) will be found look-ing out with apprehension, and yet smiling and talking cheerfully. When the movement (like a crash of thun-der) terrifies all within a hundred li, he will be (like the sincere worshipper who is not startled into) letting go his ladle and (cup of) sacrificial spirits.

I have a strong feeling that his generally involved translation was intentional. Probably he wanted to make the *I-Ching* appear difficult to understand and translate. His commentary is written in a different style: it is much more readable, being precise and lucid. But often it tends to be brief in treatment and is far from being complete in scope. A glaring instance of this is that he en-tirely ignores the meaning of the first sentence of the ancient clas-sic, which is a very important sentence setting forth the four attributes of Ch'ien, the creative principle. Apart from saying that the four attributes may be reduced to two, he says hardly anything else about them.[2]

Both Legge and Wilhelm did not attach any importance to the subject of divination. Legge considered all divination "vain" and "absurd"[3] and devoted only a few lines to the subject in the in-troduction to his translation.[4] Wilhelm's account of divination is also short and sketchy and is placed at the very end of his fat volume, as if it were thrown in at the last moment on second thought.

But divination has a close connection with the Text of the *I-Ching* and Confucius' comments on it. Blofeld gives much greater attention to divination in his work and even criticizes Jung's theory of divination.[5] However, a correct interpretation of an oracle requires a correct understanding and translation of the Text and the comments. In this respect, Blofeld's work leaves something to be desired.

For instance, in King Wen's Judgment (called "Text" by Blofeld) on the 2nd Hexagram, K'un, there is a sentence which may be transliterated thus: "Hsien mi, hou te chu." The word "hsien" here means "to lead" or "to take the initiative," and the word "hou" means "to follow" or "to follow suit." The correct translation of the sentence should be: "If one tries to lead, he will get lost; if he would be a follower, he will find his master." This interpretation is found in the Chinese commentaries and has been followed by both Legge and Wilhelm. To Blofeld, however, the word "hsien" means "at first," and the word "hou" means "later," and he translates the sentence as: "At first he goes astray, but later finds his bearings."[6]

As another instance, one may refer to a sentence in the 20th Hexagram, Kuan. The sentence appears in Confucius' explanation of King Wen's Judgment (called "commentary on the text" in Blofeld's work) and runs thus: "Chung cheng i kuan t'ien hsia." The word "kuan" here means "for others to see or contemplate," and the whole sentence should be translated thus: "Central and correct, they are shown for the world to contemplate." To Blofeld, the word "kuan" means "to look at, or look upon," and the sentence is translated as follows: "(The fifth line) is correctly centered for looking down upon the world."[7]

This and other similar examples from Blofeld show that translation of the *I-Ching* can be a very slippery affair. If the translation is at fault, the accompanying comments cannot serve as a sound basis for understanding or divination.

In 1971 Wei Tat, a well-known scholar in Hong Kong, published a work entitled *An Exposition of the I-Ching*. As his brother I am inclined to disqualify myself from passing judgment on his work;

however, it is perhaps proper for me to point out that it represents a conscientious attempt to elucidate the significant features of the *I-Ching* and to propound the philosophy underlying the two key hexagrams, Ch'ien and K'un. He was not much interested in divination but was rather enamored of what he called the metaphysical truths embodied in the classic. A unique feature of his work is the interpretation of the lines of the two hexagrams according to the principle of "analogy and correspondence," aiming at showing that the 384 lines of the 64 Hexagrams are interrelated, and that consequently all human situations and natural phenomena represented by the lines are also interrelated. Such an interpretation is an elaborate and toilsome process. Rather technical in this respect, his work seems to be for advanced students of the *I-Ching*, though perhaps he did not intend it to be so. In the course of his study, he collected numerous Chinese commentaries on the classic; after he passed into the Great Beyond in 1977, that vast collection of commentaries, together with his many other books, was donated to the City Library of Hong Kong for use by other scholars. In the preparation of my work, I availed myself of quite a number of his findings concerning the symbolism and philosophy of the *I-Ching*.

I first read the *I-Ching* in Chinese, the version by the philosopher Chu Hsi. Later I compared it with other versions, including some by contemporary scholars written in mingled classical and colloquial Chinese. To be frank, I did not fall in love with the book on the first reading. Like Legge, I was bewildered by the confusing arrangement of the first and most important hexagram, Ch'ien. Then there were the laconic judgments on the many hexagrams by King Wen, couched in archaic terminology and clumsy syntax. They appeared to me rather dull and dry.

I was, however, encouraged and inspired by the various comments usually attributed to Confucius. They led me on and on in my reading. The Duke of Chou's interpretations of the lines of the hexagrams also appealed to me as very interesting and instructive. They constantly refer to the reversals of fortune: how ill fortune changes into good and vice versa; or to the evolution of fortune: how a good or ill fortune unfolds from a small beginning to a climax and then begins to change again in a different direction.

Not infrequently the illustrations or symbolisms are very cleverly thought out. There is a wealth of quiet humor and subtle irony in them. They also radiate wisdom. They strongly support what Lao Tzu has said in the *Tao Teh Ching*: "Misfortune is what fortune leans on. Fortune is where misfortune conceals itself."

Furthermore, the *Ta Chuan*, or *Great Treatise*, and to a lesser extent, the *Shuo Kua*, or *Remarks on Trigrams*, struck a responsive and sympathetic chord in my heart. These works are traditionally attributed to Confucius. They abound in noble and inspirational ideas expressed with great literary beauty and in a grand and pontifical style. One does not need to read them twice or between the lines to feel the high moral tone, the mystic flavor and enigmatic mystery.

Thus the *I-Ching* gradually revealed its charm and wisdom and mystery to me. But all along I had no inclination or desire to translate it or to do a commentary on it, since I was well aware of the vast amount of time and labor needed and rather doubtful of my own capacities for the task. Later, however, after reading some English works on the subject and pursuing some further study, I grew by degrees less diffident and more foolhardy, rushing in where more sapient scholars hesitated to tread.

In tackling the gigantic task, my first care was to ascertain the meaning of the passages to be translated. My next was to put them in straighforward English. My purpose was to present a translation that is both faithful to the original and intelligible to general readers. This turned out to be not as simple and easy as it sounds.

Usually I tried to benefit by the Chinese commentaries available to me, but I did not always feel satisfied with the interpretations found in them. In such cases I could only make bold to use my own judgment. Two notable instances of this kind were in connection with the two words "yung chiu" (lit., "use nine") at the end of the Ch'ien Hexagram, and "yung liu" (lit., "use six") at the end of the K'un Hexagram. I considered at least four interpretations from the Chinese commentaries concerning those two little expressions,[8] but none of them sounded convincing to me. So I ventured to set forth an interpretation of my own, for whatever it may be worth.

I count it extremely fortunate that in the course of my research I came upon some diagrams which are highly enlightening and fascinating. The one most worthy of special mention is Leibniz' diagram of his binary system in relation to a diagram of the 64 Hexagrams devised by Shao Yung, a noted philosopher of the Sung dynasty. There are several other diagrams relating to various subjects, most of which have never before appeared in other English works on the *I-Ching*.

Now I should like to discuss the arrangement of my translation, and that of the ordinary Chinese version of the classic. In the latter version, five of the Ten Wings, or Appendixes (*Shih I*), are interspersed with the Text so that the works of all four authors are brought into juxtaposition. The four authors are: Fu Hsi, a legendary sage-ruler; King Wen, father of the Chou dynasty; his son, the Duke of Chou; and Confucius, the great sage. The five Wings related to the Text are: the First and Second Wings, consisting of Confucius' explanations of King Wen's judgments on the integral hexagrams; the Third and Fourth Wings, consisting of Confucius' comments on the Duke's explanations of the individual lines of the hexagrams; and the Seventh Wing, called *Wen Yen* (lit., "Comment on the Words") and consisting of Confucius' extended comments on the text of the first two hexagrams. Apart from this extra Seventh Wing, the account of each of the first two hexagrams is arranged very much like that of each of the remaining sixty-two. The arrangement of each account is in the following order: (1) the figure of the hexagram, traditionally ascribed to Fu Hsi; (2) *T'uan*, or King Wen's judgment on the hexagram; (3) *T'uan Tzu*, or Confucius' explanation of the *T'uan*; (4) *Tah Hsiang Chuan*, or Confucius' explanation of the Major Symbolism, (i.e., the symbolic significance of the whole hexagram); (5) *Yao Tzu*, or the Duke's explanation of the individual lines; and (6) *Hsiao Hsiang Chuan*, or Confucius' comment on the Duke's explanation (Minor Symbolism). The names of the four authors, however, are not shown in the arrangement.

This anonymity has misled many people into thinking that the *I-Ching* is the work of a single author. Legge was probably misled in this way at first, and this misunderstanding caused him considerable difficulty. The point is that the language of the Text is rather archaic, while that of the Wings is not without literary beauty and in some cases may be considered quite modern. Besides, the Wings are much richer in content. With his keen discrimination and delicate literary taste, Legge must have quickly discerned the great difference. How could the work of one author display such difference in style and content? At first, he must have felt greatly perplexed. Later he discovered the various authorships and claimed that he had solved the mystery of the *I-Ching*. Then he strongly contended that the Wings should be separated from the Text, and considered such separation the clue to the solution of the mystery.[9]

In my work, therefore, I consider it necessary and desirable to make clear and distinct the authorships of the various parts which constitute the account of each hexagram. For this purpose, instead of using the Chinese terms or their translations to mark off the various parts, I simply use (1) name of the hexagram; (2) King Wen's judgment on the hexagram; (3) Confucius' explanation of King Wen's judgment; (4) Symbolic significance as noted by Confucius; (5) Duke of Chou's explanation of the individual lines; and (6) Confucius' comment on the Duke's explanation.

As has been noted, the first two hexagrams each have an extra section called *Wen Yen*. Instead of using this term or its translation, I simply use "Confucius' extended comment on the text." This method of arrangement will, I think, prove convenient and useful to the reader.

Further, it may be well to point out that in the Chinese text, Line 1 (bottom line) of a hexagram is called "ch'u" (initial, or beginning), and Line 6 (top line) is called "shang" (top, or upper). Also, Yang is denoted by the numeral 9 ("chiu"), and Yin by the numeral 6 ("liu"). Thus "ch'u chiu" means Line 1, Yang; "shang liu" means Line 6, Yin. Lines 2, 3, 4, 5 are respectively denoted by the Chinese numerals for "erh, san, ssu, wu." Thus Line 2, Yin, is called "liu erh"; Line 3, Yang, is called "chiu san"; and so on. In my work I do not follow this denotation: I simply use "Line 1, Yin (or Yang); Line 2, Yang (or Yin)," and so on. All this is for the sake of easier reading and comprehension. There is little sense in following any traditional mechanical pattern if it turns out to be a hindrance rather than a help.

This work on the *I-Ching* covers only the Text and the five Wings, (Appendixes) directly related to it. The remaining five Wings, including the *Ta Chuan*, or *Great Treatise*, will be published as a separate volume.

Before concluding, I should like to express my thanks to Prof. Jay G. Williams, a noted scholar in the field of religion and philosophy, for the introduction which he graciously undertook to write for my book. I also wish to express my indebtedness to Mr. Alfred Saunders, President of Newcastle Publishing Company, for his deep interest in my work, and to Mr. Hank Stine, my editor, for his careful editing of the manuscript and his many suggestions and corrections conducive to its improvement. Last, I must not forget to thank my friend Dr. Chang Chung-yuan, Professor emeritus of the University of Hawaii, for lending me some books for reference.

Needless to say, the author himself is responsible for any defect or deficiency that may be found in his work. There is no claim here that the work is perfect and flawless. It is entirely possible that in time some scholar or scholars may feel dissatisfied with the present volume and may produce another translation and commentary that will do even fuller justice to the intrinsic virtue of the glorious *I-Ching*.

By its very nature, this work has exacted considerable study, time, and patient labor in its preparation and publication.

However, if it can in any way contribute to a deeper and better understanding of the inherent virtue of the glorious *I-Ching*, all the efforts that have been invested in it will not be regarded as having been in vain.

Needless to say, the author himself is responsible for any misstatements and misinterpretations that may be found in his work.

Henry Wei

San Francisco
1986

HOW TO USE THE *I-CHING*

THE TRADITIONAL Chinese method of consulting the *I-Ching* for divination is with the use of yarrow stalks, the manipulation of which allows time for concentration and meditation on the question to be asked as the hexagram is laboriously constructed. This method is described in detail in Part I of this volume.

However, today's readers do not always have the time or inclination for such a drawn-out procedure, and there are other, quicker ways of using the *I-Ching* which are just as effective in the long run. Today, in the West as well as in China, the most popular method is the tossing of coins. All you need is three identical coins of any denomination, which are tossed six times. The first toss gives you the *bottom* or *first* line of the first trigram. The second toss will give you the second line, which is placed *above* the first. All the lines are built from the *bottom up*. Thus, when you have completed three tosses, you have constructed your first trigram. Three more tosses will give you your second trigram, on top of the first. Together, these two trigrams form a hexagram.

The coins equate to the individual lines in the hexagram as follows:

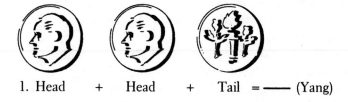

1. Head   +   Head   +   Tail   = ⸺ (Yang)

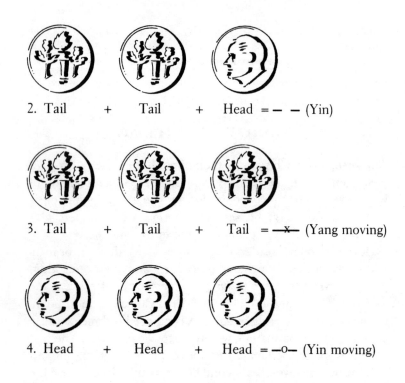

2. Tail   +   Tail   +   Head = — — (Yin)

3. Tail   +   Tail   +   Tail = —x— (Yang moving)

4. Head   +   Head   +   Head = —o— (Yin moving)

Some practitioners may prefer to have two tails and one head equal Yang, etc.; any arrangement may be utilized, so long as all possible combinations are assigned a value.

Complications arise with the last two categories above, which produce so-called "moving lines" or "changing lines." These are lines which change from Yang to Yin or vice versa. For example, say you throw the coins six times and come up with the following hexagram: ☰☷ Line 6 is a moving line (Yang changed to Yin); therefore, the hexagram is changed to this new one: ☷☷ *Both* hexagrams must now be taken into account in determining the outcome of the situation in question. The same thing applies to any Yin lines which are changed to Yang.

When you have constructed all six lines (two trigrams), you will have the hexagram(s) which is/are pertinent to your question.

Then, merely turn to that/those hexagram(s) in Part II of this book and read the interpretations of the trigrams, the hexagrams themselves, and the individual lines. It is up to you to determine how their meanings apply to your situation. More general advice on interpretation can be found in Part I of this book.

The meanings and their application to you will never be immediately clear, for each hexagram has layer upon layer of meaning, but a little conscientious study and concentration on the problem will usually result in some exceedingly beneficial insights and revelations. The more you apply your intuition to the advice of the *I-Ching*, the more it will have to say to you. Good luck!

PART I
A KEY TO THE MYSTERY

Chapter 1

THE TRIGRAMS: THEIR GENESIS AND MEANING

THE *I-CHING*, unlike other books, began in symbols—in trigrams (a figure with three horizontal lines) and hexagrams (a figure with six horizontal lines). These figures form the basic structure or skeleton of this mysterious classic. Its written text and the comments on that text came much later.

Throughout Chinese history it was generally agreed that Fu Hsi, a legendary sage-ruler of China in misty antiquity, drew the Eight Trigrams. Under what circumstances was Fu Hsi supposed to have drawn these trigrams? In the *Ta Chuan* (*Great Treatise*), an important Wing (Appendix) of the *I-Ching*, there is a revealing passage which may be translated as follows:

> In remote antiquity, when the world was under his rule, Pao Hsi (Fu Hsi) upon looking up contemplated the signs in the heavens and upon looking down contemplated the ways and processes of the earth. He noted the fine designs in birds and beasts and the varied qualities of the soil. He derived knowledge from his own person near at hand and from objects far away. He then began to devise the Eight Trigrams so as to set forth the virtues of the divine spirits and to simulate the conditions of the myriad things.[1]

In Fu Hsi's time there was as yet no written language in China. So, in attempting any composition, he could not go to a library to gather data and information as we do. He could obtain useful data only from his environment, nature, and the human scene. As he was apparently an intelligent and intuitive person, he learned a great deal from surveying the world and contemplating the heavens before he devised the Eight Trigrams.

There are two other passages in the *Great Treatise* relating to the genesis of the trigrams. The following one is especially noteworthy:

> In the *I* system, there is the T'ai Chi (Supreme Ultimate), which produces the Two Primal Forms. The Two Primal Forms produce the Four Emblems. The Four Emblems produce the Eight Trigrams. The Eight Trigrams determine good and evil fortune. Good and evil fortune give rise to great works.[2]

This passage is a description of the various steps leading to the formation of the Eight Trigrams. The T'ai Chi is usually represented by a circle, although technically, as the Supreme Ultimate, it is impossible to symbolize, for it is considered ineffable.

The T'ai Chi gives rise to the Two Primal Forms: —— and — —, representing respectively Yang, the active cosmic principle, and Yin, the passive cosmic principle.

The Two Primal Forms are the source of the Sixty-Four Hexagrams which constitute the basis of the *I-Ching*, beginning with the Four Emblems. These Emblems are: ══, ═ ═, ═ ═ and ═ ═, respectively called Major Yang (T'ai Yang), Minor Yin (Shao Yin), Minor Yang (Shao Yang), and Major Yin (T'ai Yin). They progress logically from the most active to the most passive form.

The Eight Trigrams are: Ch'ien ☰, K'un ☷, K'an ☵, Li ☲, Chen ☳, Sun ☴, Ken ☶, and Tui ☱.

The last two sentences of the above passage refer to the use of the *I-Ching* system for divination. Utilized for this purpose, the *I-Ching* is supposed to guide people to follow the path of good and eschew the ways of evil, consequently assisting them to achieve success, or at least to avoid failure.

As can be seen from the lineal symbols, the Four Emblems are formed by doubling each of the two basic lines, —— and — —, and then placing each of the two lines over the other. The Eight

Trigrams are formed by placing each of the two basic lines over the Four Emblems. The following diagram should furnish a clear illustration of the entire process:

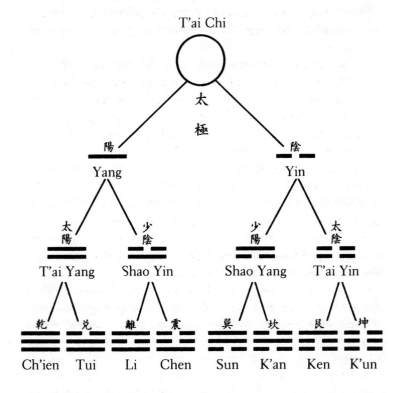

The two Chinese words for Yang and Yin originally connote brightness and darkness respectively and refer especially to mountains and rivers. The northern side of a mountain is called Yin and the southern side Yang, but in the case of a river the northern side is Yang and the southern side Yin. (Occultists attribute this to the fact that the southern side of a mountain and the northern side of a river are charged by the solar [Yang] current or force, while the north side of a mountain and the southern side of a river are characterized by the earth [Yin] current.) Whatever the reason for this tradition, through the years Yin and Yang have come to symbolize the idea of dual opposites: Yin represents what is receptive, negative, static, female, weak, and soft; Yang represents what is active, positive, dynamic, male, strong, and rigid.

In the Introduction to his translation of the *I-Ching*, James Legge criticizes the use of the circle as a symbol for T'ai Chi, saying that it "appears very unsuccessful" and "must be pronounced a failure."[3] He contends that by no stretch of the imagination can a circle be made to produce two such lines as ——— and — —. This merits some comment.

The passage involved appears to be symbolic, rather than literal, and seems to refer not to the production of material lines on a page, but to a symbolic expression that the Supreme Ultimate, or Eternal Tao, (godhead, or ultimate reality) differentiates into the Two Cosmic Principles Yin and Yang. The T'ai Chi itself is ineffable. It is beyond the capacity of the human senses to experience or the human mind to comprehend. It literally cannot be symbolized; how can *nothing* be symbolized? The circle represents an attempt to symbolize the "unsymbolizable," but could a more successful sign be conceived? It should be noted that the circle is almost the same as the sign for zero, which for ages has been used in the mathematics of many lands. Moreover, in symbolism and in nature initial and matured forms do not necessarily show a logical sequence in their development. A chicken is hatched from an egg. An oak comes from an acorn. Man himself develops from a single cell, hardly visible to the naked eye (which initially splits up spontaneously into two new cells, just as the T'ai Chi initially differentiates spontaneously into the Two Cosmic Principles).

The third passage in the *Great Treatise* concerning the genesis of the Eight Trigrams refers to the *Ho T'u*, or *River Map*, and the *Lo Shu*, or *Lo Script*. It may be translated as follows:

> Heaven produces the divine things; the sage studied
> their nature. Heaven and earth cause things to change
> and transform; the sage followed their example. Heaven
> hangs out the signs to reveal good or ill fortune; the sage
> made symbols after them. The Yellow River sent forth

the map and the Lo River sent forth the script; the sage
studied their nature.[4]

Here, "the sage" probably refers to Fu Hsi. The first portion of
this passage says essentially the same thing as the preceding
passage.

According to legend, the *River Map* (a diagramatic arrangement
of the Eight Trigrams) was supposed to have originated in a highly
mysterious manner, being borne on the back of a dragon-horse
which emerged from the Huang Ho, or Yellow River. Below is one
ancient artist's conception of this event:

Less fantastic but more enigmatic is the version with white and black circles to represent Yang and Yin, arranged in a set pattern in which the white circles represent Yang and the black ones represent Yin.

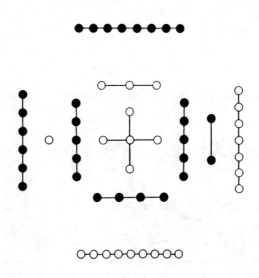

Whatever its origins, it was traditionally believed that the map definitely existed and had once been on display at the royal court in the early part of the Chou dynasty (1122–255 B.C.).[5] Centuries later, Confucius spoke of it with some reverence: "The phoenix has not come and the river has not sent forth any map. Would this be the end of me?"[6]

Some commentators on the *I-Ching*, notably Legge and Richard Wilhelm, attach little importance to the map. Legge dismisses it entirely, stating that "it seems a waste of time"[7] to discuss it. Wilhelm, on the other hand, suggests that the map furnishes a clue, not to the development of the Eight Trigrams, but to the development of the so-called Five Elements.[8]

Traditional Chinese commentators, who were usually conservative and gave credit to ancient tradition, attached great importance to the map. In his *I Hsueh Hsi Hsin (Study of the I [Ching] Purifies the Heart)*, Ren Ch'i-yun, a scholar of the Ch'ing dynasty, first rearranges the map from a square to a circular form to show how it can be transformed into a diagram of the T'ai Chi, and then shows how the Eight Trigrams can be derived from this diagram.[9] His rearrangement is as follows:

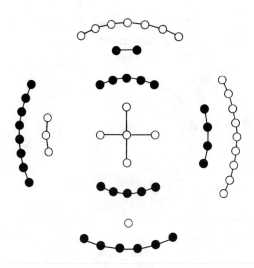

It will be observed that the five Yang circles and the ten Yin circles are grouped together to form the center of the scheme. The Yang numbers 1, 3, 7, and 9 proceed clockwise from the inner section to the outer circumference. The Yin numbers 2, 4, 6, and 8 also go clockwise from the inner section to the outer circumference, but along a different orbit. On this basis, the map can be transformed into a cosmogonic plan (a chart showing how Yin and Yang interact to create the cosmos, or reality). This plan, though it seems to have some defects, appears on the whole well conceived and revealing and is presented here to show how meaning can be extracted from an apparent enigma:

THE YELLOW-RIVER MAP
showing
THE FORMATION OF THE EIGHT TRIGRAMS

This map is drawn from the point of
view of an observer facing southward.

Meaning of the Cosmogonic Plan

The central disc represents the T'ai Chi. It contains within itself the five Yang marks and the ten Yin marks. This signifies that it has two aspects: Yin and Yang.

The white portion (indicated by the Yang numbers, 1, 3, 7, and 9) represents the Yang aspect manifesting itself from within outwards (beginning from the point indicated by the number 1) and increasing and expanding until it reaches its fullest extent, when its polar opposite, Yin, automatically begins to manifest itself. The black portion (indicated by the numbers 2, 4, 6, and 8) represents the Yin aspect (appearing at the point indicated by the number 2) increasing and expanding until it reaches its fullest extent, when Yang automatically begins to manifest itself.

The white portion (indicated by the Yang numbers 1 and 3) represents the initial stage of the manifestation of the Yang principle. Manifestation takes place from within outwards, from the center to the periphery. Therefore, at its initial stage the Minor Yang (Shao Yang) is in the inner section near the center. The white portion (indicated by the Yang numbers 7 and 9) represents the full growth of Yang. It therefore appears in the outer section at the circumference and is called Major Yang (T'ai Yang).

Similarly, the black portion (indicated by the Yin numbers 2 and 4) represents the Minor Yin (Shao Yin), or the Yin aspect in its initial stage of manifestation. The Yin aspect, too, manifests from within outwards. Therefore, the Minor Yin appears in the inner section near the center. The remaining black portion (indicated by the Yin numbers 6 and 8) represents Yin in the fully developed stage. It is, therefore, found in the outer section at the circumference and is called Major Yin (T'ai Yin).

As can be observed in the plan, when Yang is born and gradually expands and increases, Yin gradually decreases until a point is reached at which Yang has grown to its fullest extent and Yin seems to have passed away. At that point the re-manifestation of Yin begins. Similarly, when Yin gradually expands and increases, Yang gradually decreases and begins to pass away until a point is reached at which total darkness reigns without any Yang light at

9

all. At that point the manifestation of Yang begins again. This is the operation of the great principle of the alternate waxing and waning of Yin and Yang. It is the Law of Cyclic Reversion.

The Plan and the Eight Trigrams

The cosmogonic plan furnishes a basis for the construction of the Eight Trigrams in the following manner:

(1) The topmost section in the south, where Yang has manifested itself to the fullest extent just before the rebirth of Yin, is best represented by the Ch'ien trigram: ☰ (all three Yang lines).

(2) The lowest section in the north, where Yin has manifested itself to the fullest extent just before the rebirth of Yang, is best represented by the K'un trigram: ☷ (all three Yin lines).

(3) The section in the northeast (lower left corner), which contains one part of the newborn Yang inside and two parts of the grown-up Yin outside, is best represented by the Chen trigram: ☳ (one Yang line inside and two Yin lines outside).

(4) The portion to the southeast (upper left corner), where there are two parts of grown-up Yang inside and one part of the remaining Yin outside, is best represented by the Tui trigram: ☱ (two Yang lines inside and one Yin line outside).

(5) The portion in the southwest (upper right corner), where there are one part of newborn Yin inside and two parts of grown-up Yang outside, is best represented by the Sun trigram: ☴ (one Yin line inside and two Yang lines outside).

(6) The northwest section (lower right corner), where there are two parts of grown-up Yin inside and one part of the remaining Yang outside, is best represented by the Ken trigram: ☶ (two Yin lines inside and one Yang line outside).

(7) The Yang-growing section in the east (left side), the intermediate stage between Chen (N.E.) and Tui (S.E.), is best represented by the Li trigram: ☲ (two Yang lines enveloping one Yin line in the middle).

(8) The Yin-growing section in the west (right side), the intermediate stage between Sun (S.W.) and Ken (N.W.), is best symbo-

lized by the K'an trigram: ☵ (two Yin lines enveloping one Yang line in the middle).

Thus, all the Yang lines of the Eight Trigrams correspond to the Yang sections of the *River Map* arrangement and all the Yin lines correspond to the Yin section. In this way, the Eight Trigrams come into being.

The *Lo Script*

Although the *Lo Script* was mentioned along with the *River Map*, there was, in fact, a considerable time gap between them. The emergence of the map was supposed to have occurred at the time of Fu Hsi (circa 3,300 B.C.). The *Lo Script* was believed to have emerged from the Lo River in Honan province during the time of Yu the Great, before he became king and founded the Hsia dynasty (2,205–1766 B.C.). This makes it very unlikely that it had anything to do with Fu Hsi drawing the Eight Trigrams.

According to K'ung An-kuo (circa 200 B.C.), a descendant of Confucius, while Yu was fighting the vast flood a tortoise came up from the river "bearing on its back a script and a plan of nine divisions, both of which were marked with the numbers up to nine."[10] The numbers shown on the script are in various groups of white and black circles arranged in a set pattern somewhat similar to that of the *River Map*. The existing version looks like this:

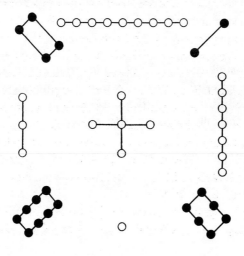

How the Eight Trigrams can be derived from this script is a complicated process. Ren Ch'i-yun did it in a rather laborious manner, indicating how hard he tried to make some sense out of the script. He first arranged the Yang circles on the four sides in a circular form. He then adduced the interactions of the Five Elements (water, fire, wood, metal, and soil) to identify each of the eight groups of circles in the script with its corresponding trigram. By way of illustration, he set forth the following scheme:[11]

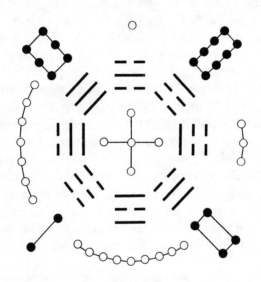

The *Lo Script* received little attention from either Legge or Wilhelm. The latter reproduced it without comment, while Legge substituted numbers for the various groups of circles and presented the following arithmetical puzzle:

4	9	2
3	5	7
8	1	6

The puzzle lies in the fact that "the numbers from 1 to 9 are arranged so as to make 15 in whatever way we add them."[12] Credit for the discovery belongs to Chu Hsi, a noted philosopher of the Sung dynasty; Legge called it the *"reductio ad absurdum"* of the *Lo Script*. In a sense he is right, for the puzzle is irrelevant to the Eight Trigrams. However, the puzzle does not end with only nine numbers, but shows how the square of *any odd number* can be arranged into such a puzzle. For instance, the square of 5 and 7 can be arranged in the following ways:

						30	39	48	1	10	19	28
17	24	1	8	15		38	47	7	9	18	27	29
23	5	7	14	16		46	6	8	17	26	35	37
4	6	13	20	22		5	14	16	25	34	36	45
10	12	19	21	3		13	15	24	33	42	44	4
11	18	25	2	9		21	23	32	41	43	3	12
						22	31	40	49	2	11	20

Every row of figures in the above tables, whether horizontal, vertical or diagonal, adds up to the *same* sum. Why so? Nobody seems able to give a reason. Those familiar with astrology will no doubt recognize the similarity between these tables and the so-called "squares of the planets," just as there are similarities between the arrangements of the hexagrams and certain other figures in traditional Western occultism; however, there is no evidence of any occult significance behind the *I-Ching* or the imagery of its hexagrams.

Trigrams and Symbolisms

Before the mystical sage Fu Hsi drew the Eight Trigrams, he contemplated the heavens and surveyed the earth to discern what forces or agencies were responsible for changes in the world and the universe. It is understandable, therefore, that four of the Eight Trigrams symbolize natural forces or phenomena and four symbolize material things on earth.

The Ch'ien trigram ☰ symbolizes heaven or the creative principle. Its three lines are all Yang, suggesting the perfect power and unfailing strength of heaven.

The K'un trigram ☷ ☷ symbolizes the earth. Its three lines are all Yin, suggesting the submissiveness and yielding nature of the earth. The shape of the trigram also reveals its symbolism: it shows a hollow channel in the middle, which things can go through, indicating the capacity as well as the receptivity of the earth.

The K'an trigram ☵ symbolizes water flowing in a stream or river. The two Yin lines represent earth or banks, while the Yang line in the middle represents something dynamic and moving. The trigram therefore signifies a stream or river flowing between two banks. As water may cause flood, shipwreck, and drowning, the trigram also signifies danger. Another reason for this interpretation is that the Yang line is imprisoned between two Yin lines, suggesting that something bright is obscured by dark forces.

The Li trigram ☲ symbolizes fire and light. It shows a Yin line inside and two Yang lines outside. Here Yin signifies darkness and Yang signifies light. The trigram therefore suggests something dark giving off light, such as a piece of burning coal or wood. By association of ideas, the trigram also signifies intelligence, brilliance, or enlightenment. As the trigram shows a Yin line leaning on two Yang lines, like a female between two males, it also signifies dependence or attachment.

The Chen trigram ☳ symbolizes thunder. It shows a Yang line below two Yin ones. The Yang line represents something dynamic and explosive trying to break forth from its prison. The two Yin lines are indicative of the earth. The trigram therefore signifies some mighty force attempting to break out through the earth. Hence the notion of thunder. The Chinese believe that thunder is the spring outbreak of the Yang force which, during the winter months, has been hidden, accumulating in the depths of the earth. For obvious reasons, the trigram also signifies motion.

The Sun trigram ☴ symbolizes wind and also penetration. It looks like an object with a hole at the bottom, through which entrance or penetration may be effected. Wind is the most penetrative element in nature, entering every chink and crevice. Another reason for this symbolism is that the Yin line below the two Yang lines indicates something weak, or the line of least resistance.

The Ken trigram ☶ symbolizes mountain. The top line (Yang) signifies something concrete and solid, while the lines beneath (Yin) signify the earth, creating the notion of mountain. The trigram also denotes obstruction, obstacle, or stoppage.

The Tui trigram ☱ symbolizes marsh. The two upper lines resemble the upper portion of the K'an trigram ☵, which signifies water. The bottom line (Yang) represents a hard bed of earth, hence the notion of a marsh. The trigram shows something weak at the top or on the outside and something strong and firm inside. This suggests outward gentleness and inward strength or firmness—the sign of a pleasant personality. Thus, the trigram also denotes delight and satisfaction. Another reason for this interpretation is that the top Yin line resembles a mouth, which is the organ for enjoying good food and indulging in delightful conversation.

Other Symbolisms of the Trigrams

We have seen the principal symbolisms of the Eight Trigrams, together with their main attributes. Numerous others are set forth in the Eighth Wing, entitled *Shuo Kua (Treatise on Remarks about Trigrams)*. They constitute a guide *par excellence* to the study of *I-Ching* symbolism, and Chinese commentators have given logical interpretations for each of them. Legge and Wilhelm, however, found them hard to comprehend. Legge asked: "Why are tui and khan [K'an] used to represent water in different conditions, while khan, moreover, represents the moon? How is sun set apart to represent things so different as wind and wood?"[13] To Chinese commentators the answer is very simple. Tui ☱ represents, more or less, stagnant water in a marsh, while K'an ☵ represents water flowing between two banks. The reason why

K'an can also represent the moon is that the middle Yang line signifies light, and the two Yin lines signify the earth, as well as darkness. The trigram therefore signifies a light on earth in darkness (at night). This light is obviously the moon. Why the Sun trigram ☴ symbolizes wind has already been explained. It symbolizes wood because the top two lines, or upper part, are Yang, while the bottom line, or lower part, is Yin. Yang signifies something dynamic and mobile, like leaves. Yin signifies something static or quiescent, like roots. In nature, what is immovable at the bottom and flexible at the top? A tree—the source of wood.

The Eight Trigrams have also been viewed as constituting a family of six children together with the parents. Chapter 10 of the *Treatise on Remarks about Trigrams* contains a passage which may be translated as follows:

> Ch'ien means heaven; therefore it is designated father. K'un means earth; therefore it is designated mother. Chen represents K'un's first demand on Ch'ien, getting a son; therefore Chen is called the first son. Sun represents Ch'ien's first demand on K'un, getting a daughter; therefore Sun is called the eldest daugher. K'an represents K'un's second demand on Ch'ien, getting a son; therefore K'an is called the middle son. Li represents Ch'ien's second demand on K'un, getting a daughter; therefore Li is called the middle daughter. Ken represents K'un's third demand on Ch'ien, getting a son; therefore Ken is called the youngest son. Tui represents Ch'ien's third demand on K'un, getting a daughter; therefore Tui is called the youngest daughter.[14]

An illustration of the passage appears as follows:

K'un's first demand on Ch'ien: ☷ → ☰ = ☳ Chen, first son
Ch'ien's first demand on K'un: ☰ → ☷ = ☴ Sun, first daughter
K'un's second demand on Ch'ien: ☷ → ☰ = ☵ K'an, second son
Ch'ien's second demand on K'un: ☰ → ☷ = ☲ Li, second daughter
K'un's third demand on Ch'ien: ☷ → ☰ = ☶ Ken, third son
Ch'ien's third demand on K'un: ☰ → ☷ = ☱ Tui, third daughter

The following table may be conducive to a general grasp of the Eight Trigrams:

Trigram	Symbolism	Attribute	Family relations
☰ Ch'ien	Heaven	Strength, creativity	Father
☷ K'un	Earth	Meekness, receptivity	Mother
☵ K'an	Water	Danger, difficulty	Second son
☲ Li	Fire, light	Elegance, intelligence	Second daughter
☳ Chen	Thunder	Motion, agitation	Eldest son
☴ Sun	Wind, wood	Penetration, pliancy	Eldest daughter
☶ Ken	Mountain	Obstruction, stoppage	Youngest son
☱ Tui	Marsh, mouth	Pleasure, eloquence	Youngest daughter

CHAPTER 2

THE MYSTIQUE OF THE HEXAGRAMS

A HEXAGRAM IS a figure with six horizontal lines. At first sight, it consists of only two trigrams, but actually it may be said to consist of four. Let us take the 11th Hexagram, T'ai, symbol of peace and prosperity, to illustrate:

The bottom line is regarded as the first line, or Line 1; the line above is Line 2, and so on. The lower trigram, also called the inner, is composed of Lines 1, 2, and 3. The upper trigram, also called the outer, is composed of Lines 4, 5, and 6. Lines 2, 3, and 4 also constitute a trigram: so do Lines 3, 4, and 5. These are called interior trigrams, or "hu kua" in Chinese. Sometimes they are called nuclear trigrams, but the word "nuclear," while fashionable, is not quite approriate. It means central, but obviously there is no central trigram in a hexagram.

So we see that there are really four trigrams in the structure of a hexagram, and consequently much more symbolic significance in it than in a trigram. When employing the *I-Ching* for divination, a hexagram usually emerges as the end result and serves as a spiritual messenger or symbolic oracle. Sound counsels, important warnings, and forebodings of good or ill fortune are all supposed to lurk in the resulting hexagram, only waiting to be unlocked and deciphered.

As the oracle conveyed by a hexagram usually involves wisdom concerning proper conduct and right living, it may also be regarded as a suggestive source of ethical principles and moral ideals. The hexagrams, therefore, are worthy of study even apart from divination.

The subject of the Sixty-Four Hexagrams usually calls forth two historical questions: Who made them? Who named them? To both questions the Chinese commentators have no unanimous answer.

With regard to the first question, some commentators, including the great historian Ssuma Ch'ien, say that it was King Wen, father of the Chou dynasty. Others, including Wang Pi, K'ung An-kuo, and Chu Hsi, maintain that it was Fu Hsi. Still others believe it was either Emperor Yu of the Hsia dynasty or Shen Nung, the legendary sage-ruler after Fu Hsi.[1] There seems to be a better reason to believe that Fu Hsi created the hexagrams. For one thing, of all the claims to authorship, Fu Hsi's seems to have aroused the least controversy, inasmuch as he has also been credited with creating a primitive system of writing and with teaching people how to tie knots as an aid to memory.

Each of the Sixty-Four Hexagrams has a name. Again, some commentators assert that it was Fu Hsi who named them, but a far greater number of others contend that it was King Wen. This view is undoubtedly the correct one, for each of the sixty-four names is indicative of an already advanced stage in the development of Chinese writing. In Fu Hsi's time, China had only the crudest system of writing, if it could be called that at all. China did not have a written language until the time of Huang Ti, known as the Yellow Emperor (circa 2,000 B.C.), when Ts'ang Chieh, a minister of the emperor, invented the *Liu Shu*, or six scripts: *Hsiang hsing*, (pictograph); *Chih shih* (ideograph); *Hsing sheng* (harmony or similarity of sound; onomatopoeia); *Hui I* (ideosuggestion); *Chuan chu* (change of intonation); and *Chia chieh*, (inference; literally, lending or borrowing).

A hexagram's name is no mere label. The meaning of each name corresponds to the meaning of the hexagram, pointing up its intrinsic significance. Whoever named them possessed a keen insight into the significance of hexagrams and a clear understanding of their meaning. For example, the 15th Hexagram ䷎ was named Ch'ien, meaning humility, because it is composed of the K'un trigram (signifying the earth) above and the Ken trigram (signifying a mountain) below. A mountain usually stands high above the earth. But in the Ch'ien Hexagram it takes a position below that of the earth, suggesting someone of exalted position deferring to one of lower position, thus showing the virtue of humility. The 36th Hexagram ䷣ is named Ming Yi, meaning light obscured or intelligence darkened. Here, the upper trigram is K'un (signifying the earth), while the lower trigram is Li (signifying light). Together they suggest light concealed beneath the earth; hence, the idea of intelligence darkened or light obscured.

Speaking of names, it may well be asked who first coined the names "trigram" and "hexagram." It must be one of the I-Ching's first two Western translators, P. Regis and P. Angelo Zottoli, both of whom translated the I-Ching into Latin. According to James Legge, Regis' work (now unavailable for general reference) appeared at the beginning of the eighteenth century, and P. Zottoli's in 1880. In his work, P. Zottoli has expressed a general view of the I-Ching, referring to the peculiar features of the Chinese classic as follows:

> Quid igitur tandem famosus iste *Yi King*? Paucis accepe: ex linearum qualitate continua vel intercisa; earumque situ, imo, medio, vel supremo; mutuaque ipsarum relatione, occursu, dissidio, convenientia; ex ipso scilicet trigrammatum corpore seu forma, tum ex trigrammatum symbolo seu imagine, tum ex trigrammatum proprietate seu virtute, tum etiam aliquando ex unius ad alterum hexagramma varietate, eruitur aliqua imago, deducitur aliqua sententia, quoddam veluti oraculum continens, quod sorte etiam consulere possis ad documentum obtinendum, moderandae vitae solvendove dubio consentaneum.[2]

The words *trigrammatum* and *hexagramma* are undoubtedly the precursors of the English "trigram" and "hexagram."

In passing, it may be worthwhile to point out that the English spellings of some of the hexagrams are identical and should be noted with care in order to avoid confusion. Following is a complete list of those hexagrams which have similar spellings and which are indicated by their sequential numbers:

Ch'ien: 1st and 15th;
K'un: 2nd and 47th;
Pi: 8th and 22nd;
Chien: 39th and 53rd;
Sun: 41st and 57th;
Yi: 27th and 42nd;
Chieh: 40th and 60th.

In Chinese, the names of these hexagrams cause no confusion, for the Chinese words, or characters, are entirely different. In speech they are distinguished by their intonation.

Formation of Hexagrams

The formation of hexagrams may appear to be a very simple process. Just add three lines to a trigram or put one trigram over another, and you have a hexagram. However, the formation of hexagrams has a logical basis, and is not as simple as it appears. In fact, it is often rather involved. A passage in the *Shuo Kua Chuan* (*Treatise on Remarks about Trigrams*) sheds some light on this subject:

In remote antiquity, when the sages devised the *I* system, their purpose was to make it in accord with the principles of nature and destiny. Therefore, they determined the way of heaven and called it Yin and Yang. They determined the way of earth and called it weakness and strength. They determined the way of man and called it benevolence and righteousness.

They combined the Three Powers and doubled them. Thus, in the *I* system the diagram is completed in six lines.

A distinction in place was made between Yin and Yang. Progressively the weak and the strong (lines) were used to occupy each place. Thus, through six layers of places in the *I* system, a picture (of the Sixty-Four Hexagrams) was completed.[3]

These passages indicate two ways of forming hexagrams. The first is indicated in the sentence, "They combined the Three Powers and doubled them." Every trigram represents the Three Powers. Its top line represents heaven, its middle line represents man, and its bottom line represents earth. The three lines are doubled, creating a figure of six lines (a hexagram), because heaven alternatively shows light and darkness, or day and night; man is divided into male and female; and earth consists of land and water. In a hexagram, Lines 1 (bottom line), 3, and 5 are considered Yang, or strong, while Lines 2, 4, and 6 are considered Yin, or weak. So heaven (top two lines), man (middle two lines), and earth (bottom two lines) each possess a Yin and a Yang aspect. It can thus be seen that the formation of hexagrams as symbols of mutation or change has a clear, logical basis.

Legge, apparently unaware of the significance of the above passage, said that it was "merely the play of fancy, and confuses the mind of the student."[4] He looked upon the formation of hexagrams as mere arithmetical manipulation: "No Chinese writer has tried to explain why the framers stopped with the Sixty-Four Hexagrams, instead of going on to 128 figures of 7 lines, 256 of 8, 512 of 9, and so indefinitely."[5] Actually, it was somewhat audacious of Mr. Legge to assume that he was familiar with all of the Chinese commentators on the *I-Ching*. In fact, there appear to be a number of reasons why there are *exactly* sixty-four hexagrams.

One of these reasons is indicated in the second paragraph quoted above. This passage inspired Shao Yung (1011–1077), a noted philosopher of the Sung dynasty (960–1279), to make the following diagram[6] (which appears in neither Legge's nor Wilhelm's work):

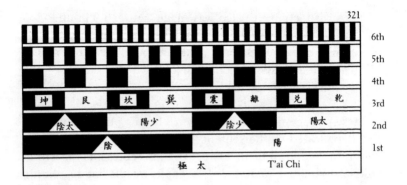

This is an ingenious way of deriving the Sixty-Four Hexagrams, and imparts a sense of mystery. (The three numerals 1, 2, and 3, above the top right corner, are for explanatory purposes only.) Just below the numeral 1 is a narrow white space beneath which is another white space twice as wide. This in turn is followed by four white spaces of successively increasing widths. Together, the six white spaces constitute the Ch'ien Hexagram ☰. Just below the numeral 2 is another series of spaces of increasing widths. The top space, being black, denotes a Yin line. These six spaces constitute the Kuai Hexagram ䷪. Beneath the numeral 3 is a similar series of six spaces in which the second is black and the other five are white. They constitute the Ta Yu Hexagram ䷍. In the same manner, the remaining sixty-one hexagrams can be traced in the diagram.

Yet another method by which the hexagrams are formed can be seen by placing each of the Eight Trigrams upon all of the Eight Trigrams, one by one. This process results in the creation of exactly sixty-four hexagrams. Again, this is no mere mechanical manipulation, but enlarges the range of symbolism for the interpretation of natural phenomena and human situations.

The Eight Trigrams are obviously limited in their symbolic capacity. The symbolization of moral qualities, human relationships, and complex life situations is beyond their scope. No trigram alone can symbolize such notions as "separation," "sunrise," or "a boy-meets-girl scene." But a hexagram can. For example, separation is symbolized by the K'uei Hexagram ☲☱. The upper trigram, Li, signifies fire, which moves upward; the lower trigram, Tui, signifies water in the marsh, which flows downward. Fire and water move in opposite directions, creating the notion of separation. Sunrise is symbolized by the Tsin Hexagram ☲☷. The upper trigram, Li, here signifies light or the sun, and the lower trigram, K'un, signifies the earth. The hexagram therefore clearly indicates that light (or the sun) has risen over the earth. A boy-meets-girl scene is symbolized by the Hsien Hexagram ☱☶. As has been noted, the Eight Trigrams can be viewed as a family of six children: the Tui trigram, upper trigram of the Hsien Hexagram, denotes the youngest daughter; the Ken trigram, lower trigram of the hexagram, denotes the youngest son. The hexagram as a whole, therefore, indicates a young man assuming a lower, more humble position, as if worshipping the young girl above him. All the correlative lines, i.e., Lines 1 and 4, 2 and 5, and 3 and 6, are all in polar relation to each other, one being Yin and the other Yang, attracting and responding to each other and further reinforcing the idea of a meeting between a young couple.[7]

There are some hexagrams whose component trigrams present a symbolism that at first can seem contrary to common sense. Legge, with his scientific turn of mind, appears to have had some difficulty with these. The Ta Ch'u Hexagram ☶☰, with its upper Ken trigram (mountain) and its lower trigram, Ch'ien (sky or heaven), suggesting the sky or heaven beneath or within a mountain, gave him particular trouble. "We are ready to exclaim," says Legge, with an overtone of ridicule that betrays the irritation his logical mind must have felt, "and ask, 'Heaven, the sky, in the midst of a mountain!' Can there be such a thing?"[8] Legge failed to realize that to be effective, symbolism, like fairy tales, cannot always accord with common sense. Anyone who reads Legge's introduction to the *I-Ching* is likely to come away with the impression that he actually had little regard for this classic. In this respect, he was quite different from Richard Wilhelm, C. G. Jung, and Hermann Keyserling, all of whom cherished a high regard for the *I-Ching*.

The Hexagrams and the Binary System

We have previously referred to the rather mysterious diagram worked out by the philosopher Shao Yung setting forth the formation of the Sixty-Four Hexagrams. Curiously, this diagram fits exactly into a distinctive arithmetical system invented by an outstanding European philosopher and mathematical genius more than six centuries later. Baron Gottfried Wilhem von Leibniz (1646–1716) discovered differential calculus concurrently with Sir Isaac Newton. The arithmetical system he invented is called the binary, or dyadic, system of numeration. It uses only the symbols 1 and 0. If 1 is used to stand for the Yang line ——, and 0 for the Yin line — —, the numbers from 0 to 63 in the system will be found to coincide with the lines of the Sixty-Four Hexagrams, according to their sequence in the mysterious diagram.

Leibniz himself discovered this coincidence, but only by chance. He sent his binary system to a Jesuit in Peking, who, apparently a learned Sinologue, quickly realized the strange correspondence between the system and the *I-Ching* diagram. When he sent the diagram to Leibniz, the scientist also recognized the correspondence. He subsequently developed a high degree of respect for Fu Hsi and became interested in Chinese writing.

The hexagrams constitute the key tool for divination. What has the binary system to do with divination? Leibniz was keenly interested in symbolic logic and set a high value on the mathematical demonstration of philosophical ideas. Of course, as some (most notably John Mitchell) have claimed, it is possible that for the ancients such seeming opposites as mathematics and divination were part of one unified system; however, few serious scholars support this view.

Although it has some relevance to computers, the binary system is not widely known. The following table shows how the first twelve numbers are represented in the system:

1	2	3	4	5	6	7	8	9	10	11	12
1	10	11	100	101	110	111	1000	1001	1010	1011	1100

The subsequent numbers are derived in the obvious manner. If the Yang line —— is substituted for 1 in the binary system and the Yin line — — for 0, the Sixty-Four Hexagrams, as set forth in Shao Yung's diagram, will coincide with sixty-four numbers in the binary system, as demonstrated in the following scheme:

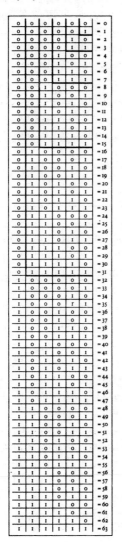

o	o	o	o	o	o	= o
o	o	o	o	o	1	= 1
o	o	o	o	1	o	= 2
o	o	o	o	1	1	= 3
o	o	o	1	o	o	= 4
o	o	o	1	o	1	= 5
o	o	o	1	1	o	= 6
o	o	o	1	1	1	= 7
o	o	1	o	o	o	= 8
o	o	1	o	o	1	= 9
o	o	1	o	1	o	= 10
o	o	1	o	1	1	= 11
o	o	1	1	o	o	= 12
o	o	1	1	o	1	= 13
o	o	1	1	1	o	= 14
o	o	1	1	1	1	= 15
o	1	o	o	o	o	= 16
o	1	o	o	o	1	= 17
o	1	o	o	1	o	= 18
o	1	o	o	1	1	= 19
o	1	o	1	o	o	= 20
o	1	o	1	o	1	= 21
o	1	o	1	1	o	= 22
o	1	o	1	1	1	= 23
o	1	1	o	o	o	= 24
o	1	1	o	o	1	= 25
o	1	1	o	1	o	= 26
o	1	1	o	1	1	= 27
o	1	1	1	o	o	= 28
o	1	1	1	o	1	= 29
o	1	1	1	1	o	= 30
o	1	1	1	1	1	= 31
1	o	o	o	o	o	= 32
1	o	o	o	o	1	= 33
1	o	o	o	1	o	= 34
1	o	o	1	r	1	= 35
1	o	o	1	o	o	= 36
1	o	o	1	o	1	= 37
1	o	o	1	1	o	= 38
1	o	o	1	1	1	= 39
1	o	1	o	o	o	= 40
1	o	1	o	o	1	= 41
1	o	1	o	1	o	= 42
1	o	1	o	1	1	= 43
1	o	1	1	o	o	= 44
1	o	1	1	o	1	= 45
1	o	1	1	1	o	= 46
1	o	1	1	1	1	= 47
1	1	o	o	o	o	= 48
1	1	o	o	o	1	= 49
1	1	o	o	1	o	= 50
1	1	o	o	1	1	= 51
1	1	o	1	o	o	= 52
1	1	o	1	o	1	= 53
1	1	o	1	1	o	= 54
1	1	o	1	1	1	= 55
1	1	1	o	o	o	= 56
1	1	1	o	o	1	= 57
1	1	1	o	1	o	= 58
1	1	1	o	1	1	= 59
1	1	1	1	o	o	= 60
1	1	1	1	o	1	= 61
1	1	1	1	1	o	= 62
1	1	1	1	1	1	= 63

T'ai

Chi

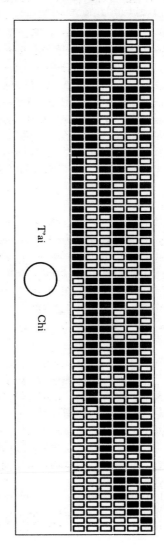

27

This scheme, which must have been designed by Leibniz himself, shows his keen insight into the formation of the hexagrams.

Legge, on the other hand, considered this to be mere arithmetical or algebraic manipulation. He says:

> The addition to each of the trigrams of each of the two fundamental lines produces 16 figures of four lines; dealt with in the same way, these produce 32 figures of five lines; and similar operation with these produces the 64 hexagrams, each of which forms the subject of an essay in the text of the *Yi*. The lines increase in an arithmetical progression whose common difference is 1, and the figures in a geometrical progression whose common ratio is 2. This is all the mystery [sic] in the formation of the lineal figures; this, I believe, was the process by which they were first formed; and it is hardly necessary to imagine them to have come from a sage like Fu-hsi. The endowments of an ordinary man were sufficient for such a work.[9]

What Legge fails to understand is that the Sixty-Four Hexagrams resulting from manipulation of the two fundamental lines (as demonstrated in Shao Yung's diagram and apprehended by Leibniz) are all *different* from one another, unique in their combinations of Yin and Yang lines, and therefore unique in their symbolic significance.

Another Coincidence with the Binary System

The following diagram has traditionally been attributed to Fu Hsi and appears in many Chinese works on the *I-Ching*. It has mystified many readers. Students of Tibetan mysticism may have thought it a charming mandala, but it was probably not intended as a mandala, though it may fittingly serve as one. The Chinese in general believe that it is a symbol of heaven and earth, the circle representing heaven and the square representing earth. Until modern times the Chinese believed that heaven was spherical and earth square, as indicated in the popular saying, "T'ien yuan, ti fang."

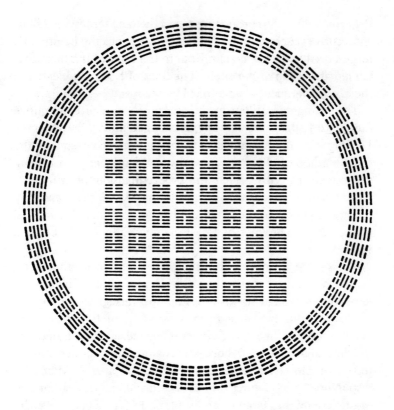

It is not proposed here to ascertain the general symbolism of this diagram, but to point out again the mysterious coincidence between it and the binary system worked out by Leibniz. The coincidence can be clearly shown by changing the Yang line of a hexagram into 1 and the Yin line into 0. Now it can be seen that at the bottom of the circle is the hexagram K'un with six Yin lines; if each of these lines is changed into 0, the result is 000000, which represents 0 in the binary system. The hexagram to the right of K'un is Po; if its lines are changed into either 1 or 0, the result is 000001, which represents 1 in the binary system.

The hexagram succeeding Po is Pi; if its lines are changed into 1 or 0, the result is 000010, which represents 2 in the binary system. By the same method of changing lines, the hexagram after

Pi become 000011, representing 3, and the next represents 4. The consecutive series of numerals ascends counter-clockwise up to 31, represented by the hexagram Kou, to the right of the hexagram Ch'ien at the top of the circle. The lines of Kou, if subjected to the above method, become 011111.

The hexagram Ch'ien begins another series of consecutive numerals. Its lines are all Yang; if changed into 1, they become 111111, which corresponds to 63 in the binary system. By the same method of changing lines, the series of consecutive hexagrams, starting with Ch'ien and proceeding counter-clockwise, stand for the consecutive numerals from 63 to 32, represented by the hexagram Fu, to the left of the hexagram K'un at the bottom of the circle. The lines of Fu, if changed into 1 or 0, become 100000.

The square arrangement of the Sixty-Four Hexagrams by Fu Hsi shows another curious correspondence with the binary system. This series begins with the topmost hexagram on the left-hand side: K'un. Proceeding from left to right on that line and on every succeeding line in the proper sequence, it will be found that the hexagrams, if their lines are changed into either 1 or 0, represent the consecutive numbers in the binary system corresponding to the figures 0 to 63. For instance, the first, or topmost, line of hexagrams represents: 000000, 000001, 000010, 000011, 000100, 000101, 000110, 000111, corresponding to 0, 1, 2, 3, 4. 5, 6, 7.

It will be noted that in the circular arrangement any two diagonally opposite hexagrams always represent two figures which add up to 63. Actually, there is no mystery here. Remember that the series of consecutive numbers on the right side is on an *increasing* scale, while that on the left side is on a *decreasing* one. In such an arrangement, whenever a number on the right side increases by 1, its opposite number decreases by 1.

What is mysterious and mystifying is this: Why is it that the arrangement of the Sixty-Four Hexagrams, whether circular or square, created by the legendary sage Fu Hsi more than 5,000 years ago, can be transformed into sixty-four consecutive numbers in the binary system conceived by Leibniz in the eighteenth century?

Could it be, as some zealous Buddhists would believe, that Leibniz was a reincarnation of Fu Hsi? Or as occultists believe, could it be that a single hidden source links all the world's wisdom systems? Could it merely be that sages and seers often attain the same truths but express them in different ways in different times and places? Or is the correspondence between the designs of these two men purely coincidence?

There is another square arrangement of the Sixty-Four Hexagrams which is ascribed to King Wen. It is as follows:

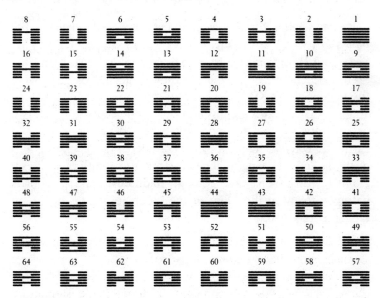

Beginning with the Ch'ien Hexagram on the right side of the bottom row, and reading leftward with all the rows in the proper sequence, we find the Sixty-Four Hexagrams in the same order as they appear in all the traditional Chinese versions of the *I-Ching*. If translated into binary numbers, they represent the following figures:

2	16	23	58	17	34	0	63
4	8	61	47	7	56	55	59
32	1	41	37	3	48	25	38
28	14	45	18	30	33	57	39
20	10	53	43	40	5	60	15
26	22	24	6	31	62	35	49
13	44	52	11	9	36	29	46
21	42	12	51	50	19	54	27

We can see that this arrangement has no correspondence to the binary system. Does this mean that Fu Hsi's arrangements of the Sixty-Four Hexagrams are truer to the nature of things than King Wen's? Apparently not, for all the traditional Chinese versions of the *I-Ching* adopt King Wen's arrangement, in which the Ch'ien and K'un Hexagrams are given priority and occupy the first two places in the series. They represent Yang and Yin, or heaven and earth, respectively. Thus, they are considered the key hexagrams of the *I-Ching*. Having followed the order of the first two hexagrams in King Wen's arrangement, traditional *I-Ching* scholars naturally followed the order of the other hexagrams in the arrangement as well.

CHAPTER 3

THE BIRTH OF THE TEXT

THE TEXT OF THE *I-Ching* was born in prison during a troubled revolutionary period in ancient China. In the *Great Treatise (Ta Chuan)* there is a passage which refers to this event:

> Did not the *I* study arise toward the end of the Yin dynasty when the virtue of Chou had attained its peak and when King Wen was having trouble with Choe? For this reason, its words intimate a sense of peril, suggesting how peril may be changed into peace and how ignoble ease may end in ruin.[1]

The "Yin dynasty" is also called the Shang dynasty (1766–1122 B.C.); Chou was then a principality in the western part of the kingdom. King Wen was the Chou prince at that time, and Choe was the last king of the Shang dynasty, then on the throne. King Choe was a tyrant who squandered the wealth of the state by building grand palaces and resorting to other extravagances to amuse his queen, T'a Chi, who happened to be very difficult to please. Hers was a perverted personality: she took delight in sadism, and the king often subjected people to various kinds of torture in order to make her smile. Consequently, the land was gripped by terror, and the people groaned under intolerable oppression. A brother of the king, who deplored the situation, described it thus:

> The house of Yin can no longer exercise rule over the land. The great deeds of our founder were displayed in a former age, but through mad addiction to drink we have destroyed the effects of his virtue. The people, small and great, are given to highway robberies, villainies

33

another in violating the laws. There is no certainty that criminals will be apprehended. The lesser people rise up and commit violent outrages on one another. The dynasty of Yin is sinking in ruin; its condition is like that of one crossing a large stream, who can find neither ford nor bank.[2]

From this description we may gain a fairly clear notion of the general disorder and misery that beset the kingdom then. Meanwhile, the Chou principality, in what is now the area around Sian in Shensi province, was rising in power and prosperity. Its prince, later King Wen, an exceedingly wise and benevolent ruler, was eager to deliver the people from their bondage. He was particularly compassionate toward the elderly. Centuries later, both Confucius and Mencius praised him in glowing terms. In the book *Mencius* there are frequent remarks that any ruler who followed the political wisdom of King Wen would, in a matter of five to seven years, enjoy power and prosperity along with his people. Such panegyric remarks reflect the wisdom and popularity of King Wen while he was still a prince, during the time of King Choe. Although King Wen remained loyal and never showed any sign of rebellion, his popularity and ability nevertheless aroused the envy and hatred of the tyrant, who threw him into prison at a place called Yu Li (in the present province of Honan) in the year 1143 B.C.

It was while he was in prison that King Wen worked on the hexagrams. Most probably he was using them for purposes of divination. At that time, his life was hanging in the balance. The fate of his principality, too, was shrouded in doubt and uncertainty, and that must have caused him additional anxiety. Furthermore, the whole kingdom was in a state of confusion, and in the turmoil his principality might have the chance of toppling the Shang house and inheriting the Mandate of Heaven. Under the circumstances, anyone in the King's position would have had a burning desire to steal a peep into the future and obtain some foreknowledge of what was to come. As a master in the art of divination, how could he resist the temptation?[3]

The hexagrams upon which King Wen rendered judgments, then, must have been those which came from his manipulation of milfoil stalks in prison for his own divinations. After he had obtained a hexagram he would study its component trigrams and lines very carefully to try and make it "speak" to him and reveal the significance, or oracle, it was supposed to convey. As Legge puts it: "Each hexagram assumed a mystic meaning and glowed with a deep significance. He made it tell him of the qualities of various objects of nature, or of the principles of human society, or of the condition, actual and possible, of the kingdom."[4] This means that King Wen's judgment on a hexagram represents ideas suggested to him by the hexagram, not his own pre-existing ideas expressed by means of the hexagram. This is probably why his judgments are usually terse and rather enigmatic but heavy with significance.

There seems to be no doubt that King Wen could draw out the meaning of the hexagrams in this way, for he was a unique man of destiny. He became the father of the Chou dynasty, which lasted well over eight hundred years and was the longest in the annals of China. This alone is marvelous enough, but even after his dynasty had ended, its culture, thanks to Confucius, has continued to exert its benign influence on the Chinese people down to the present day.

Such an extraordinary historical figure must have been endowed with exceptional intelligence and tremendous intuitive discernment. In the course of time, as he made repeated use of the art of divination, he would inevitably study each hexagram's component trigrams and their individual lines, deducing rules for their interpretation. It is likely that he was also acquainted with the earlier Lien Shan and Kuei Ts'ang systems of change and followed their rules to interpret the hexagrams. This conjecture is based on the fact that early in the Chou dynasty, decades after the death of King Wen, there was still in its government a minister called the Grand Diviner (T'ai Pu), whose duty it was "to take charge of the rules of the three systems of change, namely, the Lien Shan, the Kuei Ts'ang and the Chou *I*."[5]

The word "rules" here deserves some special notice, for it indicates that the two earlier systems of Lien Shan and Kuei Ts'ang (later lost, perhaps forever) had developed certain rules for interpreting the hexagrams and for deducing ideas from them. Since King Wen was a great scholar as well as a great statesman, it is very likely that he had studied these rules with great care and may even have modified and incorporated them into the Chou system. Whether stemming from his own intuition and intelligence or from the rules of the previous two systems, or from both, King Wen's judgments on the hexagrams have been regarded with reverence by almost all later students of the *I-Ching*. He spent about a year in prison before he was released through the intercession of a friend, so he had ample time to go over all sixty-four hexagrams and write down a judgment on each of them.

The judgments King Wen appended to the hexagrams are usually in the nature of some advice or counsel on what action to take or what course to adopt when dealing with a given situation. Such phrases as "good fortune; evil fortune; no error; occasion for repentance; repentance vanishes; advantage to see the great man; advantage to cross the great stream; nothing advantageous; nothing disadvantageous; perseverance good; advantage to persevere; perseverance evil; perseverance regretful" frequently appear.

From these phrases it may clearly be seen that good fortune is the general goal and evil fortune is something to be avoided or prevented. While evil fortune is considered positively undesirable, error or repentance must also be guarded against or eliminated. Advantage or disadvantage usually refers to the action to be taken or the course of action to be carried out. Sometimes we are advised to "cross the great stream," that is, to attempt some gigantic task suggested by the reading. Sometimes we are warned not to go ahead with any plans by the words "nothing advantageous" or just the word "evil." The phrases "perseverance good (chen chi)" or "advantage to persevere (li chen)" give two instructions. One is that the course already adopted is a good one and should be continued. The other is that the course may be difficult now, but if persevered in will lead to good fortune eventually. "Perseverance evil (chen hsiung)" or "perseverance regretful (chen lin)" mean that the course currently followed should be abandoned or altered. "Advantage to see the great man" implies that there is someone involved—"the great man" with wisdom, wealth, influence, or power which he will be glad to use in helping us succeed in some specific task or escape some difficult situation.

In general, King Wen's judgment or counsel suggests whether fortune or misfortune will be the outcome of a given event or plan, and whether the person concerned should advance or retreat or remain steady and refrain from any reckless moves. King Wen's judgments on the Sixty-Four Hexagrams constitute the primary and principal portion of the Text of the *I-Ching*.

The Duke of Chou

The other portion of the Text was written by King Wen's son, Tan, who later became famous as the Duke of Chou. Like his father, the Duke also had a difficult period in his life. After King Wen died, another of his sons, an elder brother of the Duke known to posterity as Wu Wang, or King Wu, led a revolution against the Shang dynasty. Wu Wang was an able leader: prior to launching the revolution, he issued a proclamation strongly denouncing the moral depravity and oppressive measures of the tyrant Choe, in order to arouse public opinion in his favor.

Consequently, he succeeded in overthrowing the tyrannical regime and established the Chou dynasty with the Duke, his younger brother, as prime minister. King Wu died in 1116 B.C., leaving only a thirteen-year-old son as heir. A lad that young was obviously too inexperienced to perform the duties of a ruler, so his uncle, the Duke of Chou, decided that the young king should devote himself to studies under the guidance of instructors, while he (the Duke) acted as regent. This was a wise decision. Soon, however, rumors arose that the Duke was a potential usurper and wanted to be king himself.

Hurt by such rumors, he resigned from the regency and spent a period of time in retirement. It was probably during this period that he found consolation in the *I-Ching* and took up divination in order to obtain prophetic information concerning his own future and that of the kingdom. There can be little doubt that he had a deep knowledge of the art considered so important in his time.

The Duke was no less a genius than his father. As Legge has pointed out, he was "a patriot, a hero, a legislator and a philosopher."[6] He was also a musician and a great military leader who once personally led an army to suppress a serious revolt. Even Confucius admired him and made no secret of the fact. The Duke apparently had an analytical mind: he did not follow his father's example of treating each hexagram as an integral whole; instead, he directed his attention to the individual lines. To a man so highly gifted and so vastly learned, the lines of the various hexagrams would virtually come alive with meanings and implications. As he concentrated on the lines, a sort of mystic communion with them may have occurred.

Each line would, in accordance with certain well-developed rules familiar to him, reveal its symbolism or evoke some image in his psyche. He would then write down his symbolic interpretation or explanation of the line. Consequently, after his study of all the lines of the Sixty-Four Hexagrams, he had amassed a great wealth of commentary and interpretation. Like his father's judgments on the integral hexagrams, his symbolic explanations of the individual lines have been considered sound and correct and have been used as oracles by almost all students of the *I-Ching* who have followed him. As might be expected, his lineal interpretations of a hexagram always harmonize with King Wen's judgment on the hexagram.

These lineal interpretations refer to a large variety of things, including men and women, boys and girls, birds and beasts, natural phenomena, material objects, and the many situations and accidents of human life. They are not only much more numerous but also much more specific than King Wen's judgments. As counsels, however, they are similar to those judgments in that they also suggest the advantages or disadvantages of any given situation or course of action.

The Duke's lineal interpretations of the Sixty-Four Hexagrams constitute the secondary portion of the Text of the *I-Ching*. Every lineal interpretation represents a life situation subject to change. A hexagram, therefore, represents six changing life situations linked together and indicating some process of change.

Legge's logical mind also appeared to have trouble with some of the symbolisms the Duke derived from those lines, for he wrote, "According to our notions, a framer of emblems should be a good deal of a poet, but those of the *Yi* only make us think of a dryasdust."[7]

It seems rather odd to compare the English notions of poetic emblems in the nineteenth century with Chinese oracular symbolisms of 1100 B.C. In interpreting the individual lines of a hexagram, the Duke was not writing poetry but trying to clarify arcane symbols for the purpose of divination and moral edification.

CHAPTER 4

CONFUCIUS AND THE TEN WINGS

As a system of symbolism, the *I-Ching* is essentially based on the trigrams drawn by Fu Hsi (circa 3000 B.C.) and later developed into hexagrams. Fu Hsi was traditionally believed to be a sage-ruler of ancient China. Some modern Sinologues, however, consider him as merely a mythical figure, for according to their scholarship, Chinese history cannot date back beyond the beginning of the Shang dynasty (1766–1122 B.C.). But this piece of scholarship now seems to have been discredited. Toward the end of July 1986, the *China Daily*, a newspaper in Beijing (formerly Peking), reported that the tombs, temples, and monasteries unearthed in Liaoning Province have been ascertained by the China Archeological Society to be the relics of over 5,000 years ago, indicating that at that time an organized state had already existed in China. If so, then Fu Hsi may possibly have been a historical figure, living in or before 3000 B.C.

As a book the *I-Ching* did not begin to take shape until the latter part of the twelfth century, when King Wen and the Duke of Chou wrote the Text, as described in the preceding chapter. But scholars do not consider the book to have been completed until the *Shih I* (Ten Wings or Appendixes), believed to be the work of Confucius (551–479 B.C.), had been added to it. In the traditional form of the book, five of the Ten Wings are printed together with the Text. They are: the First and Second Wings, called *T'uan Chuan*, or *Treatise on Judgments* (consisting of comments on King Wen's Judgments on hexagrams); the Third and Fourth Wings, called *Hsiang Chuan*, or *Treatise on Symbolisms* (consisting of comments on the Duke's explanations of the individual lines); and the Seventh Wing, called *Wen Yen*, or *Comments on the Words* (featuring a deeper study of the first two hexagrams, Ch'ien and K'un). The remaining five Wings are printed separately, apart from the Text. They are: the Fifth and Sixth Wings, called *Ta Chuan*, or *Great Treatise*; also called *Hsi Tzu*, or *Appended Remarks* (dealing mainly with philosophical and metaphysical concepts); the Eighth Wing, called *Shuo Kua Chuan*, or *Treatise on Remarks about Trigrams* (consisting of notes on the formation of trigrams and hexagrams, their use for divination, and the many things symbolized by each trigram); the Ninth Wing, called *Hsu Kua Chuan*, or *Treatise on the Sequence of Hexagrams* (showing how the meaning of one hexagram leads to the meaning of the succeeding hexagram); and the Tenth Wing, called *Tsa Kua Chuan*, or *Treatise on Miscellaneous Hexagrams* (featuring a comparison and contrast of the meanings of hexagrams).

Since its completion as a book, the *I-Ching* has been regarded by scholars as an important fount of knowledge and wisdom. As such, it has occupied the close attention of numerous Chinese scholars through the centuries and has elicited thousands of learned treatises and commentaries. Among these commentators, it was generally agreed that the Ten Wings were mainly the work of Confucius. However, in his introduction to the *I-Ching*, Legge advances the thesis that the Ten Wings could not have been "from the style or pencil of Confucius."[1]

On this question, it is hardly possible to render any conclusive verdict. Pending the discovery of irrefutable archeological evidence, the question can be approached in only two ways: internal evidence through textual criticism, or inference from circumstantial evidence. Legge relies mainly on textual criticism, maintaining that internal evidence favors his contention. His strongest evidence is the phrase "the Master said," which appears in both the *Great Treatise* (Fifth and Sixth Wings) and the *Wen Yen* (Seventh Wing). Legge calls it "the fatal formula." His argument is that if Confucius were the author of those Wings, he would not have used the phrase to refer to himself.

However, centuries before Legge, Chu Hsi, a philosopher of the Sung dynasty, offered an alternative explanation for the phrase. According to Chu Hsi, the Appendixes having all been made by Confucius, he ought not to use the formula, "the Master said"; it may be presumed that it is a subsequent addition to the Master's text. But Legge was not satisfied and insisted that at best only what followed that phrase was by Confucius.[2]

A brief analysis of that little phrase will perhaps elucidate the issue, and show that Legge's argument is not so sound as it may at first appear. The word "Master" patently presupposes a disciple or disciples. It indicates that it was some of Confucius' disciples who used that phrase when quoting him. This in turn means that Confucius was studying the *I-Ching* with the help of some of his disciples. The following passage from the Confucian *Analects (Lun Yu)* may also be cited as evidence: "The Master's elegant discourses with his disciples were poetry, history and the observance of ceremonies."[3] If Confucius were wont to discourse with his disciples on cultural subjects in the prime of his life, was it likely that he would omit the *I-Ching* when he began its study during his latter years?

Because of his advanced age, Confucius was eager to complete this study, and it is probable that he enlisted the help of some of his disciples in the project. If so, then it would have been one of his disciples quoting Confucius who used the phrase "the Master said." In other words, some of Confucius' disciples very probably participated with him in writing the *Great Treatise* and the *Wen Yen,* but what they wrote would have been either inspired or directed by Confucius. They may have taken down material Confucius dictated during his lectures or things he said during their frequent sessions with him. In this light, the *Great Treatise* and the *Wen Yen* may be considered essentially the work of Confucius.

After establishing what he considers a valid case against Confucius being the author of the *Great Treatise* and the *Wen Yen,* Legge states: "Possibly there is no sound reason for holding the Confucian origin of the other seven (Wings)."[4] This reasoning smacks of "guilt by association" and is tantamount to saying that if three dunces are found among ten schoolboys, the other seven are probably also dunces.

Legge also cites several other pieces of internal evidence which he feels demonstrate that the Ten Wings were not "from the pencil of Confucius." He writes: "The first three paragraphs of this Appendix [Wen Yen] are older than its compilation, which could not have taken place till after the death of Confucius, seeing it professes to quote his words."[5] As he points out in the same context, Chu Hsi has offered an explanation for this criticism, but he remains unconvinced.

In another context, Legge states that the two Chinese words for Yin and Yang "do not present themselves" in the first two Wings (his Appendix I, for he rearranged the Ten Wings into seven Appendixes).[6] "We first meet with the names Yin and Yang in the Great Appendix (Treatise)."[7] His contention is that the first two Wings and the Great Treatise were by two different authors, one of whom could not have been Confucius. But here his scholarship is clearly at fault. The names Yin and yang definitely appear in the first two Wings in connection with the 11th Hexagram, T'ai, and the 12th Hexagram, P'i. Incidentally, Richard Wilhelm, who made the same oversight, was probably misled by Legge.[8]

Elsewhere, Legge refers to and translates the following passage from the Wen Yen: "The family that accumulates goodness is sure to have superabundant happiness, and the family that accumulates evil is sure to have superabundant misery."[9] He considers such a teaching un-Confucian and so could not have been composed by Confucius. He states, "The language makes us think of the retribution of good and evil as taking place in the family, and not in the individual; the judgment is long deferred, but it is inflicted at last, lighting, however, not on the head or heads that most deserved it."[10] Thus he makes a distinction, prevalent in Western countries, between the head or heads (parent or parents) and the family (children).

The Chinese do not make any distinction between the family and its head or heads. The Text merely uses the word "family" and does not say that the evil deeds of the heads will produce evil effects on the family. In Confucian ethics, the household ("chia," translated as "family" by Legge) includes *all* the members therein and is a closely knit social unit. Its members have a mutual concern for one another. The weal or woe of one member is shared by all the others. How can parents enjoy happiness individually without seeing that their children are also happy? How can children suffer misery individually without their parents suffering too? The passage in question plainly means that the good or evil deeds accumulated by *any* member of a household will produce corresponding effects on the entire household. Such a teaching cannot be considered un-Confucian. In fact, a similar idea appears in Christian ethics. According to Alexander Yelchaninov, a Russian high priest:

> When, because of the merits of one being, Christ says that "now salvation hath come to this house," these words mean that the eternal character of our earthly ties, the ties of blood, is recognized in the next world. The merits, the sufferings, of one being save his relations—how consoling and significant are these words, what an eternal value they give to our earthly life.[11]

Permit me now to set forth my own conviction concerning Confucius' authorship of the Ten Wings. I do not claim that my conviction is necessarily correct; the readers must consider both sides of this controversy and decide the issue for themselves.

In the *Analects* there is indeed a suspect passage which was translated by Legge as follows: "If some years were added to my life, I would give fifty to the study of the *Yi*, and might then escape falling into great errors."[12] As it stands, the passage is patently absurd, for Confucius was about seventy years of age when he made that remark. Surely he did not expect to live fifty years longer. Besides, though the *I-Ching* can be a hard nut to crack, it would not necessarily take Confucius fifty years to study it. In his annotation of this passage, Chu Hsi cites the opinion of another scholar to the effect that the two Chinese words for "wu shih" (fifty) in the passage are an erroneous separation of the word for "chu," meaning "finish" or "complete." This means that the sentence, "I would give fifty to the study of the *Yi*," should be "I would complete or finish the study of the *Yi*."

Whether corrupt or not, the passage clearly indicates Confucius' intense interest and high regard for the *I-Ching*.

Confucius was an indefatigable scholar and teacher, as he makes clear more than once in the *Analects*.[13] He wanted not only to improve himself but also to improve others. When he was over seventy, he looked back on his life with this self-appraisal:

> When I was fifteen, I made up my mind to study;
> At thirty, I set myself on a firm course;
> At forty, I was no longer perplexed by doubts;
> At fifty, I knew the will of Heaven;
> At sixty, I could readily understand what I heard;
> At seventy, I could follow the desires of my heart without transgressing the norm.[14]

This declaration shows that the entire life of Confucius was a progressive pilgrimage toward truth and the highest excellence. Confucius was one who never felt too old to study and learn. According to Ssuma Ch'ien, the great historian, Confucius studied the *I-Ching* so diligently that the leather belt for keeping the bamboo pages together gave way three times from wear and tear.[15]

Confucius also spoke of the *Ho T'u*, or *River Map*, which was supposed to have inspired Fu Hsi to draw the Eight Trigrams. He says, "The phoenix has not come and the river (Yellow River) has not sent forth any map. Would this be the end of me?"[16] The question seems to suggest that he felt his life or salvation would somehow depend on the map.

Confucius and Divination

Did Confucius believe in divination? There is evidence that he did and that subsequently he paid some attention to the counsel he received. In commenting on the remark, "Inconsistent in his virtue, a man will be visited with disgrace," Confucius says, "This is simply because he neglects the practice of divination."[17] One reason why Confucius might have been interested in divination, beyond its obvious use in forecasting the future, is that its practice requires perfect sincerity and truthfulness as well as reverence, and sincerity and reverence were virtues highly regarded by Confucius and his disciples.

In China, divination is an art with very ancient roots. By the beginning of the Chou dynasty (1122–255 B.C.), it already had a history of nearly two thousand years. The Text of the *I-Ching* now available to us was once called the *Chou I*, or the Chou system of change. As the *Chou I* formed a major feature of Chou culture, of which Confucius was an ardent admirer, he could not have ignored or neglected it. On one occasion he even says, "The Chou dynasty has the two preceding dynasties for reference and review. How elegant and exuberant are its cultural features! I follow Chou."[18]

Confucius considered it his life's mission to edit and preserve all cultural works of the Chou dynasty in order to hand them down in correct and proper form for the edification of posterity. He had edited such works as the *Book of History* and the *Book of Poetry*. Would he be likely to make an exception of the *Chou I*, which he considered to be so important? The following passage from the *Li Chi* (*Records of Rites and Ceremonies*) strongly suggests he did not:

> The Master said: "When you enter a country, you can tell its typical culture. If the people show themselves to be kind and gentle and sincere, they have been instructed in the *Book of Poetry*; if they are magnanimous and well acquainted with the past, they have been instructed in the *Book of History*; if they are generous and honest, they have been instructed in the *Book of Music*; if they are thoughtful and taciturn and observant, they have been instructed in the *Book of Changes*."[19]

The last sentence clearly indicates that Confucius had studied the *Book of Changes* very carefully, at least deeply enough to be familiar with its influence on human character.

Last, let us consider Confucius' attitude toward the two authors of the Text of the *I-Ching*, King Wen and the Duke of Chou. He once said this of King Wen: "He had in his possession two-thirds of the kingdom while serving the Yin (Shang) house. The virtue of Chou may be said to have attained its highest peak."[20] This was a tribute to King Wen, for he was the prince of the Chou principality at that time. That Confucius' admiration for the Duke of

Chou was equally great may be gathered from the following remark: "A man may have talents and abilities as charming as those
of the Duke of Chou; yet if he be proud and mean, his other qualities are not worth contemplating."[21]

Indeed, Confucius was so fascinated by the life and work of the
Duke that he used to dream of him frequently in his youth. In his
declining years, Confucius once lamented, "Serious is the state of
my deterioration. It has been a long time since I no longer saw the
Duke of Chou in my dreams."[22] Confucius was born more than
six hundred years after the Duke. That he would dream of an
historical figure so far away in time must be considered an un-
usual event in history as well as in psychology. It shows that his
admiration for the Duke must have lodged in the depths of his
soul.

The First Six Wings

Legge aside, is it conceivable that a man so filled with respect
and admiration for King Wen and the Duke of Chou could resist
the temptation to study and expound their greatest works, the
Text of the *I-Ching*? The above two comments alone are sufficient evidence to convince me personally that Confucius must
have edited and commented upon the Text. The application of
that European device, Occam's Razor, suggests that the First and
Second Wings (consisting of explanations of King Wen's judgments on the hexagrams) and the Third and Fourth Wings (consisting of comments on the Duke's explanations of the individual
lines) were in all probability written by Confucius himself. As for
the Fifth and Sixth Wings, often called *Ta Chuan*, or the *Great
Treatise*, there are reasons for believing that they were probably
composed by Confucius in collaboration with his disciples. After
writing the first four Wings, Confucius may have become concerned that he might not live long enough to finish his study unless he enlisted help in his research and composition. Moreover,
the *Great Treatise* required wider research and greater labor. It
does not deal with the Text alone but also delves into related subjects such as divination, philosophy, ethics, and even the arts and

crafts. Under the circumstances, Confucius may very well have enlisted the assistance and cooperation of his disciples, making the *Great Treatise* the result of a cooperative research enterprise in which he played the leading part.

The Seventh Wing

What has been said of the Fifth and Sixth Wings may be said also of the Seventh Wing, called *Wen Yen*. The *Wen Yen* is an extended study of the first two hexagrams, Ch'ien and K'un. These are the two key hexagrams of the whole *I* system and have considerable significance. Confucius had already commented on them in the first four Wings; after studying his comments, his disciples may have discovered many subtle points about which they would have liked to have been further enlightened by the Master. In subsequent discussions, questions were probably raised and answers given; hence the *Wen Yen*, in which the phrase "the Master said" often occurs.

The Eighth Wing

The Eighth Wing, the *Shuo Kua Chuan, or Treatise on Remarks about Trigrams,* seems designed for use in divination. It deals with the growth of milfoil stalks, which were used in divination, the formation of hexagrams from trigrams, the functions of the trigrams, and especially the symbolisms of the trigrams. In his introduction Legge expresses a strong admiration for the first section, saying that it is sufficiently worthy to be regarded as "from the pencil of Confucius." The latter part, however, which lists the numerous things each of the Eight Trigrams symbolizes, draws sharp criticism.

I believe that the first part must have been written by Confucius, while the latter part was prepared by his disciples, but actually, the latter part may have been the work of the Duke of Chou. According to some Chinese commentators, nearly all the symbolisms of the trigrams listed in this Wing are used by the Duke in his explanations of the individual lines of the Sixty-Four Hexagrams. The compiler of the Wing may have simply picked out these symbolisms and classified them under the various trigrams.

Legge saw these symbolisms as silly and trivial, and Wilhelm endorsed his view. But symbols are enigmatic things: they may be compared to mathematical signs or music scores. People who have had no training in music or mathematics cannot help but be baffled and irritated by their apparently enigmatic symbol systems. But to those who know their meaning they are an instantly recognizable language that allows them to do great work. Mathematicians make use of symbols to solve complicated problems in physics and help land men on the moon; musicians employ them to produce stirring and inspiring melodies and symphonies. Much the same may be said of the symbolisms found in the *I-Ching*. People who take a patient interest in them will find them a fertile source of ideas and guidance in personal conduct and moral evolution.

The Ninth Wing

The Ninth Wing is called *Hsu Kua Chuan,* or *Treatise on the Sequence of Hexagrams.* Sequence means the order in which the hexagrams are arranged. Fu Hsi and King Wen arranged them in one way and Shen Nung and Huang Ti arranged them in another. These two different arrangements may have aroused the curiosity of Confucius or his disciples and caused them to wonder if the matter of sequence had any significant underlying rationale. Their study led them to conclude that the hexagrams as arranged by King Wen present a smooth transition in meaning from the first hexagram to the last. Whether this was actually King Wen's original intent, no one knows, but it is indeed an ingenious arrangement and strings the hexagrams together in an orderly fashion like a beautiful strand of pearls.

The Tenth Wing

After the Ninth Wing was composed, the Tenth, *Tsa Kua Chuan,* or *Treatise on Miscellaneous Hexagrams,* came almost as a matter of course. It was probably born of the realization that hexagrams not lying adjacent to each other, and even in some spaces far apart, could have a relationship or yield a revealing contrast. As usual, Legge considered this Wing useless: "The student will learn nothing of value from it."[23]

Chinese commentators, however, have observed that the meanings this Wing assigns to the sixty-four names of the hexagrams are meant as clues to help interpret the significance of apparently unrelated hexagrams. For example, the meaning given the name of the 3rd Hexagram, Chun, is "seeing," or "perception." Thus, whenever the idea of "seeing" or "perception" appears in the text of any hexagram, that hexagram will be found to be closely correlated with the Chun Hexagram, even if they are separated by a wide distance.[24]

The evidence upon which the views presented in the preceding paragraphs are based seems to me a strong support of the thesis that the Ten Wings represent ideas springing principally from the mind of Confucius, if not actually flowing from "the pencil of Confucius."

Chapter 5

THE SYMBOLIC SYSTEM OF CHANGE

At the very beginning of his *Tao Teh Ching,* Lao Tzu calls Eternal Tao the unnameable originator of heaven and earth. This is similar to the idea expressed in the *I-Ching* when it says that the T'ai Chi engenders the Two Primal Forms, —— and — —.[1] The Two Forms symbolize Yin and Yang, Yin being the passive cosmic principle and Yang the active. These two principles are considered to be constantly at work in space and time, interacting and cooperating with each other to produce the ever-changing phenomena of the universe. They manifest themselves as Spirit and Matter, Father and Mother, Day and Night, Light and Darkness, Motion and Rest, Dynamic and Static, and other dualities familiar to us in daily life.

The T'ai Chi itself, however, is usually held to be beyond the grasp of the human intellect and consequently inexpressible in any human tongue. This is perhaps why neither Fu Hsi, King Wen nor Confucius ever tried to symbolize it. But centuries later, in the first part of the tenth century, a Taoist priest by the name of Ch'en T'uan prepared a *Wu Chi T'u (Diagram of the Ultimateless),* in which he represented the Wu Chi, or Infinite, by a circle. The term "Wu Chi" first appears in Chinese literature in Chapter 28 of Lao Tzu's *Tao Teh Ching,* so Ch'en may have been inspired by Lao Tzu in creating the diagram. Not long afterwards, Chou Tun-yi (1017–1073), father of Neo-Confucianism, got hold of the *Wu Chi T'u* and changed its name to *T'ai Chi T'u* without changing the diagram but giving it a different interpretation from that of the Taoist priest.[2]

Diagram Of The Ultimateless
Wu Chi T'u

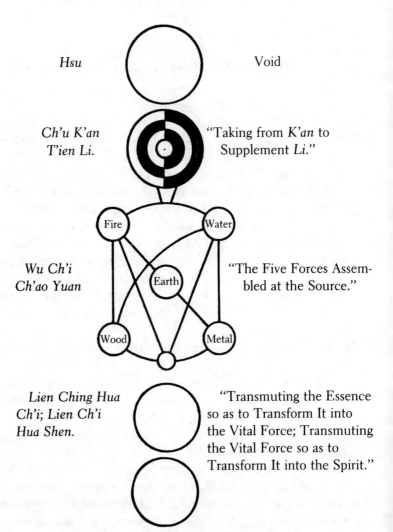

Hsu — Void

Ch'u K'an
T'ien Li. — "Taking from *K'an* to Supplement *Li*."

Wu Ch'i
Ch'ao Yuan — "The Five Forces Assembled at the Source."

Lien Ching Hua
Ch'i; Lien Ch'i
Hua Shen. — "Transmuting the Essence so as to Transform It into the Vital Force; Transmuting the Vital Force so as to Transform It into the Spirit."

"Doorway of the Mysterious Female"
Hsuan P'in Chih Men

THE T'AI CHI T'U
DIAGRAM OF THE SUPREME ULTIMATE

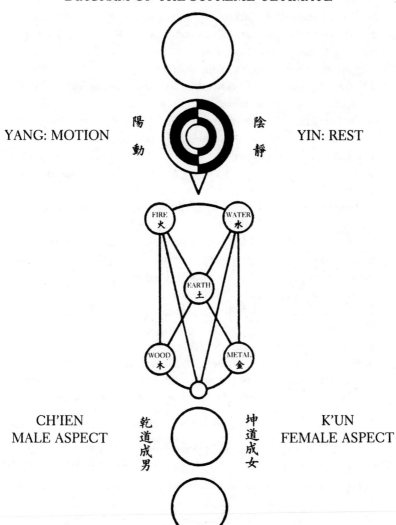

YANG: MOTION 陽動　　　陰靜 YIN: REST

FIRE 火　　WATER 水

EARTH 土

WOOD 木　　METAL 金

CH'IEN
MALE ASPECT
乾道成男　　坤道成女
K'UN
FEMALE ASPECT

CREATION OF ALL THINGS
萬物化生

It was Fu Hsi, the legendary sage-ruler of prehistoric China, who is believed to have first used the two lines —— and — — to symbolize Yin and Yang. Having done so, he probably manipulated the two lines in various ways in order to simulate the interplay of the two cosmic principles and create new symbols. He may have first placed one Yang line over another, and one Yin line over another, and then one Yang over a Yin, and one Yin line over a Yang. This manipulation resulted in the formation of the Four Emblems: ≡≡, ≡ ≡, ≡ ≡, ≡ ≡. The first is called T'ai Yang, symbolizing the sun; the second is called T'ai Yin, symbolizing the moon, both sun and moon being important agencies of change. The last two are respectively called Shao Yang and Shao Yin (literally, young Yang and young Yin), symbolizing the early spring sun and the crescent moon.

However, this system of symbols is still rather restricted in scope. Man himself is also an important agency of change; consequently, Fu Hsi is said to have manipulated the Four Emblems to form trigrams by adding to each of them first the Yang line and then the Yin line. Thus the Eight Trigrams came into being. Every trigram represents the Three Powers: the bottom line represents earth; the middle line, man; and the top line, heaven.

Each of the Eight Trigrams is an integral whole, representing a different agency of change: Ch'ien represents heaven; K'un, earth; K'an, water; Li, fire; Chen, thunder; Sun, wind; Ken, mountain; and Tui, marsh. Thus, cosmic and natural agencies of change are represented and brought into the *I* system of change.

The Five Elements

The Wu Hsing, the so-called Five Elements (water, fire, wood, metal, and earth), are not specifically mentioned in the *I-Ching* but are concealed in some of the trigrams: water is indicated in K'an; fire in Li; wood in Sun; metal in Ch'ien; and soil (earth) in K'un. They are popularly considered agencies of change by the Chinese because they both foster and subdue each other in cyclic fashion: water promotes the growth of trees or wood; wood is used as fuel to produce fire; fire burns things into ash to form soil (earth); soil develops and nurtures metal in its mines; and metal supports dew and moisture to form water. On the other hand, water quenches fire; fire melts metal; metal cuts wood; wood can be made into a plow to churn the soil; and soil can obstruct and dam up water.

The Creation of the Hexagrams

Further contemplation appears to have led Fu Hsi to realize that each of the Three Powers has two polar aspects: heaven shows light and darkness; earth displays land and water; and mankind divides into two sexes, male and female. And both aspects have a part to play in producing changes in the universe. To represent this, Fu Hsi doubled each of the lines in the trigram, and the hexagram was born. He then manipulated the Eight Trigrams through all the permutations by placing each one over itself and over each of the others, thus obtaining the Sixty-Four Hexagrams.

With the creation of the hexagrams the symbolic structure of the *I* system was complete, every level throughout the structure linked to some cosmic principle or agency of change, and the whole so designed as to simulate the natural system of change operating in the universe.

Whether or not Fu Hsi followed the above process of manipulating the two basic lines —— and — — is, of course, a matter of conjecture, but it is he who is traditionally regarded as the author of the trigrams and hexagrams.

The Significance of the Six Lines

However, even the Sixty-Four Hexagrams were considered inadequate to represent the numerous situations in human life and in the world in general. But here the genius of the Duke of Chou came into play. He did not attempt to expand the hexagram, but observed that *each* of the six lines could be viewed as having a symbolic significance of its own. This added six symbols to each hexagram and 384 symbols to the Sixty-Four Hexagrams. This number of symbols was considered sufficient to represent all of the complex situations of life, and no important commentator has seen fit to add to it since. Each lineal symbol represents a dynamic, changing life situation, its possible changes determined by its relationship to the other lines, as well as to the trigrams and the hexagrams.

Interpretation of the Hexagrams

Interpretation of a hexagram as a whole lies in considering the mutual influence of its two component trigrams. Every hexagram has its major symbolism, or symbolic significance, which sets forth and helps interpret its meaning.

As for the interpretation of the individual lines, the process is more elaborate. The lines of a hexagram begin their sequence from the bottom up. Take for example the 3rd Hexagram, Chun:

The bottom line is the first line, or Line 1. Then come Lines 2, 3, 4, 5, and 6.

The trigram above is called the upper or outer trigram, and the one below is called the lower or inner trigram. From the lower trigram to the upper is said to be "going out or up." From the upper trigram to the lower is said to be "coming in or down." Since the bottom line is the first line, the rising tendency is always from the first line up, and the falling tendency from the top line down. The bottom (first two) lines represent the two aspects of earth (land and water); the middle two lines represent the two aspects of man (male and female); and the top two lines represent the two aspects of heaven (light and darkness).

A hexagram not only has six lines but also six *places*. While the six lines of a hexagram are different in nature and arrangement from those of every other hexagram, the six places of a hexagram are fixed and the same in all the hexagrams. The first, third, and fifth places are called Yang; the second, fourth, and sixth places are called Yin. Thus, the six places are also governed by the Two Cosmic Principles.

A Yang line in any of the three Yang places is said to be in its *correct* place or position. The same may be said of a Yin line in any of the three Yin places. If a Yang line is in any of the Yin places, or if a Yin line is in any of the Yang places, its position is said to be *incorrect*. Naturally, it is better for a line to be in a correct position. In real life, a correct position means one which is congenial to a person's temperament and skills. For instance, a medical student who later becomes a doctor is in a correct position; if he is forced to become a soldier, his position becomes an incorrect one.

Even more important than correct position is *central* position, which is denoted by the middle line of the lower and upper trigrams. As it lies between the two extremes of a trigram, this line is considered to be symbolic of moderation, reason, the middle path, the Golden Mean. As a central position is usually also a favorable or advantageous one, the middle line of each trigram indicates favorable circumstances for action and consequently the power or authority to act.

A line may occupy both a correct and a central position: for instance, a Yang line in the fifth place, or a Yin line in the second place. Such a line is highly auspicious, indicating both congeniality and the authority to act. If a line is in a correct but not central position, it symbolizes congeniality without authority. If a line is in a central but incorrect position, it symbolizes authority without congeniality.

The three lines of the lower trigram stand in *correlation* with the three lines of the upper one: Line 1 correlates with Line 4, Line 2 with Line 5, and Line 3 with Line 6. If the correlates are of a different nature, one Yin and the other Yang, they are said to form a harmonious relationship and augur good fortune. The underlying reason is that there is a natural attraction between the elements symbolized by Yin and Yang. If the correlates are of the same nature, both Yin or both Yang, mutual repulsion or antagonism is said to exist between them, as it does with similar poles of a magnet or any other polar twins, and the auspice is considered unfavorable. There are, however, some exceptional cases, depending on the general significance of the hexagram. In these cases (see Lines 3 and 6 of the 26th Hexagram, the symbol of restraint), the two correlates are compared to birds of the same kind that flock together and get along well.

Any two adjacent lines of a hexagram are called *associates*. Their significance is more or less the same as that of the correlated lines. The bottom and top lines naturally represent the low and high points of a thing, or the beginning and end of a process. The bottom line, therefore, may represent the toes or feet of the body, a child, or the commencement of a career; the top line may represent the head or face, the leader of a team, the roof of a house, or the terminal stage of a development.

The top line, however, never signifies the greatest good fortune; for according to the philosophy of the *I-Ching*, when a thing has reached its extreme point, there is bound to be a decline or setback. What signifies the optimum good is Line 5. This is usually the most important line of a hexagram. It usually constitutes the lord, or ruling line, of a hexagram because it tends to determine the hexagram's general meaning or significance. The fifth line usually denotes a ruler, whether king, queen, or regent, and inferentially, the highest authority of any social organization. As its correlate is Line 2, the latter usually denotes an official. As Line 4 is near Line 5, it denotes a high official, minister, or power who is normally close to the ruler.

Line 4 being at the base of the upper trigram, and Line 3 being at the top or end of the lower trigram, they are said to be indicative of a transitional stage which in most cases is not a good auspice because it means encountering new circumstances, which consequently require new adjustments and adaptations.

Apart from the lower and upper trigrams, each hexagram also has two interior trigrams, the lower one formed by lines 2, 3, and 4; the upper by lines 3, 4, and 5. So far as significance is concerned, an interior trigram is like the lower or upper trigrams and is interpreted in more or less the same way (according to the relationship of its lines and the Yin or Yang nature of the lines and their places).

The Eight Trigrams are considered one family with two parents, three sons, and three daughters. Just as each member of the family exerts influence on themself and the others, so each line of a trigram determines its own significance as well as the significance of other lines and of the hexagram.

In certain cases, the line under interpretation will even change to its opposite, (i.e., from Yin to Yang and vice versa). This kind of change may cause surprise or perplexity. According to the philosophy of the *I-Ching*, no situation remains stationary; every situation is in a state of flux. In order to foretell what changes the future will bring, the line must be changed to reflect the new or altered situation; once it is changed, a new trigram and a new hexagram are formed, relating to the prospects in store. In social life, an occasion may arise when a man is powerless to change the circumstances or the people confronting him. Then it is necessary and desirable for him to change his own attitude or position and adapt himself to the circumstances or to other people so as to maintain harmony and a working system.

In the *Ta Chuan*, or *Great Treatise*, it is said that a Yang trigram has more Yin lines, while a Yin trigram has more Yang lines.[3] This clearly shows that integral trigrams are also divided into two categories: Yang and Yin. The Yin or Yang nature of a trigram also affects the meaning of the hexagram in which it appears and of its own individual lines.

There is another and rather advanced method of interpreting the lines of a hexagram: "analogy and correspondence" demonstrates that the Sixty-Four Hexagrams, with their 384 individual lines, are organically connected and interrelated. But this method is too technical and complicated to be set forth here.[4]

From what has been said above, it may be observed that in the *I-Ching* both the symbols and the rules for their interpretation have a logical basis which is derived from the T'ai Chi, the Two Cosmic Principles Yin and Yang, and other agencies of change in nature, as well as from self-evident truths and common sense. As the *Shuo Kua Chuan*, or *Treatise on Remarks about Trigrams*, says: "In remote antiquity, when the sages devised the *I* system, their purpose was to make it in accord with the principles of nature and destiny."[5]

Although each of the Sixty-Four Hexagrams is made up of only six lines which are either Yin or Yang in nature, it embodies many symbolisms and involves a large body of rules for interpretation. Some hexagrams have more Yang lines than others, some have more Yin lines than others, and some have an equal number of Yin and Yang lines. But each hexagram has its own unique arrangement of Yin and Yang, and this arrangement gives it and each of its lines a unique significance. As Wilhelm puts it: "The hexagrams and lines in their movements and changes mysteriously reproduce the movements and changes of the macrocosm."[6] In this sense the *I-Ching* is unique and distinctive as both a symbolic system and a philosophy of change.

King Wen and the Duke of Chou

While the hexagrams are traditionally attributed to Fu Hsi, the *I-Ching* makes no mention as to whether the rules of interpretation were inherited from the earlier Lien Shan or Kuei Ts'ang systems, or laid down by King Wen and the Duke of Chou. Since the rules were deduced from the nature and position of the lines of a hexagram and its component trigrams, it may be said that a hexagram also follows those rules in revealing its secrets. In rendering judgments on the hexagrams, King Wen was guided not by his personal notions and inclinations, but by those rules. The same may be said of the Duke of Chou in explaining the individual ines. As King Wen and the Duke were great sages, they were believed to be especially gifted to receive the oracles accurately, so that their interpretations themselves were also regarded as oracles for divination.

In the *Great Treatise*, it is said that "T'uan (individual hexagram) refers to symbolism, and Yao (individual line) refers to change."[7] King Wen's judgments on hexagrams stress symbolism and foretell the general aspect or prospect of a given situation; while the Duke's explanations of the individual lines stress the changes represented by the lines. Each line represents a life situation, and each situation bears within itself the seed of change, for no situation will remain stationary. The six lines of a hexagram, therefore represent a sequence of six changing situations, each carrying some indication of what the subsequent change will be and the reason for it. In the Sixty-Four Hexagrams, there are 384 lines representing the same number of life situations. Consequently, the Text of the *I-Ching* is really a vast system containing most of the major situations found in life and all the processes by which change occurs. This system follows certain sound and definite rules, thereby furnishing guidelines for human action.

The symbolic system of change described in the previous pages may very possibly have been what King Wen and the Duke of Chou found it to be in their time. They put flesh and blood into it by writing judgments on the hexagrams and explaining the individual lines. Thus, the Text of the *I-Ching* came into being.

It was probably this Text that aroused the interest of both Lao Tzu and Confucius. Many scholars have expressed the general notion that the *I-Ching* was the fount of both Taoism (Taoist school of philosophy) and Confucianism.

In conclusion, I would like to point out that according to an ancient script called *chuan*, the Chinese word for *I* is composed of two radicals: the upper one is evolved from the original symbol for sun, the lower from the original symbol for moon. In the *Great Treatise* it is said that "the sun having gone, the moon comes; the moon having gone, the sun comes. Sun and moon alternately take the place each of the other and there arises brightness or luminosity."[8] The Chinese word for *I*, therefore, signifies the periodic changes caused by the sun and moon. By inference it indicates the operation of the eternal Law of Periodicity and symbolizes the cycles of phenomenal change in the universe.

CHAPTER 6

DIVINATION: THEORY AND PRACTICE

DIVINATION AS TAUGHT in the *I-Ching* was practiced in China at a very early date, possibly not long after the dawn of her civilization. Chinese tradition regards Fu Hsi as the earliest of the legendary sage-rulers and the author of the Eight Trigrams, which were designed for divination. As stated in the *Great Treatise*, or *Ta Chuan*: "The Eight Trigrams determine good and ill fortune. Good and ill fortune give rise to great works."[1]

According to the *Shu Ching (Book of History)*, divination was a common practice at least as early as the twenty-third century B.C. and involved the use of tortoise shells.[2] This would seem to show that the art may have been quite well advanced around the beginning of the Hsia dynasty (2205–1766 B.C.). Originally, milfoil or yarrow stalks were used, not tortoise shells. The latter were widely used during the Shang or Yin dynasty (1766–1122 B.C.), and some of their remains have been uncovered by archeologists in modern times. But later the milfoil stalks became popular again, perhaps out of a benevolent desire to spare the tortoise.

The ancient sages believed in the existence of divine spirits and even sought to come in contact with them through divination with the milfoil stalks, which were thought to be of divine origin. The *Great Treatise* says: "Heaven produces the divine things (milfoil stalks and tortoise shells), and the Sage studied their nature."[3] The stalks and shells were considered divine apparently because they were believed to have the mysterious power of conveying oracles in the process of divination. (The milfoil plant still grows in the vicinity of the tomb of Confucius in Ch'u Fou, a town in Shantung Province.)

The Study of Divination

The above quotations seem to indicate that divination in ancient China was treated as a very serious matter and may have been conducted as a sort of sacrament whereby men sought divine aid and guidance for coping with certain situations in life. In practicing divination, therefore, one had to be very serious and sincere and adopt a reverential attitude as if it were a ceremony carried out in the presence of a divine being. Such an attitude was apparently considered conducive to obtaining divine or spiritual influence and also to make one more responsive to it. This may sound like superstition, but psychologically, it makes sense: even if what are regarded as divine spirits or the Divine Being are merely projections of one's own subconscious or unconscious mind, a sincere desire for guidance may have the effect of reaching and awakening one's own power, inducing it to reveal secrets as yet veiled in the mysterious future. As the *Chung Yung*, a well-known Confucian classic, says: "Perfect sincerity is capable of foreknowledge."[4] From the Confucian point of view, sincerity and reverence are important virtues, and a virtuous person is considered the best qualified to practice the art of divination.

It is not surprising, therefore, that in ancient times even the sages and the superior men took up divination. In the *Great Treatise* there appears this remark: "In the *I-Ching* there can be found four aspects of the way of the sages, and one of them is divination."[5] In this same *Treatise* it is also said that the study of divination occupied a great part in the daily life of the superior man: "Thus the superior man, when relaxing at home, will contemplate the symbols and study the explanations; and, when about to take any action, will contemplate the changes and the auspices."[6]

That divination was believed to be perfectly reliable as a means of unveiling the future may be gathered from the following passage in the *Treatise*:

> Therefore, when the superior man is about to undertake some task or to make some forward move, he writes

up an inquiry in so many words and consults the *I* (personified). The *I* receives the command like an echo reflecting a sound. Whatever the subject under consultation may be, whether faraway or nearby in locality, whether mysterious or profound in nature, the *I* offhand knows what the future destiny will be.[7]

In ancient China divination was held to be a respectable practice by its experts, the superior men who studied it every day. In later years, however, the practice was often abused superstitiously and for mercenary ends. Nevertheless, its true value has continued to command credence. In Japan, for instance, during the reign of Emperor Meiji, the Genro (council of elderly statesmen) regularly consulted the *I-Ching* for revelations concerning high affairs of state. Even in the present century, a number of eminent savants, notably C. G. Jung and Herman Keyserling, have been favorably impressed by the *I-Ching* method of divination and have testified to its efficacy.[8]

The Procedure of Divination

There was a certain procedure to be followed in *I-Ching* divination, which is described in Chapter 9, Section I, of the *Great Treatise*. The procedure presented in the following pages is broadly based on the content of that chapter and on some passages from the *I Hsueh Ch'i Meng* (*Beginner's Guide to the Study of the I-Ching*) by Chu Hsi, a noted philosopher of the Sung dynasty.

At the very outset, one should note that divination is not to be dabbled in frivolously for a new sensation or as a parlor game, but should be used only to resolve some serious issue or determine the outcome of some plan or situation.

In order to successfully utilize the *I-Ching* as a source of divination and guidance, it is first necessary to put one's inquiry into proper form. The inquiry should be couched in the form of a question that can be answered either in the affirmative or the negative. It is best not to couch this question in terms that are too definite or specific, such as: Will my salary be raised twenty percent from the beginning of next month? Rather it should be couched in more general and flexible terms, such as: Will the plan under consideration meet with good fortune in the foreseeable future? Will the victim of the accident eventually recover from his injuries?

The ancient instructions for consulting the oracle suggest that the diviner observe some abstinences and purify himself through ritual bathing to help achieve the proper attitude of humility and sincerity. Next, the diviner should attire himself in special robes. Having done this, he should light incense sticks in an incense-burner set on a clean table placed against the northern wall of the room. Above this table should be a picture of Fu Hsi or of the Eight Trigrams.

According to tradition, the burning of incense is supposed to have mystic significance: the rising smoke is considered a sign of reverence for the Divine Being, and its sweet smell is said to signify the Divine Presence. In this holy atmosphere the diviner then carefully takes out the bunch of fifty milfoil stalks and the copy of the *I-Ching* kept pure especially for the occasion. The stalks are placed in the center of the table, in front of the incense-burner, and the *I-Ching* is placed on the left, with pen and paper on the right.

Now the actual consultation begins: the diviner stands respectfully before the table, reverently invoking the spirit of Fu Hsi or King Wen or the Duke of Chou (or all three) while earnestly praying for revelation and guidance concerning the question he has formulated. At what he feels to be the proper moment,[9] the diviner takes up one stalk from the bunch and puts it aside. This stalk plays no further part in the process, for it is supposed to represent the Absolute, which, being all in all, does not enter into any process of creation or change and which, in fact, is above and preceeds it. The remaining forty-nine stalks are then divided into two portions at random to represent the Two Cosmic Principles Yin and Yang. (The number 49, however divided, always produces two different numbers, one odd and one even, to represent Yin and Yang.)

Having divided the forty-nine stalks into two portions, the diviner then places one portion on the right side of the table and the other portion on the left. He next takes one stalk from the portion on the right and inserts it between the little finger and the ring finger of the left hand (symbolizing heaven, earth, and man). Then he takes all the stalks in the portion on the left in his left hand and (still keeping the stalk between the last two fingers of his right hand) uses the right hand to draw the stalks out of the left, four at a time (to represent the four seasons). When there are four or fewer stalks remaining in the left hand, this remainder is inserted between the ring finger and the middle finger of the left hand (representing the intercalary month, which occurs once in three years). The discarded stalks (which remain held in the right hand) are now placed back on the left side of the table.

The diviner then uses his left hand (with the stalks still between his ring and middle finger) to pick up the portion of stalks he placed on the right, repeating the whole process again, taking four stalks at a time from the left hand with the right hand, and this time inserting the remainder between the middle finger and the forefinger of the left hand (representing the other intercalary month, which occurs during the next two years, for according to the lunar calendar there are two such months in five years). Now the discarded stalks, held in the right hand, are placed back on the right side of the table. The sum of the stalks now held between the fingers of the left hand is either 9 or 5. (In this system the number 5 is easier to obtain than the number 9.) The various possibilities are as follows:

$$1 + 4 + 4 = 9$$

$$\text{or } 1 + 3 + 1 = 5$$

$$\text{or } 1 + 2 + 2 = 5$$

$$\text{or } 1 + 1 + 3 = 5$$

These stalks are now laid aside for the time being (usually in front of the incense-burner), and the number 9 or 5 is written down on a chart, thus completing the first manipulation.

After this, the remaining stalks are gathered together again to form one heap which will number forty or forty-four stalks. This heap is then divided and manipulated in exactly the same manner as before. When finished, the sum of the stalks held between the fingers of the left hand will be either 8 or 4 (the chances between them being equal), made up as follows:

$$1 + 4 + 3 = 8$$

$$\text{or } 1 + 3 + 4 = 8$$

$$\text{or } 1 + 1 + 2 = 4$$

$$\text{or } 1 + 2 + 1 = 4$$

These stalks are then laid before the incense-burner and their sum written down beside the first. The diviner then repeats this process for a third time. The sum of the stalks held between the fingers of the left hand at the end of this manipulation will be either 8 or 4. Again the sticks from the left hand are placed before the chart and their sum written down.

Now sufficient data has been generated to establish the first of the six lines of a hexagram. The nature of this line is provided either by the three numbers which have been noted down or by the total of the two portions of stalks left over after the third manipulation. This figure is always equal to the difference between 49 and the sum of the three numbers noted down on the chart. When this figure is divided by 4, the quotient is always one of four numbers, namely, 6, 7, 8, or 9. These numbers are those of the Ssu Hsiang, or Four Emblems: Major Yang and Minor Yang, Major Yin and Minor Yin.

The number 9 signifies Major Yang, indicating a positive line that transforms into its opposite. As such, it will change into Yin. (Thus, if 9 is obtained, a Yang line —— with the special mark "o" in the middle is drawn [——o——] to show that this line is to be transformed.) The number 6 signifies Major Yin, indicating a negative line that moves. As such, it will change into Yang. (If 6 is obtained, a Yin line — — with the special mark "x" in the middle is drawn [——x——] to show that the line is to be transformed into Yang.) However, if either 7 or 8 is obtained, only a simple Yang line —— or a simple Yin line — — is drawn (the 7 signifying Minor Yang and the 8 signifying Minor Yin). These two lines are supposed to be at rest and therefore not taken into account in the interpretation of the individual lines.

From a glance at the three numbers he has obtained, an experienced diviner can tell at once what line is to be drawn. If he finds them to be, say, 5, 4, 4, he draws a Major Yang line, because $5 + 4 + 4 = 13$. Subtract this from 49, and the difference will be 36. Divide 36 by 4, and the quotient will be 9. Similarly, if he finds 9, 8, 8 on the paper, he draws a Major Yin line, because

$$9 + 8 + 8 = 25$$
$$49 - 25 = 24$$
$$24 \div 4 = 6$$

Groups of numbers such as 5, 4, 8 and 9, 4, 4 represent Minor Yin lines, while such groups as 5, 8, 8 and 9, 8, 4 represent Minor Yang lines, because in all these cases, the quotient is either 8 or 7.

To make up each of the six lines of a hexagram requires three manipulations of the stalks. Thus, eighteen manipulations are necessary to build up a hexagram. The resulting hexagram represents the *I-Ching*'s oracle on the situation about which the diviner is consulting it.

Transformation of Lines

The next question to be considered is the transformation of the Major Yang and Major Yin lines, if any. Naturally, every hexagram has the following possibilities: one in which no transformation takes place, the hexagram consisting entirely of "non-moving" lines (Minor Yang or Minor Yin); one in which all six lines are to be transformed, the hexagram consisting entirely of "moving" lines (Major Yang or Major Yin); six in which only one line is to be transformed; and fifty-six in which more than one line (from two to five) are to be transformed. In this way every hexagram can be brought into relation with every other hexagram. In other words, every hexagram is capable of being transformed into each of the other sixty-three hexagrams; and as there are sixty-four hexagrams altogether, the total number of possible transformations for the whole system of symbols is 64 × 64, or 4,096, which is considered sufficient to represent all the basic combinations to be found in most situations in nature and human life.

Whenever transformation is necessary, a new hexagram is drawn which is called "Chih Kua" (as distinguished from the original hexagram, which is called "Pen Kua"). For example, if the Ch'ien Hexagram ☰ is obtained, and its second line is to change to Yin, the transformed hexagram will be T'ung Ren ☰, whose meaning must also be taken into account in determining the outcome of the situation in question. Again, if Lines 2 and 5 of Ch'ien are changed into Yin, the transformed hexagram will be Li ☲, which must be taken into account by the diviner.

When these hexagrams have been obtained, the divination is at an end. The diviner then offers sincere thanks to the spirits who guided his hand and returns the *I-Ching* and the stalks to their respective places. This done, he proceeds to interpret the oracle.

The Rules of Interpretation

The general rules of interpretation are as follows:

(1) When the hexagram obtained consists entirely of non-moving lines (none of its lines are to be transformed), the diviner takes into account only the idea represented by the hexagram as a whole as set down in the Major Symbolism (symbolic significance of the hexagram), and in the judgment on it by King Wen and the explanation by Confucius of the judgment.

(2) When the hexagram obtained shows one moving line (when one line is to be transformed), not only the Major Symbolism and King Wen's judgment must be taken into account, but also the Duke of Chou's explanation of the moving line and, in addition, both King Wen's judgment and the Major Symbolism of the hexagram into which the original hexagram is transformed. In such a case, the original hexagram indicates the starting point of the development which, by reason of the influences of the moving line,

will later change into the situation represented by the transformed hexagram.

(3) When two lines in the hexagram obtained are to be transformed, not only the Major Symbolism of the hexagram and King Wen's judgment must be considered, but also the Duke's explanations of the two changing lines, with special attention given to the significance of the upper line.

(4) If the hexagram obtained shows three lines to be transformed, its treatment is the same as in Rule 3. The three moving lines represent the three principal stages in the development of the situation of the consulting party.

(5) If the hexagram obtained shows four moving lines, the treatment is the same as in Rule 3, with special attention paid to the lower of the two *untransformed* lines in the *transformed* hexagram. (This rule is given by Chu Hsi in his *I Hsueh Ch'i Meng*; however, many experienced diviners believe that the meanings of the two hexagrams as a whole and of the four moving lines should also be studied for probable revelations.)

(6) If the hexagram obtained shows five moving lines, its treatment is relatively simple. According to Chu Hsi, only the Duke's explanation of the *untransformed* line of the *transformed* hexagram should be studied for guidance. However, most experienced diviners disagree with Chu Hsi here, too, and maintain that the meanings of the two hexagrams as a whole and of the five moving lines should also be taken into account.

(7) If the hexagram obtained consists entirely of moving lines, its treatment is also relatively simple. Although it is advisable to consider the meaning of the original hexagram and of its lines, only King Wen's judgment on the *transformed* hexagram need be considered in interpreting the prognosis for the consulting party.

The oracles conveyed by the hexagrams of the *I-Ching* are not necessarily fatalistic in nature. Other oracles, notably those from the Temple of Apollo at Delphi, presage manifestations of inexorable Fate, against which man seems helpless, as the story of Oedipus clearly shows. The oracles obtained from the hexagrams, however, are usually counsels as to what the wisest and most harmful courses are in various life situations. They point out the ways to gain good fortune and ward off trouble. They leave man free to determine his own destiny. As man is a spiritual being, endowed with initiative and free will, he can choose to be guided by the oracle and follow a course of action that will set in motion new forces that can modify events in his favor, thus changing from a passive puppet of Fate to an active conspirator with it.

Part II
TEXT AND RELATED APPENDIXES

The CH'IEN Hexagram
(Symbol of Creativity)

1st  乾

In Chinese philosophy and metaphysics, Ch'ien represents the creative cosmic principle and usually pairs with K'un, the receptive cosmic principle, just as Yang pairs with Yin, heaven with earth, and spirit with matter or nature. Generally speaking, Ch'ien, Yang, heaven, and spirit are interchangeable terms and have the same connotations. They suggest such qualities as vastness, strength, power, motion, light, and intelligence and may be regarded as omnipotent, omniscient, and omnipresent.

In the world of human relationships, they connote the male as antithetical to the female, father as antithetical to mother, husband as antithetical to wife, ruler as antithetical to minister, and master as antithetical to servant.

In individual man, they connote his energy, moral strength, and mental faculties as opposed to the body and the senses.

Confucius calls Ch'ien the greatest strength in the universe. Great strength engenders great and continuous motion. The creative principle is thus viewed as the most dynamic power in the universe, creating and transforming all things. It influences and governs the vast and distant masses of the nebulae no less precisely than it does the microcosmic laws of the atom. Most mysteriously, it works within man as his creative energy, making him a potential sage capable of serving as an effective agent of the Creator and a moral leader of his fellow men.

To symbolize this creative principle, either Fu Hsi or King Wen devised a hexagram with six Yang lines and named it Ch'ien. Each

Yang line, being straight and continuous, suggests strength and motion. Three such lines form the Ch'ien trigram, and together they reinforce each other, suggesting immense strength and constant motion. The Ch'ien Hexagram is formed by placing two Ch'ien trigrams one above the other. The new figure with the combined trigrams suggests inexhaustible strength and ceaseless motion, an apt symbol of the creative principle as the primal originator and eternal transformer of all things in the universe.

KING WEN'S JUDGMENT ON THE HEXAGRAM:

The T'uan was a prehistoric animal in China noted for its keen sensitivity and sharp horns. In the original Chinese Text of the *I-Ching*, the judgment on a hexagram is called a *T'uan*, signifying keen intelligence and deep insight.

In contemplating the Ch'ien Hexagram, King Wen rendered his judgment in only five words: "Ch'ien: *Yuan, Heng, Li, Chen*." The first word refers to the creative principle, symbolized by the hexagram. The last four words denote its four attributes. These five words constitute the first sentence of the *I-Ching* and may be translated as follows:

Ch'ien, the creative principle, is great and originative (Yuan), pervasive and prospering (Heng), advantageous and benefiting (Li), correct and firm (Chen).

The word *"Yuan"* in Chinese means primordial, original, initial, head, chief, top, or peak. It is, therefore, aptly descriptive of the creative and originative attributes of Ch'ien.

After things have been created, the creative force (Ch'ien) does not leave them as they are, but continues to change and transform them. Ch'ien pervades the universe and is the force that underlies the growth and flourishing of all things. This fostering and vitalizing attribute is called *"Heng"* by King Wen. Heng in Chinese means pervasive, prosperous, flourishing, successful—a suitable name for the attribute.

Ch'ien is in perpetual motion: as it moves it continues to act upon things. After their initial growth, things move on to a higher stage of development: plants become mature and bear fruit; children become adults. The beneficial influence which underlies the phenomenon of fruition and maturity is another attribute of Ch'ien. King Wen calls it *"Li."* In Chinese this word consists of two radicals, or root components, the left one meaning grain and the right one meaning knife, thereby suggesting harvesting, reaping profit, or obtaining benefit.

To become wealthy or attain success is one thing; to stay wealthy or retain success is another. Either may turn out to be a misfortune in disguise. After a goal has been reached, there is often a setback or a tendency to decline, just as plants begin to wither after their mellow glory in the fall. To cope with this tendency requires circumspection and careful consideration. Yet precisely at the hectic moment of success, people are apt to be overly optimistic and ambitious and rush into reckless ventures which may lead to their downfall. To avoid such dangers requires fortitude and firmness of mind as well as correct attitudes and policies, so that instead of overplaying our hand we can plan with prudence and judiciously conserve our resources for a new cycle of activity and progress, just as plants withdraw and store up their vitality in the roots in preparation for new life in the spring. This attribute of fortitude, or "firm correctness," is called *"Chen"* by King Wen. In Chinese the word usually means chastity and purity, but also implies fortitude, firmness of mind, rectitude, and moral integrity and aptly characterizes the fourth and final attribute of Ch'ien.

Through the centuries, there have been many controversies among commentators on the *I-Ching*. One such concerns the four attributes of the creative principle. Some authorities, including Confucius, maintain that the four words, *Yuan, Heng, Li,* and *Chen*, signify four separate attributes; others contend that they represent only two, because the first two words often appear together as a phrase in the Text, and so do the last two. Chu Hsi, a famous philosopher of the Sung dynasty, is among the latter group, but he appears to contradict himself when he says that the four attributes correspond to the four seasons of the year:

The budding forth of things into life is manifestation of the attribute of origination, and among the seasons it corresponds to spring. The growth and development of things is manifestation of the attribute of pervasion, and among the seasons it corresponds to summer. The attainment of fruition is manifestation of the advantageous and benefiting attribute, and among the seasons it corresponds to autumn. The storing up of nature's resources and energy is manifestation of the attribute of firm correctness, and among the seasons it corresponds to winter.

Whether or not this interpretation is sound would be difficult to say, but it does show that Chu Hsi considered *Yuan, Heng, Li* and *Chen* as four attributes, not two.

Ren Ch'i-yun, a scholar of the Ch'ing dynasty, has advanced some interesting interpretations concerning the four words. He says that the four attributes of Ch'ien correspond to the four main stages of man's life: childhood, maturity, old age, and death. In another interpretation, he says that the first two attributes (*Yuan Heng*) represent the outflow of the Yang principle from rest to activity, or from unity to multiplicity, and the last two attributes (*Li Chen*) represent the inflow of the Yang principle from multiplicity to unity, or from activity to rest. It is impossible to verify whether this rather metaphysical interpretation is what King Wen had in mind, but Hindu philosophy teaches a similar doctrine.

King Wen's judgment on the Ch'ien Hexagram sets forth his theory of creation in which Ch'ien is envisioned as ceaselessly active, forever creating, vitalizing and sustaining things, and mysteriously determining every phase of cyclical phenomenal change.

CONFUCIUS' EXPLANATION OF KING WEN'S JUDGMENT:

1. *Vast indeed is the great originative power of Ch'ien. To it all things owe their beginning. It thus commands the entire heaven.*
This paragraph explains the first attribute of Ch'ien, *Yuan*.

Confucius seems to be filled with awe as he contemplates the universe. Here, he implies that Ch'ien is the original cause not only of all things on earth but also of the sun, moon, and the countless stars in heaven ("commands the entire heaven"). In fact, it is heaven itself.

2. *Clouds move. Rain is distributed. The myriad things assume their changing forms.*

This second paragraph explains the second attribute, *Heng*. It sets forth a vivid illustration of how Ch'ien prospers all things, causing them to flourish and grow in all their myriad forms. Water is necessary to life, whether of plants or animals, and rain is the most important source of water. Confucius, however, refers not only to rain and its distribution but also to the movement of clouds. He apparently wants to direct people's attention to the infinite expanse of heaven and its immense beneficence. Ch'ien (heaven) not only causes all things to flourish and grow but continues to support their lives so that they may fulfill their natures.

3. *The Sage amply understood the end and the beginning and discerned six situations in accord with the spirit of the times. He rode the six dragons, each at the proper time, and drove through the sky.*

This paragraph explains the third attribute, *Li*. ("The Sage" is probably either Fu Hsi or King Wen.) The terms "six situations" and "six dragons" clearly reflect the six lines of the Ch'ien Hexagram, and it was either Fu Hsi or King Wen who first devised the hexagram to represent six different situations, each according to a different set of circumstances. The Sage obviously understood well the basic principles of life ("the end and the beginning" of things). Ch'ien is active and creative; the Ch'ien Hexagram, therefore, was intended by the Sage as a guide to creative action for himself and the people. Through long and rigorous study, the Sage could make use of the guidelines with great ease. He understood the prophetic indications of each line so well that he knew immediately which line to follow in any given situation. To him the six lines were indeed like six dragons. He knew which one to ride at a given time and drove them, as it were, through the sky.

4. *The way of Ch'ien ever effects changes and transformations. Each man should rectify his nature and destiny accordingly and*

preserve his harmony with the Grand Concord. Then it will be advantageous to stay firm and correct.

This paragraph explains the fourth attribute, *Chen.* As the way of Ch'ien causes the entire universe to remain in a state of constant flux, change is always current in everyone's life. The problem then arises of how to deal with this. Confucius instructs us to follow the path suggested by the firmness of the six lines of the Ch'ien Hexagram, maintaining our own inner integrity while constantly rectifying and readjusting ourselves to remain in harmony with what our changing situation in life brings (harmonizing "with the Grand Concord"). In this state of flux, the most advantageous course is to firmly adhere to the correct course of truth.

5. *The Sage elevates himself above the myriad things and will bring peace to all nations.*

This paragraph refers to the subject of Line 5 of the hexagram. This is the most important and auspicious line, the so-called *ruler* or *ruling line* of the hexagram, indicating great good fortune and highly favorable circumstances for action. Any average person finding himself in such circumstances will attain success of some sort. But when a Sage, or one sage enough to follow the way of the *I-Ching*, with his consummate virtues and extraordinary abilities, happens to be in such circumstances, he will inevitably become a ruler and translate his benevolent aspirations into living realities for his own satisfaction and for the welfare of the people ("peace to all nations").

SYMBOLIC SIGNIFICANCE OF THE HEXAGRAM AS NOTED BY CONFUCIUS:

Heaven's movement is steady and strong. The superior man is inspired thereby to strive ceaselessly to strengthen and improve himself.

There are various conceptions of heaven. In Western literature the term "starry heavens" frequently appears, indicating more than one heaven. The Buddhists believe there are thirty-three heavens (and eighteen hells). According to the *I-Ching*, there is only one heaven, for heaven means the Yang power or Spirit, and there is only one Spirit pervading all space. Why then does the Ch'ien Hexagram consist of two Ch'ien trigrams, *each* signifying heaven? The two trigrams do not mean there are two heavens; they signify the idea of heaven daily renewing itself. With every new dawn there is a new heaven. This eternal renewal demonstrates the inexhaustible strength and power of heaven and furnishes inspiration to the superior man to likewise exert himself ceaselessly for self-improvement. In this respect, the superior man may be likened to Wordsworth's "Happy Warrior"

> Who, not content that former worth stand fast,
> Looks forward, persevering to the last,
> From well to better, daily self-surpast.

Emperor T'ang, founder of the Shang dynasty, practiced this kind of daily self-renewal. On his bathing tub was engraved: "If you can one day renovate yourself, do so from day to day. Yea, let there be daily renovation" (Legge's translation).

DUKE OF CHOU'S EXPLANATION OF THE INDIVIDUAL LINES (a) AND CONFUCIUS' COMMENT THEREON (b):

Line 1, Yang:

(a) *The hidden dragon does not act.*

(b) *"The hidden dragon does not act." This is because its Yang power is submerged underground.*

Line 1 (Yang) represents a dragon. Since the first two lines of a hexagram represent the earth, and Line 1 represents the underground, the line further suggests a dragon hidden underground. It does not act because its low position does not allow much room for it to move about. In the human world, such a dragon symbolizes an able person who remains inactive because of unfavorable circumstances.

Line 2, Yang:

(a) *The dragon appears in the field. It is advantageous to see the great man.*

(b) *"The dragon appears in the field." Its virtue is diffused far and wide.*

Line 2 represents the surface of the earth as well as a dragon, indicating a dragon seen in the field. This line, being the central one of the lower trigram, also represents man. Its central position signifies that the man is possessed of the central cardinal virtues. Furthermore, it is the correlate of Line 5, which represents the sage-ruler. The man it denotes is a great man, and his virtues make it advantageous for people to see and be inspired by him. This interpretation, favored by Wang Pi and other *I-Ching* scholars, was disapproved of by Cheng K'ang-sheng, a leading scholar of the Han dynasty. He maintained that the correct interpretation implies that it is advantageous for the subject of Line 2, who has just emerged from seclusion and obscurity, to go forth and become acquainted with some great man (such as the sage-ruler of Line 5) in order to gain recognition or receive some benefit. Confucius seems to have favored the former interpretation, for he says that the subject of Line 2 has diffused his influence far and wide.

Line 3, Yang:

(a) *The superior man is intensely active all day long. At nightfall, he still seems to be alert and apprehensive. The situation is perilous, but there will be no error.*

(b) *"Intensely active all day long." He reviews over and over again the path he is following and returns to it in case of deviation.*

The subject of Line 3 realizes he is in a perilous situation. The line occupies a position that is correct (Yang in a Yang place) but not central, indicating that its subject cannot express himself as freely as he wants. Moreover, the line occupies the top of the lower trigram—beyond heaven signified by the top two lines, beyond earth signified by the bottom two lines, and only at the edge of the world of man. Its subject can neither enjoy the blessings of heaven nor establish a firm abode on earth. His situation is therefore rather perilous; he must be very careful about how he proceeds in order to avoid error or blame.

Line 4, Yang:

(a) *The dragon would leap up now and then while in the cavern. No error.*

(b) *"Would leap up now and then while in the cavern." It will be no mistake to advance.*

Line 4 symbolizes an insecure and uncertain situation. It is neither in a central position nor correctly placed, being a Yang line in a Yin position. Furthermore, it is at the base of the upper trigram, indicating a stage of transition involving new adjustments. Its subject does not find himself in a comfortable situation but is nevertheless tempted to soar by the sight of heaven just above him. So he acts like a dragon in a cavern that "would leap up now and then" but is forced to return to the cavern.

According to Wang Pi, the most advantageous course for one in such a situation is to purify himself of selfish desires and let his every "leap upward" be motivated by a noble, altruistic purpose. Confucius says of this line that it is proper for the subject to advance. This opinion seems sound, for movement from Line 4 to Line 5 means movement from an incorrect and noncentral position to a correct and central one. If this move is motivated by a high altruistic purpose, it is likely to succeed. Some other *I-Ching* scholars have suggested that the line in this place indicates that the subject should look for opportunities that will come at particular moments.

Line 5, Yang:

(a) *The dragon is flying in the sky. It is advantageous to see the great man.*

(b) *"The dragon is flying in the sky." The great man is actively pursuing his creative career.*

Line 5 is the ruling line of the Ch'ien Hexagram and as such signifies Yang power. It is both central and correct (Yang in a Yang Place) and is in the realm of heaven, represented by the top two lines. Its central position in the upper trigram also represents man, suggesting man in heaven. Further, the line denotes the stage at which the Yang power is manifesting intensely without going to the limit. Its subject is a truly great man, a sage-ruler. As Confucius' comment indicates, he is manifesting his greatness, fulfilling his destiny, and attaining the crowning glory of his spiritual life. It is decidedly advantageous to see such a great man.

Line 6, Yang:

(a) *An arrogant dragon has occasion for repentance.*

(b) *"An arrogant dragon has occasion for repentance." What is at its fullest cannot last long.*

An arrogant person, symbolized by the arrogant dragon, is apt to be too eager to advance. He is therefore highly liable to transgress the proper limit in his actions and consequently encounter difficulties which will cause him to repent. But repentance is a good thing: a repentant person usually desires to correct his errors. To parody Alexander Pope: To err is human, to repent, divine.

What is the correct course after repentance? According to the Ancients: Seek a new cycle of activity and humble oneself by beginning over in a low position.

When he says, "What is at its fullest cannot last long," Confucius refers to the Law of Cyclic Reversion, according to which Yang, having manifested to its maximum extent, will inevitably revert to its polar opposite, Yin.

Nine used up:

(a) *There is seen a drove of dragons devoid of heads. Good fortune.*

(b) *"Nine used up." It is the virtue of heaven not to assume leadership all the time.*

After explaining Line 6, the Duke of Chou adds this extra paragraph. Such an extra paragraph is unique to the first two hexagrams, Ch'ien and K'un.

What is the meaning of this extra paragraph? This question has called forth at least four different explanations from *I-Ching* scholars throughout the centuries. They all fail to give any reason why an extra paragraph was added only to the Ch'ien and K'un Hexagrams and not to any of the remaining sixty-two. At least there is no explanation that commands general acceptance. The inconclusive nature of the controversy tempts this writer to advance a new explanation, which may not necessarily be the right one, but is in harmony with both the context of the extra paragraph and the basic teachings of the *I-Ching*.

The term "Yung chiu" in the Chinese text literally means "Use nine," but it should more properly be translated as "Nine used up." The numeral 9 denotes Yang, or Yang power. Nine used up, therefore, means that Yang has manifested to its maximum extent. The context shows that this is the natural remark for the Duke of Chou to make, for he has just explained Line 6 of the hexagram, which signifies that Yang has advanced to its extreme limit. What then? "There is seen a drove of dragons devoid of heads." Dragons are dynamic male creatures symbolizing Yang, and their heads are the Yang portions of their bodies. Dragons devoid of heads, therefore, have lost their dynamic masculine attributes and have become passive female creatures symbolizing Yin. In other words, the Yin influence has emerged.

According to the Law of Cyclic Reversion as taught in the I-Ching, this emergence of Yin inevitably occurs after Yang has manifested to its maximum extent. Symbolically, the Ch'ien Hexagram is no more, and the K'un Hexagram symbolizing Yin comes into being. This fact is always taken into consideration in the process of divination based on the I-Ching.

This also explains clearly why the Duke of Chou adds an extra paragraph only after the lines of the Ch'ien and K'un Hexagrams; for *only these two*, respectively representing Yang and Yin, are involved in the Law of Cyclic Reversion.

In commenting on the extra paragraph at the end of the Ch'ien Hexagram, Confucius says that it is not the virtue of heaven to assume leadership all the time. This also refers to the Law of Cyclic Reversion, according to which Yang, after its maximum manifestation, yields leadership to Yin. One commentator has expressed the view that Yang, or heaven, never shows itself outwardly as a leader. This individual seems to have confused heaven with the Absolute, or T'ai Chi, from whence heaven originally derived its being.

The I-Ching teaches that harmony should always be maintained between the influence of Yin and Yang and that any prolonged excess of one over the other is unpropitious. Therefore this replacement of Yang by Yin is considered good fortune. In Line 6 of the Ch'ien Hexagram, its subject has already exceeded the proper limit and should be concerned with repenting his transgression. If instead of repenting, Yang continues to advance, the situation will become disastrous. But if Yang, after its fullest manifestation, reverts to Yin, the opposite pole, then the two are waxing and waning correctly, thereby maintaining the eternal harmony that allows the manifestation of Tao. This is undoubtedly good fortune.

CONFUCIUS' FURTHER EXPLANATION OF KING WEN'S JUDGMENT:

In the Chinese Text, this section is called *Wen Yen*. These two words literally mean "Literary Sayings," or "Comment on the Words." Both these interpretations were considered objectionable by the traditional Chinese commentators, who felt that these titles could have been equally applicable to Confucius' other comments in the *I-Ching*. Liang Wu Ti, emperor of the Liang dynasty, once suggested that "Wen" in the title meant King Wen and that *Wen Yen* simply meant "King Wen says." However, he overlooked the fact that there is a later section, also called *Wen Yen*, commenting on the Duke of Chou's explanation of the individual lines of the hexagram. For the above reasons, the term "Confucius' Further Explanation" is used here. This is not a translation of the two words "*Wen Yen*," but refers only to the nature of its contents.

1. *What is called* Yuan, *the great originative attribute, is the supreme good. What is called* Heng, *the pervasive and prospering attribute, is a combination of what is beautiful. What is called* Li, *the advantageous and benefiting attribute, is the harmony of what is right. What is called* Chen, *the attribute of firm correctness, is the essential factor in the management of affairs.*

The reason why *Yuan* constitutes the first attribute of Ch'ien is obvious, for its function is to originate or give birth to all things. Without it, nothing can be or could have been created, and the three other attributes would have no *raison d'être*. It is, however, not only the source of all things but also, as Confucius sees it, the supreme good, or the best of all that is good. Confucius must have believed that Ch'ien is essentially good and that this goodness is behind all creation, especially the creation of man. Hence the well-known Confucian doctrine that human nature is naturally good, a doctrine which Mencius, the greatest sage after Confucius, developed with great brilliance in his own works.

In commenting on *Heng,* the second attribute of Ch'ien, Confucius tells us that this process of fertile and burgeoning growth is a combination of everything that is beautiful. All things are beautiful during their initial burst of life. In summer, when plants are in full bloom, they radiate fragrance and beauty all around, eloquent evidence that *Heng* is indeed the heart of that which is beautiful.

In commenting on *Li,* the third attribute, Confucius says that those things which are truly fruitful or beneficial are in harmony with what is right. He implies that *Li* inspires this harmonious collaboration, or at least is the result of such collaboration. For the maturation or fruitful development of things to occur, the right factors must converge. In autumn plants mature and bear fruit, thereby yielding benefit or advantage. What contributes to this fruition? It is the harmonious collaboration of such factors as fertile soil, favorable weather, and the proper method of cultivation. In the realm of man, the *Li* attribute suggests that only when mind and body are working together harmoniously can he think and act rightly, and only when he can act rightly can he fulfill his life's dream.

The fourth and last attribute, *Chen,* is linked by Confucius to the management of affairs through firm correctness (correctness implying not only a correct course but a correct position). A position is considered correct when it suits the aptitude and abilities of its occupant. But correctness alone is not enough; to succeed it must be coupled with firmness. The course of human affairs, whether personal or social, is seldom smooth-flowing and is often punctuated by obstacles, failures, and disappointments. In this regard, it is significant that *Chen* corresponds to winter. In winter plants wither, while nature in general presents a bleak and menacing aspect. To wither suggests death, and in a deeper sense means withdrawing the life force underground to the roots where it is stored and preserved for the renewal of life in the spring. In the natural course of events a man may find himself, like a plant in winter, overtaken by adversity. If he is to save and preserve his resources (mental and physical) for the next campaign in the warfare of life, he may have to withdraw from active participation for awhile and suffer hardship and loss. To survive this disheartening situation, he must display fortitude in the management of his affairs, firmly following a correct course. If he is weak-minded and allows himself to waver, failure and disaster will surely follow.

2. *The superior man, exemplifying benevolence, is qualified to be the leader of men; combining in himself what is beautiful, he is qualified to be a model of propriety; able to benefit all things, he is qualified to harmonize what is right; being firm and correct, he is qualified to manage affairs ably.*

"Exemplifying benevolence" means maintaining a benevolent attitude toward people and actively working for their welfare. Such a man will command the love and support of the people and so become their leader.

Combining within himself all that is beautiful (i.e., good, worthy), the superior man is able to act in a way proper to any occasion and creating the idea of propriety.

To benefit all things is very difficult, and requires a strong sense of what is just or right. Within human society there are all kinds of people, and their interests are often in conflict. To benefit all and render each individual his just due requires the ability to harmonize and resolve these conflicts. Only the superior man who puts all lesser interests aside and considers it his duty to benefit everyone is able to do so.

Even in the absence of difficulties and obstacles, the successful management of human affairs requires a steady purpose, firm determination, and undeviating perseverance. Uncertainty, lack of confidence, and frequent change of mind and direction will almost inevitably end in failure. Only the superior man who possesses the wisdom and faith to remain firmly on the correct course is fit to manage human affairs.

3. *The superior man who practices these four virtues furnishes reason for the remark that he personifies the four attributes of Ch'ien:* Yuan, Heng, Li, Chen.

The four virtues (benevolence, propriety, rightness, and wisdom-faith) are strongly linked here to the four attributes of Ch'ien, with benevolence corresponding to *Yuan* because *Yuan* is the supreme good; propriety corresponding to *Heng* because *Heng* is the producer of beauty; rightness corresponding to *Li* because *Li* inspires the harmony of what is right; and wisdom-faith (two different but closely related virtues: wisdom determines correctness and faith determines firmness of purpose) corresponding to *Chen* because *Chen* denotes both correctness and firmness.

This correspondence between the four virtues and the four attributes of Ch'ien has some special significance from the standpoint of spiritual cultivation. It is believed that he who practices and personifies the four virtues will become identified with Ch'ien (heaven, or spirit).

4. *What is called the great originative attribute of Ch'ien creates things and prospers their growth.*

Here, the two attributes *Yuan* and *Heng* are referred to. *Yuan* is what originates or creates things and *Heng* is what prospers their growth. These are closely related, one without the other having little or no effect.

5. *Beneficence and firm correctness refer to nature and feelings.*

Li, the attribute of benefit, and *Chen*, the attribute of firm correctness, are coupled together as belonging to the realm of the nature and feeling of things. There are countless things in the universe. Each has its own nature and reacts to external stimuli accordingly. It is this condition that prevents the cosmos from becoming a chaos.

6. *Ch'ien creates and is able to benefit the world with what is beautiful and beneficial. Yet it does not speak of the benefits it bestows. It is great indeed.*

The first sentence of this paragraph is full of inspiration and hope, telling us that Ch'ien (heaven) wills all creation to be good and beautiful. The next two sentences may be taken as a paean to the greatness and magnanimity of Ch'ien as well as a hint as to how we should conduct ourselves.

7. *How great indeed is Ch'ien, the creative cosmic principle! Strong, vigorous, central, and correct, it is the pure, genuine quintessence.*

This passage refers to the fifth line of the hexagram, as indicated by the two words "central" and "correct," for Line 5 is the only line that is both central (occupying the central position of the upper trigram) and correct (a Yang line occupying a Yang position). The subject of this line is usually taken to be a wise, able, benevolent, and brilliant ruler—a sage-ruler, a philosopher-king, the Confucian conception of man at his highest perfection. Such a man has truly placed himself in tune with Ch'ien, or what Confucius calls the quintessence, the inner vitality of things. This term may be better understood by considering the following lines from the *Tao Teh Ching*:

It (Tao) may seem receding afar and darkening,

Yet within it there is an essence.

This essence is very real.

Inside is something invariably vital.

8. *The six lines help lay bare the meaning of the hexagram in such a way as to make the meaning correspond "sidewise" to the ramifying situations.*

This refers to the explanation of the six individual lines given by the Duke of Chou, which points out clearly the situation confronting the subject of each line and how the subject should conduct himself in order to deal with it properly. The explanation makes the meaning of the hexagram clearer by extending it "sidewise" to comment on particular cases.

9. *The great man rides the six dragons, each at the proper time, and drives through the sky. Clouds move and rain is distributed. Peace reigns in the world.*

"The great man" is the sage-ruler denoted by Line 5 of the Ch'ien Hexagram. He understands the meanings of the six lines so well that he can choose the proper one to guide him through whatever crisis may confront him. The six lines are so useful to him and so completely at his disposal that they may be regarded as "six dragons" he has mastered, each of which stands ready to carry him through the sky whenever the need should arise.

Clouds and rain are the main source of water on earth. Since water is essential to life, its distribution is an apt symbol of general blessings from heaven or of a great ruler. With such blessings the world will enjoy peace.

CONFUCIUS' FURTHER COMMENT ON THE DUKE OF CHOU'S EXPLANATION OF THE INDIVIDUAL LINES:

There are four groups of these comments, here marked a, b, c, d. In the Chinese Text, each group includes comment on all six of the lines. Here the four comments on each line are put together in the same place to facilitate comparison. Groups b and c also contain comments on the extra paragraph after Line 6.

Line 1, Yang:

(a) *Line 1 suggests that the hidden dragon does not act. What does this signify? The Master said: "It signifies a person with the powers of a dragon but living in seclusion. He is not to be changed by the world, nor does he want to attain fame. He can withdraw from the world without regret, nor would he regret if he met with no approval. In happy times, he carries out his principles; in times of trouble, he lays them aside. Firm as a rock, he cannot possibly be uprooted from his moral position. Such is the hidden dragon."*

This is the first of six paragraphs which consist of questions, apparently by disciples of Confucius, and answers by the Master himself. Here the question concerns the "hidden dragon" denoted by Line 1 of the Ch'ien Hexagram. Confucius compares the dragon to a virtuous man living in seclusion who firmly adheres to what he considers to be the truth. Such a man is less eager for fame than for the truth. He will be glad to offer his services to the world when circumstances are in accord with what he feels is right. Otherwise, he simply retires and hides his light under a bushel, as the saying goes.

(b) *"The hidden dragon does not act." The position is low.*

The low position is indicated by Line 1, which symbolizes the underground. Such a position is unsuitable for action.

(c) *"The hidden dragon does not act." The Yang force is laid up and buried deep.*

Confucius' comment points out the motive of the dragon in remaining inactive, namely, the concealment and conservation of its Yang or masculine power for manifestation at the proper time.

(d) *The superior man considers the perfection of virtue as his activity, which can be seen in his daily conduct. What is called concealment refers to one's seclusion with as yet no recognition, and to one's activity with as yet no possibility of success. That is why the superior man does not act.*

The superior man's first care is to cultivate virtue; his next is to manifest it in the world. Before he emerges from seclusion, he must consult not only his own virtue and ability, but must also pay special attention to time and circumstance. According to the I-Ching, these two factors are very important. If they are favorable and there is the possibility of his activities being successful, the superior man will come out and serve his fellow men; otherwise, he will remain in obscurity, enjoying the satisfaction of knowing he has not strayed from his proper path. Such a man will not swim with the social or political current if it does not accord with his own path.

Line 2, Yang:

(a) *Line 2 suggests that the dragon appears in the field and that it is advantageous to see the great man. What does this signify? The Master said: "It signifies a man endowed with the powers of a dragon and trying to be correct in his central position. He is truthful even in his ordinary speech and cautious even in his ordinary conduct. He guards against depravity in order to preserve his sincerity. He labors for the good of the world but does not brag about it. His virtue is vast and radiates a transforming influence. The I-Ching says: 'The dragon appears in the field. It is advantageous to see the great man.' This saying refers to the virtue of a king."*

Line 2 occupies a central position, but is not correct (Yang in a Yin place). Its occupant must make an effort to become correct, careful, and cautious, even in his ordinary speech and conduct, so as to guard against the possibility of moral depravity, a potential hinted at by his incorrect position. He tries to do good to his fellow men but does not brag about it. His virtue, however, exerts a silent influence and is a source of inspiration, so it is advantageous to see him.

(b) *"The dragon appears in the field." The time does not need him.*
He has made his debut in the world and his virtue is shining, but the time is not quite ripe; he must still wait for an opportunity to arise.

(c) *"The dragon appears in the field." The world receives adornment and enlightenment.*
The visible dragon signifies the emergence of the superior man from seclusion. His emergence indicates that the proper moment has finally arrived for him to display his virtues and talents.

(d) *The superior man studies to gather wisdom, raises questions for the sake of discrimination, rests in his wisdom with magnanimity, and practices it with benevolence. The* I-Ching *says: "The dragon appears in the field. It is advantageous to see the great man." This saying refers to the virtue of a king.*
The superior man is a potential ruler, for he possesses the virtue of a king. Conscientious in his search for knowledge and wisdom, he seeks them not just for himself but also for the welfare of his fellow men.

Line 3, Yang:

(a) *Line 3 suggests: "The superior man is intensely active all day long. At nightfall he still seems to be alert and apprehensive. The situation is perilous, but there will be no error." What does this signify? The Master said: "The superior man aims at moral advancement and vocational improvement. Faithfulness and truthfulness are his means of moral advancement. Tending his speech till it becomes sealed with sincerity is how he remains steady in his vocation. He knows what goal to reach and reaches it, thereby satisfying the initial prompting of his heart. He knows where to end and ends there, preserving what is righteous. For this reason, he is not proud while holding a high position and not worried while holding a low one. Therefore, he is intensely active and puts himself on the alert when the occasion arises. In this way, though in a dangerous situation, he will be free from error."*
Confucius' comment points out clearly that the aim and aspiration of the superior man is always, first, to cultivate his own moral

advancement, and second, to cultivate his vocational skills, that he might better serve humanity. As long as he does so, no matter how perilous the situation in which he finds himself, he will remain free from error and ensure his success. At the same time, the superior man remains ready to seize any favorable opportunity that comes his way and will not let it slip through his fingers.

(b) *"The superior man is intensely active all day long."* He goes *about his work.*

The superior man keeps himself busy preparing for his task in life.

(c) *"The superior man is intensely active all day long."* He keeps *pace with the time.*

Confucius' comment shows that the superior man wants to stand in the forefront of time, not lie in sloth and lag behind.

(d) *Line 3 is doubly strong but does not occupy a central position. Its subject is neither in heaven above nor in the field below. Therefore, he must be intensely active and on the alert as occasion arises. In this way, though in a perilous situation, he will be free from error.*

This line is called doubly strong because first, it occupies a Yang position, and second, it borders on the upper Yang trigram. However, some commentators attribute this remark to the fact that the line itself is Yang, occupying a Yang position. This makes some sense but is not quite satisfactory because Line 4 is also called doubly strong even though it does *not* occupy a Yang position.

Line 3 has already left the earth denoted by the first two lines, yet is still beneath the top two lines, which represent heaven. It is neither in heaven nor in the field. This position is perilous, so its subject must be prepared to act when the occasion demands.

Line 4, Yang:

(a) *Line 4 suggests: "The dragon would leap up now and then while in the cavern. No error." What does this signify? The Master said: "There is no permanent position for him, whether above or below. This is not because he is depraved in nature. There is no steady course for him, whether to advance or to retreat. This not because he is alienated from his fellows. The superior man wants to be timely*

*in his moral advancement and vocational improvement. Therefore,
he is free from error."*

Here, the question concerns the situation of the superior man
when he is fluctuating in his movement, like the dragon which
"would leap up now and then." Confucius answers that the fluctuating movement arises not because the man lacks resolve but
because he has no permanent position nor any steady course to
follow at the present time. He is still watching for an opportune
moment to advance. Meanwhile, he continues to gather his
strength and works to improve himself.

The subject of Line 4 is very near the ruler (Line 5). It is not safe
for him to make any reckless move, for in so doing he may offend
the ruler.

(b) *"The dragon would leap up now and then while in the cavern."
It wants to test its own power.*

The occasional leap of the dragon in the cavern suggests that
it is testing its power to rise and soar. Likewise, the superior man
tests himself before assuming any responsibility or task. Such self-
testing is necessary to avoid failure and ensure success.

(c) *"The dragon would leap up now and then while in the cavern."
The way of Ch'ien is undergoing a transformation.*

Line 4 has passed from the lower Ch'ien trigram and reached
the beginning stage of the upper Ch'ien trigram. It clearly indicates a transformation of the Ch'ien or Yang forces and as such
represents a transitional stage of special importance. When faced
with this kind of transition, one must not advance recklessly. On
the other hand, one should not remain completely inactive, either.
At such a stage the possibility for both success and failure exists.
So one should make an exploratory move now and then, just as
the dragon does when it leaps up from the cavern. If the move reveals an encouraging prospect, one should act accordingly.

(d) *Line 4 is doubly strong but does not occupy a central position.
Its subject is neither in heaven above, nor in the field below, nor
among men on the middle plane. He is therefore in perplexity. Perplexity leads to doubt and caution; hence, no error.*

This line is called "doubly strong" because it belongs to the upper trigram, a symbol of strength, and is in contact with Line 3 of the lower Ch'ien trigram, also a symbol of strength. Since they are instrumental in the union of the two Ch'ien trigrams, Lines 3 and 4 intensify and reinforce each other's strength.

This line obviously symbolizes a highly uncertain and precarious situation. Its subject, therefore, is right to feel perplexed and to exercise caution and prudence in his movement.

Line 5, Yang:

(a) *Line 5 suggests: "The dragon is flying in the sky. It is advantageous to see the great man." What does this signify? The Master said: "Notes of the same key echo one another. Creatures of the same nature seek one another. Water flows towards what is wet. Fire turns towards what is dry. Clouds accompany the dragon. Winds accompany the tiger. When a sage appears, all creatures look up to him. What is rooted in heaven draws near to what is above. What is rooted in earth draws near to what is below. Thus, each thing goes with its kind."*

In the *I-Ching* "clouds" and "dragons" are represented respectively by the K'an and Chen trigrams, both Yang symbols. So in this sense clouds and dragons are said to be of the same nature. On the other hand, "wind" and "tiger" are respectively represented by the Sun and Tui trigrams, which are both Yin. So wind and tiger are considered to be of the same nature.

"Like attracts like," and in this way the moral excellence of the sage-ruler (Line 5), draws the people to him and makes them conscious of their own potential goodness and greatness, inspiring them to follow his example.

(b) *"The dragon is flying in the sky." One is ruling from the supreme position.*

The subject of Line 5 is a wise and able ruler who finds himself in highly favorable circumstances to carry out his policies for the welfare of the people. He may well feel like a dragon enjoying its flight in the sky.

(c) *"The dragon is flying in the sky." His position is based on his heavenly virtues.*

Here, the flying symbolizes a man with sublime virtues acting as ruler. His virtues shine forth and justify his enthronement.

(d) *The great man is he whose virtue harmonizes with that of heaven and earth; whose brilliance harmonizes with that of the sun and moon; whose orderly progression harmonizes with that of the four seasons; and whose fortune or misfortune harmonizes with that of the gods and demons. He may act in advance of heaven, but heaven will not act contrariwise. He may act after heaven does, but then he will do so in unison with heaven's rhythm. Even heaven will not oppose him. How much the less will men! How much the less will the gods and demons!*

The *I-Ching* constantly stresses the importance of a correct and central position to success. A correct position means one commensurate with its occupant's talents and temperament. A central position means one invested with authority. Even the manager of a small store needs such a position in order to be successful. But when the sublime virtues, brilliant talents, and extraordinary abilities of a sage are conjoined with a supreme ideal, as well as with a correct and central position, the result is extraordinary indeed. Such is the case with the subject of Line 5 of the Ch'ien Hexagram. This Yang line not only occupies a position both central and correct (Yang in a Yang place) but also occupies a place in the sphere of heaven (the top two lines of the hexagram). In this position a great sage will achieve supreme fulfillment as a human being, realizing all his highests aspirations and most noble dreams and will attain Grand Harmony with his surroundings, so that he automatically carries out the will of heaven in all circumstances. Thus his actions will conform to heaven's will and satisfy the needs of men. With ease and serenity he will sail through life as a ruler, with no opposition from gods, demons, or his fellow men.

Line 6, Yang:

(a) *Line 6 suggests: "The arrogant dragon has occasion for repentance." What does this signify? The Master said: "The subject of the line is noble but has no appropriate position. He is in a lofty spot but has no people under his rule. Worthy men in low places can give him no support. Therefore, if he makes any move, he will have to repent."*

The lines of the hexagram give an indication of the Master's meaning. Line 6 is supposed to be an ancestor of the ruler in Line 5. He is noble indeed but has no proper position; this is indicated by the fact that Line 6 occupies an incorrect position (Yang in a Yin place). Its subject is in a lofty spot because Line 6 is at the top of the hexagram, but he has no people under his control, for all the subjects belong to the ruler (Line 5). Finally, he can receive no support from worthy men because Line 6 and Line 3 (its correlate), fail to form a harmonious relationship. The subject of Line 6, therefore, is more or less isolated while in a dangerous position, so any move he makes will lead to regret.

(b) *"The arrogant dragon has occasion for repentance." There is disaster in pushing matters to the extreme limit.*

Arrogance in itself is a dangerous attitude. It can create even more harm when it causes one to resort to radical measures and push a situation to the extreme limit. But repentance, if sincere, can be a lesson learned and so a saving grace.

(c) *"The arrogant dragon has occasion for repentance." His course has ended with the end of the opportune span of time.*

Confucius' comment shows that an opportune moment or favorable circumstance does not last long. One should anticipate its end and act accordingly in order to avoid error and remain free from regret.

(d) *What is called arrogance knows to advance but knows not to retreat, knows preservation but knows not perdition, knows gain but knows not loss.*

Isn't it only the sage who knows to retreat as well as to advance and knows perdition as well as preservation, without deviating from what is correct? Isn't it only the sage who can do so?

Confucius illustrates his answers with the headstrong movements of the arrogant dragon or the proud, overbearing man. Such movements are bound to exceed the proper limit and consequently lead to setbacks and failures because the headstrong do not know how to retreat or give ground. Having achieved the heights, they heedlessly continue to plunge on, forgetting the Law of Cyclic Reversion, which says that everything, when reaching an extreme point, inevitably reverts to its opposite pole. Thus, in Chapter 9 of the *Tao Teh Ching*, Lao Tzu gives this advice: "Retire after achieving success and winning renown. This is the way of heaven." Most people seldom possess the wisdom to know how far they can go and to stop there and turn around. Only the sage is wise enough to do so without regret or hesitation.

Extra paragraph: Nine used up by Ch'ien's originative attribute Yuan:

(a) *There is no comment on the extra paragraph in group a.*

(b) *"Nine used up by Ch'ien's originative attribute* Yuan." *The world is enjoying peace and good government.*

The reason behind Confucius' comment seems to be that the creative power of Yang (denoted by nine) has been used to its ultimate potential and its mission of spreading enlightenment has been fulfilled. Peace is also indicated by the Ch'ien Hexagram's subsequent replacement by the K'un Hexagram, symbolizing the Yin principle, whose attributes are meekness, quiescence, and conciliation.

(c) *"Nine used up by Ch'ien's originative attribute* Yuan." *The ordinance of heaven will become apparent.*

Nine, as usual, denotes Yang. The inherent virtue of Yang may be taken as the ordinance of heaven. Yang knows when to advance and when to retreat. It can assert itself and bend itself, according to the innate freedom it possesses. When it has waxed to the limit, Yang does not exercise its leadership further but yields it to Yin. Such is the ordinance of heaven, demonstrating the movement of Tao according to the Law of Cyclic Reversion.

In conclusion, it might be well to point out why the numeral 9 stands for Yang and the numeral 6 stands for Yin. There is some metaphysical significance underlying these designations. In the *Great Treatise* it is said that heaven (Yang) is One —— and earth (Yin) is Two — —. One potentially embodies Two. The Ch'ien (Heaven) trigram has three Yang lines ☰, each of which embodies Two — —, and $3 \times 2 = 6$. This potential number 6 plus the actual number $3 = 9$. The K'un (earth) trigram has only three divided lines ☷ ☷ and nothing else. $3 \times 2 = 6$.

The K'UN Hexagram
(Symbol of Receptivity)

2nd 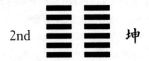 坤

K'UN IS THE RECEPTIVE cosmic principle and is similar in essence to Yin, earth, nature, and matter. In contrast to Ch'ien, the creative cosmic principle, it connotes such quiescent or feminine attributes as weakness, passivity, stillness, meekness, docility, obedience, submissiveness, darkness, and inertness.

In the mundane world, it represents the wife, the mother, the minister in relation to the ruler, the servant, and others in a subordinate position.

In regard to the individual, it represents the body, the senses, and the appetites.

In the *Great Treatise* Confucius calls K'un "the greatness in the universe."

KING WEN'S JUDGMENT ON THE HEXAGRAM:

K'un is great and originative, pervasive and prospering, advantageous and benefiting, having the firm correctness of a mare. When a superior man has some forward move to make, he will get lost if he tries to lead; but if he would be a follower, he will find his master. His advantage lies in getting friends in the west and south and losing them while in the east and north. Good fortune will be his if he calmly stays firm and correct.

K'un, with its six Yin lines, represents what is weak and static in the universe. The Yin line (a straight but broken line) is considered weak because, being broken and inert, its motion is interrupted.

Three such lines form the Yin trigram, suggesting weakness and inertness strongly reinforced. The K'un Hexagram is formed by placing two K'un trigrams one above the other. When Yin lines are stacked in this manner, they form a central channel, suggesting the idea of receptivity and the association with things feminine. This figure indicates that K'un is ever ready for penetration and pervasion by the Ch'ien (Yang) force. It also suggests hollowness and a capacity for containing and storing. This arrangement demonstrates why the sages thought K'un the ideal symbol of both the primal womb and the infinite capacity of the universe.

According to King Wen's Judgment, K'un possesses the same four attributes as Ch'ien. This is because Ch'ien and K'un are eternal partners in the process of creation. After creation, all that exists embodies both the Ch'ien and K'un principles. As Lao Tzu has said, "The ten thousand things carry Yin and embrace Yang." The creative or originative attribute, along with the other three that follow it, are therefore common to and shared by both Ch'ien and K'un.

A mare is a female horse and is often forced into service bearing a heavy burden. Its primary characteristics are endurance and docility. A person with these characteristics seems born with a will to serve, which can be a very desirable asset. The mare also devotes itself completely to its mate, the stallion (the Ch'ien trigram). For this reason, it may aptly be called chaste, an example of "firm correctness."

King Wen's admonition on the most advantageous geographical location in which to seek friends has given rise to some controversy. Non-Chinese translators generally render it as being advantageous to find friends in the west and south, and to lose or forego friends in the east and north. This is literally correct, as can be seen from the following transliteration of the Chinese text: "Li, hsi nan te p'eng, tung pei sang p'eng." However, this rendering fails to capture the true sense. To explain more fully, King Wen arranged the following diagram (which in Chinese fashion places south at the top of the page):

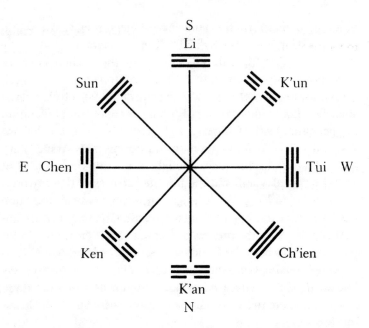

Here, the three Yin trigrams, Sun, Li, and Tui, lie in the west and south, and so are considered friends or prospective friends of K'un in the southwest. The three Yang trigrams, Chen, Ken, and K'an, lie in the east and north, and so are considered strangers, not friends or prospective friends of K'un.

In this diagram friends are people of the same nature, whether Yin or Yang. In the situation symbolized by the K'un Hexagram, the position of the superior man is Yin in nature rather than Yang, as in the Ch'ien Hexagram. He cannot become a friend of the Yang people in the east and north; in essence he has no friends in that quarter. Therefore, it is incorrect to say that he loses or foregoes friends there. How can one lose what he does not have? Instead, it is better to say that he does not possess friends in the east and north.

King Wen's Judgment on the current situation is that K'un (Yin) should not lead or take any initiative on its own but should follow the lead of Ch'ien (Yang). Here, the most advantageous course for the superior man is to fulfill his destiny as a Yin force and seek a

Yang master to the east and north. If his Yin friends are willing to journey with him and serve the Yang master, well and good. If they are not able or willing to accompany him, he should still make the journey, even if he must do so alone, without companions. In such a case he will be losing the friends he leaves behind when he goes east and north. However, to remain firm in his resolve to find and follow a Yang master and serve him in a humble position is the most important course. To do so, as the Judgment clearly indicates, is the advantageous path in the situation of which this hexagram speaks, and will surely bring good fortune.

CONFUCIUS' EXPLANATION OF KING WEN'S JUDGMENT:

1. *Perfect indeed is K'un's originative capacity. To it all things owe their birth, as it submissively receives potency from heaven.*

K'un, as well as Ch'ien, plays an essential role in the cosmic creative process. All things owe their birth not merely to Ch'ien but also to K'un. The roles of Ch'ien and K'un, though, are different, complementing each other. Ch'ien originates in the sense that it sets the creative process into motion by infusing the germs of life into K'un, but this process cannot function without K'un to develop these germs, perfect them, and produce them in the proper form. K'un is like a womb that receives the fecundating potency emanating from Ch'ien and transforms it into living realities. Thus the creative attribute of Ch'ien is called *originative power*, and that of K'un is called *originative capacity*.

2. *K'un carries all things in the vastness of its capacity. Its power matches the infinite power of Ch'ien. What it enfolds is vast, bright, and grand. Through it the various kinds of things all grow up and prosper.*

Here, Confucius comments on the pervasive and prospering attributes of K'un. K'un is not only a co-partner in the creation of all things, it also contains and sustains them after their creation. The life it enfolds is infinite in variety, manifesting itself in a radiant glory when the myriad things prosper and grow.

3. *The mare is an earthly animal. It roams the earth without limit. Gentle, docile, beneficial, as well as firm and correct, it sets an example which the superior man may follow.*

According to the *Shuo Kua* (*Remarks on the Trigrams*), the cow is a K'un symbol. Here, a mare is chosen as a K'un symbol because it embodies all the essential qualities that a cow symbolizes (i.e., gentleness, calmness, submissiveness). In addition it is gifted with swiftness of foot and the superior strength necessary for those who would place themselves in the service of any Ch'ien entity. For instance, a servant or minister should be not only loyal and obedient but also strong and vigorous enough to bear responsibilities patiently over a long time, much as a mare carries heavy loads over a long distance. The mare, therefore, serves as a model for the superior man to follow.

4. *If he tries to lead, he will get lost and miss the proper path. If he would be a follower, he will find a master with ease. He gets friends in the west and south; this is because he moves among his kinsfolk. He loses his friends while in the east and north; this eventually will result in rejoicing.*

More or less the same paragraph appears in King Wen's Judgment. The last sentence reinforces the idea that it is advantageous for the superior man, or the K'un subject, to leave his friends in the southwest and go to the northeast in search of a Yang lord or master.

5. *The good fortune of calmly staying firm and correct reflects the unlimited capacity of the earth.*

In Confucius' view the good fortune one enjoys by patiently remaining firm is similar to the benefits the earth receives from heaven. In such a manner, the wife may receive beneficence from her husband and the servant or minister from his master or lord.

In this paragraph Confucius may be speaking of spiritual cultivation. By remaining docile and serene during meditation, one may contact the divine influence which flows from heaven, or from Yang, the active cosmic principle.

SYMBOLIC SIGNIFICANCE OF THE HEXAGRAM AS NOTED BY CONFUCIUS:

K'un denotes the contour and condition of the earth. The superior man is inspired thereby to consolidate his virtues so as to support and endure all things.

The K'un Hexagram consists of two trigrams, each of which signifies the earth. The double symbol, however, does not mean there are two earths; instead, it stands either for renewal of the earth with each new dawn or the vast capacity and great depth of the earth which carries all things, or both. From the example of large-heartedness (or vast capacity) of the earth, the superior man learns that he should "consolidate (develop and gather together) his virtues" so that he is morally strong enough "to support and endure all things," especially his fellow men. The Chinese place man among the ten thousand things, as indicated by the well-known saying, "Man is the most spiritual or intelligent of all the ten thousand things" ("Ren wei wan wu chih ling").

DUKE OF CHOU'S EXPLANATION OF THE INDIVIDUAL LINES (a) AND CONFUCIUS' COMMENT THEREON (b):

Line 1, Yin:
(a) *One treads on hoarfrost. Solid ice is approaching.*
(b) *"One treads on hoarfrost. Solid ice is approaching." The Yin, or dark power, is beginning to gather. If allowed to go its own way, it will lead to the approach of solid ice.*

If the hexagram is taken to signify the human body, then the bottom line (Line 1) signifies the feet. Since the first two lines of every hexagram represent the earth, and K'un being Yin denotes coldness, the three notions—feet, earth, and coldness—combine to suggest "treading on hoarfrost."

The line in the present situation shows that things begin with a little hint; if allowed to evolve unchecked, they will grow and become larger. A wise man should be alert to recognize the first signs of any such situations and to weigh carefully whether they should be allowed to develop unchecked.

Line 2, Yin:
(a) *Straightforward, foursquare, and great. No need to repeat any effort, yet there will be nothing disadvantageous.*

(b) *The movement indicated in Line 2, Yin, is from straightforwardness to foursquareness. "No need to repeat any effort, yet there will be nothing disadvantageous." This shows the glorious way of the earth.*

The first three words in the Chinese text ("Chu, fang, ta") have evoked various explanations from traditional Chinese commentators. Literally, these words mean "straight, "square," and "big" and may be taken as an apt description of the earth. Straight may rightly be extended to mean a square, for a square consists of a compact assemblage of parallel straight lines on the same plane. Square is what the Chinese, until modern times, always conceived the earth to be, as indicated by the well-known saying, "T'ien yuan, ti-fang" ("Sky round, earth square"). That the earth is considered to be big needs no explanation. This description also relates to Line 2, for symbolically the line signifies the surface of the earth. However, the description conveys little significance and does not seem to fit into the rest of the Text.

Another interpretation is that the motion of heaven is straightforward, and consequently, the motion of the earth should be straightforward too. But when this explanation comes to the word "square," it fails to be reasonable and convincing.

The meaning of the first three words would seem to be, then, as here translated, "straightforward," "foursquare," and "great." These are essentially Yang qualities, but K'un or Yin is always responsive to Yang and fulfills what Yang initiates. This suggests that what is straightforward will become foursquare, fair, or impartial, and finally great in moral or spiritual excellence.

Since Line 2 occupies a central as well as a correct position, its subject is especially rich in those moral qualities. Therefore, he is said to show correct and direct response to Ch'ien (Yang). Consequently, he makes no errors and does not have to revise or repeat his motions. Such harmonious and spontaneous cooperation with Yang will surely mean good fortune in every sense ("the glorious way of the earth").

Line 3, Yin:

(a) *Concealment of one's bright talents could be the firm and correct course. If one happens to be in the king's service, one should bring his tasks to a successful conclusion but should claim no credit.*

(b) *"Concealment of one's bright talents could be the firm and correct course." Talents should manifest at the proper time.*

"One may happen to be in the king's service." This means one's wisdom is bright and grand.

Line 3 occupies a position neither central nor correct (Yin in a Yang place), indicating a precarious situation. Its correlate, Line 6, is also Yin and therefore offers no harmonious cooperation, so the subject of Line 3 is more or less isolated. In such a precarious situation, a man should conceal his talents, in order to avoid envy and criticism, and continue firmly on a correct course. If in the king's service, the subject should do his duty but should shun exaltation of his personal achievements.

To do one's duty is in a way to manifest one's "bright talents" at the proper time; to do so without pride, vainglory, or self-satisfaction is to indicate one's wisdom.

Line 4, Yin:

(a) *A tied-up sack. No blame. No praise.*

(b) *"A tied-up sack. No blame." This means that caution will ward off injury.*

K'un stands for earth, which contains all things, a container. According to the *Shuo Kua* (*Remarks on the Trigrams*), K'un also represents cloth, among other things, so the two ideas combine to suggest a cloth container or sack. Moreover, if the line is transformed into a Yang line, the Yu Hexagram is formed, which looks like a sack tied at the neck.

A tied-up sack suggests a shut-up mouth, which in turn suggests silence or reticence. Line 4 (Yang) is not central and does not form a harmonious relationship with its correlate (Line 1), signifying an insecure and inauspicious situation. It is also at the base of the upper trigram, which signifies a transitional stage, involving new adjustments. This line usually denotes a minister near the ruler (Line 5). The ruler here is also Yin, and this means little mutual attraction between ruler and minister. In such an uncertain and insecure situation, the subject of Line 4 should be very cautious in his speech in order to ward off injury.

Line 5, Yin:

(a) *Yellow undergarment. Great good fortune.*

(b) *"Yellow undergarment. Great good fortune." Beauty exists in the interior.*

This line suggests a yellow undergarment because it is at the center of the upper trigram, K'un (earth), and in China yellow is considered the color of the earth. Second, the line, being Yin, represents a female ruler, a queen. In the Chou dynasty, whose founder was a principal author of the *I-Ching*, only the queen was privileged to wear a yellow undergarment.

Why does the yellow undergarment and the queen's wearing it promise great good fortune? The central position of Line 5 in the upper trigram usually denotes moderation or the Golden Mean, especially when its occupant is a female. A moderate ruler is prone to love the people and listen to advice. Another reason for this in-terpretation is given by Confucius: "Beauty exists in the interior." K'un is a symbol of beauty, and Line 5 is at the center of a K'un trigram. It aptly signifies qualities of inner beauty such as kind-ness, grace, intuition, tact, and tolerance, all of which are con-ducive to good government and thus, great good fortune.

Line 6, Yin:

(a) *Dragons are fighting in the wilderness. Their blood is dark blue and yellow.*

(b) *"Dragons are fighting in the wilderness." The course has come to the terminal point.*

This is a Yin line at the top of a Yin hexagram. How can it rep-resent dragons, which are masculine Yang creatures? The answer is that the line represents the extreme development of Yin power, which has become so strong that its subject is liable to forget to act according to its Yin attributes and assume those of Yang, thereby becoming a pseudo-dragon. According to the Law of Cy-clic Reversion, Line 6 represents the point in time when the Yang forces will reappear. If the subject of the line behaves in a recep-tive fashion like a Yin creature, there will be no fighting. But if he acts like a pseudo-dragon and becomes aggressive, conflict between him and the real dragon is bound to take place. Line 5 signifies the capital of the country, as the queen and her palace are there, while Line 6 lies beyond the capital, hence the image of the wilderness or an undeveloped suburb.

Dark blue is the color of heaven, symbolized by the true dragons, and yellow is the color of earth, symbolized by the pseudo-dragons. As both dark blue and yellow blood has been shed, both sides have suffered injuries.

In the human realm, the fighting of the dragons can represent various situations, such as the struggle between the superior men, or true statesmen, and the petty men, or crafty politicians mounting their forces to seize power. Or it may represent a military struggle between rebel forces and government troops. It may even represent the struggle between enlightened reason and burning passion within the individual. Each of these struggles may be compared to "solid ice," which is gradually built from the frost (Line 1).

Yin used up:

(a) *It is advantageous to be ever firm and correct.*

(b) *"Yin used up. Ever firm and correct." This is for the purpose of achieving the grand consummation.*

Again, as with Ch'ien, the Duke of Chou adds an extra paragraph after Line 6: "Yin used up" means Yin has waxed to its utmost extent and exhausted its power. According to the Law of Cyclic Reversion, Yang will reappear. Symbolically, the K'un Hexagram has used up all its power and vanished, to be replaced by the Ch'ien Hexagram, a fact always to be taken into consideration when interpreting any divination based on the I-Ching. Yang should reappear in a way that is firm and correct, so as to continue to wax.

Confucius says that a firm and correct course is necessary for attaining a "grand consummation." This would seem to mean that Yang should remain firm and correct until it manifests its power to the greatest extent. Morally speaking, a man who has switched from the darkness of Yin to the light of Yang should remain firm and correct until the Yang power in him has increased to such a point that he becomes an enlightened person. Similarly, a bad man who has reformed should remain firm and correct until he has become a thoroughly good person.

This extra paragraph is added only to the Ch'ien and K'un Hexagrams because only these two hexagrams are involved in the Law of Cyclic Reversion.

CONFUCIUS' FURTHER EXPLANATION OF KING WEN'S JUDGMENT:

1. *K'un, the receptive cosmic principle, is perfectly pliant, yet its motion is strong. It is perfectly still, yet its power manifests in the right direction.*

K'un is passive and therefore pliant. As such, it exists solely to receive the influence of Ch'ien (the creative principle). But even as K'un yields to Ch'ien's dynamism, by nature it must be strong enough to receive Ch'ien's force or no consummation can take place. Thus, K'un harmonizes with Ch'ien.

K'un is not the rival of Ch'ien, but its ideal partner and perfect complement. It is the vehicle through which Ch'ien expresses its true power and significance. It must be receptive to the influence of Ch'ien in order to fulfill its cosmic nature. As Ch'ien is always correct and spontaneous in the manifestation of its power, so is K'un.

2. *By being a follower, it finds its master and pursues its regular course. It embosoms all things, and what it transforms is radiantly glorious.*

K'un cannot lead and should not attempt to lead, but by following and obeying Ch'ien it fulfills its highest destiny. Once impregnated by Ch'ien's masculine energy, it becomes a veritable womb within which Ch'ien's energies are transformed and evolved into the ten thousand things in all their respective forms, in accordance with the originating impulse of Ch'ien. The result is indeed radiant glory, for there are infinite marvels and beauties in the four kingdoms—human, animal, vegetable, and mineral—of the universe.

3. *The way of K'un, is it not yieldingly submissive? It receives potency from heaven and acts in accord with the times.*

During the union between K'un and Ch'ien, K'un is very submissive and receives the creative force from Ch'ien. It then acts out a cycle that can be symbolized by the procession of the various seasons. The mating of K'un and Ch'ien is symbolically said to occur in winter, a time when all things, notably plants, are on the decline or have already withered, rendering necessary and making possible the renewal of life. In the depth of winter, the winter solstice, K'un reaches its fullest extent. The moment for the turn of the cycle is at hand, and the resurgence of Ch'ien begins. This is indeed the ideal time for union. Spring is the sprouting time, when fresh shoots, green buds, and early flowers come forth, inspiring us with the promise of beauty. The time for the flowering of things is summer, when the plants finally burst into luxuriant life on every hand, in an exuberance of beauty that stuns the senses. The time when things mature and bear abundant fruit is autumn. Thus, when in accordance with the time K'un makes itself receptive to the influence of Ch'ien, it begins again the cycle of rebirth, germination, flowering, and fruition that manifests in the ten thousand things.

CONFUCIUS' FURTHER COMMENT ON THE DUKE OF CHOU'S EXPLANATION OF THE INDIVIDUAL LINES:

Line 1, Yin:
The household which accumulates good deeds is sure to have a superabundance of happiness. The household which accumulates evil deeds is sure to have a superabundance of distress. The reason why a minister kills his king or why a son kills his father does not arise suddenly in a single morning or a single evening, but follows a gradual course of development, only it has not been discerned at an early date. The I-Ching says: "One treads on hoarfrost. Solid ice is approaching." This refers to the gradual course of natural developments.

Writing about Line 1 of the hexagram, the Duke of Chou refers to the gradual development of frost into solid ice. Confucius draws a parallel from this with human life, maintaining that such events as regicide and patricide also develop gradually from small beginnings. It is important to remain alert for the signs of such a development and to deal with them in the proper manner.

The first two sentences clearly express the Hindu idea of karma. In Chinese thought, the idea is expressed in the popular saying, "Plant melons, reap melons; plant beans, reap beans." In Christianity, "As ye sow, so shall ye reap."

Line 2, Yin:

"Straightforward" denotes rectitude. "Foursquare" denotes righteousness. The superior man maintains a respectful attitude in order to attain uprightness within and practices righteousness in order to square with what is without.

Respectfulnss and righteousness having been established, he is no longer isolated in his virtue.

Straightforward, foursquare, and great, he need not repeat any of his efforts, and yet they will be in no wise disadvantageous. This shows he has no doubts concerning what he does.

The Text refers to the motion of K'un in unison with that of Ch'ien. Since it is acting according to its nature, K'un's motion is also straightforward and foursquare, like that of Ch'ien. Confucius brings this notion into the context of human moral cultivation, suggesting that man's outward conduct and inner attitude should be harmonious. Righteous conduct should flow from an upright character.

In order to cultivate an upright character, a man must maintain a respectful attitude toward those he encounters and resolve to remain firmly on a correct course. His character resting on this sound foundation, he will be free from doubts about himself and his actions will be straightforward and fair. Such a man's virtues cannot help but influence his fellow men and make him great.

According to some Chinese authorities, including Jen Ch'i-yun, Ch'ien represents respectfulness and K'un represents righteousness. As K'un follows Ch'ien, so righteousness stems from respectfulness, or inner rectitude.

Line 3, Yin:
The Yin subject of Line 3 has handsome talents but keeps them concealed. If with them he enters the king's service, he does not claim credit for his achievements. This is the way of the earth, of the wife, and of the minister. The way of the earth is not to claim success for itself, but to act as an agent to bring matters to a proper conclusion.

Line 3 occupies a highly awkward and unfavorable position, which is neither central nor correct (Yin in a Yang place). It also fails to form a harmonius relationship with its correlate (Line 6). However, as Yang is related to the good and beautiful, this line is said to enfold beauty. But because of its position, the subject should avoid self-aggrandizement and ostentation. Instead he should be self-effacing like K'un, which fulfills the creative impulse of Ch'ien without calling attention to itself.

Line 4, Yin:
When heaven and earth interact to cause changes and transformations, plants and trees flourish in luxuriance. When interaction between heaven and earth is shut off, worthy men retire into obscurity.
The I-Ching says: "A tied-up sack. No blame. No praise." It refers to caution and reticence.

When there is harmony between heaven and earth, all creatures thrive and prosper. When disharmony occurs, worthy men (and inferentially all goodness and beauty) realize that their affairs can no longer prosper and that the time has come to retreat.

Line 4 is Yin in a Yin place and occupies the middle of the hexagram, surrounded by Yin lines. It therefore suggests a dark period or a political situation. In such a situation, sensible people consider it advisable to shut up like "a tied-up sack."

Line 5, Yin:
The superior man is "yellow," or sincere, at the center of his being and can penetrate to the inner reason of things. He takes care to poise his person in the correct position. The beauty which lies within him diffuses fitness and freedom through his four limbs and manifests outwardly in his vocation. This is beauty at its highest excellence.

Line 5 of a hexagram usually denotes a ruler, but need not always signify a king. In this case it represents a regent, for it is Yin, which suggests subordination. This regent is probably the Duke of Chou himself, who acted as regent to the young king, Ch'eng Wang, for six years and who had to be careful to act in the correct manner at all times to avoid giving his enemies the opportunity to discredit him.

Since this is a Yin line where a Yang line should be, its subject must take care to be correct. History says that while regent, the Duke usually put on a yellow undergarment to show that he was inferior in position to the king (the king alone could wear a yellow uppergarment).

To Confucius, who was an ardent admirer of the Duke of Chou, the yellow undergarment has a different and very significant connotation. It connotes the inner spiritual essence of the superior man. Because yellow is the color of the earth in Northern China (especially around the Yellow River), it was considered the correct color, signifying wisdom and sincerity. Yellow center (hu-ang chung), therefore, signifies the center of consciousness of the superior man. It is through the development of wisdom and virtue that man opens this center and apprehends the inner truth of things, achieving an inward beauty that transforms his being and all his outward conduct.

Line 6, Yin:

When Yin fancies itself the equal of Yang, there is bound to be a battle. Because of dissatisfaction with the idea that Yang no longer exists, mention is made of the dragon, a Yang symbol. As the Yin creature has not yet separated from its kind, mention is made of blood, a Yin symbol. What is referred to as "dark blue and yellow" is a mixed mess of heaven and earth. Heaven is dark blue. Earth is yellow.

K'un (Yin) should and usually does occupy a subordinate place. However, Line 6 represents Yin at the height of its power, when it has almost completely supplanted Yang. In such a situation, it is easy for Yin to become carried away and feel itself the equal or superior of Yang. According to Confucius, when this happens there is sure to be a big fight. For Yang will never let itself be dominated by Yin, especially when its time of renewal comes after the fullness of the eclipse.

In the Text, the Duke of Chou speaks of a "battle between dragons." Here, the Yin force is indicated by a dragon, a Yang symbol, because when Yin has grown to its utmost, its power is so great that it almost appears to be Yang. Blood, a Yin symbol, is used to characterize the battle because the Yin force is regarded as Yang only due to its unseemly self-assertion. In fact, blood is Yin in nature, as this symbolism reminds us. Finally, the term "dark blue and yellow" is explained as signifying the chaos created by this conflict between heaven and earth, symbolized by genuine dragons and pseudo-dragons.

The maximum manifestation of Yin, represented by Line 6 of this hexagram, occurs at the winter solstice, on December 22 (a day that comes in the early part of the eleventh month of the Chinese lunar year). This is the shortest day and the longest night of the year. From midnight on, however, the days grow longer and longer, signifying that Yang is making its return and has begun to wax. This represents the Law of Cyclic Reversion in operation. It is not, as some commentators maintain, the result of the battle of the dragons. This battle is merely coincidental, for Line 6 of the Ch'ien Hexagram also shows the operation of the Law of Cyclic Reversion (signifying the return of Yin), yet there is no mention of any battle. The true meaning of Line 6 of both hexagrams is a reminder of the danger of letting extraordinary power lead to reckless arrogance that can tempt a man to push matters too far and so bring about his undoing.

The CHUN Hexagram
(Symbol of Initial Difficulty)

3rd  屯

THE LOWER TRIGRAM of this hexagram is Chen, signifying thunder. The lower interior trigram (Lines 2, 3, 4) is K'un, signifying earth. Together the two trigrams signify thunder breaking forth from the earth. The upper trigram, K'an, however, signifies obstruction, or the domain of danger. The whole hexagram, therefore, signifies thunder encountering obstruction ahead. Hence the idea of difficulty or distress.

KING WEN'S JUDGMENT ON THE HEXAGRAM:

The Chun Hexagram indicates great success and prosperity. Advantageous to be firm and correct. Do not act unless there is some possibility of success in doing so. Advantageous to establish principalities.

When thunder crashes through the earth, it means that the Yang force has gratified its impulse, indicating great success. But the situation is not yet quite settled; so a firm and correct course should be followed, and reckless moves that might unsettle things should be avoided. At such times, it is always advantageous to seek the aid of friends and associates ("establish principalities").

CONFUCIUS' EXPLANATION OF KING WEN'S JUDGMENT:

Difficulty arises when the strong and the weak begin intercourse. Action amidst danger may lead to great success if it be firm and correct.

The action of thunder and rain (signified by the lower and upper trigrams) fills the void. When heaven causes a troublous situation, the ruler should establish principalities and not rest in self-satisfaction.

The lower trigram, Chen, is derived from the K'un trigram ☷ ☷ when its first line is changed into Yang (☳); in other words, after K'un has had its first intercourse with Ch'ien. Hence the image "the strong and the weak begin intercourse." Usually the initial intercourse involves some difficulty. However, such an act is fundamental in beginning any new activity, and one should not be discouraged by the initial difficulty or danger, but should remain firm and correct to achieve success.

The lower trigram, Chen, signifies thunder and the upper, K'an, also signifies water or rain; hence the image of "the action of thunder and rain."

SYMBOLIC SIGNIFICANCE OF THE HEXAGRAM AS NOTED BY CONFUCIUS:

The idea behind Chun is derived from raincloud (K'an) over thunder (Chen). The superior man is inspired thereby to put his affairs into proper shape.

The hexagram suggests a close atmospheric condition. The sky is overcast with rainclouds and thunder is rumbling below, but as yet there is no rain and things remain unsettled. The superior man may find his personal affairs in a similarly unsettled condition; if so, he should make every effort to put them into proper shape.

DUKE OF CHOU'S EXPLANATION OF THE LINES (a) AND CONFUCIUS' COMMENT THEREON (b):

Line 1, Yang:

(a) *One hesitates to advance. Advantageous to remain firm and correct. Advantageous to establish principalities.*

(b) *Though "hesitant to advance," one yet aims to do what is correct. Noble in rank, he stoops to deal with the lowly, thereby winning the great support of the people.*

Line 1 is Yang in a Yang place, but at the bottom of the hexa-gram. It signifies a person of great ability and dynamic character in a low position. He is inwardly strong enough to advance, but in his present lowly position it is disadvantageous for him to do so. In his situation success is best assured by firmly remaining in his position and continuing to discharge his obligations in a cor-rect manner, while gathering support for the future.

If Line 1 is transformed into a Yin line, the lower trigram be-comes K'un (territory, people), and the entire hexagram becomes Pi (friendly association). Thus the idea of dealing with people in a good spirit (stooping "to deal with the lowly, thereby winning the great support of the people").

Line 2, Yin:

(a) *She seems to be in distress and unsteady motion. The horses of her carriage, too, seem to be jolting. What she sees is not a high-wayman but a suitor. She, a chaste maiden, declines the marriage offer. After ten years she will then be married.*

(b) *The distress indicated in Line 2, Yin, is due to the line riding over a strong Yang line. "After ten years she will then be married." This means there will be a return to the normal situation.*

Line 2 occupies a position both central and correct (Yin in a Yin place). Its subject is a meek person, averse to radical action (fol-lows the middle way), who must cope with a person of strong character (Line 1). Such a man is naturally unsure of himself and his course tends to waver, like a horse driven by an inexperienced rider.

As a Yin line in a Yin place, Line 2 also signifies a pure-hearted virgin who is careful in choosing a mate. She elects to wait for ten years before considering marriage. Ten is the number of fullness and represents a cycle; thus the tenth year (the time necessary for the present situation to complete itself and the next to begin) is supposed to be the time when the present uncertain situation will return to normal. Line 2 also forms a harmonious relationship with its correlate (Line 5, Yang). This clearly indicates the possi-bility of marriage. Hence, the idea that "after ten years she will then be married."

Line 3, Yin:

(a) *One hunts deer without a forester to guide him, and only goes deep into the forest. A superior man who can discern the faint initial sign of a coming event would prefer to quit. Advance will cause regret.*

(b) *"One hunts deer without a forester to guide him." This means he is eager to chase the game. "The superior man would prefer to quit. Advancement will cause regret." This is because to advance will lead to a hopeless situation.*

Line 3 is a Yin line sandwiched between two other Yin lines. Its correlate (Line 6) is also Yin, so there can be little harmony or cooperation between them. Its subject is weak and lonely, like a hunter going into the forest without a guide. In addition, the upper trigram, K'an, usually signifies a dangerous cavern. To advance toward such a cavern is a course of utter folly. In such a situation the superior man knows the wiser course is to retreat.

Line 4, Yin:

(a) *A man on horseback appears to be in trouble. He is seeking marital relations. Advancement will be auspicious. There will be advantage in every move.*

(b) *To go out and seek the desired object shows clear discernment.*

This line is Yin in a Yin place. Its subject is gentle and passive in character and tends to be indecisive in his movements, like an inexperienced rider on horseback. The line, however, forms a harmonious relationship with its correlate (Line 1, Yang), so if its subject makes the effort to approach the subject of Line 1 concerning marriage or a political alliance, the result will be very advantageous. Confucius considers such a course a wise one.

Here, Line 4 (the minister) is Yin, while Line 5 (the ruler) is Yang. This means ruler and minister will get along harmoniously. If the subject of Line 4 succeeds in forming an alliance with the subject of Line 1, and both work together for the ruler, the result will be highly advantageous.

According to the *Shuo Kua Chuan* (*Treatise on Remarks about Trigrams*), the lower trigram, Chen, represents the eldest son. If Line 4 is transformed into a Yang line, the upper trigram, K'an, will become Tui, which represents the youngest daughter. Hence the idea of "seeking marital relations."

Line 5, Yang:

(a) *The distribution of handsome gifts or fat favors involves difficulty. A firm and correct posture in regard to small matters will be auspicious; in regard to weighty matters it will lead to evil.*

(b) *"Difficulty in the distribution of handsome gifts" means that the distribution has not been brought to the public light.*

Here, Line 5 (the ruler) occupies a position both central and correct (Yang in a Yang place), denoting a ruler of great ability and wisdom. However, it is situated between two Yin lines: its subject (the ruler) is liable to encounter difficulties in the diffusion of his light, that is, in the execution of his enlightened policies. So it is advantageous for him to devote his energies only to the pursuit of small matters, not great ones.

Line 6, Yin:

(a) *A man on horseback appears to be in trouble. Tears of blood seem to stream from his eyes.*

(b) *"Tears of blood seem to stream from his eyes." How can such a condition be prolonged?*

Line 6 is Yin in a Yin place, and its subject is a weak, timid person. It also occupies the top or extreme limit of the hexagram, indicating that there is no place to go. A weak, timid person on horseback finds such a situation frightening and full of peril ("tears of blood seem to stream from his eyes"). Blood is signified by the upper trigram, K'an, according to the *Shuo Kua.* What is the way out for a person in such a perilous situation? He must reform himself and change his course. As Confucius implies, such a situation is fraught with danger and should not be allowed to continue.

The MENG Hexagram
(Symbol of Ignorance)

4th  蒙

THE LOWER TRIGRAM, K'an, signifies water, and the upper, Ken, signifies mountain. Water beneath the mountain suggests an underground spring or fountain where the water remains pure and undefiled. Such water symbolizes the innocence, pure heart, or undeveloped intelligence of children. Hence the name Meng means an innocent or ignorant child (not a fool, as one translator would have it).

KING WEN'S JUDGMENT ON THE HEXAGRAM:

The Meng Hexagram indicates prosperity and success. Not that I seek the ignorant youth, but that the ignorant youth seeks me. The first time he seeks guidance from divination, I tell him. When he asks again and again, he is irreverent and I do not answer. Advantageous to be firm and correct.

An ignorant child is not a stupid child; his intelligence is as yet undeveloped. With that intelligence he can learn and succeed, but he must be eager to learn and willing to make the effort to go out and seek his teacher instead of waiting for the teacher to come to him. If he is serious and sincere, his teacher will be glad to teach him. If he is not, he will be psychologically unready to receive any teaching, and his teacher will not accept him as yet. As for the teacher, it is advantageous for him to remain firm and correct until the student comes to him.

123

CONFUCIUS' EXPLANATION OF KING WEN'S JUDGMENT:

The Meng Hexagram suggests danger lurking beneath the mountain and blocking progress. This is the significance of the hexagram.

"The hexagram indicates prosperity and success." For prosperity and success will result when action is taken at the right time. "Not that I seek the ignorant youth, but that the ignorant youth seeks me." This means there must be concordance of wills. "The first time he seeks guidance from divination, I tell him." This is because of the strong and central position (as indicated by Line 2, Yang). "When he asks again and again, he is irreverent and I do not answer." For to be irreverent is to remain ignorant.

To help innocent youths cultivate their correct nature is the meritorious task of a sage.

Confucius first refers to the symbolism of ignorance. The Lower trigram signifies danger, and the upper trigram signifies a mountain. Danger begets fear, and mountain constitutes a great obstacle. Fear and obstacle signify the child's state of mind.

Confucius then explains that the way to develop the child's mind and banish ignorance is to be sure that the teaching is timely and suitable to the age of the child. The child must also have the will to learn and a beginner's reverence and sincerity. Symbolically, this is the situation shown by Lines 2 and 5.

Line 5 is in the center of the upper trigram, Ken, which represents a young child. The line therefore signifies the center or heart of a child and being Yin, further signifies a humble or docile heart. Line 2 is Yang (strong) and occupies the central position of the lower trigram. It represents the will to teach, or something worth teaching, as well as the teacher. As it forms a harmonious relationship with its correlate (Line 5, Yin), together the two signify a child willing to learn and a teacher willing to teach: a concordance of wills. In furthering this project, an irreverent attitude is generally considered inimical to learning or teaching.

As Confucius points out, the ultimate goal of teaching or learning is the cultivation of the child, which is considered the noble task of a sage.

SYMBOLIC SIGNIFICANCE OF THE HEXAGRAM AS NOTED BY CONFUCIUS:

The idea of Meng is derived from a spring issuing forth from below a mountain. The superior man is inspired thereby to act with firm resolve to foster virtue.

Water coming from a spring below a mountain is pure, symbolizing the innocence and pure heart of a child. The superior man realizes that just as water needs to be directed into the proper channels to be made useful, so the pure nature of a child needs to be guided properly if it is to learn the value of virtue. The superior man, therefore, is determined to cultivate virtue himself and to foster virtue in the character of children.

DUKE OF CHOU'S EXPLANATION OF THE LINES (a) AND CONFUCIUS' COMMENT THEREON (b):

Line 1, Yin:

(a) *In educating ignorant youths, it is advantageous to use punishment. To go on with their education without resorting to punitive instruments will lead to regret.*

(b) *"Advantageous to use punishment" means it is necessary to enforce the correct law.*

Line 1 occupies an incorrect position (Yin in a Yang place), indicating a subject who feels uncomfortable and insecure with his situation. If the entire hexagram represents a man's life span, then the bottom line represents a youth. In educating a youth, it is sometimes necessary to apply punishment to make him conform to what is considered appropriate.

Line 2, Yang:

(a) *Auspicious to treat ignorant youths with forbearance. Auspicious to take a wife. The son able to support the family.*

(b) *"The son able to support the family." This is suggested by the correspondence of the strong (Line 2) with the weak (Line 5).*

Line 2 occupies a position that is incorrect (Yang in a Yin place) but central. The central position of a trigram often denotes a man with executive ability. In this case, it denotes a teacher, and the four surrounding Yin lines represent his students. The situation, therefore, is advantageous to him. A Yang line surrounded by Yin lines also suggests a man surrounded by women, indicating propitious circumstances for taking a wife. The same symbol also represents a big brother who is taking care of his brothers and sisters. As Line 2 is Yang in the lower trigram, K'an, it denotes the second son. Normally the responsibility to support the family should be assumed by the elderly person (Line 5), but as this line is Yin, signifying a female, the responsibility falls on the son (Line 2). Since the two lines correlate harmoniously, their subjects will work together as a team.

Line 3, Yin:

(a) *Do not marry a woman who, upon seeing a man with plenty of gold, is unable to retain her self-possession. There will be nothing advantageous.*

(b) *"Do not marry the woman." This is because her conduct is improper.*

This line occupies a position neither central nor correct (Yin in a Yang place). The subject of such a line usually feels dissatisfied and is emotionally unstable. If the line is transformed into Yang, the lower trigram will become Sun, which signifies the eldest daughter. Now the upper trigram is Ken, which signifies the young son, hence the image of a possible marriage. Line 3 also forms a harmonious relationship with its correlate (Line 6, Yang); there is some mutual attraction between their subjects. This reinforces the idea of a possible marriage. According to the *Shuo Kua*, Ch'ien (Yang) signifies gold, among other things, suggesting that the subject of Line 3 sees gold in her possible mate (Line 6, Yang).

Line 4, Yin:

(a) *An ignorant youth in difficulties. He will have regret.*

(b) *"The regret of the ignorant youth" is due to his being far from realities.*

Being Yin in a Yin position, this line indicates meekness and weakness. It is also sandwiched between two more Yin lines, indicating a lack of mutual attraction with its neighbors. Moreover, it fails to form a harmonious relationship with its correlate (Line 1, Yin). Its subject is a weak person in an isolated and helpless position who has no opportunities to learn and whose intelligence remains undeveloped. Confucius says that he is removed from reality.

Line 5, Yin:

(a) *The ignorant youth will meet with good fortune.*

(b) *"The good fortune of the ignorant youth" is the result of his docility and humility.*

This line is Yin and occupies a central position in the upper trigram, indicating its subject to be an obedient and receptive youth who is inclined to follow the middle course. The line also forms a harmonious relationship with its correlate (Line 2, the teacher). Its subject is in an advantageous and fortunate position.

Line 6, Yang:

(a) *The innocent youth is given some violent blows. There is no advantage in acting as an aggressor. There is advantage in guarding against aggressive action.*

(b) *"There is advantage in guarding against aggressive action," because this will make both high and low follow the natural course.*

This line is strong (Yang) and occupies the top, or extreme limit, of the hexagram. It is also close to three Yin lines (representing three weak persons). Further, the upper trigram, Ken, signifies "hand." All this clearly indicates a violent man committing aggression against weak people by using his hand. The person who receives the violent blows is most likely the subject of Line 5 (the student), for he is nearest to the aggressor. The subject of Line 3 is least likely to be smitten, for he is a harmonious correlate or partner of the subject of Line 6 (the aggressor). Confucius may have had this in mind when he says that the advantage of guarding against aggressive action by maintaining a harmonious relationship is that both high and low (such as the subjects of Lines 3 and 6) will follow the natural course.

The HSU Hexagram
(Symbol of Waiting)

5th  需

Hsu MEANS "WAITING," waiting for auspicious circumstances to occur before taking any action. The lower trigram, Ch'ien, signifies strength but encounters great danger ahead, as signified by the lines of the upper trigram, K'an. In K'an, Line 5 occupies a central and correct position but is hemmed in by two Yin lines, signifying evil influences. Its subject is waiting for the assistance of the strong forces signified by the three Yang lines of the lower trigram.

KING WEN'S JUDGMENT ON THE HEXAGRAM:

The Hsu Hexagram indicates innate sincerity, brilliant success, and prosperity. Good fortune will stem from a firm and correct course. Advantageous to cross the great stream.

The Judgment has special reference to Line 5, which usually denotes a ruler. As its position is both central and correct, it denotes a great ruler, inwardly sincere, who will attain great success and prosperity if he is firm in following a middle course. Such a man will be successful even in crossing "the great stream," that is to say, in carrying out his great plans.

CONFUCIUS' EXPLANATION OF KING WEN'S JUDGMENT:

The hexagram suggests waiting because of danger ahead. Strong and vigorous and yet inclined to keep away from any snare, one by right should be free from distress and despair.

"The hexagram indicates innate sincerity, brilliant success, and prosperity. Good fortune will stem from a firm and correct course." This is seen from the correct, central, and heavenly position. "Advantageous to cross the great stream" means that any forward move will be crowned with success.

Yang is usually strong and dynamic in its movement, yet here, represented by the lower trigram, it is not reckless and takes care to avoid falling into the snare represented by the upper trigram. Such wise as well as cautious conduct enables it to be free from distress and despair.

The second paragraph dwells on the auspicious qualities ("central, correct") of the position which Line 5 occupies. The position is also called "heavenly" because the top two lines of a hexagram represent heaven.

SYMBOLIC SIGNIFICANCE OF THE HEXAGRAM AS NOTED BY CONFUCIUS:

The idea behind Hsu is derived from rainclouds (upper trigram) high in the sky (lower trigram). The superior man is inspired thereby to eat and drink and be merry.

The situation symbolized by the hexagram is one of waiting. The sky is overcast with rainclouds, but rain is slow in coming. Rain is usually considered a blessing, because it yields the water so necessary to life and therefore represents good fortune.

The lower interior trigram (Lines 2, 3, 4) is Tui, which signifies both "mouth" and "pleasure," hence suggesting the image "eat, drink and be merry." Taken together with the previous paragraph, this shows that the superior man considers it wise to enjoy life along the way and not refrain from it until his good fortune arrives.

DUKE OF CHOU'S EXPLANATION OF THE LINES (a) AND CONFUCIUS' COMMENT THEREON (b):

Line 1, Yang:
(a) *Waiting in the suburb. Advantageous to be steadfast in one's purpose. Then there will be no error.*

(b) *"Waiting in the suburb" means to avoid the risk of making any difficult move. "Advantageous to be steadfast in one's purpose" means one has not lost the normal course.*

Being at the bottom of the hexagram, this line represents the edge of a tract of land. Hence the image of a "suburb" where the waiting takes place. The line is Yang in a Yang place, indicating that its subject is strong and eager to advance. But danger (represented by the upper trigram, K'an) is threatening. Under such circumstances, an attempt to advance will not prove advantageous. The wisest course is to be patient and steady, avoiding any reckless move.

Line 2, Yang:

(a) *Waiting on the sand. Some petty criticisms will arise. Eventually there will be good fortune.*

(b) *"Waiting on the sand" indicates one inwardly free and confident and occupying a central position. Though "some petty criticisms will arise," one will meet with good fortune in the end.*

This line denotes a sandy beach, nearer the zone of danger (the upper trigram). The lower interior trigram, Tui, signifies "mouth." Impending danger often causes people to criticize one another in an attempt to shift or place blame, hence the idea of "petty criticisms." But as the danger is still at a distance, eventually there will be good fortune.

Line 3, Yang:

(a) *Waiting in the mud. Causing the approach of robbers.*

(b) *"Waiting in the mud" means calamity is at the outskirts. Since "the approach of robbers is caused" by oneself, one will avoid defeat if one is reverent and cautious.*

This line shows that its subject has moved to the brink of danger (the upper K'an trigram), where its proximity tempts the robbers to approach. One who is not afraid to expose himself to robbers possesses the courage to find ways to overcome them if he remains careful and alert.

Line 4, Yin:

(a) *Waiting in the blood. Coming out of the cavern.*

(b) *"Waiting in the blood" shows one to be docile and obedient to orders.*

This line usually denotes a minister in the service of the ruler (Line 5). Here, it is Yin, denoting a receptive and obedient minister, trusted by the ruler. Blood, as a sign of danger, is signified by the upper trigram, K'an. So although he may stray into the danger zone (become covered with blood), he will emerge from it unscathed.

Line 5, Yang:

(a) *Waiting before wine and food. Firm correctness will lead to good fortune.*

(b) *"Wine and food. Firm correctness will lead to good fortune." This is because of the central and correct position.*

Line 5 may be considered the center of danger, for it is in the center of the K'an trigram. But it also denotes a strong, able, virtuous ruler, for it is a Yang line in a Yang place and occupies a central and correct position. Furthermore, the ruler is served by a loyal and obedient minister (as denoted by Line 4). Such a ruler is well able to ward off the dangers. Meanwhile, he can enjoy good food and drink while he waits for the coming of good fortune.

Line 6, Yin:

(a) *Falling into the cavern. There come three uninvited guests who, if treated with respect, will bring good fortune in the end.*

(b) *"Uninvited guests coming. Respect shown to them will bring good fortune in the end." This is because no great mistake has been made, though the position occupied is inappropriate.*

This line is Yin and at the extreme limit of the hexagram. It indicates a weak person who has nowhere to go in fleeing the danger that threatens him. However, Line 6 forms a harmonious relationship with its correlate (Line 3, Yang), indicating a strong and responsive partner who will come to the rescue, bringing along the two other strong men represented by Lines 1 and 2. Hence the image of "three uninvited guests."

The SUNG Hexagram
(Symbol of Litigation)

6th  訟

THE LOWER TRIGRAM, K'an, represents danger or deep water. The upper, Ch'ien, represents strength. The hexagram signifies a situation in which the strong intends to come down to quell the danger, while the danger lurks underneath and seeks to subvert the strong. The Chinese word for Sung is composed of two simpler words: the left one means "speak" and the right means "public." Together they mean "argument in the open," hence the idea of litigation.

KING WEN'S JUDGMENT ON THE HEXAGRAM:

The Sung Hexagram indicates one who is inwardly sincere but is facing opposition. Caution and moderation will lead him to good fortune. Pushing any matter to the limit will be disastrous. Advantageous to see the great man. Not advantageous to cross the big stream.

The ruling line of the hexagram is Line 2, Yang. It represents a truthful person surrounded by dark influences, resulting in litigation. In litigtion one should be satisfied with a reasonable settlement and refrain from pushing matters to the limit.

The subject of Line 5 is a wise ruler or a great man, and it would prove advantageous for the litigants to see him, for such a man will render a fair verdict in their dispute.

CONFUCIUS' EXPLANATION OF KING WEN'S JUDGMENT:

The hexagram suggests strength above and danger below. Danger threatening the strong results in litigation.

"The hexagram indicates one who is inwardly sincere but is facing opposition. Caution and moderation will lead him to good fortune." This is because the strong (Line 2) comes and occupies a central position. "Pushing any matter to the limit will be disastrous." This is because litigation should not be pursued to the ultimate end. "Advantageous to see the great man." This means that he in the central and correct position (Line 5) should be highly respected. "Not advantageous to cross the big stream." For there is danger of falling into the cavern.

When a weak person is threatened by danger, he will avoid conflict or litigation. But when a strong, powerful person is so threatened, he will surely go to court.

Line 2 is Yang and occupies a central position, indicating a reasonable course which leads to good fortune. Line 5 is central and correct and in the portion of the hexagram representing heaven, indicating a great man or a wise ruler, one whom it is advantageous to see. The upper trigram, Ch'ien, signifies metal, and the lower trigram, K'an, signifies water. Metal sinks in water, suggesting that it is not advantageous to attempt big things ("cross the big stream").

SYMBOLIC SIGNIFICANCE OF THE HEXAGRAM AS NOTED BY CONFUCIUS:

The idea behind Sung is derived from sky (upper trigram) and water (lower trigram) going in opposite directions. The superior man is inspired thereby to deliberate carefully at the very beginning in the conduct of his affairs.

Sky is airy and air tends to rise upward, while water tends to flow downward. The opposing directions of their movements signify people who are far apart in their opinions, causing disagreement or litigation. From this the superior man learns that differences of opinion should be avoided. Thus he deliberates carefully at the very beginning of things so that all will be clear and in order and no misunderstanding can arise later to cause any dispute.

DUKE OF CHOU'S EXPLANATION OF THE LINES (a) AND CONFUCIUS' COMMENT THEREON (b):

Line 1, Yin:
(a) *Not pushing the matter in hand to the end. A few explanations. Good fortune eventually.*

(b) *"Not pushing any matter in hand to the end." This means litigation should not be prolonged. Through "a few explanations," they will make the argument clear.*

Line 1 occupies an incorrect position (Yin in a Yang place) and lies at the bottom of the hexagram. This indicates that its subject is weak and in a lowly, difficult position. In such a case, it is not advantageous for him to pursue any dispute to the end. Instead, the wisest course is to explain his position and clarify the controversy.

Line 2, Yang:
(a) *Not able to continue the litigation. One backs down and flees to a small town with only three hundred families. Will incur no untoward incidents.*

(b) *"Not able to continue the litigation. Backs down and flees." This shows that a lowly fellow who sues a person high above him brings disaster to himself with his own hands.*

This line is incorrectly placed and forms an antagonistic relationship with its correlate (Line 5, the ruler). Line 2's subject is no match for a man in this position, but is sensible (as is indicated by his central position) and knows he cannot hope to win any dispute with his superior, so he backs down. Confucius considers him rather unwise to have sued his superior in the first place.

Line 3, Yin:
(a) *Living on old virtues. Firm and correct. The perilous situation will end in good fortune. One may be in the king's service but will*

not presume on any achievement.

(b) *"Living on old virtues." This shows that obedience to his superior brings him good fortune.*

Line 3 occupies a position neither central nor correct (Yin in a Yang place) and is sandwiched between two Yang lines. Its subject is a weak person in an insecure position, menaced by strong neighbors. The line, however, forms a harmonious relationship with its correlate (Line 6, Yang). This means that its subject is supported by some influential person and will therefore move from his perilous situation to good fortune. This is especially true if he is obeidient to his supporter and content to live by the moral heritage of hs ancestors. He should remain humble, even if he finds himself in the service of the king and achieves some success.

Line 4, Yang:

(a) *Not able to continue the litigation. He resumes his original aim and follows sublime principles. He changes his mind and rests in a firm and correct course. There will be good fortune.*

(b) *"He resumes his original aim and follows sublime principles. He changes his mind and rests in a firm and correct course." This means he has not fallen into error.*

This line occupies a position that is incorrect (Yang in a Yin place) and indicates a state of transition (being above the lower trigram and on the edge of the uppr one). Its subject, therefore, tends to be impulsive in his actions and uncertain in his aims. At first, he may bring a lawsuit against an opponent, then change his mind and turn to the right course. Such a man frees himself from error.

Line 5, Yang:

(a) *The litigation ends in great good fortune.*

(b) *"The litigation ends in great good fortune." This is because of the central and correct position.*

This line nearly always augurs good fortune. In this hexagram it occupies a position both central and correct (Yang in a Yang place). It denotes a great and able ruler who will be victorious in any litigation.

Line 6, Yang:

(a) *One may have a leathern belt conferred on him. But in a single morning he may be deprived of it three times.*

(b) *Receiving a robe (i.e., becoming an official) as a result of litigation. This nevertheless is not entitled to any respect.*

This line is Yang at the extreme limit, indicating a radical and contentious person eager to attain his objectives through litigation. But he has reached the pinnacle of his career and his fall is imminent. Even if he wins a lawsuit or obtains a government position or other reward as the result of one litigation, he is not entitled to any respect and will lose what he gains before long.

The SHIH Hexagram
(Symbol of Armed Forces)

7th  師

THE UPPER TRIGRAM, K'un, denotes meekness or gentleness. The lower trigram, K'an, denotes danger. Meekness outside coupled with danger inside suggests an army, whose nature is to show order and discipline outside while containing danger inside. Line 2 is the only Yang line in the hexagram and represents the general, or commander. Line 5 represents the ruler as usual, and the four other Yin lines represent the soldiers. Hence the idea of armed forces.

KING WEN'S JUDGMENT ON THE HEXAGRAM:

The Shih Hexagram indicates firm correctness. Veteran leadership will bring good fortune. There will be no error.

The Judgment sets forth the two essential requirements for a good army: first, its objective as well as its strategy must be both correct and just; second, it must be commanded by able and experienced officers.

CONFUCIUS' EXPLANATION OF KING WEN'S JUDGMENT:

Shih, the name of the hexagram, means multitude. Firm means correct. Ability to employ the multitude to enforce correct measures will realize the kingly way in the world.

The strong (Line 2) occupies a central position and enjoys favorable response (Line 5). Dangerous exploits are launched smoothly and

agreeably. When they are used to distress (lit., poison) the evil forces in the world and are espoused by the people, there will be good fortune. What error would there be?

The first part of the explanation stresses the importance of the rank and file. It suggests that a general with the ability to keep a large army firmly on a correct and just course can bring about peace and prosperity in the world.

The second part explains how an army can be free from error and meet with good fortune. It refers to Line 2, a Yang line occupying a central position, indicating an able general commanding a strong army and following a moderate course. Such an army can both cope ably with the danger (represented by the lower trigram, K'an) and will receive support from the people. With this foundation, an army is sure to conquer the lawless elements in the world.

SYMBOLIC SIGNIFICANCE OF THE HEXAGRAM AS NOTED BY CONFUCIUS:

The idea behind Shih is derived from water (lower trigram) collecting underneath the earth (upper trigram). The superior man is inspired thereby to be kind to the people and build up the masses.

Water hidden under the earth may be compared to soldiers potentially existing among the people. The superior man is wise enough to treat the people well, thereby strengthening his position as well as that of the masses.

DUKE OF CHOU'S EXPLANATION OF THE LINES (a) AND CONFUCIUS' COMMENT THEREON (b):

Line 1, Yin:

(a) *An army should set out with discipline. Poor discipline leads to disaster.*

(b) *"An army should set out with discipline." This is because loss of discipline will cause disaster.*

Discipline is important to an army, especially at the beginning of a campaign. Line 1 is Yin (weakness) and occupies the lowest position of the hexagram, indicating something like disorder at the beginning. Both the Duke of Chou and Confucius, therefore, sound a warning, stressing the importance of discipline to preserve order in an army.

Line 2, Yang:

(a) *The general is in the army. Good fortune. No error. The king has issued three decrees to him.*

(b) *"The general is in the army. Good fortune." This means he has received favors from heaven. "The king has issued three decrees to him." This shows the king is concerned about the numerous regions in his kingdom.*

This Yang line occupies a central but incorrect position (Yang in a Yin place). It is also the only Yang line in the hexagram; in other words, the only strong man. It is therefore he who must take up the position of general. The line correlates harmoniously with Line 5, Yin (the ruler), indicating that the general is high in royal favor. He thus has three royal decrees issued to him, each conferring a great honor. In return, the general is expected to bring peace to all regions of the kingdom.

Line 3, Yin:

(a) *An army led by a number of incompetent officers will meet with evil.*

(b) *"An army led by a number of incompetent officers will meet with evil." This means there will be considerable lack of success.*

This line is neither central nor correct (Yin in a Yang place), and its subject tends to be wayward and prone to feelings of insecurity. The line is also above Line 2 (the general), which suggests that its subject is haughty and wants to surpass the general. Thus, he is prone to criticize the tactics of the general and interfere in the conduct of military affairs. Naturally, an army led by this kind of officer is sure to meet with ill fortune.

Line 4, Yin:

(a) *An army in strategic retreat. No error.*

(b) *"An army in strategic retreat. No error." This means the normal course has not been lost.*

This line occupies a position that is correct (Yin in a Yin place) but not central. This means that its subject is not advantageously placed to act, but knows his proper duties and follows a moderate course. He does not underestimate the enemy but leads his army on a detour to avoid a frontal encounter. Line 4 usually indicates a stage of transition and uncertainty, involving change and new considerations. But this change is merely an adjustment, and the normal course or basic strategy is retained.

Line 5, Yin:

(a) *There are birds and beasts in the field. Their presence serves as a good pretext to seize them. If the eldest son leads the army while younger relatives serve as incompetent officers, there will be evil if the situation persists.*

(b) *"The eldest son leads the army." This is because he acts from a central position. "Younger relatives serve as incompetent officers." This means that the assignment of military duties has not been done in a proper way.*

Line 5 always occupies a central place and usually denotes a ruler. Here, because the line is Yin, the ruler is a queen or a weak person who is unlikely to pursue an aggressive policy, and takes action for defence only when invasion is imminent ("birds and beasts in the field"). In such a situation, this line's subject has to rely on the loyal support of the able general, (Line 2) with whom she forms a harmonious relationship.

According to the *Shuo Kua*, the bottom of the Chen trigram represents "eldest son." Here, Line 2 (Yang, male) is at the bottom of the lower interior trigram, Chen (Lines 2, 3, 4), and so represents the eldest son. The ill-placed Line 3 represents the younger relatives, haughty and wayward fellows who consider themselves smarter than the general and should never be allowed to interfere in the conduct of any military campaign.

Line 6, Yin:

(a) *The supreme ruler issues decrees, some concerning the establishment of states, and some the inheritance of clan headship. The mean people should not be employed.*

(b) *"The supreme ruler issues decrees." This is for the purpose of rewarding meritorious achievements correctly and properly. "The mean people should not be employed." This is because such people are bound to cause trouble and confusion in the country.*

This line is at the extreme end of the hexagram, indicating that the war is over and the king is victorious and truly great. He then proceeds to reward his ministers and generals according to their merits. He appoints some of them to positions as governors of states; others, leaders of clans. He shows a sincere desire to pacify the country by taking care not to employ people of mean character, who are apt to put their own interests before those of the nation, creating disharmony and disorder.

The PI Hexagram
(Symbol of Neighborliness)

8th  比

IN CURRENT CHINESE, the word for Pi usually means "compare" or "contrast," and less commonly, "associate." In ancient China Pi was the name of a social unit or neighborhood organization comprising five different clans and headed by a chief executive. The Pi Hexagram exactly symbolizes such a neighborhood organization. The only Yang line, Line 5, represents the chief executive, while the five Yin lines represent the five clans.

KING WEN'S JUDGMENT ON THE HEXAGRAM:

The Pi Hexagram indicates good fortune. Deliberate carefully and reverently. If basically good, persistent and chaste or firm, there will be no error. People from regions of unrest will come. Latecomers will face misfortune.

The Judgment refers essentially to Line 5, which occupies a central and correct position, signifying a great and wise ruler. This line also has a harmonious correlate in Line 2, which is Yang. The two lines, therefore, symbolize a close association which presages good fortune. However, the leader should periodically review his virtues so as not to let his character weaken or be corrupted and to remain free from blame. A leader of this sort is sure to attract people from troubled regions seeking a wise ruler for themselves. Latecomers, attracted only by the bounty his policies have produced, should not be rewarded.

CONFUCIUS' EXPLANATION OF KING WEN'S JUDGMENT:

The hexagram signifies good fortune. The word "Pi" means assitance, with people below obeying those above.

"Deliberate carefully and reverently. If basically good, persistent, and chaste or firm, there will be no error." This is because the strong occupies the central heavenly place (Line 5). "People from regions of unrest will come." This means that high (Line 5) and low (Line 2) respond to each other favorably. "Latecomers will face misfortune." This is because their course has exhausted its power.

Line 5 (Yang in a central heavenly place) denotes a strong ruler who should periodically review his virtues. The harmonious correlation of Line 2 with Line 5 indicates the coming of people from the troubled regions. Line 6, at the extreme limit of the hexagram, represents the latecomers whose course has exhausted its power.

SYMBOLIC SIGNIFICANCE OF THE HEXAGRAM AS NOTED BY CONFUCIUS:

The idea behind Pi is derived from water (upper trigram) above earth (lower trigram). The ancient kings were inspired thereby to set up numerous states and maintain cordial relations with the princes.

Water is essential to life and civilization. It gives rise to communities and corporate living. In fact, all civilizations began in river valleys. The sign of water on earth, therefore, induced the ancient kings to think of setting up states and appointing rulers.

DUKE OF CHOU'S EXPLANATION OF THE LINES (a) AND CONFUCIUS' COMMENT THEREON (b):

Line 1, Yin:

(a) *One has sincerity in associating with people. No error. A heart filled with sincerity like a water jug filled with water will induce favorable responses and other good fortunes.*

(b) *The association indicated in Line 1 means there are other good fortunes.*

This line is the first in the hexagram, so it signifies the sincerity which is usually present at the beginning of an association or union. Any union based on sincerity will remain free from blame. However, the position Line 1 occupies is neither central nor correct (Yin in a Yang place), and it fails to form a harmonious relationship with its correlate (Line 4). Its subject finds himself in an isolated, insecure position, although he sincerely desires to associate with people. Becaue of his sincerity, he may yet be rewarded in some way.

Line 2, Yin:

(a) *Association originates inwardly from the heart. Firm correctness will lead to good fortune.*

(b) *"Association originates inwardly from the heart." This means no loss of self-respect.*

This line forms a harmonious relationship with its correlate (Line 5, the ruler), indicating that its subject's desire for union is sincere and comes from the heart. As he is sincere and has no ulterior motive, he does not lose his self-respect.

Line 3, Yin:

(a) *Association with people of questionable character.*

(b) *"Association with people of questionable character." Isn't this a sad and lamentable thing?*

This line is badly situated. Its position is neither central nor correct (Yin in a Yang place) and it does not form a harmonious relationship with its correlate (Line 6). It is also hemmed in by its neighbors (two Yin lines), weak and sinister characters. Its subject, therefore, is in an unhappy and unfavorable position.

Line 4, Yin:

(a) *Association with outsiders. A firm and correct course will lead to good fortune.*

(b) *"Association with worthy people from the outside." This is because of obedience to superiors.*

Line 4 (the minister) is Yin in a Yin place, suggesting a loyal and obedient minister. However, it fails to form a harmonious relationship with its correlate (Line 1) and, further, it lies above the lower trigram in the upper or outside trigram. All this indicates that its subject has left his home base and is in contact with outsiders. In addition, Line 5 (the ruler), also in the outside trigram, is Yang in a central and correct place, denoting a strong and wise ruler and suggesting that the minister is associated with a highly placed outsider, or ruler, to whom he is loyal and obediant, for there is much mutual attraction and happy cooperation between them. This is indeed good fortune.

Line 5, Yang:

(a) *Magnificent association. The king is hunting and pursues his game in three directions, leaving the front direction for the hunted to escape. The townspeople are not disturbed and do not have to raise any warning. There will be good fortune.*

(b) *The "good fortune from magnificent association" is due to the central and correct position. Giving up those animals that flee and getting those that come along is indicated by "leaving the front direction for the hunted to escape." "The townspeople do not have to raise any warning." This shows that the leaders are directing the people in the right way.*

This line occupies a position both central and correct (Yang in a Yang place) and forms a harmonious relationship with its correlate (Line 2, Yin), as well as with Line 4 (Yin, the minister). Its subject, therefore, is a wise and brilliant ruler who shows affection even to beasts. Such benevolence inspires and unifies his people.

Line 6, Yin:

(a) *No initiative toward association. There will be evil.*

(b) *"No initiative toward association." This means there will be no good end.*

This line is Yin in a Yin position, indicating its subject to be weak, prone to follow rather than lead. Since Line 3 (its correlate) is also Yin, they do not form a harmonious relationship; and since the line is also placed above Line 5 (the ruler), its subject may be overbearing and hostile toward his superior. Such a subject seriously lacks the qualifications for leadership.

The line is at the extremity of the hexagram. Beyond lies the unknown. This situation, coupled with the lack of harmonious associates, bodes evil ("there will be no good end").

The HSIAO CH'U Hexagram
(Symbol of Mild Restraint)

9th  小畜

THE MEANING OF this hexagram is "mild restraint," and it is not difficult to make out this meaning from its lines. Line 4 is the ruling line, the only Yin line, and occupies a Yin place, indicating that it exercises only a weak influence or restraint over the five strong Yang lines.

KING WEN'S JUDGMENT ON THE HEXAGRAM:

The Hsiao Ch'u Hexagram indicates success and prosperity. Thick clouds appear but do not turn into rain. They are spreading from our western border.

The fact that a weak line can succeed in restraining five Yang lines indicates harmonious relations which bode well for success and prosperity. The phrase "our western border" indicates some political significance in the Judgment, which was written toward the end of the Shang dynasty when King Wen was prince of the Chou principality. Rain is usually a symbol of blessing, and rain-clouds a symbol of potential blessings. Clouds over the Chou principality, which lay to the west of the Shang capitol, but not yet melting into rain meant that the Chou principality was a potential source of restraint and blessings to the kingdom, but as yet its influence over the kingdom was only slight. Later, when the Chou dynasty had superseded the Shang, this potential was realized for the betterment of the land.

CONFUCIUS' EXPLANATION OF KING WEN'S JUDGMENT:

The hexagram shows that the weak has obtained its proper place and receives favorable response from both above and below. This is called Hsiao Ch'u.

With vigor and adaptability, the strong occupy the central positions and carry out their aspirations. Hence success and prosperity.

"Thick clouds but no rain" means there is still movement onward. "From our western border" shows that the distribtution of rain is not yet widespread.

Line 4 is expressive of the meaning of the hexagram as a whole, for it is both Yin in a Yin place and receives harmonious response from all the Yang lines. This indicates that success and prosperity will come about as the result of vigor (lower trigram) coupled with adaptability (upper trigram), and because the strong (Lines 2 and 5) occupy central positions and carry out their aspirations. Line 4, which is Yin and represents dark clouds, is at the bottom of the upper trigram, indicating that the clouds are still moving up but have not yet dissolved into rain.

SYMBOLIC SIGNIFICANCE OF THE HEXAGRAM AS NOTED BY CONFUCIUS:

The idea behind Hsiao Ch'u is derived from wind (upper trigram) high in the sky (lower trigram). The superior man is inspired thereby to beautify his illustrious virtues.

Wind is fitful and does not last long. Besides, for all its seeming might, it blows in only a small part of the infinite expanse of the sky. Hence the idea of "small storage" or "mild influence." The superior man notes that clouds must be dispersed by wind before heaven can appear in its pure blue aspect. This inspires him to polish and perfect his character so that it will appear as pure as blue heaven.

DUKE OF CHOU'S EXPLANATION OF THE LINES (a) AND CONFUCIUS' COMMENT THEREON (b):

Line 1, Yang:

(a) *One resumes one's own course. What error can there be? There will be good fortune.*

(b) *"One resumes one's own course." This rightly means good fortune.*

This line is Yang in a Yang place, indicating its subject to be a person of dynamic character, eager to advance. But as it forms a harmonious relationship with its correlate (Line 4), Line 1's subject does not advance recklessly but returns to the proper course of moderation when circumstances require. He will thus be free from error and enjoy good fortune.

Line 2, Yang:

(a) *One resumes one's proper course through the influence of association. This is good fortune.*

(b) *"One resumes one's proper course through the influence of association." This means that nevertheless, one's integrity has not been lost.*

Line 2 occupies a position that is central but incorrect (Yang in a Yin place), indicating that its subject is strong and active, yet not prone to go to extremes, and will follow the middle path of moderation. In addition, the line is a close associate of Line 1 (also Yang), and the subjects of both lines tend to follow a moderate path, as if one is dragging the other along.

Line 3, Yang:

(a) *The spokes have gone off from the wheels of the wagon. Husband and wife are not in harmony.*

(b) *"Husband and wife are not in harmony." This shows that the husband cannot treat his wife properly.*

Line 3 is in most cases a sign of ill fortune. Here, it occupies a position neither central nor correct (Yang in a Yin place). Hence its subject tends to feel uncomfortable and insecure. The line is also at the top of the lower trigram, Ch'ien, suggesting its Yang power is increased. For all these reasons, the subject of the line is apt to make reckless moves and cause trouble like that which results when the spokes of a wagon wheel break off. Such an act would disturb the harmony in any close partnership, such as that between husband and wife. This is why Confucius lays blame on the husband (Line 3).

The lower trigram, Ch'ien, signifies something circular; hence the idea of "wheels." It also signifies a husband, while the upper trigram, Sun, signifies a wife. Hence the image of "husband and wife."

Line 4, Yin:

(a) *One is inwardly sincere. Blood has vanished and anxiety gone. No error.*

(b) *"One is inwardly sincere. Anxiety has gone." This is because one's aspirations harmonize with those of one's superior.*

Line 4 is the only Yin line in the hexagram and occupies a Yin place. In addition, it is the first line of the upper trigram, Sun, which signifies docility. This indicates that its subject is sincere and submissive and possesses sufficient Yin virtues to neutralize the surrounding Yang forces, thus keeping them in a state of peaceful coexistence.

The line usually denotes a minister in service to the ruler (Line 5). This minister can easily find favor, as his aspirations harmonize with those of the king. Line 4 also forms a harmonious relationship with its correlate (Line 1, Yang), and there is mutual attraction between it and its neighbor (Line 3). Trusted by the king and enjoying support from the people and close associates, the minister can succeed in dispelling anxiety and preventing conflict ("blood has vanished"). This is indicated by the fact that none of the four trigrams in the hexagram (lower, upper, and the two interior trigrams) is K'an, the symbol of blood.

Line 5, Yang:

(a) *One's inward sincerity attracts people to him. He becomes wealthy through cooperation with his neighbor.*

(b) *"One's inward sincerity attracts people to him." This means that not only he himself will be wealthy.*

This line occupies a position both central and correct (Yang in a Yang place), denoting a wise leader or ruler. While his sincerity draws his neighbor (Line 4) to him, his neighbor is also one of sincere and loyal character. Through cooperation they both become wealthy or meet with success.

Line 6, Yang:

(a) *Rain has fallen and has ceased. Loads of lofty virtue. The wife, while firm and correct, is grave. The moon is almost full. The superior man will meet with disaster if he embarks on any venture.*

(b) *"Rain has fallen and has ceased." This means that virtue has been accumulated, as it were, by the load. "The superior man will meet with disaster if he embarks on any venture." This means he should have misgivings.*

This line is at the end of the hexagram. It signifies that the rain has ceased. Rain is usually considered a blessing, so a heavy rainfall is likened to the accumulation and growth of character ("loads of virtue"). The wife (Line 4) has been doing well in mildly restraining her Yang neighbors. Her influence is growing, like the moon becoming full. But now she appears grave, for she must deal with the subject of Line 6. This is the last of the five Yang lines of the hexagram, indicating great and dynamic power, and is at the extreme limit of the hexagram. Its subject is exceedingly strong and active, tending to be tough, haughty, and aggressive, and may be heading toward conflict with his wife. The situation is very uncertain. The superior man has misgivings and hesitates to advance for fear of mishap.

The LU Hexagram

(Symbol of Cautious Tread)

10th  履

THE CHINESE WORD for Lu means "treading" or "stepping." The ruling line of the hexagram is Line 3 (Yin), which is on the plane of man (the two middle lines), denoting a weak man or woman. Since the bottom two lines of any hexagram signify earth, the position of Line 3 (Yin) over Line 2 suggests a weak person treading gingerly on the earth.

KING WEN'S JUDGMENT ON THE HEXAGRAM:

The hexagram indicates a man treading on the tail of a tiger which does not bite him. Prosperity and success.

If the whole figure represents a tiger, Line 1 at the bottom represents the tiger's tail. The subject of Line 3 may be said to be treading on it because Line 2 represents the surface of the earth where the tail lies. The lower trigram, Tui, however, stands for pleasure or satisfaction. The subject of Line 3, at the top of Tui, is therefore considered pleased or satisfied, indicating that he has not been bitten by the tiger. Hence the idea of prosperity and success.

CONFUCIUS' EXPLANATION OF KING WEN'S JUDGMENT:

The hexagram shows the weak treading on the strong.
There is pleasure and docile response to the Yang power. Hence prosperity and success for him who treads on a tiger's tail and does not get bitten.

The strong is in a central and correct position. He sits on the kingly throne without any self-reproach. He is brilliant and enlightened.

The upper trigram, Ch'ien, is Yang, signifying great strength or power, and the lower trigram, Tui, signifies pleasure. Yang is an awe-inspiring as well as a loving power. To be able to respond to it with a joyful feeling is to be free from harm ("treads on a tiger's tail and does not get bitten").

The last paragraph refers to Line 5 (Yang), which occupies a central and correct position. Its subject is a great and brilliant ruler who ascends ("treads on") the throne with no pangs of conscience. His intelligence is denoted by the lower interior trigram, Li (Lines 2, 3, 4), which stands for light or enlightenment.

SYMBOLIC SIGNIFICANCE OF THE HEXAGRAM AS NOTED BY CONFUCIUS:

The idea behind Lu is derived from heaven above (upper trigram) and marsh below (lower trigram). The superior man is inspired thereby to discriminate between high and low and to calm the minds of the people.

The sky is up high and the marsh is down low, both where they ought to be. From this, the superior man learns to make distinctions between the duties of high and low. Without knowing such distinctions, the people may feel confused about their proper responsibilities and relationships, leading to psychological unrest and social disharmony. By making such distinctions, the superior man sets the minds of the people at rest.

DUKE OF CHOU'S EXPLANATION OF THE LINES (a) AND CONFUCIUS' COMMENT THEREON (b):

Line 1, Yang:

(a) *One advances by treading his usual proper path. No error.*

(b) *"The advance by treading one's proper path" means carrying out one's wishes alone.*

This line occupies the correct position (Yang in a Yang place) but lies at the bottom of the hexagram and fails to form a harmonious relationship with its correlate (Line 4, Yang). Therefore, its subject does not relate amicably to the subject of Line 4. Instead, he remains in his low place and lives a simple life, making no error.

Line 2, Yang:

(a) *Treading a plain and easy path, a reclusive person with firm correctness meets with good fortune.*

(b) *"A reclusive person with firm correctness meets with good fortune." This is because his heart remains unperturbed.*

Here, Line 2 occupies a position incorrect (Yang in a Yin place) but central, indicating a subject who follows a middle course and maintains his integrity with a serene heart. The line is in a rather low position and fails to form a harmonious relationship with its correlate (Line 5, the ruler), suggesting that its subject is reclusive, for although in a low position, he does not desire to serve the ruler.

Line 3, Yin:

(a) *One who can see with only one eye and walk, though lame of one leg, treads on a tiger's tail and gets bitten. This is evil. A daring fellow enters into the service of a great king.*

(b) *"A one-eyed man can see," but this does not mean that his vision is clear. "A lame man can walk," but this does not mean that his steps are firm. "The evil of being bitten by a tiger" is due to the fact that one's position is inappropriate. "A daring fellow enters into the service of a great king." This shows that his will is strong.*

This line occupies a position neither central nor correct (Yin in a Yang place), indicating a weak person in an awkward position who is unsure of himself and apt to act recklessly on the spur of the moment. Though he has only one good eye and is lame, he is still active and gets about. Such a person is likely to "tread on a tiger's tail and get bitten." This is an evil outcome indeed. However, the line forms a harmonious relationship with its correlate (Line 6, Yang) at the top of the upper trigram, Ch'ien, signifying a powerful king. Its subject, therefore, may impulsively go through danger to success in the service of his ruler.

The upper interior trigram, Sun (Lines 3, 4, 5), signifies legs, and the lower interior trigram, Li (Lines 2, 3, 4), signifies eyes.

Line 4, Yang:

(a) *One treads on a tiger's tail. He acts very cautiously and apprehensively. Good fortune in the end.*

(b) *"He acts very cautiously and apprehensively. Good fortune in the end." This means his wish has been realized.*

This line usually denotes a minister. Here, its position is neither central nor correct (Yang in a Yin place), nor does it form a harmonious relationship with its correlate (Line 1), indicating a minister in highly unfavorable circumstances. Its neighbor (Line 5, the ruler) is also Yang, so there is no mutual attraction between them. This shows a minister in an isolated and insecure position who does not enjoy the confidence of the ruler. Such a man may well feel he is treading on a tiger's tail. The subject must act "very cautiously and apprehensively" if he wishes to meet with good fortune.

Line 5, Yang:

(a) *One treads with decisive steps. He is firm and correct and awe-inspiring.*

(b) *"One treads with decisive steps. He is firm and correct and awe-inspiring." This is because his position is correct and appropriate.*

Here, Line 5 (the ruler) occupies a position both central and correct (Yang in a Yang place), denoting a great and powerful ruler who acts with decision and determination, presenting a firm and awe-inspiring appearance.

Line 6, Yang:

(a) *Review the steps already taken and examine the foreboding signs. If they are orderly and well-formed, there will be supreme good fortune.*

(b) *"Supreme good fortune" in the top position. This is a matter for great rejoicing.*

Being Yang and at the peak of the hexagram, this line represents a strong man who has climbed to the top. But the line does not occupy the correct position (Yang in a Yin place), indicating that its subject will feel uncomfortable and insecure. Looking back, he reviews the path he has followed, examining the various signs and omens. If his course is found to have been the right one, there will be occasion for rejoicing.

The T'AI Hexagram
(Symbol of Prosperity)

11th  泰

ANYONE FAMILIAR WITH Chinese folklore will remember the popular saying at the beginning of the Chinese New Year: "San Yang Ch'i T'ai" ("Three Yangs initiate peace and prosperity"). "Three Yangs" refers to the three Yang lines of this hexagram, which are supposed to blaze a path to prosperity because they are dynamic. Their onward course is bound to be successful and smooth-sailing, for the only opposition they face is very weak, as indicated by the three Yin lines constituting the upper trigram. This is why the T'ai Hexagram is identified with the first month of the lunar year, when spring returns and things begin to grow and flourish.

The ruling lines of the hexagram (Lines 2 and 5) each occupy the central position of their respective trigrams and form a harmonious relationship with each other, suggesting prosperity and smooth sailing.

KING WEN'S JUDGMENT ON THE HEXAGRAM:

The T'ai Hexagram indicates that what is small goes out and what is great comes in. There will be success and prosperity as well as good fortune.

The lower trigram of any hexagram represents the inside, and the upper trigram represents the outside. The lower trigram is Yang, signifying what is great or strong and is supposed to have come in from the outside. The upper trigram is Yin, signifying what is weak and small and is supposed to have gone out from the inside. The outgoing course of the Yin and the incoming course

155

of the Yang cross each other smoothly, indicating success and prosperity.

CONFUCIUS' EXPLANATION OF KING WEN'S JUDGMENT:

"The hexagram indicates that what is small goes out and what is great comes in. There will be prosperity and success as well as good fortune." This means that heaven and earth are in union and the ten thousand things correspond satisfactorily, and that people high and low are in communication and have similar aspirations. What is Yang is inside, and what is Yin is outside. Inward strength is coupled with outward docility. The superior men are in, the inferior men are out. The way of the superior man is waxing, while that of the inferior man is waning.

Confucius here brings King Wen's Judgment into the context of natural phenomena and human society. To him the Judgment suggests what is desirable, or what causes prosperity, in each of these two fields.

SYMBOLIC SIGNIFICANCE OF THE HEXAGRAM AS NOTED BY CONFUCIUS:

The idea behind T'ai is derived from the union of heaven (lower trigram) and earth (upper trigram). The ruler is inspired thereby to determine and fulfill the ways of heaven and earth and to assist the unfoldment of their ways in a proper manner for the moral and physical transformation of the people.

This hexagram, with the K'un trigram over the Ch'ien trigram, signifies the union of heaven and earth, or the interplay of Yin and Yang. Such contact always means peace and prosperity. According to a common Chinese saying, it is only when Yin and Yang are in harmony that rain will descend. The superior man realizes that in order to ensure harmony and blessings (rain) in his own life and the lives of those around him, he should learn to understand the ways of heaven and earth (the immutable natural laws).

DUKE OF CHOU'S EXPLANATION OF THE LINES (a) AND CONFUCIUS' COMMENT THEREON (b):

Line 1, Yang:
(a) *Some herbs are pulled up together, because of their intertwining roots. Ventures will be propitious.*
(b) *"Some herbs are pulled up and ventures will be propitious." This is because one's aim is directed outward.*

All the lines of the lower trigram, being Yang, are in harmony with their Yin correlates in the upper trigram. These happy correlations signify a well-integrated family or other social group who have grown as close together as the intertwining roots of herbs. As Line 1 begins the hexagram, its subject is viewed as starting the cooperation for prosperity ("herbs are pulled up . . . intertwining roots"). To do this, he has to go out and work ("one's aim is directed outward").

Line 2, Yang:
(a) *Patient and magnanimous toward people from all regions. Willing to swim across a river. Remembering people far away. Practicing no favoritism among friends. Thus one prefers to follow the middle path.*
(b) *"Patient and magnanimous toward people from all regions. One prefers to follow the middle path." This is because he is enlightened and magnanimous.*

This line is incorrect (Yang in a Yin place), but occupies a central position and forms a harmonious relationship with its correlate (Line 5), which also occupies a central position, suggesting that the subject of the line follows the middle path closely and is inwardly enlightened. He wants to be just and fair to everyone. To do his duty, he is willing to take a great risk ("swim across a river").

Line 3, Yang:
(a) *No plain which does not turn into a slope. No outgoing which does not lead to a turning around. Fortitude and perseverance ward off errors. Unstinted sincerity leads to enjoyment of happiness.*
(b) *"No outgoing which does not lead to a turning around." This is due to the interaction between heaven and earth.*

This line is at the top of the lower trigram, Ch'ien, and just below the bottom of the upper trigram, K'un, signifying the contact or interplay between heaven and earth (Yin and Yang), the Law of Cyclic Reversion. As a result of the operation of this law, the vast wheel of history keeps turning round and round, giving birth to the enormous vicissitudes of human life. To cope with these requires sincerity as well as fortitude and perseverance.

Line 4, Yin:

(a) *One descends like a bird flapping its wings. He cannot become rich single-handedly, but has to rely on his neighbor. He needs no exhortation about sincerity.*

(b) *"One descends like a bird flapping its wings. He cannot become rich single-handedly." This shows lack of substance or means. "He needs no exhortation about sincerity." This is because his desires flow from his heart.*

This line is Yin at the bottom of a Yin trigram, suggesting weakness personified. Its subject cannot become rich with his own poor resources but must rely on the strength of his neighbor (Line 3), whom he comes down to join ("descends like a bird flapping its wings"). He does this naturally, without any hypocrisy, for it is the correct path in such a situation. Line 4 being Yin and Line 3 being Yang, mutual attraction is indicated between the two, denoting happy cooperation.

Line 5, Yin:

(a) *Emperor Yi gave his sister in marriage. Great felicity and good fortune.*

(b) *"Great felicity and good fortune." This is because they occupy central positions and realize their wishes.*

Emperor Yi was a noted emperor of the Shang dynasty who gave his sister in marriage to a worthy man. This was considered a happy marriage in those times. Line 5 represents the sister of the emperor, and Line 2 represents the worthy man. As Yin and Yang they form a harmonious relationship. Since the two lines each occupy a central position, their subjects tend to follow the Golden Mean and the promptings of their hearts. The lower interior trigram (Lines 2, 3, 4) is Tui (a young daughter), and the upper interior trigram (Lines 3, 4, 5) is Chen (an eldest son). Hence the image of marriage.

Line 6, Yin:

(a) *City wall falls into the moat. Do not resort to armed force. Issue orders to warn the local populace. Persistence or reluctance to change will cause regret.*

(b) *"City wall falls into the moat." Its destiny is in trouble.*

The upper trigram is K'un (territory and its people). Hence the image of "city" and "city wall." The line is Yin, occupying the highest limit of the hexagram. This suggests the high city wall, which is weak at the top and falls down. The collapse of the wall is a bad omen, indicating that the city or country is on the decline and in trouble. In such a case, it is inadvisable to use armed force or other extreme means. It is necessary, however, to institute reforms and arouse the people to support their country, otherwise decline will ensue.

The P'I Hexagram
(Symbol of Adversity)

12th  否

THE GENERAL STRUCTURE of this hexagram is the reverse of the preceding T'ai Hexagram. Here, the Ch'ien trigram is above and the K'un trigram below, symbolizing an adverse prospect in which the onward course of the weak (the lower trigram) is blocked by the strong (the upper trigram), causing mutual obstruction or difficulty. Hence the idea of adversity.

KING WEN'S JUDGMENT ON THE HEXAGRAM:

This hexagram indicates the presence of depraved people. The situation is not favorable to the firm and correct course of the superior man. What is great goes out, what is small comes in.

What is great (signified by the upper Ch'ien trigram) is supposed to have gone out (departed from the "inside," or lower trigram). What is small (signified by the lower K'un trigram) is supposed to have come in (moved to the lower location). Together they suggest a situation in which the superior men are no longer in power, while the inferior men have come in to replace them.

This hexagram is identified with the seventh month of the lunar year, when all things in nature begin to decline and decay.

CONFUCIUS' EXPLANATION OF KING WEN'S JUDGMENT:

"The hexagram indicates the presence of depraved people. The situation is not favorable to the firm and correct course of the superior

man. What is great goes out, what is small comes in." This means that heaven and earth are in disunion and the ten thousand things do not correspond satisfactorily. It also means that people high and low are not in communication, and the world has no states worthy of the name. What is Yin is inside, and what is Yang is outside. Inward pliancy is coupled with outward vigor. The inferior men are in, the superior men are out. The way of the inferior man is waxing, while that of the superior man is waning.

Confucius interprets King Wen's Judgment in terms of natural phenomena, human society, and moral development.

SYMBOLIC SIGNIFICANCE OF THE HEXAGRAM AS NOTED BY CONFUCIUS:

The idea behind P'i is derived from the disunion between heaven (upper trigram) and earth (lower trigram). The superior man is inspired thereby to practice the virtue of frugality in order to avoid hardship. He cannot be tempted by glory and wealth.

Just as the preceding T'ai Hexagram (with the Ch'ien trigram under the K'un) signifies the union of heaven and earth and augurs prosperity, so the P'i Hexagram (with Ch'ien above K'un) signifies the reverse, or the disunion of heaven and earth, and so augurs adversity. In times of adversity, the superior man wards off hardship by practicing frugality and resisting all temptations to pursue self-glorification and wealth. Instead, he will turn to the enjoyment of simple and virtuous living.

DUKE OF CHOU'S EXPLANATION OF THE LINES (a) AND CONFUCIUS' COMMENT THEREON (b):

Line 1, Yin:

(a) *Some herbs are pulled up together because of their intertwining roots. A firm and correct posture will lead to good fortune and success.*

(b) *"Some herbs are pulled up, and a firm and correct posture will lead to good fortune." One intends to serve the king.*

The Duke of Chou's comments about Line 1 of this hexagram are similar to those he made about Line 1 of the preceding hexagram. In both hexagrams the lines of the upper and lower trigrams all form harmonious relationships with their correlates (herbs with intertwining roots).

The subject of the first line of either hexagram is supposed to pull up herbs with intertwining roots (lead a movement). In the T'ai Hexagram the movement is toward attaining prosperity. Here, the movement is aimed at eliminating adversity. Thus the subject of Line 1 assumes a firm attitude because, as Confucius says, he has the interests of the king in mind. If he possesses the fortitude to remain on the correct course, it will lead to good fortune.

Line 2, Yin:

(a) *Forbearance and submissiveness are for the inferior man a means to secure good fortune. A great man in adversity will manage to attain prosperity and success.*

(b) *"A great man in adversity will manage to attain prosperity and success." This is because he is not perturbed by the mob.*

This line occupies a position both central and correct (Yin in a Yin place), signifying such virtues as patience and obedience. Its subject is a great man who follows the path of reason, pursuing the middle or moderate course and treating people with forbearance. In times of adversity, unlike the inferior man, he concerns himself more with maintaining his integrity and virtue than the search for fame and fortune. Not so the inferior man who, in adversity, acts submissively to attain lucre.

Although Line 2 forms a harmonious relationship with its correlate (Line 5, the ruler), it is hemmed in by two Yin lines, signifying dark and adverse influences. Its advance may also encounter opposition from Line 4 (Yang).

Line 3, Yin:

(a) *One is enduring shame.*

(b) *"One is enduring shame." For his position is not proper.*

The subject of Line 3 will bear insults and endure humiliation, for this line occupies a position neither central nor correct (Yin in a Yang place). The line's influence is also very weak because it is the last of the three Yin lines in the lower trigram. In addition, it must withstand the full impact of the obstruction (the three Yang lines) just above it.

Line 4, Yang:

(a) *There is a command to follow. No regret. People will support him and share his happiness.*

(b) *"There is a command to follow. No regret." This is because his aspirations will be realized.*

This line also occupies a position neither central nor correct (Yang in a Yin place), representing a stage of transition and uncertainty. Its subject is in highly unfavorable circumstances and afraid of making mistakes. He is usually a minister in service to the ruler denoted by Line 5, but here, being Yang in nature, he is not particularly attracted to the ruler, who is also Yang.

Fortunately, this line forms a harmonious relationship with its correlate (Line 1, Yin). Since the subject of Line 1 has started the movement toward eliminating adversity, the subject of Line 4 may have received some encouragement or commands from him. Because he follows these commands, the subject of Line 4 will find all his aspirations realized. He will possess an abundance of joy and happiness to share with those who support him.

Line 5, Yang:

(a) *Adversity has ceased. The great man enjoys good fortune. "Would it perish? Would it perish? Let it be tied to the sturdy mulberry trees."*

(b) *"The good fortune of the great man" is due to his correct and proper position.*

This line is both central and correct (Yang in a Yang place), denoting a wise and powerful ruler under whose rule adversity has come to an end. Yet he has not forgotten the bitter experience of adversity and acts to ensure that his good fortune and felicitous status will long endure ("tied to the sturdy mulberry trees").

Line 6, Yang:

(a) *Adversity has been knocked down. Adversity came first, but joy follows in its wake.*

(b) *Having reached its extreme limit, adversity will be knocked down. How can it last long?*

This line is at the extreme end of the hexagram, suggesting that the limits of adversity have been reached, as is inevitable according to the Law of Cyclic Reversion. If the line is transformed into Yin, the upper trigram becomes Tui, signifying pleasure and satisfaction. Hence the image of joy following in adversity's wake.

The T'UNG REN Hexagram
(Symbol of Comradeship)

13th  同人

THE MEANING OF THIS hexagram is "human union" or "fellowship." The upper trigram, Ch'ien, signifies heaven; the lower trigram, Li, signifies fire. Fire goes upward to heaven, suggesting man's tendency to associate with his fellow men. Line 2 forms a harmonious relationship with its correlate (Line 5, Yang) and as the only Yin line, is supposed to charm the other Yang lines, who are drawn to it by natural attraction. Hence the idea of comradeship.

KING WEN'S JUDGMENT ON THE HEXAGRAM:

This hexagram indicates that comrades appear in the open field. There will be prosperity and success. Advantageous to cross the great stream. Advantageous for the superior man to be firm and correct.

The sight of a number of comrades in the field suggests the open manifestation of universal and unselfish love, teaching cooperation and success in the conquest of mutual difficulties. Such an attitude will also lead to harmonious conduct on the part of all.

CONFUCIUS' EXPLANATION OF KING WEN'S JUDGMENT:

The hexagram shows that the weak (Line 2) obtains the correct and central position and responds docilely to the strong (Line 5). Hence the name of the hexagram, T'ung Ren, meaning "comrades."

"The hexagram indicates that comrades appear in the open field. There will be prosperity and success. Advantageous to cross the great stream." This is the action of the strong creative principle, Ch'ien. Elegance and brilliance coupled with vigor, and favorable response between those in correct and central positions (Lines 2 and 5), signify the correctness or rectitude of the superior man. Only the superior man can comprehend and prosper the aspirations of the world.

Line 2 occupies a position both central and correct. In addition, it is a harmonious correlate of Line 5 and the only Yin line among five Yang lines.

Line 5 is Yang in a Yang place and occupies a central position, signifying a great ruler who inspires universal and unselfish love. The lower trigram is Li (light), and the upper trigram is Ch'ien (strength), suggesting brilliance with vigor or enlightenment. Moreover, Lines 2 and 5 are harmonious correlates which occupy both correct and central positions, denoting reasonableness, moderation, and the Golden Mean. All these attributes are indicative of the inner rectitude of the superior man and enable him to help fulfill the aspirations of the people.

SYMBOLIC SIGNIFICANCE OF THE HEXAGRAM AS NOTED BY CONFUCIUS:

The idea behind T'ung Ren is derived from fire (lower trigram) below heaven (upper trigram). The superior man is inspired thereby to distinguish things according to their kinds and species.

Fire rises to the sky, symbolizing the tendency of man to aim high and to work with his fellows to accomplish great tasks. In the same way, the superior man considers it important to study humanity closely in order to distinguish and discover those of like mind.

DUKE OF CHOU'S EXPLANATION OF THE LINES (a) AND CONFUCIUS' COMMENT THEREON (b):

Line 1, Yang:
(a) *Comrades appear at the door. No error.*
(b) *Comrades are going outdoors. Who would blame them?*

If the entire hexagram represents a house, the first line represents the door. The appearance of comrades at the door indicates that they are eager to seek out others of their own temperament and are setting forth to do so. This is only natural. "Who would blame them?"

Line 2, Yin:

(a) *Comrades are among their clansmen. There will be regret.*

(b) *"Comrades are among their clansmen." This course will lead to regret.*

Line 2 forms a harmonious relationship with its correlate (Line 5, Yang), indicating that the subjects of the two lines are clansmen and that their association is based on this fact. Such an association smacks of favoritism and is therefore to be avoided.

Line 3, Yang:

(a) *Weapons are concealed in the bushes. One ascends a high hill. For three years he does not make any headway.*

(b) *"Weapons are concealed in the bushes." This is because the enemy is strong. "For three years he does not make any headway." How can he take any action?*

Line 3 is Yang in a Yang place, indicating that its subject will be headstrong and aggressive. Since it does not occupy a central position, its subject is not inclined to moderation but tends to act impulsively. In addition, it fails to form a harmonious relationship with its correlate (Line 6, Yang), suggesting a possible conflict between them.

According to the *Shuo Kua*, the Li trigram (which here occupies the low place) stands for "soldier" or "armor," suggesting concealed soldiers or weapons. The soldiers are concealed because of the danger represented by their much stronger enemy (represented by Line 6). For this reason, they take no action until the danger passes (symbolically, "three years").

Line 4, Yang:

(a) *"One goes up to the city wall. He cannot launch any attack. There will be good fortune.*

(b) *"One goes up to the city wall." This is because he could not possibly conquer his enemy. What is "good fortune" is that he will be impelled by distress to follow other principles.*

This line, being neither central nor correct (Yang in a Yin place), signifies a transitional and uncertain stage. Furthermore, it forms an antagonistic relationship with its correlate (Line 1, Yang). The subject of Line 4 is in unfavorable circumstances and is therefore reluctant to act overtly and attack his enemy. If he follows a moderate course, however, he will meet with good fortune.

Line 5, Yang:

(a) *The comrades first howl and wail, then laugh. Their great forces are victorious and they meet and unite.*

(b) *The first action of the comrades is due to their sincerity and candor. "Their great forces meet and unite." This means that both their forces are victorious over the enemy.*

This line occupies a position both central and correct (Yang in a Yang place), representing a great and powerful ruler. It also forms a harmonious relationship with its correlate (Line 2, Yin), indicating that the subjects of the two lines are eager to meet and unite. Their common aspiration, however, is frustrated by the subjects of Lines 3 and 4. The two, therefore, join forces to overcome their opponents. During the battle, their forces at first howl with fury amid the danger, but after victory they meet and laugh.

Line 6, Yang:

(a) *Comrades gather in the suburb. There is no occasion for regret.*

(b) *"Comrades gather in the suburb." This means that their ambition has not been realized.*

This line occupies the top position of the hexagram ("the suburb"). It fails to form a harmonious relationship with its correlate (Line 3, Yang), indicating that its subject lacks support and cooperation and that his forces are weak. Hence the comrades are either driven to the suburb by their opponents or gather there themselves to plan some action. In either case, their aspirations have not been fulfilled, but at least they have made no mistake to cause them future regret.

The TA YU Hexagram
(Symbol of Great Wealth)

14th  大有

THE MEANING OF THIS hexagram is "great or vast in possessions."
Yin signifies what is small, and Yang signifies what is great. Here,
Line 5, Yin, occupies the position of the ruler and possesses all
that is signified by the five Yang lines. Hence the idea of vast
possessions.

KING WEN'S JUDGMENT ON THE HEXAGRAM:

This hexagram indicates great prosperity and success.
Naturally, great prosperity and success correlate with vast
possessions.

CONFUCIUS' EXPLANATION OF KING WEN'S JUDGMENT:

*This hexagram shows that the weak has obtained the place of honor
and is in a grand central position, with people high and low responsive to him. Hence the name "Ta Yu," meaning vast possessions.*

*His virtues include strength and vigor coupled with elegance and
brilliance. He (Line 5) docilely responds to heaven (Line 2) and acts
in accord with the times. Hence great prosperity and success.*

The first paragraph explains the meaning of vast possessions.
It refers to the central position of the ruler (Line 5) and to the
harmonious relation between this line (Yin) and the other lines
(Yang).

The second paragraph refers to the symbolism of the two component trigrams as well as of Lines 2 and 5. The ruler (Line 5) is said to be inwardly strong (inner or lower trigram Ch'ien) and outwardly elegant (outer or upper trigram Li). Then, as Line 5 forms a harmonious relationship with Line 2 (Yang), and as Line 2 correctly occupies the central place of the lower trigram Ch'ien (all Yang, heaven), the ruler is said to be docilely responsive to heaven. Such a ruler, of course, will enjoy great success and possess immense wealth.

SYMBOLIC SIGNIFICANCE OF THE HEXAGRAM AS NOTED BY CONFUCIUS:

The idea behind Ta Yu is derived from fire (upper trigram) high in the sky (lower trigram). The superior man is inspired thereby to suppress the evil and exalt the good and follow the beneficent will of heaven.

Fire is a source of light. Fire high in the sky suggests light shining over a vast expanse of the earth, symbolizing both vast possessions and darkness banished. From this, the superior man learns to cultivate ("exalt") what is good in order to suppress evil. This is the will of heaven.

DUKE OF CHOU'S EXPLANATION OF THE LINES (a) AND CONFUCIUS' COMMENT THEREON (b):

Line 1, Yang:
(a) *Harm stems from lack of relations, not from error. Fortitude will ward off error.*
(b) *Line 1, Yang, of this hexagram shows harm stemming from lack of relations.*

Line 1 (Yang) does not occupy a central place and is farthest from Line 5 (the ruler and the seat of royal favor). Nor, being Yang, does it possess any attraction for its correlate (Line 4) or for the other three Yang lines. Hence the image of "lack of relations" or close associations. Although this situation harms the subject, it is inherent in his position and is not due to any error on his part.

Line 2, Yang:

(a) A *big wagon for loading things. Some forward move in sight. No error.*

(b) *"A big wagon for loading things" means that things can be accumulated in the center without any possibility of mishap.*

According to the *Shuo Kua*, the lower trigram, Ch'ien, stands for something like a wheel. Line 2 occupies a central position and being Yang, suggests strength which can sustain heavy things or "a big wagon" where "things can be accumulated in the center without any possibility of mishap." "Some forward move in sight" suggests that the subject may find a way out of the situation that will lead to fortune or success. The probability is further indicated by the fact that the line correlates harmoniously with Line 5 (the ruler), and so its subject may well hope to be bathed in royal favor.

Line 3, Yang:

(a) A *duke honored with a feast by the emperor. Inferior people cannot deserve such honor.*

(b) *"A duke honored with a feast by the emperor." Inferior people so honored will do harm.*

Line 3 is Yang in a Yang place and at the top of the lower trigram, denoting a high and powerful official ("a duke"). The upper interior trigram (Lines 3, 4, 5), Tui, stands for "mouth," "food," and "pleasure." Hence the image of "a feast."

The line, like the symbolism itself, refers to the suppression of the evil and the exaltation of the good. Those of good character and noble aspiration should be honored by the emperor, while the mean and petty should remain in his disfavor.

Line 4, Yang:

(a) *One shies away from excessive influence. No error.*

(b) *"One shies away from excessive influence. No error." This is due to his clear and judicious discrimination.*

This Yang line has advanced beyond the lower Ch'ien trigram, indicating tremendous strength and power. Since Line 5 (the ruler) is Yin, denoting a queen or regent, and Line 4 usually denotes a minister, its Yang nature ensures mutual attraction and harmony between them, indicating that the minister holds, or can hold, great power and influence. Line 4 is neither correctly nor centrally placed and also lies at the bottom of the upper trigram, representing a stage of transition. In addition, it is antagonistically correlated with Line 1, suggesting lack of harmony. Therefore, its subject shies away from displaying his power and influence because he does not feel secure or comfortable in his position. He prefers instead to hide his light under a bushel.

The line is in the upper trigram, Li, which usually denotes "light," "eye," or "eyesight." Hence the idea of reviewing things carefully for "clear and judicious discrimination."

Line 5, Yin:

(a) *One's sincerity evokes sincerity from others. One's majestic mien leads to good fortune.*

(b) *"One's sincerity evokes sincerity from others." This is because sincerity can stimulate others' wills. "One's majestic mien leads to good fortune," because it commands easy obedience and renders preparation unnecessary.*

Here, Line 5 (the ruler) is Yin, signifying a queen. As it lies in the center of the trigram Li, symbol of light, it suggests that the queen is highly intelligent and enlightened. Since this line also occupies a central position and commands five Yang lines, it indicates that the queen possesses genuine humility and sincerity; this impresses others, winning her their loyalty and support. Yet despite her influence, she conducts herself with a majesty and dignity that endears her to her minister and supporters, for it makes serving her an easy and pleasant task.

Line 6, Yang:

(a) *One receives blessings from heaven. Good fortune. Nothing disadvantageous.*

(b) *The "good fortune" indicated in Line 6 of the hexagram means blessings descending from heaven.*

The top two lines of any hexagram represent heaven, and the topmost represents highest heaven, suggesting the image of "blessings descending from heaven."

Since the entire hexagram signifies great wealth or vast possessions, the top line signifies immense wealth and great advantage. Under such an auspice, all undertakings lead to good fortune.

The CH'IEN Hexagram
(Symbol of Humility)

15th 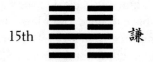 謙

THE UPPER TRIGRAM IS K'un (the earth), and the lower is Ken (mountain). A mountain ought to tower above the earth, but here it is placed below the earth, symbolizing people of high position or character who place themselves below their inferiors. Hence the idea of humility.

KING WEN'S JUDGMENT ON THE HEXAGRAM:

The hexagram indicates prosperity and success. The superior man will have a good end.

A humble disposition facilitates both social and business intercourse and is conducive to success and prosperity. But to be of lasting effect, such humility should be genuine and consistent, not spurious and sporadic. Only a superior man can remain humble from beginning to end.

CONFUCIUS' EXPLANATION OF KING WEN'S JUDGMENT:

"The hexagram indicates prosperity and success." The way of heaven descends to give relief, thus manifesting its brilliant light. The way of earth, while low in position, moves upward to exert its influence.

The way of heaven deflates the puffed-up and benefits the humble. The way of earth overturns the puffed-up and supports the humble. Demons and gods distress the puffed-up and bless the humble. The way of man detests the puffed-up and likes the humble. Humility

adds glory to a position of honor, and while in a low position it cannot be bettered. Hence the good end of the superior man (as mentioned in King Wen's Judgment).

The top line of any trigram represents heaven, the middle line represents man, and the bottom line represents the earth. Here, Line 3 is also Yang, signifying the course or way of heaven. In addition, it is placed above the two lower lines, suggesting heavenly influence descending to earth to give relief to man. The upper trigram, K'un, is lowly in nature and yet occupies the upper level, indicating that the earthly influence has risen to harmonize with the heavenly influence and fulfill the grand process of creation. Thus humility is said to be becoming to both the high and the low, but pride can only lead to a downfall.

SYMBOLIC SIGNIFICANCE OF THE HEXAGRAM AS NOTED BY CONFUCIUS:

The idea behind Ch'ien is derived from a mountain below the earth. The superior man is inspired thereby to take away from where there is too much and add to where there is too little, and to weigh things with a view to making them equitable in distribution.

A mountain below the surface of the earth clearly symbolizes the idea of self-abasement or humility. Inspired by this example, the superior man sets out to bring abundance and scarcity, high and low, into balance.

DUKE OF CHOU'S EXPLANATION OF THE LINES (a) AND CONFUCIUS' COMMENT THEREON (b):

Line 1, Yin:

(a) *The superior man intensifies his humility. He may make use thereof to cross the great stream. Good fortune.*

(b) *"The superior man intensifies his humility." He humbles himself in order to cultivate his virtues.*

This line, being Yin, indicates humility. In this case, since it is also at the lowest level of the hexagram, it denotes extreme humility. Thus the superior man cultivates humility not only when performing important public tasks but also when alone, in order to improve himself morally and spiritually.

Line 2, Yin:

(a) *Humility bruited abroad. A firm and correct posture will lead to good fortune.*

(b) *"Humility bruited abroad. A firm and correct posture will lead to good fortune." This means that what is in the center of his heart has been realized.*

This line is Yin in a Yin place and occupies a central position, which usually denotes a subject who pursues a middle course in a highly visible situation. This signifies a man whose humility has been recognized by the community. According to Confucius, this humility issues from the heart (is sincere) and has been realized in the subject's actions.

Line 3, Yang:

(a) *Hard-working and humble, the superior man will have a good end. Good fortune.*

(b) *"The hard-working and humble superior man" will win the homage and submission of all the people.*

This line lies in the center of the lower interior trigram, K'an (Lines 2, 3, 4), which stands for danger. It is also Yang in a Yang place, indicating great strength. Hence the image of "hard-working." Its subject must work hard because he is menaced by danger. The superior man works hard and humbly for the welfare of the people, thus winning their hearts and ensuring a successful outcome.

The line is also the top line of the lower trigram, Ken, signifying cessation ("a good end").

Line 4, Yin:

(a) *There is nothing that is not advantageous. Humility sways action.*

(b) *"There is nothing that is not advantageous. Humility sways action." This means there is no violation of the basic principles.*

Here, Line 4 (the minister) finds itself above a strong, bright man (Line 3, Yang) and lying in the zone of danger (lower interior trigram, K'an). However, its subject, as indicated by its Yin (receptive) nature, is humble and obedient, the very virtues which will serve him best if he wishes success and good fortune to come to him.

Line 5, Yin:

(a) *One is not wealthy but can avail himself of the resources of his neighbors. It is advantageous for him to use force for punitive purposes. None of his moves will not be advantageous.*

(b) *"To use force for punitive purposes." This is for chastising those who refuse to submit.*

Line 5 (the ruler) is Yin, indicating a weak leader in an impoverished condition. However, as denoted by his central position, he is a sensible man who pursues a reasonable and moderate course, thus winning the support of his neighbors and his people. Such a ruler can afford to use force to chastise recalcitrant rebels or a hostile foreign country without seeming oppressive or tyrannical.

Line 6, Yin:

(a) *Humility bruited abroad. It will be advantageous to use the armies to chastise the towns in the state.*

(b) *"Humility bruited abroad." This shows one's aspiration has not been realized. One may "use the armies." This is for "chastising the towns in the state."*

The upper trigram, K'un, represents both territory and humility. Line 6, being at the extreme end, signifies that this humility has been seen and recognized, even to the far ends of the country. Such humility is advantageous even when waging a military campaign, for it shows that the campaign is just and has been resorted to only with reluctance and because of much provocation.

The YU Hexagram

(Symbol of Satisfaction)

16th 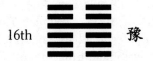 豫

THE WORD "Yu" has several meanings, including "satisfaction," or "gratification." Here, the upper trigram is Chen (thunder), and the lower is K'un (the earth), suggesting thunder breaking forth from the earth, or the gratification of an impulse. Hence the idea of satisfaction.

KING WEN'S JUDGMENT ON THE HEXAGRAM:

The hexagram indicates advantage in establishing principalities and marching out the armies.

The lower trigram, K'un, also stands for masses of people. Together with Chen (thunder), this suggests something noisy and stirring, like an army emerging from the masses. Such a situation augurs the possibility of war and favors the enlisting of supporters and assistants ("establishing principalities") to ensure peace and happiness for all.

CONFUCIUS' EXPLANATION OF KING WEN'S JUDGMENT:

The hexagram suggests that a strong personality receives favorable response and carries out his will. Movement is made smoothly.

The hexagram shows that movement is made smoothly. Thus heaven and earth move in a similar way. How much the more so should move the establishment of principalities and the direction of armies!

Heaven and earth move smoothly; therefore the sun and moon do not err in their courses and the four seasons do not deviate from theirs. The sage moves smoothly; then punishments and penalties will be well-defined and the people will submit to them. Great indeed is the timeliness and significance indicated by the Yu Hexagram.

Line 4 (the minister), the only Yang line in the hexagram, is in general harmony with the five surrounding Yin lines which indicate docility. Further, it forms a harmonious relationship with its correlate (Line 1), indicating outside support. Therefore its subject is a strong personality who receives support and a favorable response from all sides. Such a man can surely easily realize his aspirations and enjoy a sense of satisfaction.

The next two paragraphs imply that underlying every smooth-flowing operation is the law of nature, or the way of heaven or Tao. Those who find and follow it faithfully can accomplish all things smoothly. In the social realm, nothing is so difficult to handle as the administration of justice and the punishment of unlawful elements. However, if it is handled correctly, in accordance with universal law, then even the criminals themselves have no complaint. Thus the course of such a society is sure to run smooth.

The two component trigrams are K'un, which represents docility or submissiveness, and Chen, which represents thunder or motion. Hence the idea of docile movement or smooth-flowing operation.

Line 4, the only Yang line in the hexagram, signifies an able minister serving a gentle ruler who is represented by Line 5, Yin. Line 4 also forms a harmonious relationship with its correlate (Line 1), indicating that the minister enjoys support from the masses (the Yin lines). This line therefore signifies trouble-free gratification of aspiration. In addition, two component trigrams represent motion (Chen) coupled with submissiveness (K'un), which also suggests the idea of satisfaction, or gratification.

SYMBOLIC SIGNIFICANCE OF THE HEXAGRAM AS NOTED BY CONFUCIUS:

The idea behind Yu is derived from thunder bursting forth from the earth with an explosive force. The ancient kings were inspired thereby to compose music and exalt virtue and to offer them reverently to God, associating their ancestors with Him.

The positions of the two component trigrams symbolize thunder breaking out of the earth with great force and reverberating toward heaven. According to the *Great Treatise,* Chen (thunder) is a Yang trigram. This thunder, therefore, represents the sudden and joyful manifestation of the spirit of Yang. Infected by this spirit, the ancient kings were inspired to compose music and cultivate virtue and to offer thanks to heaven and their ancestors who resided there.

DUKE OF CHOU'S EXPLANATION OF THE LINES *(a)* AND CONFUCIUS' COMMENT THEREON *(b):*

Line 1, Yin:

(a) *One voices his satisfaction in public. This is an ill omen.*

(b) *Line 1 shows "self-satisfaction voiced in public." This is an "ill omen" because one's aspiration is exhausted.*

Line 1 always signifies the beginning of whatever process or situation the hexagram represents. The subject of the line here voices self-satisfaction at the very beginning, apparently because he is on good terms with the subject of Line 4 (an able and powerful minister), for the two lines form a harmonious relationship. However, such self-satisfaction indicates that the peak of one's aspiration has been reached and, according to the Law of Cyclic Reversion, this means ill fortune. This is why Confucius says that exhaustion of one's aspirations is an unfavorable omen.

Line 2, Yin:

(a) *One is firm as a rock. He decides before the day ends. His firm correctness will lead to good fortune.*

(b) *"He decides before the day ends and his firm correctness will lead to good fortune." This is because he occupies a correct and central position.*

179

This Yin line occupies a position both central and correct (Yin in a Yin place), indicating its subject to be a sensible, clear-minded leader who can make quick decisions and take decisive actions. The line is the first line of the lower interior trigram, Ken (Lines 2, 3, 4), which signifies "little rock."

Line 3, Yin:

(a) *Regret from aiming high while remaining in self-satisfaction. Tardiness in making changes will cause regret.*

(b) *"Aiming high while remaining in self-satisfaction will lead to regret." This is because the position one occupies is not suitable to him.*

This line is ill-suited, since its position is neither central nor correct (Yin in a Yang place), and it fails to form a harmonious relationship with its correlate (Line 6, Yin). In addition, being the last Yin line of the lower K'un trigram, it also signifies great weakness. The subject of Line 3, therefore, is neither happy nor comfortable in his position. As he is near the strong minister (Line 4), he may look up to him and out of envy try to worm himself into the other's favor, but he will not be trusted. Such a man should change his course soon or he will suffer misfortune.

Line 4, Yang:

(a) *There is a source of pleasure and satisfaction. Great will be the gains. Do not doubt. Friends will gather together like hair kept in place by a clasp.*

(b) *"A source of pleasure and satisfaction. Great will be the gains." This means one's aspiration is being fulfilled in great measure.*

Line 4 (the minister) is the only Yang line in the hexagram, indicating its subject to be the only strong man in the situation and suggesting that he can realize his aspirations and reap rich harvests without encountering great opposition. The line also represents a strong minister serving a weak ruler (Line 5) and forms a harmonious relationship with its correlate (Line 1), which denotes happy cooperation. However, since its position is neither central nor correct (Yang in a Yin place), its subject may be troubled by doubts and scruples. If he can cast these off, he will discover that he is supported by all his friends and will gain considerably for it.

Line 5, Yin:

(a) *One suffers from a stubborn ailment. He will usually survive.*

(b) *Line 5 shows "a stubborn ailment." This is because it rides on a strong line (Line 4). "He usually survives," for the center of his being has not yet perished.*

This line represents a weak ruler who finds a strong and ambitious minister (Line 4, Yang) placed below him. This ruler may have difficulty in dealing with his minister and may even become chronically ill, but, as indicated by his central position, he is basically a reasonable and sensible person, so his ailment will not end in death.

Line 6, Yin:

(a) *A mind clouded and weakened by pleasure. This is an established fact. Change of course will ward off error or regret.*

(b) *One in a top position but with "a mind clouded by pleasure." How can such a case be prolonged?*

This Yin line is at the extreme end of the hexagram, suggesting that its subject is weakened and spoiled by excessive pleasure. As Confucius has said, such a course cannot be allowed to continue. But if the line is transformed into Yang, then the upper trigram will become Li (light and intelligence), and the entire hexagram will become Tsin (progress). This shows that if the subject will change his course, it will bring very favorable results.

The SUI Hexagram
(Symbol of Following)

17th  隨

THE UPPER TRIGRAM is Tui (a young girl), and the lower is Chen (a young man or the eldest son), suggesting a young man who is willing to subordinate himself to a young girl. Furthermore, Tui is composed of two Yang lines beneath a Yin line, and Chen is composed of one Yang line beneath two Yin lines, symbolizing the strong subordinated to the weak. Hence the idea of following. One who is willing to follow others humbly will inspire others to follow him.

KING WEN'S JUDGMENT ON THE HEXAGRAM:

This hexagram indicates great prosperity and success. Advantageous to be firm and correct. No error.

Following blindly and without discrimination is never wise. One must follow a correct course and stick to it firmly, no matter where others are heading.

CONFUCIUS' EXPLANATION OF KING WEN'S JUDGMENT:

This hexagram suggests that the strong come and stay below the weak. Motion gives rise to pleasure. This is what the hexagram means.

"There will be great prosperity and success, and firm correctness will ward off error." The world will then follow the spirit of the

times. Great indeed is the significance of following the spirit of the times.

The lines indicate that the Yang (strong) elements come down and place themselves below the Yin (weak) elements, while the trigrams suggest that willingness to follow stems from motion (Chen) that yields pleasure (Tui).

Those who would achieve worldly success, Confucius says, must learn to perceive the social trends and currents around them ("the spirit of the times").

SYMBOLIC SIGNIFICANCE OF THE HEXAGRAM AS NOTED BY CONFUCIUS:

The idea behind Sui is derived from marsh (upper trigram) with thunder (lower trigram) beneath it. The superior man is inspired thereby to go home toward evening and dine and relax.

The symbolism indicates that thunder will break out through the marsh and when it does, waves and motion will follow. From this, the superior man learns that there are times when any sudden, impulsive move may cause great and far-reaching disturbances. In such times, he knows that the wisest course is to retire from the field and preserve his energies for a future day.

DUKE OF CHOU'S EXPLANATION OF THE LINES (a) AND CONFUCIUS' COMMENT THEREON (b):

Line 1, Yang:

(a) *A leader changes his course. Firm correctness will lead to good fortune. Going outdoors to associate with people will find its reward.*

(b) *"A leader changes his course." There is good fortune in following decent people. "Going outdoors to associate with people will find its reward." This is because he has not strayed from his correct path.*

Line 1 is a Yang in a Yang place, indicating a strong and dynamic person. Such a person naturally wants to lead, but here finds himself placed below two weak fellows (Lines 2 and 3). Such a man's prospects for moving ahead are not bright. If he seeks the assistance of others ("going outdoors"), there will be good fortune, for there is mutual attraction between the subject of Line 1 (Yang) and his neighbors (Yin). In such a situation, it is correct to seek the aid of others, and in doing so he will meet with good fortune, if only he remains firmly on a correct and congenial course.

Line 1 is below the lower interior trigram (Lines 2, 3, 4), signifying "door." Hence the image of "going outdoors."

Line 2, Yin:

(a) *She attaches herself to her little son and loses her husband.*

(b) *"She attaches herself to her little son." This is because she cannot be attached to both.*

Line 2 is Yin in a Yin place, signifying a gentle, compliant female. Line 1, being the first Yang line of the lower trigram, Chen, denotes her eldest son, and her husband is represented by Line 5 (its correlate, Yang), with which Line 2 forms a harmonious relationship. Though there is no antagonism between the woman and her husband, she is close to her son and remote from her husband; so she attaches herself to her son and loses her husband, for she cannot have both.

Line 3, Yin:

(a) *She attaches herself to her husband and loses her little son. Following such a course, she will get what she seeks. Advantageous to stay firm and correct.*

(b) *"She attaches herself to her husband." She is determined to give up what is below.*

This line occupies a position neither central nor correct (Yin in a Yang place) and fails to form a harmonious relationship with its correlate (Line 6). Its subject, therefore, is not only weak but also in poor circumstances. She prefers to be attached to her husband (Line 4) and loses her little son (Line 1). But in following her husband she gets what she wants, for her husband is a minister serving the ruler (Line 5).

Line 4, Yang:

(a) *One acquires followers and rewards. If it persists, this situation will lead to evil. But one is sincere in following the right way and his motives are clear and evident. What regret can there be?*

(b) *"One acquires followers and rewards." This state of affairs means evil. "One is sincere in following the right way." This is to show achievements in a clear light.*

This Yang line denotes a strong minister who gains "followers and rewards" because there is harmony between him and those placed below him (Line 3, Yin). His growing influence may excite the suspicion and envy of his ruler (Line 5, Yang), who is also a strong personality. Such a situation can only lead to evil.

Line 4 occupies a position neither central nor correct (Yang in a Yin place) and forms an antagonistic relationship with its correlate (Line 1, Yang). However, since it occupies the central position of the entire hexagram, this line's subject (the minister), though placed in unfavorable circumstances, is inwardly sincere and enlightened and so will escape any blame.

Line 5, Yang:

(a) *Sincerity manifesting itself in what is good and beautiful. Good fortune.*

(b) *"Sincerity manifesting itself in what is good and beautiful. Good fortune." This is because the position is correct and central.*

Here, Line 5 (the ruler) is ideally situated, since it is both central and correct (Yang in a Yang place) and forms a harmonious relation with its correlate (Line 2, Yin). There is also mutual attraction between it and Line 6. Its subject, therefore, is a sage ruler in happy circumstances. His sincerity manifests itself in good works and inspires all those around him, bringing good fortune.

Line 6, Yin:

(a) *One is detained and bound. The king presents his offerings on the Western Mountain.*

(b) *"One is detained." This shows that the one above is at the end of his resources.*

This line is weak, occupies an extreme position, and forms an antagonistic relationship with its correlate (Line 3, Yang). Its subject, therefore, is at the end of his rope and may do something desperate or even perish. For this reason he is restrained ("detained and bound") by the king's men. The king then feels he has brought all his dissident subjects back safely into the fold and has thus pacified his whole kingdom. This is a grand achievement and a grand occasion; so he offers sacrifices at the Western Mountain and gives thanks to God and his ancestors. (The Western Mountain is Ch'i Shan, or Hill, birthplace of King Wen, primary author of the *I-Ching*.)

The KU Hexagram

(Symbol of Deterioration)

18th  蠱

IN THE UPPER TRIGRAM, Ken, two Yin lines (signifying weakness) are beneath a Yang line (signifying strength). A similar situation exists in the lower trigram, Sun. Weakness beneath strength symbolizes a thing strong on the surface but weak inside. Hence the idea of deterioration or decay.

The structure of the Chinese word for "Ku" points to the same notion. The bottom radical of the word means an instrument. Above it are three identical radicals, each of which means a worm, and a worm-eaten instrument is an excellent symbol for deterioration.

KING WEN'S JUDGMENT ON THE HEXAGRAM:

This hexagram indicates great prosperity and success. Advantageous to cross the great stream. Deliberate for three days before the event and for three days afterward.

At first sight, this Judgment may appear surprising. How could a hexagram symbolizing decay presage great success and prosperity? King Wen's idea is that decay may lead to rebirth or renovation. By examining a decaying situation thoroughly and then risking the effort to correct and renew it ("cross the great stream"), success and prosperity will be ensured.

The Law of Cyclic Reversion may also be operating here. An old, antiquated order gives place to a new, progressive one. This suggests a tumultuous political era followed by a peaceful one.

SYMBOLIC SIGNIFICANCE OF THE HEXAGRAM AS NOTED BY CONFUCIUS:

The hexagram shows that the strong are above and the weak are below. Passivity (lower trigram) is coupled with inactivity (upper trigram). This is what the hexagram means.

"The hexagram indicates great prosperity and success." This means a world at peace. "Advantageous to cross the great stream." This means there are important tasks ahead. "Deliberate for three days before the event, and for three days afterward." The end of one era is the beginning of another. This is the course of heaven.

The upper trigram is Ken (mountain or inactivity); the lower is Sun (passivity or docility). When something docile is obstructed by an obstacle such as a mountain, the result is stagnation, and stagnation leads to decay. This idea is further borne out by the lines of the two component trigrams, which also suggest that the weak below are impeded by the strong above.

The second paragraph refers to the operation of the Law of Cyclic Reversion. It also implies that a dangerous situation may be resolved by tackling it with drastic action ("cross the great stream").

CONFUCIUS' EXPLANATION OF KING WEN'S JUDGMENT:

The idea behind Ku is derived from wind (lower trigram) at the foot of a mountain (upper trigram). The superior man is inspired thereby to arouse the people to cultivate virtue.

Wind at the lower slope of a mountain suggests the destruction of trees and property, but it also conveys the idea of action or stimulation. The superior man is thus inspired to arouse the people to cultivate virtue, thereby restraining them from any destructive action.

DUKE OF CHOU'S EXPLANATION OF THE LINES (a) AND CONFUCIUS' COMMENT THEREON (b):

Line 1, Yin:

(a) *One handles the failing efforts of his father. If he is a capable son, his father will be free from blame. Situation grave, but good fortune in the end.*

(b) *"One handles the failing efforts of his father." This means he aims to do his father's will.*

Generally speaking, since it occupies a position that is neither central nor correct (Yin in a Yang place) and fails to form a harmonious relationship with its correlate (Line 4), this line is inauspicious, and its subject is not a brilliant or happy person. However, in its position, though incorrect, there lies some good, since it occupies a Yang place at the beginning of the hexagram, suggesting someone who has begun his work energetically, like one who "handles the failing efforts of his father." However, the subject may have to undergo some difficulty or peril before good fortune finally ensues.

Line 2, Yang:

(a) *One handles the failing efforts of his mother. Do not be too firm and correct.*

(b) *"One handles the failing efforts of his mother." He chooses the middle course of moderation.*

This Yang line occupies a position that is incorrect but central, indicating a strong man in a good position to carry out his work. It forms a harmonious relationship with its correlate (Line 5), which is Yin, indicating a weak woman ("his mother"). All this suggests a strong man who follows a sensible course, successfully handling his mother's failing efforts without hurting her sensibilities.

Line 3, Yang:

(a) *One handles the failing efforts of his father. Some minor repentance. No serious error.*

(b) *"One handles the failing efforts of his father." In the end there will be freedom from blame.*

This line is Yang in a Yang place and fails to form a harmonious relationship with its correlate (Line 6, the father), suggesting a strong-willed subject who is likely to offend his father. Since Line 3 occupies a position that is correct but not central, though his situation is an unfavorable one from which to act, its subject ultimately follows the correct course and will succeed in freeing his father from blame.

Line 4, Yin:

(a) *One aggravates the failing efforts of his father. If he moves ahead, he will regret.*

(b) *"One aggravates the failing efforts of his father." This is because he has not found the right way to proceed with his task.*

Line 4 is Yin in a Yin place, and its correlate (Line 1) is also Yin and so offers no cooperation. Its subject is a weak, helpless person who cannot find the right way to handle his father's failing efforts. Any active move he undertakes will only make matters worse and cause him regret.

Line 5, Yin:

(a) *One handles his father's failing efforts and gains a good reputation.*

(b) *"One handles his father's failing efforts and gains a good reputation." This is because he does his father's will in a virtuous way.*

This Yin line occupies a central though incorrect position, denoting a gentle and sensible ruler who is inclined to follow the course of moderation and finds himself in favorable circumstances from which to execute his plans. In the course of correcting his father's failings, he remains in the path of virtue and so gains a good reputation.

Line 6, Yang:

(a) *One serves neither the king nor the princes. He is high-minded and exalts his own work.*

(b) *"One serves neither the king nor the princes." His aspiration is exemplary.*

This is a Yang line at the top limit of a hexagram and forms an antagonistic relationship with its correlate (Line 3), suggesting an able, high-minded person, but one who has already fulfilled his mission in the world and has retired from active life to enjoy the peace and quiet of his own pursuits.

The LIN Hexagram

(Symbol of Advent)

19th  臨

THIS HEXAGRAM SIGNIFIES the advent of the superior to inspect or supervise the inferior. The upper trigram, K'un (the earth), is above the trigram Tui (marsh), suggesting that the high comes down to the low. This symbolism is further reinforced by the bottom two strong Yang lines which are moving toward the four weak Yin lines.

KING WEN'S JUDGMENT ON THE HEXAGRAM:

This hexagram indicates great prosperity and success. Advantageous to be firm and correct. In the eighth month there will be evil fortune.

According to this Judgment, the auspicious situation indicated by the hexagram lasts for only seven months. As to why seven, and not eight or nine, some Chinese commentators have advanced a rather kabalistic explanation. It involves the counting of the lines of the K'un Hexagram which represents both moon and month. In this method, each Yin line represents one month, and the passage of each month is represented by replacing the Yin line with Yang. After six counts, or the passing of six months, the K'un Hexagram (Yin) becomes a Ch'ien Hexagram (Yang), just as the seasons pass from the six warmer months to the six colder months. With the seventh month (according to the Law of Cyclic Reversion), the entire process begins over again as the Yang lines of the Ch'ien Hexagram are replaced from the bottom, one at a time, by

Yin lines, to signify the passing of the months. Following this system, by the end of the eighth month the Tun Hexagram has been formed, with two Yin lines at the bottom beneath four Yang lines (exactly the opposite of that in the Lin Hexagram), indicating the growing strength of the Yin or dark forces. Hence the idea of a dark situation in the eighth month and afterward.

CONFUCIUS' EXPLANATION OF KING WEN'S JUDGMENT:

This hexagram shows that the strong forces begin to grow and increase.

Pleasure is coupled with docile obedience. The strong occupies the central position and receives favorable response.

Great prosperity and success from following the correct course. This is the way of heaven.

"In the eighth month there will be evil fortune." This means that the growing tendency will soon begin to wane.

In this hexagram the strong creative force (the bottom two Yang lines) is waxing. The lower trigram represents pleasure, and the upper trigram represents docility. Hence the idea of pleasure coupled with or resulting from docility.

Line 2 is Yang in a central position and forms a harmonious relationship with its correlate (Line 5, the ruler); Line 1 is Yang in a Yang place. Their subjects, therefore, are moving ahead strongly and will surely succeed because they encounter very weak opposition (the four Yin lines above). However (according to the Law of Cyclic Reversion), evil fortune will come after seven months, for though the Yang forces are growing at the present, Yin cannot be gone for long and is sure to return.

SYMBOLIC SIGNIFICANCE OF THE HEXAGRAM AS NOTED BY CONFUCIUS:

The idea behind Lin is derived from earth (K'un) above the marsh (Tui). The superior man is inspired thereby to pursue ceaselessly his teaching profession and to be patient in guarding the people forever and forever.

The earth, which is larger than the marsh, is here placed above the marsh, signifying great over small, or high over low. In the human realm, it signifies superior intelligence placed over inferior intelligence. Tui also stands for mouth, suggesting speech or teaching; K'un (earth) suggests a nearly infinite capacity to contain all things or love all people. To the superior man this indicates the wisdom of employing his knowledge to enlighten those below him and help promote their welfare.

DUKE OF CHOU'S EXPLANATION OF THE LINES (a) AND CONFUCIUS' COMMENT THEREON (b):

Line 1, Yang:

(a) *One comes with a companion. Firm correctness will lead to good fortune.*

(b) *"One comes with a companion. Firm correctness will lead to good fortune." This means they aim to pursue the correct course.*

This line is Yang in a Yang place, indicating a strong and active person. Its companion (Line 2) is Yang in a central position, indicating a strong, reasonable person in favorable circumstances. Together, they suggest bright, able companions who will realize their aspirations if they can remain true to their values while pursuing their goals.

Line 2, Yang:

(a) *One comes with a companion. Good fortune. Nothing that will not be advantageous.*

(b) *"One comes with a companion. Good fortune. Nothing that will not be advantageous." The will of heaven is yet to be fulfilled.*

The subject of this line and that of Line 1 are companions who cooperate to do good works. All their actions will be advantageous, for they are in the pursuit of a worthy goal, and those in their path (the four Yin lines) are not the type to oppose their efforts.

Line 3, Yin:

(a) *One comes in a joyful mood. There will be nothing advantageous. If he is seized with anxiety, however, he will be free from error.*

(b) *"One comes in a joyful mood." This is because his position is not suitable to him. "He is seized with anxiety." This shows his error will not last long.*

193

This line occupies a position which is neither central nor correct (Yin in a Yang place) and fails to form a harmonious relationship with its correlate (Line 6, Yin). In addition, it lies at the top of the lower trigram, Tui (satisfaction or pleasure). Its subject is not only weak and in a highly uncongenial position, but also self-satisfied and complacent. To act from this stance will not prove advantageous. If, however, such a person displays concern and remorse and acts quickly to reform himself, his difficulties will not last long.

Line 4, Yin:

(a) *One descends from on high to a low place. No error.*

(b) *"One descends from on high to a low place. No error." This is because he occupies a correct and proper position.*

This line occupies a correct position (Yin in a Yin place) and forms a harmonious relationship with its correlate (Line 1). Since it is Yin (receptivity, obedience), its subject is humble, and though occupying a more eminent position, comes down to work with a partner on a lower plane.

Line 5, Yin:

(a) *There comes wisdom suitable for the great king. Good fortune.*

(b) *"Wisdom suitable for the great king." This means practicing the Golden Mean.*

Here, Line 5 (the ruler) is Yin and occupies a central position, indicating a leader with the intelligence and wisdom to follow the course of reason in all situations, as befits a great king. Its correlate (Line 2, Yang), with which it forms a harmonious relationship, also occupies a central position, suggesting a strong minister well-placed to act. The subject of Line 5, therefore, is a wise ruler who enjoys popular support, in addition to receiving loyal and competent service from his ministers.

Line 6, Yin:

(a) *Sincerity becomes manifest. Good fortune. No error.*

(b) *"The good fortune of manifest sincerity" stems from the fact that one's aim is oriented toward the interior.*

This line is at the top of the upper K'un trigram (the earth, vast capacity, magnanimity). Its subject is like one looking down on people below ("the interior"). He is said to be concerned for ("oriented toward") those beneath him, especially toward the strong elements denoted by the bottom two Yang lines. There is no doubt that he is sincere in his concern, for he himself is in some peril, as indicated by the extreme position of the line at the end of the hexagram. However, as he is sincere, he will inspire people and meet with good fortune.

The KUAN Hexagram
(Symbol of Contemplation)

20th  觀

THE UPPER TRIGRAM (Sun) signifies wind, and the lower trigram (K'un) signifies the earth. The top two lines (Yang) represent beauty, and the four lines beneath (Yin) represent people looking up and admiring this beauty. Together they suggest wind moving above the earth, or people moving over (touring) it to view its wonder. Hence the idea of contemplation.

This idea is reinforced by the fact that the upper interior trigram (Lines 3, 4, 5) is Ken (mountain). Here, its position above K'un also suggests people looking at or contemplating a mountain. In addition, the shape of the hexagram suggests a watch tower or contemplation from above. The hexagram also indicates the displaying of something to be seen or contemplated, or the setting of an example for people to follow.

KING WEN'S JUDGMENT ON THE HEXAGRAM:

The hexagram indicates one who has cleansed his hands but has not yet offered his sacrifices. He manifests a sincerity which evokes the same from others.

Here, King Wen uses the metaphor of a priest making preliminary preparations for a religious service. He carries out this task with the sincerity and reverence such worthy work deserves and, through example, inspires those around him to do the same.

CONFUCIUS' EXPLANATION OF KING WEN'S JUDGMENT:

The hexagram indicates grand spectacles appearing above but showing signs of docility and pliancy. Central and correct in position, they are for the world to contemplate.

"The hexagram indicates one who has cleansed his hands but has not yet offered his sacrifices. He manifests a sincerity which evokes the same from others." This means that people looking up become transformed.

In contemplating heaven's spiritual course and the progress of the four seasons without deviating from it, the sage is inspired to formulate his teachings in accordance with the spiritual course, and the world willingly submits to it.

The top two lines of any hexagram represent heaven. Here, they are Yang, indicating the highest manifestation of heaven ("grand spectacles appearing above"). Further, both Yang lines (which are dominant) are well-placed, Line 6 occupying the highest position, while Line 5 is both central and correct. In addition, the upper trigram is Sun (docility). All this suggests a great and gentle ruler in a high and central position who conducts himself in such a manner that those below him are inspired to follow his example.

When such a man prepares himself for solemn ritual or prayer, his piety and sincerity inspire all onlookers to follow him on the path of virtue. When he contemplates the way of heaven, he draws profound wisdom from it and then shares this with those who turn to him of their own accord.

SYMBOLIC SIGNIFICANCE OF THE HEXAGRAM AS NOTED BY CONFUCIUS:

The idea behind Kuan is derived from wind (upper trigram) moving over the earth (lower trigram). The ancient kings were inspired to inspect the regions and observe the conditions of the people so as to formulate their teachings.

Wind sweeping over the earth penetrates every nook and corner, as if eager to examine everything. From this the ancient kings derived the idea of visiting all the lands of their kingdom to observe their condition and needs, so that wise provision could be made for the education of their people.

DUKE OF CHOU'S EXPLANATION OF THE LINES (a) AND CONFUCIUS' COMMENT THEREON (b):

Line 1, Yin:

(a) *The look of a small boy. Not blamable in small, mean men. In superior men it is something lamentable.*

(b) *"The look of a small boy indicated in Line 1" is the way of the small, mean men.*

The first line of this hexagram signifies childhood (or boyhood). Here, it is both Yin and occupies the position farthest from the top two lines, which are Yang and represent the source of enlightenment. This suggests the ignorant or innocent expression of a child. In those of small, mean character, such a look is only natural and they are not to blame for it. In the superior man, however, it is to be lamented.

Line 2, Yin:

(a) *One peeps out through a door. Advantageous for a chaste damsel.*

(b) *"One peeps out through a door. Advantageous for a chaste damsel." This is nevertheless something to be ashamed of.*

This line occupies a position which is both central and correct (Yin in a Yin place) and also forms a harmonious relationship with its correlate (Line 5, the ruler). The subject of Line 2 is an intelligent, virtuous woman or Yin person who wishes to contemplate some great man. That she does not go out-of-doors, but lets her suitor come to her indicates that she is a person of chaste and restrained character who does not commit the error of mingling indiscriminately. For one who is chaste in this fashion, a preliminary observation or investigation of a prospective suitor could prove advantageous. In terms of the strict tenets of Confucian morals, however, it is considered shameful or unseemly for a woman to peek out through the door to look at a man.

Line 3, Yin:

(a) *One contemplates his own life to see whether to advance or to retreat.*

(b) *"One contemplates his own life to see whether to advance or to retreat." This shows that he has not missed the right way.*

On the one hand, this line is inauspicious because it occupies a position neither central nor correct (Yin in a Yang place), and because it rests on the top of a K'un trigram (weakness or passivity). On the other hand, Line 3 also forms a harmonious relationship with its correlate (Line 6), which represents "contemplation from the heights" or "a great personage." The line's subject is uncertain of his position and is unable to determine whether to advance or retreat. This suggests that he has not missed the right way and may yet attain a more advantageous position. To do so, he must stop and review his past life; only in this way can he make the right choice.

Line 4, Yin:

(a) *One sees the glories of the kingdom. Advantageous to be a guest of the king.*

(b) *"One sees the glories of the kingdom." This indicates esteem shown to the guests.*

Line 4 (the minister) is Yin in a Yin place, denoting a loyal, obedient minister. It lies next to Line 5 (the ruler), and here, in harmony with the general meaning of the hexagram taken as a whole, also signifies glories being contemplated. That the minister is able to contemplate them indicates that he has creditably discharged the great responsibilities entrusted to him and is consequently enjoying royal favor.

This line also lies above the lower trigram, K'un, a symbol for earth, suggesting the minister is surveying the conditions of the kingdom, so as to keep himself informed of their development and prevent any difficulty that may arise.

Line 5, Yang:

(a) *One contemplates his own life. A superior man will have no regret.*

(b) *"One contemplates his own life." It means contemplating the people.*

This line occupies a position both central and correct, denoting a strong and enlightened king. It is also above four Yin lines and forms a harmonious relationship with its correlate (Line 2, Yin), indicating that the king rules over a contented and peaceful people. In contemplating his own condition, he must contemplate the condition of the people, for it affects his condition as well. If he determines his actions to have been those of the superior man, he will have no cause for regret.

Line 6, Yang:

(a) *One contemplates his life in a general persepctive. A superior man will have no regret.*

(b) *"One contemplates his life in a general perspective." This is because one's aspiration has not yet been realized.*

This line is Yang and lies at the top of the hexagram, indicating a bright man in a good position from which to survey life in general, as it forms a harmonious relationship with its correlate (Line 3). Its subject looks down with good will on his partner and on the world below him. While he may have no cause for regret, he is not satisfied, for many of his deepest hopes and aspirations remain unfulfilled.

The SHIH HO Hexagram
(Symbol of Punishment)

21st  噬嗑

SHIH HO MEANS "the closing of the mouth after biting through an obstacle." The top and bottom lines symbolize the lips, the Yin lines the teeth, and the remaining Yang line (Line 4) the bone or other obstacle. The lips and the upper and lower teeth will meet only after the obstacle has been bitten through. The hexagram thus represents disharmony in a group, family, or nation due to some obstruction that must be eliminated before union can be restored. It also suggests both the "punishment" the obstruction endures as it is bitten through and the punishment used to reform a criminal or a bad situation.

KING WEN'S JUDGMENT ON THE HEXAGRAM:

The hexagram indicates prosperity and success. It also shows advantage in the use of punishment and the management of prisons.
King Wen points especially to obstacles that disturb the peace and order of a society or community. These must be removed or prevented before peace and prosperity can occur.

CONFUCIUS' EXPLANATION OF KING WEN'S JUDGMENT:

The hexagram means there is something between the jaws.
"The hexagram indicates prosperity and success." The strong and the weak (lines) are equal in number. Movement (lower trigram) is coupled with intelligence or enlightenment (upper trigram). Thunder (lower trigram) and lightning (upper trigram) combine in outward

201

manifestation. The weak (Line 5) obtains the central position and acts from on high. Though the position is inappropriate, there is advantage in making use of punishment.

This hexagram has an equal number of Yin and Yang lines, suggesting balance. The two component trigrams mean movement coupled with light or brilliance (thunder and lightning). Together, they give rise to the idea of justice and punishment or severity moderated by mercy. Further, Line 5 (the ruler), though incorrect (Yin in a Yang place), occupies the upper central position, indicating a ruler who is inclined to be merciful and will apply punishment in a temperate way.

SYMBOLIC SIGNIFICANCE OF THE HEXAGRAM AS NOTED BY CONFUCIUS:

The idea behind Shih Ho is derived from thunder and lightning. The ancient kings were inspired thereby to define clearly the punishments and adjust the laws.

Thunder suggests terror and punishment, while lightning suggests brilliant intelligence capable of judicious discrimination. Thus the ancient kings were inspired to rectify and clarify the laws and to apply just and intelligent penalties.

DUKE OF CHOU'S EXPLANATION OF THE LINES (a) AND CONFUCIUS' COMMENT THEREON (b):

Line 1, Yang:

(a) *One has his feet placed in the stocks, which hide his toes from view. No error.*

(b) *"One has his feet placed in the stocks, which hide his toes from view." He is then unable to walk.*

Here, the first and lowest line of the hexagram signifies several things: In human society, it signifies the ignorant and lowly placed; from the standpoint of the human body, it represents the toes or feet. It also signifies the first crime or error committed by a strong (Yang) young fellow. He is fortunate to be caught and punished ("feet placed in the stocks") for the first time, for he learns a lesson from the experience, and will not commit further crimes (he is "unable to walk" the same path again).

Line 2, Yin:

(a) *One bites through the skin and then bites off the nose. No error.*

(b) *"One bites through the skin and then bites off the nose." This is because the line is riding on a strong one.*

This line is both Yin in a Yin place and occupies a central position, indicating a gentle and sensible person inclined to follow the path of moderation. However, the line lies above ("riding on") a Yang line (Line 1). This means that the subject of Line 2 is dealing with a tough, unruly fellow and must employ drastic or violent means in order to restrain him ("bites through the skin and then bites off the nose"). Such drastic action is the only effective course in such a situation, and the one who employs it will incur no error.

Line 3, Yin:

(a) *One bites through some dried meat and meets with something thick and tough. There will be some minor regret but no great error.*

(b) *"One meets with something thick and tough." This is because his position is not suitable to him.*

This line occupies a position that is neither central nor correct (Yin in a Yang place): its subject is a man in unfavorable circumstances who cannot act efficiently or effectively. Although the line forms a harmonious relationship with its correlate (Line 6, Yang), which normally signifies mutual attraction and harmony, in this case the subject of Line 6 is an unruly, dangerous fellow, an outcast. Because of their relationship, it is the duty of the subject of Line 3 to chastise and reform him. For a meek and gentle person, this is a difficult task (biting into a thick piece of dried meat). However, this course, though not without its toll on the subject, is the correct one. The outcast should be punished; this action will prove itself to be no error.

Line 4, Yang:

(a) *One gnaws the dried meat sticking to the bone and gets gold and arrows. Advantageous to practice fortitude and firm correctness. Good fortune.*

(b) *"Advantageous to practice fortitude and firm correctness. Good fortune." This means that the light has not yet become manifest.*

The subject of this line is even more unfavorably situated than that of Line 3, since it occupies a position neither central nor correct (Yang in a Yin place) and forms an antagonistic relationship with its correlate (Line 1). In addition, it is in the center of the upper interior trigram (Lines 3, 4, 5), which is K'an (danger). In terms of the symbolism of the hexagram as a whole, this line is the bone being bitten between the upper and lower teeth. In terms of its symbolism as an individual line, it represents a headstrong fellow whose great difficulty is to bite into the bone. The gold and arrows he receives indicate him to be a minister or judge deciding a law case. (In ancient China, litigants usually brought gold and arrows to the judge to show that they were as true as gold and upright as an arrow and that they were going to tell the truth.) Deciding this case will be as difficult as biting through a piece of bone.

The line is only on the lower edge of the upper trigram, Li (light), indicating that its subject is not yet fully enlightened on all the facts of the case. Or, as Confucius intimates, perhaps it may only be that his judicial administration is at its beginning and its light has not yet become manifest. Whatever the case, if the subject practices fortitude and correctness in pursuance of his task, he will secure good fortune.

Line 5, Yin:

(a) *One bites through dried meat and gets yellow gold. If firm and correct in the perilous situation, he will be free from error.*

(b) *"If firm and correct in the perilous situation, he will be free from error." This is because he has found the right way.*

Here, Line 5 (the ruler) occupies a central position in the upper trigram, Li (light), signifying a gentle and enlightened ruler and one who is inclined to follow the middle path of moderation. As he "gets yellow gold," he is also a judge. Yellow is traditionally considered the correct color (because of its connection with the fertile Yellow River), and gold, noted for its pure and genuine quality, signifies honest testimony. That he "gets yellow gold" indicates that the subject has the discernment to get at the truth accurately and render just decisions ("bites through dried meat"). On the other hand, the situation is not without its difficulties, since Line 5, for all its advantages, occupies a position which is incorrect (Yin in a Yang place), and this usually denotes an uncongenial atmosphere.

Also, in terms of the symbolism of the hexagram as a whole, Line 5 represents the teeth which bite through the bone (Line 4), never an easy task. But what makes the situation actually dangerous is the peril represented by the unruly outcast (Line 6). The one who must decide the case, therefore, must remain firm and correct if he is to avoid error. However, as he is an intelligent and enlightened man, the subject is sure to find the right way.

If this line is changed into Yang, the upper trigram becomes Ch'ien, which stands for gold. Hence, the idea of "yellow gold."

Line 6, Yang:

(a) *One has the cangue on his head, and his ears are hidden from view. Ill omen.*

(b) *"One has the cangue on his head, and his ears are hidden from view." This means he does not hear clearly and attentively.*

In terms of the symbolism as of the hexagram taken as a whole (the use of punishment to correct a wrong situation), this strong (Yang) line at the extreme top indicates a desperate outcast or an incorrigible criminal whose behavior requires severe punishment if he is to be discouraged. Such a man's prospects are indeed gloomy. In terms of the symbolism of the individual lines, Line 6 represents the head, suggesting that the offender's problem is related to his head, and that something prevents him from heeding warnings or learning from punishment (a "cangue on his head"), either because he cannot or will not listen ("his ears are hidden from view").

The PI Hexagram
(Symbol of Ornament)

22nd  賁

THE UPPER TRIGRAM is Ken (mountain), and the lower is Li (light or fire). Together they suggest light shining on the mountain, which presents a bright and beautiful sight. Li also represents the pheasant, whose beautiful feathers have been favored for centuries as objects of adornment. Hence the idea of ornament. The shape of the hexagram also suggests an ornament adorning a plain box.

KING WEN'S JUDGMENT ON THE HEXAGRAM:

This hexagram indicates prosperity and success. There will be some minor advantage for the forward move that is to be made.

The lower Li trigram suggests brilliance and enthusiasm, two attributes which favor movement ahead. But here the movement is obstructed to some extent by a hill or mountain (the upper trigram, Ken). Therefore, although the results are favorable, the movement will bring only minor success.

CONFUCIUS' EXPLANATION OF KING WEN'S JUDGMENT:

"This hexagram indicates prosperity and success."
The weak comes to adorn the strong. Hence prosperity and success. The strong is sent up to adorn the weak. Hence "there will be some minor advantage for the forward move that is to be made." This is the adornment of heaven.

Cultural glory sets to itself a limit. This is the adornment of humanity.

Contemplation of the adornment of heaven is helpful for ascertaining the change of seasons. Contemplation of the adornment of humanity is helpful for effecting the transformation of the world.

The upper trigram, Ken, has one Yang and two Yin lines; the lower trigram, Li, has one Yin and two Yang lines. Confucius suggests that Ken is adorned by the Yang line and Li by the Yin line. His idea seems to be that beauty requires harmony between Yin and Yang. He also indicates that originally the upper trigram was K'un ≡ ≡, and the lower trigram was Ch'ien ≡≡≡, but that somehow they exchanged a line for each other's adornment, forming the present hexagram. This harmony of Yin and Yang he considers to be the glory and adornment of heaven. Those with the wisdom to learn the lesson it teaches are certain to enjoy success.

Confucius then refers to the two component trigrams, saying that the adornment of humanity is the wisdom to realize that there are limits to cultural glory, and to restrain one's culture so that these limits will not be transgressed, for such glory requires not only harmony (K'un ≡ ≡ and Ch'ien ≡≡≡), but also balance and proportion (Ken ≡ ≡ and Li ≡ ≡). Finally, he says that just as we learn to tell the seasons by studying the stars ("adornment of heaven"), so we can learn much about world peace and order by studying those virtues that most adorn humanity.

SYMBOLIC SIGNIFICANCE OF THE HEXAGRAM AS NOTED BY CONFUCIUS:

The idea behind Pi is derived from fire under the mountain. The superior man is inspired thereby to define clearly general policies but not to be daring in deciding criminal cases.

Fire on the lower slope can illuminate a whole mountain. This suggests action that sheds light on, or clarifies, general or governmental policies. On the other hand, the mountain also serves to stop the fire. Hence the idea of action should not be carried to harmful extremes ("not to be daring in deciding criminal cases") that result in reckless judgment and unfair punishment.

DUKE OF CHOU'S EXPLANATION OF THE LINES (a) AND CONFUCIUS' COMMENT THEREON (b):

Line 1, Yang:

(a) *One adorns his toes. He lets go the carriage and walks on foot.*

(b) *"He lets go the carriage and walks on foot." This means that he ought not to ride on the carriage.*

The first line of this hexagram signifies the toes or feet. Here, Line 1 also lies at the bottom of the lower trigram, Li (light). Together the two denote light or adornment on the feet. Further, the lower interior trigram, K'an (Lines 2, 3, 4), represents wheels, and wheels suggest the idea of a carriage. Since Line 1 is just below K'an, it's subject is considered not to be riding in the carriage, either because he is unwilling or unable to do so.

Line 2, Yin:

(a) *One adorns his beard.*

(b) *"One adorns his beard." This means that one makes headway with the help of his superiors.*

This line is not only Yin in a Yin position, but also fails to form a harmonious relationship with its correlate (Line 5), suggesting something both weak and unimportant, fit only for ornament, like the beard. This symbolism is reinforced by the fact that there is mutual attraction between the line and its strong neighbor (Line 3), so that the subjects of the two lines band together like beard and chin. The subject of Line 2 is far too weak to act independently and must attach himself to his neighbor if he hopes to make any headway, just as a beard must be attached to the chin to be useful.

Line 3, Yang:

(a) *One appears with rich ornaments and a fresh make-up. Perseverance in a firm and correct course will lead to good fortune.*

(b) *"The good fortune from perseverance in a firm and correct course" means that to the end there will be no one to bully him.*

Being Yang in a Yang place, this line signifies a strong, handsome man who is attracted to and adored by two females (the Yin lines on each side). Because he has followed a firm and correct course, no one disparages his personality or contests his success. This is indeed good fortune. However, he must not let such good fortune cause him to deviate from this course, or his fine appearance will prove to be only a facade.

Line 4, Yin:

(a) *One appears adorned in plain white like a white horse with wings. He is not a highwayman. He desires to get married.*

(b) *Line 4, Yin, is in a correct place but is subject to doubt. "He is not a highwayman. He desires to get married." This means that to the end there will be no resentment.*

This Yin line occupies a correct (Yin) place and forms a harmonious relationship with its correlate (Line 1). Its subject is a gentle, meek man who desires to ally with (get married to) the subject of Line 1, but because of his modest nature does nothing to make a display of himself (traditionally, wedding finery is a raiment of gorgeous colors). He has doubts about this course, for he also feels some attraction to the subject of Line 3 (which is also Yang). But his decision will ultimately give him no occasion for repentance or regret.

Since Line 4 does not occupy a central position, its subject is not in a favorable position to take decisive action. Moreover, its place at the edge of the upper trigram denotes a transitional stage involving new circumstances and new adjustments, which makes decisive action all the more difficult.

Line 5, Yin:

(a) *An obscure scholar in his garden on a hill is adorned with a small roll of plain cloth. This is a shabby gift. Eventually there will be good fortune.*

(b) *The good fortune of the subject of Line 5 means there will be occasion for jubilation.*

This Yin line does not form a harmonious relationship with its correlate (Line 2) and is attracted instead to the strong (Yang) line just above it (Line 6), the top line of the upper trigram, Ken (mountain). Hence the image of a "garden on a hill." Since Line 5 occupies a central position, its subject is, if not a ruler, at least a person of some note (a great and brilliant scholar). As yet he is honored and adorned only with "a small roll of plain cloth." Such a gift may seem parsimonious. However, in the end there will be good fortune, for behind the giving of the gift there is good will, which may become a source of greater jubilation.

Line 6, Yang:

(a) *One adorns himself in white. There will be no error.*

(b) *"One adorns himself in white. There will be no error." This means that the leader has realized his ambition.*

This Yang line at the upper end of the hexagram indicates that the use of adornment or decoration has run its course. Its subject, having gratified his desires, is returning to simplicity, like a rainbow's colors returning to the white from which they originally issued. In the realm of human life, this line signifies a man who has resumed or recovered his true character, free from sham and ostentation.

The PO Hexagram
(Symbol of Deprivation)

23rd 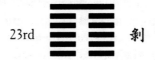 剝

IN THIS HEXAGRAM, only Line 6 (at the top) is Yang, indicating that the Yang principle has been progressively undermined by the Yin forces as their strength grows toward the maximum. The shape of the hexagram also shows that what is above has been persistently reduced in order to augment what is below. Hence the idea of deprivation.

KING WEN'S JUDGMENT ON THE HEXAGRAM:

This hexagram indicates that it is not advantageous to go ahead with any tasks or plans.

Yin forces are generally supposed to be dark and reactionary. When they wax in strength, it is considered an inauspicious occasion for taking action.

CONFUCIUS' EXPLANATION OF KING WEN'S JUDGMENT:

The hexagram means deprivation or peeling off. It means the weak are trying to change or transform the strong.

"Not advantageous to go ahead with any plans or tasks." This is because the mean people are gaining influence and increasing in number. To follow docilely and stop when necessary—this may be seen by contemplating the symbolism of the hexagram. The superior man attaches importance to the alternation of waning and waxing movements and of fullness and emptiness, for this is the way of the heavenly bodies.

Here, Confucius speaks of deprivation in terms of the encroachment on Yang by Yin. In the human world, this means that the petty, inferior men are in power and the position of the superior men is weakening. He then refers to the fact that the lower trigram, K'un, signifies docility, and the upper trigram signifies stoppage. To Confucius the Po Hexagram clearly shows the wisdom of docility, which moves forward when circumstances are favorable and stops when they are adverse (in accordance with the Law of Cyclic Reversion). The superior man knows this and makes his decisions accordingly.

SYMBOLIC SIGNIFICANCE OF THE HEXAGRAM AS NOTED BY CONFUCIUS:

The idea behind Po is derived from mountain attached to the earth. People in high places are inspired to thicken and strengthen what is below and to secure their dwellings.

Although the mountain towers above the earth, it can be reduced and leveled when men need material to thicken the surface of a road or to build walls for houses. In human terms, this suggests that the rich or powerful should work or give to benefit the poor so as to better ensure the peace and security of all.

DUKE OF CHOU'S EXPLANATION OF THE LINES (a) AND CONFUCIUS' COMMENT THEREON (b):

Line 1, Yin:

(a) *One deprives the bed of its legs. What is firm and sound will be destroyed. There will be evil.*

(b) *"One deprives the bed of its legs." This means destruction of the low foundation.*

This line is Yin and occupies a position neither central nor correct (Yin in a Yang place). It also lies at the bottom of the hexagram and fails to form a harmonious relationship with its correlate (Line 4, Yin). In addition, its neighbors (the other Yin lines) are all weak and repulsive. This suggests something extremely weak that can be easily damaged or destroyed.

If the hexagram is viewed as a symbol for a bed, the first line naturally represents the legs of the bed. To deprive a bed of its usefulness, one first removes the legs. In the human realm, this symbolizes an attempt to overthrow a regime by first subverting the allegiance of those to be found at the lower levels of society. Thus the fact that the bed has been deprived of its legs is an evil omen.

Line 2, Yin:

(a) *One deprives the bed of its edges. What is firm and sound will be destroyed. There will be evil.*

(b) *"One deprives the bed of its edges." This is because of lack of friends or associates.*

Since Line 1 represents the legs of a bed, Line 2 represents its edges. The fact that it is a Yin line suggests weakness or damage at the bed's edges, which renders it practically useless ("There will be evil"). Although the line occupies a position both central and correct (Yin in a Yin place), it forms an antagonistic relationship with its correlate (Line 5, the ruler). The subject of Line 2 therefore lacks any association with powerful or enlightening influences who could help him resist deprivation or destructive action, and through ignorance he may even unwittingly participate in the process of his own destruction.

Line 3, Yin:

(a) *One encounters the destructive process but is free from error or blame.*

(b) *"One encounters the destructive process but is free from error or blame." This is because one is dissociated from those above and below him.*

Although Line 3 occupies a position neither central nor correct (Yin in a Yang place), it forms a harmonious relationship with its correlate (Line 6, Yang). In this is an important difference between Line 3 and the Yin lines above and below it. Since its subject sympathizes with the Yang subject of Line 6 (someone or something influential and enlightening) and does not side or cooperate with the other Yin subjects, he remains free from error or blame.

Line 4, Yin:

(a) *One deprives the bed of its surface. This is an evil omen.*

(b) *"One deprives the bed of its surface." This means that the peril is imminent.*

If Line 4 represents the surface of the bed, then destruction here means that the bed is rendered practically useless ("peril is imminent").

Line 5, Yin:

(a) *Palace workers are following their leader, like fish in single file, for the purpose of obtaining royal favors. Nothing that will not be advantageous.*

(b) *"Palace workers are following their leader, like fish in single file, for the purpose of obtaining royal favors." This means that in the end there will be no resentment.*

This line represents a ruler who, though weak (Yin), occupies a central position. He is a wise and sensible person who follows a middle, or reasonable, course. Instead of contending with the strong man above him (Line 6), such a ruler assumes a conciliatory attitude. Those below him (the other Yin lines) follow his lead ("fish in single file"). Because there is already mutual attraction between Line 5 (Yin) and Line 6 (Yang), harmony develops naturally between them, and the ruler's attempt at conciliation dispels all resentments and leads to good fortune.

Line 6, Yang:

(a) *A big fruit as yet uneaten. The superior man obtains a carriage. The petty, mean men topple the house.*

(b) *"The superior man obtains a carriage." This means he is supported by the people. "The petty, mean men topple the house." This means that to the end they are of no use.*

The Ch'ien Hexagram signifies fruit. Since Line 6 looks like the last remaining Yang line of the Ch'ien Hexagram, it suggests a big fruit which has remained uneaten. This uneaten fruit in turn symbolizes a superior man, one who has learned to survive the subversive activities of those who, through envy, would bring about his downfall. However, the fact that the three Yin lines below form the trigram K'un (carriage, people), indicates that the superior man has won the loyal support of the people ("obtains a carriage"). Therefore, the attempts to subvert him fail through lack

of popular support. This is fortunate, for if men of petty character who let envy and jealousy lead them are brought to power, the
whole structure or situation represented by the hexagram (the top
line represents the top of a house) will collapse. It is useless to
hope for anything good from such men, and they should never be
employed in positions of great responsibility ("to the end they are
of no use").

The FU Hexagram
(Symbol of Returning)

24th 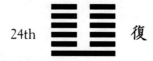 復

STRUCTURALLY, THIS HEXAGRAM is the opposite of the preceding Po Hexagram. In Po, the top Yang line has reached the summit and has nowhere to go, and so in accordance with the Law of Cyclic Reversion it returns to the bottom of the K'un Hexagram, displacing the first Yin line and forming the Fu Hexagram. Hence the idea of returning or resumption.

KING WEN'S JUDGMENT ON THE HEXAGRAM:

The hexagram indicates prosperity and success. Whether going out or coming in, one will be free from harm. Friends will come and there will be no regret. The way will revert to its starting point to repeat its course. The reversion comes on the seventh day. It will be auspicious to go ahead with one's plans.

The Judgment shows that with the resumption of the Yang cycle of manifestation (represented by Line 1), an auspicious course has been set in motion, so that the time is favorable for moving ahead. As to King Wen's remark that "reversion comes on the seventh day," the underlying idea seems to be that if Yang advances all the way through the hexagram and returns to its starting position, it will have passed through seven stages. Another explanation is that the "seven days" are actually seven months, dating from the fifth month of the lunar calendar (when the summer solstice occurs) to the eleventh month (when the winter solstice occurs). At midnight of the winter solstice (Yang), after a cycle of waning manifestation lasting seven months, a new cycle of waxing manifestation begins (the Yang line in the first position).

CONFUCIUS' EXPLANATION OF KING WEN'S JUDGMENT:

"The hexagram indicates prosperity and success." The strong Yang power has returned.

Movement will encounter and follow the smooth submissive trend; therefore, "whether going out or coming in, one will be free from harm and friends will come without any regret."

"The way will revert to its starting point to repeat its course. The reversion comes on the seventh day." This is the dynamic course of heaven.

"It will be auspicious to go ahead with one's plans." For the strong Yang power is increasing.

Does not the Fu Hexagram reveal the heart of heaven and earth?

To Confucius, the waxing cycle of Yang signifies the dynamic course of heaven. In this action, Confucius perceives the merciful "heart of heaven" working to bring about the renewal of life on earth.

The strong Yang power (Line 1) is increasing because it is following an unobstructed course ("the smooth submissive trend"), symbolically represented by the five weak Yin lines which lie in its upward path. In such circumstances, success and prosperity are ensured.

SYMBOLIC SIGNIFICANCE OF THE HEXAGRAM AS NOTED BY CONFUCIUS:

The idea behind Fu is derived from thunder (lower trigram) in the midst of the earth (upper trigram). The ancient kings were inspired thereby to close the passes connecting states on the day of the winter solstice. Merchants and travellers had to stop their journeys on that day. The king would not go out to inspect the regions.

Thunder under the surface of the earth, though just a mild rumbling that has not yet broken forth, symbolizes the glowing brightness of spring (Yang) returning after the deepest darkness of winter (Yin). The ancient kings learned to wait quietly ("close the passes") and store up the kingdom's energies while winter held sway, that all might be ready for the abundant activities of spring.

DUKE OF CHOU'S EXPLANATION OF THE LINES (a) AND CONFUCIUS' COMMENT THEREON (b):

Line 1, Yang:

(a) *One turns back after going a short distance. No occasion for repentance. Great good fortune.*

(b) *"Turning back after going a short distance" is needed for rectification of one's personality.*

Line 1 having moved down from the top of the preceding hexagram to form the present one signifies a person who corrects himself quickly after committing some error ("turns back after going a short distance"). As he is eager to rectify the situation, he will not persist in it long enough to cause blame or regret. Such an attitude can only lead to good fortune.

Line 2, Yin:

(a) *One turns back in a pleasant mood. Good fortune.*

(b) *"The good fortune of turning back in a pleasant mood" stems from one's humility toward the virtuous people below him.*

This Yin line occupies a position both central and correct. Its subject is a weak person who is resting quietly to recover health and strength. Fortune will smile on him because he is humble enough to serve "the virtuous people below him" (Line 1, Yang).

Line 3, Yin:

(a) *One turns back frequently. His situation is grave but he will be free from error.*

(b) *"The grave situation of turning back again and again" should, according to reason, be free from error.*

This line occupies a position neither central nor correct (Yin in a Yang place) and fails to form a harmonious relationship with its correlate (Line 6, Yin). The subject, therefore, is a weak, ignorant person, liable to frequent mistakes and errors in judgment.

However, he displays the willingness to correct himself each time he learns of an error and so, even when in a perilous situation, remains free from harm or blame.

Line 4, Yin:

(a) *In order to follow the middle path, one turns back alone.*

(b) *"In order to follow the middle path, one turns back alone." This is because he wants to harmonize with Tao.*

Here, Line 4 is quite favorably placed: not only does it occupy a correct position (Yin in a Yin place), but it also occupies the central position of the five Yin lines and of the upper interior trigram, K'un (Lines 3, 4, 5). In addition, this line forms a harmonious relationship with its correlate (Line 1, Yang). Thus, Line 4 indicates a meek, gentle person who lets himself be guided only by truth (Tao). Such a person opposes extremes and will turn back to follow a more reasonable course, even if he is alone in doing so.

Line 5, Yin:

(a) *One turns back with great sincerity of heart. No occasion for repentance.*

(b) *"One turns back with great sincerity of heart. No occasion for repentance." This shows self-examination from the center of one's heart.*

Here, Line 5 (the ruler) occupies an important central position, indicating a wise leader given to deep self-examination who willingly returns to the correct course when he discovers he has deviated from it. Such a leader will know no occasion for repentance.

Line 6, Yin:

(a) *One is perplexed about turning back. Evil omen. There will be trouble and disaster. If the army is set in motion against the enemy, it will eventually suffer great defeat and the ruler of the state will be in an evil plight. Even in ten years he will be unable to accomplish his task of chastising the enemy.*

(b) *"The evil of perplexity about turning back" shows that the proper path or course for a king has been violated.*

This line is the last of five Yin lines and occupies a Yin place. It also fails to form a harmonious relationship with its correlate

(Line 3) and occupies the extreme position at the top of the hexagram. Its subject may be a leader; but one who (unlike the subject of Line 5) has deviated from the kingly path of moderation and gone to extremes without correcting himself. Not having turned back in time, the subject of Line 6 has reached the point of no return (the top position of the hexagram). As the line also fails to form a harmonious relationship with its correlate (Line 3, Yin) or any of the other Yin lines, he has no associates he can call upon for help and so finds himself isolated in his difficulty. No wonder he is greatly perplexed. Misfortune or disaster lies in store for such a man and for any venture he might undertake.

The WU WANG Hexagram
(Symbol of Blamelessness)

25th  无妄

THE UPPER TRIGRAM, Ch'ien, stands for heaven, and the lower, Chen, stands for thunder. Thunder below the heavens suggests a spontaneous outburst from below, as when a man's true nature is revealed through an unexpected outburst of his innermost sentiments. In the councils of ancient times, such inner truthfulness, even if it aroused dissension, was held to be innocent of blame or censure, because it flowed from the heart or conscience. Hence the idea of blamelessness.

KING WEN'S JUDGMENT ON THE HEXAGRAM:

This hexagram indicates great prosperity and success and advantage in being firm and correct. What is contrary to the correct course will bring trouble and will not be advantageous to going ahead with one's plans.

To follow the course of inner truth and remain spiritually undefiled, no matter how difficult, leads to success. To turn aside from such a course can lead to disadvantage and disaster.

CONFUCIUS' EXPLANATION OF KING WEN'S JUDGMENT:

The hexagram suggests that strength comes from the outside and acts as the lord in the interior. Motion is coupled with strength and vigor. The strong occupies a central and correct place and is favorably responded to. Tremendous prosperity and success based on firm correctness shows the will of heaven. "What is contrary to the correct

221

course will bring trouble and will not be advantageous to going ahead with one's plans." With one's inner truthfulness gone, whither shall one turn? Without the blessing of heaven's will, how can any action proceed with success?

The lower trigram, Chen, is formed when Yang comes from the outside, that is, from the upper Ch'ien trigram, to displace the first Yin line of the K'un trigram. As the lower trigram represents the interior, the above symbolism leads to the notion that "strength comes from the outside and acts as the lord (Chen represents the eldest son) in the interior." The upper trigram, Ch'ien, signifies strength, and the lower trigram, Chen, also signifies motion, hence the auspicious idea that "motion is coupled with vigor." Further-more, Line 5 (Yang) forms a harmonious relationship with its correlate (Line 2); thus it is said that "the strong is favorably responded to." This idea is reinforced by the fact that both lines occupy central and correct positions.

These are all highly auspicious symbols indicating great prosperity and success ("the blessings of heaven's will") for the man who firmly follows the path of inner truth.

SYMBOLIC SIGNIFICANCE OF THE HEXAGRAM AS NOTED BY CONFUCIUS:

The idea behind Wu Wang is derived from thunder under heaven. All creatures act according to their endowed nature, without guilt or folly. The ancient kings were inspired thereby to manifest their abundant virtues in accord with the auspicious season and foster the growth of the ten thousand things.

In the preceding Fu Hexagram, thunder rumbled beneath the earth. In this hexagram, thunder has broken forth from the earth and resounds beneath the heavens, indicating that the Yang power has returned to earth, causing things to grow and flourish, each according to its own nature. Inspired by this penomenon, the ancient kings endeavored to cultivate their own virtues, so that they might prosper both themselves and their people.

DUKE OF CHOU'S EXPLANATION OF THE LINES (a) AND CONFUCIUS' COMMENT THEREON (b):

Line 1, Yang:

(a) *No follies. To go forward will bring good fortune.*

(b) *"Going forward with no follies" means the realization of one's aims.*

This line is Yang in a Yang place, indicating great strength and intelligence. Together with its position at the beginning (bottom) of the hexagram, this suggests man's initial innocence or original nature, which is free from error or evil. To maintain this kind of child-like innocence and bring it to all life's tasks and activities will prosper any venture and foster success and good fortune. This means the fulfillment of one's most cherished dreams.

Line 2, Yin:

(a) *Ploughing the field without thinking of harvests, and cultivating wasteland without thinking of fertile meadows. Then there will be advantage in moving forward in any direction.*

(b) *"Ploughing the field without thinking of harvests." This means that as yet there is no hankering after wealth.*

This Yin lines occupies a position that is both central and correct and forms a harmonious relationship with its correlate (Line 5, the ruler). Its subject is a meek and gentle person, possibly a minister, who loyally serves his ruler without consideration of benefit or reward. Such loyalty and unselfishness will bring good fortune in whatever ventures he may undertake.

Line 3, Yin:

(a) *Calamity not due to one's follies. A cow may have been tied up somewhere and some passersby may have led it off. The people of the district will suffer calamity.*

(b) *"Passersby have got the cow." This will involve the people of the district in calamity.*

This Yin line occupies a position neither central nor correct and lies at the extreme top of the lower trigram, Chen (motion). Its subject is an unlucky person in a tight and awkward situation.

Such a man is apt to meet with calamity through no fault of his own, even when following the course of inner truth. Others, however, may not judge him so fairly, and his situation may be likened to that of a man charged with stealing a cow, though he is innocent of such a crime.

Line 4, Yang:

(a) *Capable of maintaining a firm and correct course. No error.*

(b) *"Capable of maintaining a firm and correct course. No error." This is the natural result of one's innate innocence.*

This line is neither central nor correct (Yang in a Yin place) and forms an antagonistic relationship with its correlate (Line 1). As there is also no mutual attraction between it and its neighbor (Line 5), its subject (a minister) is in an isolated and helpless position. In addition, Line 4, being the first line of the upper trigram, denotes a stage of transition involving new adjustments. Its subject must act without help, relying only on his own judgment and strength to steer a steady course through the time of transition. Only by so doing can he avoid error or blame.

Line 5, Yang:

(a) *Sickness not due to one's follies. One need not take any medicine and will rejoice.*

(b) *"Medicine in a case free from follies" should not be tasted.*

Here, Line 5 (the ruler) is both central and correct (Yang in a Yang place) and forms a harmonious relationship with its correlate (Line 2). Its subject is a well-placed man of great strength whose actions are free from error in any difficulty ("sickness") in which he may find himself. His situation, therefore, is not due to any folly on his part, nor is any outside intervention ("medicine") necessary, because he will recover from the situation on his own. Outside remedies should also be avoided because the cause of the problem has not yet been determined.

Line 6, Yang:

(a) *Action, even if free from follies, will meet with trouble. There will be no advantage in any forward move whatsoever.*

(b) *"Action, even if free from follies" may meet with the calamity caused by exhaustion.*

Being at the top, this Yang line indicates great strength and dynamism. It also forms a harmonious relationship with its correlate (Line 4, Yin). However, because it has reached the extreme limit of the hexagram, to advance at all, even to follow the path of inner truth, is sure to bring disaster to its subject. Such danger is inherent in his position and may not be attributed to any folly on his part, but if he remains contented with his position and scales no further heights, all will be well.

The TA CH'U Hexagram
(Symbol of Great Restraint)

26th  大畜

THE UPPER TRIGRAM, Ken, stands for mountain and symbolizes obstruction; the lower, Ch'ien, stands for strength and dynamic motion. Together they suggest some onward dynamic force being restrained. In the process, this force is stored up and increases. Hence the idea of vast possessions or great restraint.

KING WEN'S JUDGMENT ON THE HEXAGRAM:

The hexagram indicates advantage in being firm and correct. Not to eat at home. Good fortune. Advantageous to cross the great stream.

The hexagram basically refers to the accumulation of virtue, which requires the ability to remain firmly on the correct path. A virtuous man should use his resources to provide food for others and not merely his own family ("Not to eat at home"). If he makes an effort ("cross the great stream") in this direction, it will prove to his advantage.

CONFUCIUS' EXPLANATION OF KING WEN'S JUDGMENT:

The hexagram suggests strength and vigor, utter solidity and refulgent light, and daily renewal of virtue.

The strong above show respect to the worthies and can restrain their vigorous motion. This shows correctness on a grand scale.

"Not to eat at home. Good fortune." The idea is to feed the worthy people.

"Advantageous to cross the great stream." This shows that one responds to heaven.

According to Confucius, this hexagram illustrates both the means and importance of accumulating virtue. Line 6 at the top is Yang, as are the first three lines, suggesting a leader in a high position who shows respect for those below him ("the worthies"). The onward course of the strong (lower trigram) is restrained by the mountain (upper trigram) from going to excess, thus preventing disaster. Not eating at home indicates eating with (sharing with) the worthies below.

The upper interior trigram, Chen (Lines 3, 4, 5), stands for thunder or motion, and the lower interior trigram, Tui (Lines 2, 3, 4), stands for lake. Motion over a lake suggests crossing a great stream. Line 2 occupies the center of the Ch'ien trigram (heaven) and forms a harmonious relationship with its correlate (Line 5, the ruler). Hence the image of "one responding to heaven."

SYMBOLIC SIGNIFICANCE OF THE HEXAGRAM AS NOTED BY CONFUCIUS:

The idea behind Ta Ch'u is derived from heaven in the mountain. The superior man is inspired thereby to increase his knowledge of the words and deeds of former sages so as to nourish his own virtue.

Heaven represents the sky or air. Air, when it accumulates into clouds, often comes to rest on mountains, where it assumes the appearance of a vast, expansive mass under restraint. This symbolism is reinforced by the fact that heaven also represents something of supreme value. Heaven in the mountain, therefore, also suggests something of great value has accumulated inside the mountain. Thus the superior man is inspired to accumulate and nourish heaven (virtues) within his own being.

DUKE OF CHOU'S EXPLANATION OF THE LINES (a) AND CONFUCIUS' COMMENT THEREON (b):

Line 1, Yang:
(a) Danger exists. Advantageous to stop moving forward.
(b) "Danger exists. Advantageous to stop moving forward." This is to avoid incurring calamity.

This is a Yang line in a Yang place at the beginning (bottom) of a hexagram and suggests a young man full of vigor who is inclined to advance. However, although the line forms a harmonious relationship with its correlate (Line 4, Yin), and their subjects normally cooperate to help each other, in the Ta Ch'u Hexagram (restraint) the subject of Line 4 is given the task of checking the advance of Line 1. It is therefore advantageous for the subject of this line to stop any advance or he will encounter disaster.

Line 2, Yang:

(a) *The axletree has fallen off from between the wheels of a carriage.*

(b) *"The axletree has fallen off from between the wheels of a carriage." This shows the center is free from blame*

This is a Yang line occupying a central position, indicating that its subject possesses a dynamic character balanced by good sense. He forms a harmonious relationship with his correlate (Line 5, Yin), whose task is to also act as a restraining influence, checking his advance. However, due to his good sense the subject of Line 2 stops, like a carriage from whose wheels the "axletree has come off." Because he cooperates, instead of acting in a headstrong manner, he commits no error.

Line 3, Yang:

(a) *The steeds are chasing one another. Advantageous to exercise fortitude and firmness and to practice daily the art of driving a chariot and of self-defense. Advantageous to go ahead with one's plans.*

(b) *"Advantageous to go ahead with one's plans." This means that people above have similar aims.*

Being at the top of the Ch'ien trigram, this Yang line suggests a person of highly dynamic character who is very eager to advance. Its subject is as impetuous as "steeds chasing one another," but his position, because not central, is unfavorable and rests just below the trigram Ken (obstruction). If the subject of Line 3 wishes to avoid disaster, he should restrain himself and follow the path of virtue. He should devote himself to his daily practices, improving and developing his position until (according to the Law of Cyclic Reversion) the time comes for him to push ahead with his own plans. Although Line 3 forms an antagonistic relationship with its correlate (Line 6, Yang), in this hexagram all the Yang lines are said to be advancing together against restraint, and the upper Yang line is considered to be sympathetic toward Line 3 ("people above have similar aims").

According to the *Shuo Kua*, the lower trigram, Ch'ien, represents good horses, giving rise to the image of "steeds" in the Text.

Line 4, Yin:

(a) *A young bull has a horizontal piece of wood over its horns. Great good fortune.*

(b) *"The great good fortune" indicated in Line 4, Yin, means there will be jubilation.*

As has been noted, the subject of this line undertakes to restrain a strong young man (Line 1, its correlate). The subject of Line 4, therefore, is in a position like that of a man who must put a horizontal piece of wood over the horns of a young bull to render him harmless. To do so represents great fortune, for danger and disaster have been prevented. This is cause for jubilation.

Line 5, Yin:

(a) *A castrated hog shows its teeth. Good fortune.*

(b) *The "good fortune" indicated in Line 5, Yin, means there will be great rejoicing.*

This line (the ruler) is Yin and occupies a central position, denoting a wise and gentle leader. However, his task is also to restrain the strong man represented by his correlate (Line 2). His position is similar to that of a man who must tame a hog by castration. Although the hog may have sharp teeth, it will be in no mood to use them. Thus disaster is avoided. This too is an occasion for rejoicing.

Line 6, Yang:

(a) *One is in command of the broad boulevards in the capital. Prosperity and success.*

(b) *"One is in command of the broad boulevards in the capital." This means that one's plans are being carried out in full force.*

Since the Ta Ch'u Hexagram represents not only restraint but vast accumulation, the Yang line at the top signifies that great strength and power have been stored up. The term "t'ien ch'u" refers to the broad boulevards in the capital of China. The implication is that the subject of Line 6 is a powerful person entrusted with important tasks and whose plans and projects are carried out in great measure.

The upper trigram, Ken, also stands for paths and roads, creating the image of "broad boulevards."

The YI Hexagram
(Symbol of Nourishment)

27th  頤

THE STRUCTURE OF THIS hexagram represents the mouth. Since the lower trigram, Chen, represents motion, Line 1, the only strong (Yang) line in Chen, symbolizes the movable lower lip and jaw. Since the upper trigram, Ken, represents a mountain or immobility, Line 6, the strong (Yang) line in Ken, symbolizes the immovable upper lip and jaw. The Yin lines in between symbolize the teeth.

A mouth naturally suggests eating and food. Hence the idea of nourishment, not only for the body but (by association) also for the soul.

KING WEN'S JUDGMENT ON THE HEXAGRAM:

The hexagram indicates that good fortune will result from firm correctness. Consider nutrition. Seek your own proper food.

It is of utmost importance to select those things which provide the necessary nutrition for survival, both spiritually and physically.

CONFUCIUS' EXPLANATION OF KING WEN'S JUDGMENT:

"The hexagram indicates that good fortune will result from firm correctness." This means that when the nourishment is proper, good fortune will result. "Consider nutrition." This means the consideration of what is to be nourished. "Seek your own proper food." This means the consideration of one's own nourishment.

Heaven and earth nourish the ten thousand things. The sage nourishes the worthies and thence all the people. Great is the time when nutrition shows its significance.

Confucius practically says that one must exercise self-restraint and firmly adhere to a correct diet. Only such firm correctness will lead to good health and good fortune. One should also select one's own diet, for not all people need the same food. The sage or the ruler, therefore, should provide food for different people, or instruct them in proper nutrition. Grand indeed will be the time when the salutary effect of proper nutrition is widespread.

SYMBOLIC SIGNIFICANCE OF THE HEXAGRAM AS NOTED BY CONFUCIUS:

The idea behind Yi is derived from thunder (lower trigram) below the mountain (upper trigram). The superior man is inspired thereby to be cautious in speech and abstemious in eating and drinking.

As the hexagram is shaped like an open mouth, the upper trigram, Ken, signifies the upper jaw, which is immovable like a mountain, and the lower trigram, Chen, signifies the lower jaw, which moves like thunder. Thus the superior man comes to think of the mouth and its uses and keeps a close guard against careless speech and improper diet.

DUKE OF CHOU'S EXPLANATION OF THE LINES (a) AND CONFUCIUS' COMMENT THEREON (b):

Line 1, Yang:

(a) *"You discard your spirit-like tortoise and look at me with your mouth open and jaws quaking."* Ill omen.

(b) *"You look at me with mouth open and jaws quaking."* This indeed is not entitled to any respect.

This line is Yang in a Yang place, indicating its subject to be a man of means who possesses more than sufficient nourishment of his own. However, he is not satisfied and yearns for more, coveting that possessed by the subject of his correlate (Line 4,

Yin), to whom he is attracted by their mutual harmony. It is the subject of Line 4, in fact, who is supposed to be speaking here ("You look at me with mouth open"). Such a greedy fellow is, of course, not entitled to respect.

This hexagram resembles the trigram Li ☲, only with greater hollowness, having four Yin lines instead of one. Li signifies a tortoise as well as light or intelligence. A tortoise is supposed to live purely on air and not need any solid or liquid food. It symbolizes the spirit, hence the subject (Line 1) is said to have spiritually deviated from the correct path ("discard your spirit").

Line 2, Yin:

(a) *One acts improperly in seeking food from people below him and faces an uphill climb in seeking it from people above him. Such efforts will lead to evil.*

(b) *The evil efforts indicated in Line 2, Yin, are due to the fact that in taking action one fails to find any kindred associates.*

This is a Yin line occupying a position both central and correct, suggesting that its subject is a well-placed person of gentle and able character. However, he does not form a harmonious relationship with the subject of his correlate (Line 5, Yin), nor is his relationship any more favorable with the subjects of Lines 1 and 6, who are strong (Yang), well-to-do people. Since the subject of Line 2 occupies a higher position than that of his stronger subordinates, their relationship is rendered awkward. In addition, he lies far below the subject of Line 6, who resides at the top of the upper trigram, Ken (mountain). In attempting to approach him, the subject of Line 2 "faces an uphill climb." Therefore, he has difficulty in seeking nourishment from both those below him and those above. In the absence of any "kindred associates," it will prove inauspicious to undertake any ventures ("seeking food").

Line 3, Yin:

(a) *One eats contrary to what nutrition requires. Persistence will mean evil. One should not take any action for ten years. There is nothing that will be in any way advantageous.*

(b) *"One should not take any action for ten years." This is because the course adopted is highly improper.*

Line 3 occupies a position neither central nor correct (Yin in a Yang place) and directly beneath the trigram Ken (mountain or great obstacle). Since it forms a harmonious relationship with its correlate (Line 6, Yang), its subject could normally expect assistance (nourishment) from his highly placed partner. But in this case the latter is far above, at the top of a mountain (Ken), and is difficult to reach. In such a situation, any expectations or plans which the subject of Line 3 might harbor can hardly be brought to fruition. He should instead devote himself to inner nourishment and wait until a time when (according to the Law of Cyclic Reversion) the present cycle has completed itself (symbolically, ten years) and a situation favorable to his own prospects has occurred.

Line 4, Yin:

(a) *One seeks food from people below him. Good fortune. He stares like a tiger and his desires are so intense as to seem chasing one another. There will be no error.*

(b) *"The good fortune of seeking food from people below" means the high officials will spread the light.*

Line 4 (the minister) is Yin and lies above the lower trigram, denoting an official who seeks nourishment from people below him, not for himself but for his country. Officials in ancient times collected taxes in the form of grain, and what the subject of this line receives he will use to maintain the welfare of the people ("spread the light"). Although he is vigorous in performing his duty ("stares like a tiger"), his motives are unselfish and he will incur no blame.

Both the interior trigrams (Lines 2, 3, 4, and Lines 3, 4, 5) are K'un (territory, people). Moreover, the entire hexagram resembles the Li trigram (light). Together, these suggest the spreading of light over the earth. The upper trigram, Ken, also signifies wild animals, and Li signifies eyes. Hence the image of "staring like a tiger."

Line 5, Yin:

(a) *One acts abnormally. Good fortune will be his if he stays firm and correct. He must not cross the great stream.*

(b) *"The good fortune that results from staying firm and correct" is due to docile obedience to superiors.*

234

Here, Line 5 (the ruler), being Yin and the last of four Yin lines, occupies a very weak position. It also fails to form a harmonious relationship with its correlate (Line 2, Yin). Its subject is a weak ruler who lacks any significant support. However, he is a gentle, sensible person who is receptive to the influence of the strong subject of Line 6, which allows him to share the latter's resources (nourishment). He will enjoy good fortune if he persists in this course, but to undertake any action on his own will not be propitious ("must not cross the great stream").

Line 6, Yang:

(a) *There is a way of nutrition. A sense of peril will bring good fortune. Advantageous to cross the great stream.*

(b) *"There is a way of nutrition. A sense of peril will bring good fortune." This means there will be great rejoicing.*

The hexagram as a whole signifies nutrition. Therefore, the presence of a Yang line at the top suggests that the need for nutrition has been fulfilled and a source of food secured. However, the extreme position of the line at the summit of the hexagram indicates the end of one cycle before the beginning of the next, and also that this source may not last long or is in danger of disruption ("a sense of peril"). Only if the subject of Line 6 realizes the situation for what it is and acts to correct it ("cross the great stream"), can he prevent it from deteriorating. By acting in time, he creates a cause for great rejoicing.

The TA KUO Hexagram
(Symbol of Excessive Greatness)

28th  大過

THIS HEXAGRAM HAS four strong (Yang) lines and only two weak (Yin) ones, indicating the preponderance of strength over weakness. Hence the idea of excessive greatness. The structure of the hexagram, with a weak line at the top, a weak line at the bottom, and four strong lines in between, resembles a pillar which is weakening at top and bottom but still remains sound and strong in the center. This also suggests the idea of strength overcoming weakness.

KING WEN'S JUDGMENT ON THE HEXAGRAM:

This hexagram indicates a wooden beam which is weakening. It favors going ahead with one's plans. There will be prosperity and success.

The Judgment refers to the state of the pillar or beam, in which the weak portions are unable to help support the strong center portion. When such a situation comes to one's notice it is advantageous to proceed with repairs and attempt to correct the situation. By restoring it to a sound condition, good fortune is ensured.

CONFUCIUS' EXPLANATION OF KING WEN'S JUDGMENT:

The hexagram shows that what is great has become excessive. "A wooden beam is weaking." This is because the beginning and the end are weak.

236

The strong elements are excessive but they occupy central positions. Flexibility coupled with satisfaction form the basis of action. This "favors going ahead with one's plans" and hence prosperity and success.

Great indeed is the time when Ta Kuo, or excessive greatness, shows its significance.

The four Yang lines, though excessively strong and tending to extremes, are tempered by their central positions. Lines 2 and 5 are in the center of the lower and upper trigrams respectively, while Lines 3 and 4 occupy the central position of the entire hexagram. This is an auspicious sign because the center always signifies moderation, justice, balance, and wisdom. In addition, the lower trigram, Sun, signifies docility or flexibility, and the upper trigram, Tui, signifies pleasure or satisfaction. One who is flexible and satisfied with life possesses enormous advantages in carrying out his plans and will meet with success.

SYMBOLIC SIGNIFICANCE OF THE HEXAGRAM AS NOTED BY CONFUCIUS:

The idea behind Ta Kuo is derived from marsh (upper trigram) covering the trees (lower trigram). The superior man is inspired thereby to stand alone without fear and retire from the world without sorrow.

The watery marsh nourishes the trees and fosters their growth. But when the water becomes excessive, as in a flood, it inundates the trees. This symbolizes a situation in which those of small, mean character have overshadowed the superior man. At such a time, the superior man refuses to follow the course his inferiors have adopted and chooses to bide his time ("retire from the world") until (according to the Law of Cyclic Reversion) the tide of events turns again in his favor.

DUKE OF CHOU'S EXPLANATION OF THE LINES (a) AND CONFUCIUS' COMMENT THEREON (b):

Line 1, Yin:

(a) *Some white herb is used as a mattress. No error.*

(b) *"Some white herb is used as a mattress." This means that weakness or pliancy is down below.*

This Yin line denotes a soft or pliant herb and its bottom position denotes the herb's use as a cushion or mattress. Hence the subject of Line 1 pliantly serves the subjects of the four (Yang) lines above. This is the correct course for one in his position.

Line 2, Yang:

(a) *A withered willow tree sends out green shoots. An old husband has got a young wife. There is nothing that will not be advantageous.*

(b) *"Old husband, young wife." This is a lopsided relation.*

The lower trigram, Sun (wood or tree), is covered by the trigram Tui (marsh); therefore the trees are said to be withered. However, Line 2 is Yang in the center of the lower trigram, indicating that its subject still has some remnant of vitality ("sends out green shoots"). In the human realm, the subject is an elderly person who still retains his strength. As there are three strong men (the other Yang lines) blocking his upward path, he turns downward toward his neighbor (Line 1), with whom he forms a harmonious relationship. Since Line 1 is Yin and occupies the first position of the lower trigram, Sun (docility), it suggests a family's first daughter ("old husband . . . young wife"). All this indicates that the excess of one and the deficiency of the other ("a lopsided relation") can be brought into adjustment and the situation rendered harmonious and agreeable for both.

Line 3, Yang:

(a) *A wooden beam is weakening, or giving way. Ill omen.*

(b) *The ill omen of a wooden beam "giving way" is due to the fact that it does not have the needed support.*

This line is Yang in a Yang place and occupies a central position in the hexagram as a whole. It is likened to a strong wooden beam in the center of the ceiling, but its very strength turns out to be a drawback. The line is just below the upper trigram, Tui (marsh), which places it under heavy pressure: it needs outside support. However, although it forms a harmonious relationship with its correlate (Line 6, Yin), that line is weak and the needed support is lacking. The wooden beam (Line 3) is in a very precarious condition.

Line 4, Yang:

(a) *A wooden beam shows great strength. If it expects support from others, it will have cause for regret. Good fortune.*

(b) *"The good fortune of a strong wooden beam" lies in that it will not give way, even if the support from below is weak.*

Like Line 3, this line is Yang and occupies a central position in the hexagram as a whole. It too is compared to a strong beam in the center of the ceiling. However, unlike the beam of Line 3, this one carries only one strong line above it and so is not subject to such tremendous pressure. It can maintain its position without much outside support. This is fortunate, for although Line 4 forms a harmonious relationship with its correlate (Line 1, Yin), that line is weak and its subject cannot be looked upon for any significant support.

Line 5, Yang:

(a) *A withered willow tree sends forth flowers. An old woman has got her learned husband. Neither blame nor praise.*

(b) *"A withered willow tree sends forth flowers." How can such a situation last long? "Old woman, learned husband." This nevertheless is something to be ashamed of.*

This line occupies a position both central and correct (Yang in a Yang place), which usually denotes a brilliant ruler or a great man. However, in the present hexagram, which symbolizes excessive greatness, Line 5, being the last of the four Yang lines, signifies a scholar who has passed his prime but still retains his vigor ("a withered willow tree" which still "sends forth flowers"). Since Line 5 and its correlate (Line 2, Yang) fail to form a harmonious relationship, forcing Line 2 to turn to the nearest Yin line (Line 1), Line 5 is likewise forced to turn for support to the nearest Yin line (Line 6). If a Yin line at the beginning of the hexagram represents a young girl or green shoots, then the Yin line at the end of the hexagram represents an old woman or the last flower of a withered tree. If the relationship between Lines 1 and 2 represents an older man marrying a young girl, then the relationship between

Lines 5 and 6 represents a young scholar marrying an older woman. Though there is no blame, there is also no praise, for according to ancient traditions the wife should be about ten years younger than the husband. Their relationship, therefore, is not wholly free from error.

Line 6, Yin:

(a) *One wades through water and reaches a depth where the water covers his head. There will be evil but no blame.*

(b) *"The evil of wading through water beyond one's height" should not cause any blame.*

This line rides on a series of Yang lines; in addition, it lies at the top of the trigram Tui (marsh). The subject of Line 6 is one who is weak or has lost his strength. Symbolically, this situation signifies a man who attempts some great task far beyond his powers ("water beyond one's height"). He may fail but should not be blamed, for he has tried his best to do something great. However, it is still possible that he may be rescued or can save himself, if only he possesses the wisdom to remain calm and not panic.

The K'AN Hexagram
(Symbol of Peril)

29th  坎

THIS HEXAGRAM CONSISTS of two K'an trigrams, one over the other. A single K'an trigram suggests a river (the Yang line) flowing between two banks of earth (the Yin lines). Water in a river is a potential source of danger. Two K'an trigrams suggest that the movement of water has doubled, which represents a great danger. Hence the idea of peril.

KING WEN'S JUDGMENT ON THE HEXAGRAM:

The trigram K'an repeated indicates one's possession of sincerity. Only let the mind be calm and free, and action taken will be highly commendable.

Sincerity is denoted by the central position of both Lines 2 and 5 in the hexagram. Sincerity leads to clarity of judgment, which reveals the correct method of coping with a perilous situation, a commendable action.

CONFUCIUS' EXPLANATION OF KING WEN'S JUDGMENT:

K'an trigram repeated means double danger.

Water flows without overflowing. It moves amid dangers without losing its faithfulness.

"Only let the mind be calm and free." This stems from the strong elements occupying central places. "Action taken will be highly commendable." This means going ahead will meet with success.

The perils in heaven cannot be surmounted. The perils on earth consist of mountains, rivers, hills, and mounds. Kings and princes

set up perils for the defense of the state. Great indeed is the timely use of perils.

Confucius first refers to the great danger signified by high water that flows along calm and full. It must remain unobsructed or it will overflow its banks. In the human realm, this suggests moving faithfully among dangers in the service of others. To do so the mind, like the river, must be calm and free. Finally, he points out that, just as natural obstacles constitute perils for those who try to cross them, so kings set up perils as obstacles to the movement of their enemies ("the defense of the state").

SYMBOLIC SIGNIFICANCE OF THE HEXAGRAM AS NOTED BY CONFUCIUS:

Water comes flowing on and on, as indicated in the K'an trigram repeated. The superior man is inspired thereby to practice frequently virtuous conduct and the art of teaching.

As water flows in an endless stream (K'an repeated), so the superior man works ceaselessly to improve his own character and to share with those around him the knowledge gained from his experience.

DUKE OF CHOU'S EXPLANATION OF THE LINES (a) AND CONFUCIUS' COMMENT THEREON (b):

Line 1, Yin:

(a) *Double peril. One falls into a pit in the cavern. There will be evil.*

(b) *"Double peril. One falls into a pit in the cavern. There will be evil." This is the evil of losing one's way.*

This line is Yin and lies at the bottom of the hexagram signifying great peril. It also occupies a place neither central nor correct (Yin in a Yang place). Its subject, therefore, is in a very insecure and uncomfortable position and is prone to be reckless. He does not follow a middle path and consequently falls "into a pit in the cavern" ("Double peril"). His condition is indeed evil and perilous.

Line 2, Yang:

(a) *One is surrounded by perils in a cavern. He may get a little of the relief he is seeking.*

(b) *"He may get a little of the relief he is seeking."* This is because he has not yet got out of the interior.

This Yang line occupies a position incorrect (Yang in a Yin place) but central, as it is sandwiched between two Yin lines. Normally, its subject would be said to be in a trap, but as he is a sensible person who follows a middle course, he will probably extricate himself.

Line 3, Yin:

(a) *One faces peril whether inward or outward. From a situation already perilous, he falls into a pit in a cavern. Effort will be of no use.*

(b) *"One faces peril whether inward or outward."* This shows that to the end there will be no success in any effort.

This line occupies an awkward position, since it is neither central nor correct (Yin in a Yang place). It also fails to form a harmonious relationship with its correlate (Line 6, Yin), so its subject is a weak and rather dull-witted person placed in very unfavorable circumstances. As Line 3 occupies the top of the lower trigram and is just below the upper one, its subject faces peril whether he turns inward or outward. For one of his limited intelligence, escape from the situation will prove impossible ("no success in any effort").

Line 4, Yin:

(a) *A bottle of wine, a bamboo basket of rice and some earthen vessels, wherewith one presents his simple offerings on the windowsill. Eventually no error.*

(b) *"A bottle of wine and a bamboo basket of rice."* This means interrelation between the strong and the weak.

This Line is Yin in a Yin place, but it does not occupy a central position and fails to form a harmonious relationship with its correlate (Line 1, Yin). This signifies a rather weak and mediocre minister who occupies an insecure position. However, he is in harmony with the subject of Line 5 (the ruler, Yang) and offers the latter his humble services ("presents his simple offerings on the windowsill"). In humbling himself, he obtains the favor of the ruler and frees himself from the difficulties of his position ("Eventually no error").

The wine and basket are signified by the K'an trigrams, while the upper interior trigram, Ken (Lines 3, 4, 5), signifies the window.

Line 5, Yang:

(a) *The cavern is not filled with water, which only reaches a certain level. There will be no error.*

(b) *"The cavern is not filled with water." This means that as yet one's heart does not feel any exaltation.*

This Yang line occupies a position both central and correct. Such a line usually denotes an able and active ruler. However, here it is at the top of the upper interior trigram, Ken (Lines 3, 4, 5), which signifies a mountain or obstruction, indicating that the water or peril has stopped rising. In fact, the line itself looks like the flat surface of a lake or river. Further, its central position denotes moderation or a middle course. All this indicates that there is no danger of the river overflowing its banks and causing a flood. The subject of the line will be safe.

Line 6, Yin:

(a) *One is bound with coarse cords and placed in the thicket of thorns. He will not be pardoned for three years. There will be evil.*

(b) *Line 6, Yin, indicates one having lost his way. For three years evil will be his lot.*

This Yin line is at the extreme top of the K'an Hexagram (water and peril), indicating that there is no space left beyond for escape. Since its position is not central, there is a tendency to make radical moves. In addition, the line fails to form a harmonious relationship with its correlate (Line 3, Yin), indicating that there will be no help from the outside. This line's subject, therefore, is like a criminal at bay or one who has lost his soul. In ancient China, such a criminal could be pardoned and released in three years, but as the subject of Line 6 has nowhere to go (no other option), he will not receive such a pardon. Such a man's situation is indeed evil.

The upper interior trigram is Ken (hands); if Line 6 is transformed into Yang, the upper trigram becomes Sun (cords or ropes). Hence the punishment described in the text ("bound with coarse cords").

The LI Hexagram

(Symbol of Light, Adherence)

30th 離

THIS HEXAGRAM CONSISTS of two Li trigrams (a Yin line between two Yang lines), one above the other. The two Yang lines represent brightness, and the Yin lines represent hollowness. Together the three lines represent a lantern which is hollow inside and casts bright light outside, or an intelligent and enlightened person (Yin) who is humble at heart. Structurally, the Yin (female) lines hold together the normally antagonistic Yang (male) lines on each side of them. Hence the idea of adherence.

KING WEN'S JUDGMENT ON THE HEXAGRAM:

This hexagram indicates advantage in being firm and correct, as well as prosperity and success. There will be good fortune in rearing a cow.

The hexagram stands for fire or light, which signifies enlightenment, intelligence, or adherence, for light must adhere to some reflective medium to be perceived. But brightness is desirable and advantageous only when present in the right degree. Excessive light must be dimmed or softened, otherwise it becomes painful and destructive (Yang must be harmonized with Yin). This softness is symbolized by Yin, which possesses the docility of a cow.

CONFUCIUS' EXPLANATION OF KING WEN'S JUDGMENT:

Li, the name of the hexagram, means adherence. The sun and moon adhere to the sky. The numerous kinds of grain, grass, and trees adhere to the earth. Double brightness adheres to what is correct, thereby transforming and perfecting what is in the world.

The weak adhere to the central and correct position. Hence prosperity and success. Therefore, there is good fortune in rearing a cow.

Brightness or brilliance (indicated by the Yang lines of the hexagram) must adhere to the correct course (indicated in the central and correct position of the two Yin lines) before it can manifest its beneficial influence in the world.

The second paragraph points out that good fortune stems from the central and correct place of the two Yin lines. Each of the Yin lines lies between two Yang lines, indicating that something soft and gentle ("a cow") is restraining or harmonizing two strong forces. This harmony is an auspicious sign.

SYMBOLIC SIGNIFICANCE OF THE HEXAGRAM AS NOTED BY CONFUCIUS:

The idea behind Li is derived from double brightness. The great man is inspired thereby to continue brightening his virtues so as to spread enlightenment to the four quarters of the land.

Since the Li trigram denotes light or enlightenment, two such trigrams placed one above the other suggest that both high and low are bathed in light. This relationship inspires the superior man to polish and develop his own character ("brightening his virtues"), both for his own improvement and that of others.

DUKE OF CHOU'S EXPLANATION OF THE LINES (a) AND CONFUCIUS' COMMENT THEREON (b):

Line 1, Yang:

(a) *One takes wrong steps in walking but maintains a reverential attitude. There will be no error.*

(b) *The "reverential attitude accompanying wrong steps" serves to dispel error.*

This Yang line at the bottom of the hexagram represents feet or ground, hence the idea of walking. Here, Line 1 is Yang and occupies its correct place, indicating that its subject is strong and dynamic. But Line 1 does not occupy a central position, so its subject is likely to wander from the right path. Since it is the first line of the hexagram, its subject is just starting his journey and is unfamiliar with the route. He remains vigilant and cautious as he proceeds; consequently, though he makes wrong moves, as every beginner will, he acts to correct himself and thus avoid error.

Line 2, Yin:

(a) *One appears with a yellow radiance. There will be great good fortune.*

(b) *"The great good fortune of appearing with a yellow radiance" stems from obtaining the middle way.*

This line occupies a position both central and correct (Yin in a Yin place). Such a line in the lower trigram normally signifies the center of the earth, which in China is considered to be yellow. In addition, yellow is considered the correct color, because it is the royal color. Since Li signifies adherence or brightness, the subject of Line 2 is said to be wearing a yellow robe and makes a radiant appearance. In other words, he adheres to the correct path. This line's central position also indicates that he is a gentle, reasonable person who will follow a middle course. Great good fortune is such a man's lot.

Line 3, Yang:

(a) *One is on the decline like the setting sun. If he does not sing to the accompaniment of a clay instrument, he groans and sighs like an eighty-year-old man. This is an ill omen.*

(b) *"One is on the decline like the setting sun." How can such a condition last long?"*

This line occupies a position that is correct (Yang in a Yang place) but does not form a harmonious relationship with its correlate (Line 6, Yang). Further, its place at the top of the lower Li trigram (the sun), signifies a setting sun. Its subject, therefore, is a man whose life is on the decline and who must depend on his own judgment because he receives no outside help. He is liable to deviate from the correct path, either from lamenting his situation ("groans and sighs") or reacting foolishly to it (singing with a clay instrument). If he continues long in this manner, disaster will surely result.

Line 4, Yang:

(a) *Something comes all of a sudden. It flames up, dies down, and is discarded.*

(b) *"Something comes all of a sudden." This means that the thing can nowhere find any tolerance.*

This strong (Yang) line occupies a position neither central nor correct (Yang in a Yin place) and fails to form a harmonious relationship with its correlate (Line 1, Yang). Line 4 denotes a strong-willed person who does not follow a middle course and is prone to act rashly and go to extremes. Line 4 usually denotes a minister serving the ruler (Line 5). However, in this case the ruler is weak (Yin); his strong minister is tempted to take radical action on his own (something "flames up"), thereby causing a crisis for the kingdom and bringing ruin upon himself. Such rashness proves intolerable to the people and he finds no supporters ("is discarded").

The lower trigram, Li, stands for fire, and the lower interior trigram, Sun (Lines 2, 3, 4), stands for wind and trees. Fire fanned by wind sets the trees ablaze. Hence the image of something that "flames up, dies down, and is discarded."

Line 5, Yin:

(a) *One sheds tears in torrents and utters dismal groans. There will be good fortune.*

(b) *The "good fortune" indicated in Line 5, Yin, is due to adherence to kings and princes.*

Line 5 (the ruler) is Yin in a Yang place, and occupies a central position. Its subject is a kind but active ruler who sheds tears of compassion because he cannot do as much as he wishes to promote the welfare of his people. On the other hand, he is hemmed in on both sides by stronger men (Lines 4 and 6) who may oppose and block his plans. However, he will meet with good fortune, for he pursues the middle course.

The Li trigram also signifies eyes, while the upper interior trigram, Tui (Lines 3, 4, 5), signifies mouth. Hence the images of "tears" and "groans."

Line 6, Yang:

(a) A *king directs his armies in a punitive expedition. This exploit is praiseworty. He aims to crush the leaders of his foes, not to capture their shameful followers. There will be no error.*

(b) *"A king directs his armies in a punitive expedition." This is for the purpose of rectifying the conditions of the state.*

Being at the top of the hexagram, this Yang line denotes a king on his throne. As the hexagram is a symbol for light, the king is an enlightened one who, when engaged in an armed conflict, wishes to seize and punish only the leaders of his enemies, not capture and kill their soldiers. His major goal is to correct the abuses of the opposing state, not punish its citizens. Since his actions are good and just, he remains free from blame.

Li also represents armor and soldiers. Hence the images of armies and a punitive expedition.

The HSIEN Hexagram
(Symbol of Mutual Influence)

31st 咸

THE LOWER TRIGRAM, Ken, represents a young son; the upper, Tui, represents a young girl or daughter. Together they represent the union between the sexes and in a larger sense, human fellowship or mutual influence.

KING WEN'S JUDGMENT ON THE HEXAGRAM:

The hexagram indicates prosperity, success, and advantage in maintaining a firm and correct posture. There will be good fortune in marrying a young girl.

Beneficial associations ("marrying a young girl") are only possible when those invovled are careful to follow the path of rectitude and treat others fairly at all times.

CONFUCIUS' EXPLANATION OF KING WEN'S JUDGMENT:

Hsien, the name of the hexagram, means to influence or excite. The weak lies above, the strong below. The two forces respond to and influence each other, thereby forming a union. Pause is coupled with satisfaction. The male subordinates himself to the female. Hence prosperity, success, and advantage in maintaining a firm and correct posture, and good fortune in marrying a young girl.

Heaven and earth influence each other, thereby transforming and producing the ten thousand things. The sage influences the heart of the people, and consequently the world enjoys peace and harmony.

Observe the effects of what is influenced, and there can be seen the innate disposition of heaven and earth as well as of the ten thousand things.

The upper trigram, Tui, is Yin (a Yin trigram has more Yang lines), and the lower, Ken, is Yang (a Yang trigram has more Yin lines). Together they represent the harmony (mutual influence) between Yin and Yang. According to this symbolism, Tui signifies pleasure or satisfaction, and Ken signifies pause or cessation. A pause after a union ending in pleasure signifies success and happiness. Confucius considers the subordination of the strong to the weak (Ken below Tui) a contributing factor in man's success.

Finally, Confucius points out that all things mutually influence each other (both for good and ill), and that by observing how things are influenced and what influences them, we can learn much about them and about the ways of nature. A sage takes the idea of influence and applies it by attempting to influence for the better the people he meets.

SYMBOLIC SIGNIFICANCE OF THE HEXAGRAM AS NOTED BY CONFUCIUS:

The idea behind Hsien is derived from marsh (upper trigram) above the mountain (lower trigram). The superior man is inspired thereby to receive people or their views with a humble heart.

This suggests the idea of mutual benefit through mutual influence. The marsh is supported by the mountain, and the mountain receives water from the marsh to nourish its trees and plants. To the superior man this signifies that he is as dependent on those below as they are on him. Therefore, he meets them with true humility and wins their hearts, demonstrating mutual influence between high and low.

DUKE OF CHOU'S EXPLANATION OF THE LINES (a) AND CONFUCIUS' COMMENT THEREON (b):

Line 1, Yin:
(a) *One moves his big toes.*
(b) *"One moves his big toes." His mind is oriented outward.*

If the entire hexagram represents the human body, Line 1, at the bottom, represents the toes or feet. Motion of the toes indicates the desire to move forward. This line forms a harmonious relationship with and is attracted to its correlate, Line 4, and its subject is said to be moving in the direction of the subject of Line 4 ("outward").

Line 2, Yin:

(a) *One moves the calves of his legs. Ill omen. Staying in one's proper place will lead to good fortune.*

(b) *Despite the "ill omen, staying in one's proper place will lead to good fortune." This shows docile obedience dissipating injury.*

If Line 1 represents the feet, then Line 2 represents the calves of the legs, which do not move by themselves but derive their motion from the feet. Since the line is Yin, the calves are also weak, and any attempt they make to move forward will not be propitious. If they remain where they are ("staying in one's proper place") and do not attempt to advance on their own, they will meet with good fortune.

Line 3, Yang:

(a) *One moves his thighs and clutches at those following him. Advancement will cause regret.*

(b) *"One moves his thighs." This shows that one nevertheless does not want to stay in the same place. As he aims to follow other people, what he holds fast is rather low.*

Line 3 represents the thighs, which like the calves, cannot move by themselves but depend on the feet and calves for their motion. Here, however, the line is Yang, indicating a strong subject who is inclined to move instead of remaining in the same place. He is attracted to his correlate (Line 6), with whom he forms a harmonious relationship. However, Line 3 is at the top of the lower Ken trigram (obstruction) and its upward course is blocked by two strong Yang lines above. This line's subject cannot advance easily but must depend on his followers (Lines 1 and 2), with whom he is in harmony. But to rise by the influence of others is rather shameful and bound to lead to regret. The fact that he is a follower, rather than a leader, indicates that he has no great ideals ("what he holds fast is rather low").

Line 4, Yang:

(a) *There will be good fortune in being firm and correct. Repentance will disappear. One vacillates about whether to advance or retreat, but his associates will go along with his ideas.*

(b) *"There will be good fortune in being firm and correct, and repentance will disappear." This means that as yet no injurious interactions have been felt. "Vacillation about whether to advance or retreat," means that one has not yet become enlightened and great.*

This Yang line occupies a position neither central nor correct (Yang in a Yin place). Being above the lower trigram and at the base of the upper one, it also signifies a transitional stage. Its subject, therefore, is a weak person who is erratic in his movements. He can move forward to serve the ruler (Line 5) or retreat to join his friend (Line 3), but he is wavering and cannot make up his mind. During a difficult period of transition, such a man should endeavor to remain firmly on a correct course and not let doubts sway him. That he has doubts, according to Confucius, is because he has not yet achieved wisdom and fails to grasp the whole situation.

Line 5, Yang:

(a) *One moves the flesh above the heart and in the upper part of the spine. No cause for regret.*

(b) *"One moves the flesh above the heart and in the upper part of the spine." This means one's mind is oriented toward the far end.*

This line represents the flesh above the heart. Its subject, being Yang, wants to move and influence people. As he cannot easily move backward, being blocked by two strong fellows (Yang lines), he sets his sights instead on the Yin line at the top (far end) of the hexagram (Line 6), with whom he naturally forms a harmonious relationship. In this there is no cause for blame.

Line 6, Yin:

(a) *One moves the jaws and tongue.*

(b) *"One moves the jaws and tongue." He is blabbing about nonsense.*

Being at the top of the trigram Tui (mouth), this line represents the lips. Hence the image of "moving jaws and tongue," which suggests idle talk or empty gossip.

The HENG Hexagram
(Symbol of Lasting, Steadiness)

32nd 恆

THIS HEXAGRAM REPRESENTS steady or long-lasting good fortune. The upper trigram, Chen (with its first Yang line), signifies the eldest son, and the lower trigram, Sun (with its first Yin line) signifies the eldest daughter. Together the two trigrams signify an adult couple who have attained a stable, happy relationship. The fact that three lines of the lower trigram form harmonious relationships with their correlates in the upper trigram also suggests that the situation is long-lasting and beneficial. This idea is reinforced by the fact that the upper trigram, Chen, represents motion or activity, signifying one working outside the home, and the lower trigram, Sun, represents obedience and docility, signifying one working inside the home. Together they denote a stable situation in which the husband works outside to secure support for the family while the wife attends to the household duties.

KING WEN'S JUDGMENT ON THE HEXAGRAM:

The hexagram indicates prosperity and success, absence of regret, and advantage in being firm and correct. Advantageous to go ahead with one's plans.

Things that are lasting and steady come from remaining firmly on the correct path. To advance in such a manner can only bring success.

CONFUCIUS' EXPLANATION OF KING WEN'S JUDGMENT:

Heng, the name of the hexagram, means steadiness or lasting. The strong are in the upper place; the weak are in the lower. Thunder and wind are getting along well together. Passive docility is coupled with dynamic motion. All the strong and the weak enjoy favorable response or harmonious correlation. This is the meaning of the hexagram.

"The hexagram indicates prosperity and success, absence of regret and advantage in being firm and correct." This is because the way has been in operation for a long time. The way of heaven and earth is steady and eternal and does not stop.

"Advantageous to go ahead with one's plans." This means that the termination of one cycle will lead to the beginning of another.

The sun and moon, having obtained heaven, can shine perpetually. The four seasons, through change and transformation, can perpetuate their act of achievement. The sages, having been long in following the way, can complete the transformations in the world. Observe what has been long-lasting and there can be seen the innate disposition of heaven and earth, as well as of the ten thousand things.

Strength above (Chen) is coupled with docility below (Sun), and thunder (Chen) interplays with wind (Sun). The general harmony here between motion and docility, plus that between the individual lines of the trigram, indicates good fortune.

Pursuing the path of virtue (firm correctness) involves changes and progress, never stagnation. Where the inferior man sees only an ending, the superior man sees only a moment between the completion of one cycle and the beginning of the next, just as the end of one season is but the beginning of the next. The superior man, through long study of the way of nature, knows how to complete social and psychological transformations. By observing those social patterns (transformations) that last, the track of the superior man can be discerned.

SYMBOLIC SIGNIFICANCE OF THE HEXAGRAM AS NOTED BY CONFUCIUS:

The idea behind Heng is derived from thunder (upper trigram) and wind (lower trigram). The superior man is inspired thereby to stand firm and not change his way of life.

This hexagram represents the interplay of thunder and wind. Wind carries the sound of thunder wherever it blows, while thunder tends to heighten the force of the wind. Observing this, the superior man learns to stand firm in the face of life's storms and not let them affect or alter his inner nature.

DUKE OF CHOU'S EXPLANATION OF THE LINES (a) AND CONFUCIUS' COMMENT THEREON (b):

Line 1, Yin:

(a) *One very eager to attain steadiness. Persistence will lead to evil. Nothing advantageous in any way.*

(b) *The evil of being "very eager to attain steadiness" lies in seeking the profound at the very beginning.*

The first line indicates a beginner or a beginning step. Here, it is Yin and attracted to its correlate (Line 4, Yang), with whom it forms a harmonious relationship. However, its course is obstructed by two strong lines. Its subject is a rather rash person, for who but the reckless would attempt, at the very outset, to form a steady relationship with a distant partner? Such rashness, if persisted in, can only lead to misfortune.

Line 2, Yang:

(a) *Repentance will disappear.*

(b) *"Disappearance of repentance" indicated in Line 2, Yang, is because of ability to stay long in the middle course.*

This Yang line occupies a position that is central but incorrect (Yang in a Yin place). Its subject is a strong, able person with some authority to act, but his abilities and talents are unsuitable for the situation into which he has been placed. However, since he follows a moderate course and avoids radical actions, he makes no great mistakes and creates no cause for regret.

Line 3, Yang:

(a) *One is unsteady in his virtue. This may invite insult from some people. Persistence will lead to regret.*

(b) *"One is unsteady in his virtue." Nowhere will he find tolerance.*

This Yang line occupies a position correct (Yang in a Yang place) but not central, suggesting a subject with a strong, dynamic character who finds himself in an unfavorable position from which to act. Therefore, he is apt to be indecisive and stray from the middle course ("unsteady in his virtue"). If he persists in this fashion, he is bound to cause ridicule wherever he goes.

Line 4, Yang:

(a) *A field without game.*

(b) *One has long been in a wrong place. How can he get any game?*

This is the last of three consecutive Yang lines, indicating exceptional strength and lying within the upper trigram, Chen (strong motion). Its subject is a very strong, dynamic person who is eager to act and advance. However, this line occupies a position neither central nor correct (Yang in a Yin place) and this, together with its position at the bottom of the upper trigram, represents a transitional stage of uncertainty. To advance in such a situation would be as futile as to hunt in a field without game.

Line 5, Yin:

(a) *Steadiness in being virtuous and chaste. Good fortune in the case of a woman. Evil in man.*

(b) *A woman will meet with good fortune in being chaste. This means she will follow only one husband in life. A man's duty is to establish what is righteous. For him to follow the example of a woman will be evil.*

This is a Yin line occupying a position central but incorrect (Yin in a Yang place) and denoting a gentle person who follows a middle course. The subject of Line 5, if female, will be an ideal woman, for in ancient China a woman had to be chaste and marry only one husband. (The upper trigram, Chen, signifies an eldest son, and the lower trigram, Sun, signifies an eldest daughter. Hence the image of marriage.) If the subject is male, however, he will meet with difficulty, for a man should not be meek and chaste like a woman. He must be strong and decisive in order to establish the right life for himself and those who rely upon him.

Line 6, Yin:

(a) *One makes strong efforts to be steady. Evil omen.*

(b) *"To make strong efforts to be steady" while in a high place will fall far short of success.*

This is a Yin line at the extreme top of the hexagram, indicating that steadiness is at an end. Line 6 is also the top line of the trigram Chen (strong motion), which means that whatever steadiness there is has been greatly shaken. In such a precarious position, it would be futile to make any effort to maintain the stability of one's position. Such an effort will only lead to failure ("fall far short of success").

The TUN Hexagram

(Symbol of Retreat)

33rd 遯

ANY MOVEMENT INDICATED by a hexagram starts from the bottom (Line 1). Here, there are two Yin lines at the bottom, suggesting that the Yin (dark) forces are moving forward and growing in strength, while the Yang (bright) forces are withdrawing. Hence the idea of retreat (regression of the good and bright). In the natural sphere, retreat means the waning of the Yang influence after the summer solstice, as indicated by the gradual shortening of the days. In the human realm, it usually means the retreat of worthy, honorable people before the growing power of small, mean people or corrupt politicians.

KING WEN'S JUDGMENT ON THE HEXAGRAM:

The hexagram indicates prosperity and success. Minor advantage may accrue from being firm and correct.

The Judgment shows that retreat from a corrupt government or difficult situation is the wisest course and may even lead to advantage in remedying the situation later on.

CONFUCIUS' EXPLANATION OF KING WEN'S JUDGMENT:

"The hexagram indicates prosperity and success." This means that retreat is conducive to prosperity and success. The strong is in the proper place and receives favorable response. Action proceeds in accord with the time.

"Minor advantage may accrue from being firm and correct." The reason is that sinister forces are gradually growing.

Great indeed is the timely significance of retreat denoted by the hexagram.

There are times when to advance would be a disaster, and only in withdrawal lies any hope of later success. Line 5 is Yang (strong) and occupies a central as well as correct position. It also forms a harmonious relationship with its correlate, or partner (Line 2). The subject of Line 5, therefore, is a wise and great man in an important position who is free to advance or retreat as the situation demands. He may accomplish something by standing firm in the face of the rising dark forces (the two Yin lines), but considers it wiser to keep out of their way for the time being ("retreat is conducive to prosperity"). Wise are they who understand the significance of retreat.

SYMBOLIC SIGNIFICANCE OF THE HEXAGRAM AS NOTED BY CONFUCIUS:

The idea behind T'un is derived from mountain (lower trigram) below the sky (upper trigram). The superior man is inspired thereby to keep far away from the inferior, mean people and to assume a solemn but not resentful attitude.

"Mountain below the sky" suggests a mountain rising to a great height from the earth, as if to rival the sky in greatness. But the sky always eludes the mountain and however high it towers, rises above it. In the same manner, the superior man always remains aloof in the presence of those of lesser character and assumes a correct and formal manner with them which is wholly free of disapprobation or resentment.

DUKE OF CHOU'S EXPLANATION OF THE LINES (a) AND CONFUCIUS' COMMENT THEREON (b):

Line 1, Yin:
(a) *A tail in retreat. Situation perilous. Do not make any forward move in any direction.*

(b) *"Perilous situation of a tail in retreat." If no forward move is made, what calamity can there be?*

Line 1 occupies a position neither central nor correct (Yin in a Yang place). It is also a Yin line at the bottom of the lower Ken trigram (mountain or stoppage). Its subject, therefore, is a weak person in an unsuitable position, beset by unfavorable circumstances. Such a man should refrain from making any forward move; in fact, he should beat a retreat from the situation as soon as possible, for he does not possess the resources to cope with it and may be overwhelmed by it ("a tail in retreat").

Line 2, Yin:

(a) *One holds so fast to his determination that it looks like being bound by an unbreakable thong made from the hide of a yellow ox.*

(b) *"One holds so fast to his determination that it looks like being held by a yellow ox." This means that he is adamant in his determination.*

This line is Yin in a Yin place and occupies a central position. It signifies a gentle, sensible person who follows a middle course and whose determination to retreat from a distasteful situation is unshakable.

Line 2, being Yin, represents the K'un trigram, which signifies a cow or ox. The lower trigram, Ken, signifies hand. The color of earth represented by K'un is yellow. All this gives rise to the concept of being "bound by a thong made from the hide of a yellow ox." Hence great determination.

Line 3, Yang:

(a) *One retires from a post to which he seems to be tied. He will find himself in affliction and in peril. Good fortune will stem from caring for one's servants and concubines.*

(b) *"The peril of retiring from a post to which one seems to be tied" means there will be affliction and weariness. "Good fortune will stem from caring for one's servants and concubines." This means one should not try to accomplish great tasks.*

This line, at the top of the Ken trigram (obstruction or stoppage), forms an antagonistic relationship with its correlate (Line 6). Its subject is beset by enemies and faces an immovable obstruction. In such a situation, to advance, or even maintain one's position, is impossible. He should retire to his own estates and devote his energies to their improvement ("caring for one's servants and concubines"). However, this is a Yang line in a Yang place; its subject is strong and dynamic, and so is reluctant to leave his post, though to remain can only lead to disaster.

Line 4, Yang:

(a) *Retirement with gladness. Auspicious for the superior man, otherwise for the petty, mean man.*

(b) *The superior man "retires with gladness"; the petty, mean man is incapable of so doing.*

This line is not only Yang but belongs to the upper Ch'ien (Yang) trigram; it also forms a harmonious relationship with its correlate (Line 1). Its subject is a man of strong decision and determination who enjoys the support of others. However, the subject of Line 4 may encounter difficulty with the Yang ruler (Line 5). But such is his character that if he must, he can retire from the contest without resentment. This means good fortune. To those of petty character, on the other hand, retirement is never an opportunity, only a cause for bitterness, resentment, and reluctance.

Line 5, Yang:

(a) *Graceful retirement. Firm correctness will lead to good fortune.*

(b) *"Graceful retirement. Firm correctness will lead to good fortune." This is because one has correct aspirations.*

This Yang line occupies a position not only correct, but also central in the upper Ch'ien trigram (strength, intelligence). It also forms a harmonious relationship with its correlate (Line 2, Yin), which occupies a similar position in the lower trigram. Its subject is an able, active, enlightened leader who commands wide and efficient support. He can retire gracefully and with dignity, never deviating from the middle path or forsaking his noble aspirations. Such a man will surely meet with good fortune.

Line 6, Yang:

(a) *One retires in affluence. There is nothing that will not be advantageous.*

(b) *"One retires in affluence. There is nothing that will not be advantageous." This is because there is no room for doubt.*

This Yang line caps the upper Ch'ien trigram and perches on the extreme top of the entire hexagram. It is also the last of the four consecutive Yang lines. All this signifies a very strong, successful man who has reached the end of his career, has many achievements to his credit, and has amassed great wealth. Under these circumstances, there is no reluctance on his part to retire ("no room for doubt"). Such an action always means good fortune.

The TA CHUANG Hexagram
(Symbol of Great Strength)

34th 大壯

THE FOUR YANG LINES in the lower portion of this hexagram indicate that the strong, bright forces are advancing en masse, displaying tremendous strength and power. Further, the upper trigram is Chen (thunder) and the lower is Ch'ien (the sky). Together they represent thunder booming in the sky, which always symbolizes great strength and power.

KING WEN'S JUDGMENT ON THE HEXAGRAM:

The hexagram indicates advantage in being firm and correct.
Great strength and power alone are not enough, for by themselves they can be misused. Only one who has the will to restrain them and keep them to the course of right can employ them to advantage.

CONFUCIUS' EXPLANATION OF KING WEN'S JUDGMENT:

The hexagram shows that greatness means strength. Motion is coupled with vigor and therefore strong.
"The hexagram indicates advantage in being firm and correct." Greatness means uprightness. Uprightness and greatness will reveal the disposition of heaven and earth.
One form of greatness is moral strength ("Greatness means uprightness"), which, when set in operation, can transform the world. To follow the upright path is always advantageous. One

with the character to do so will ultimately find himself in harmony with heaven and earth.

SYMBOLIC SIGNIFICANCE OF THE HEXAGRAM AS NOTED BY CONFUCIUS:

The idea behind Ta Chuang is derived from thunder high in the sky. The superior man is inspired thereby not to take any step which is contrary to propriety.

Thunder breaking forth from the earth and rolling in the sky suggests tremendous force and power or greatness. This inspires the superior men to seek moral greatness by conquering their lower nature and following the right path. As Confucius once said: "Conquer yourself and return to propriety." Such self-conquest requires considerable mental strength and moral power.

DUKE OF CHOU'S EXPLANATION OF THE LINES (a) AND CONFUCIUS' COMMENT THEREON (b):

Line 1, Yang:

(a) *Strength is in the toes. Any venture will, of a truth, result in evil.*

(b) *"Strength is in the toes." This will surely end in exhaustion.*

The bottom line of a hexagram represents the foot or toes. Here, Line 1 is Yang in a Yang place, suggesting strong toes, and strong toes suggest and invite movement. Its subject is a strong, active person who wants to move ahead and begins his actions by moving his toes. However, he is in an unfavorable position, for he does not occupy a central position and fails to form a harmonious relationship with his correlate (Line 4, Yang). In such a situation, any attempt on his part to advance will lead only to failure and misfortune.

Line 2, Yang:

(a) *Good fortune will accrue from firm correctness.*

(b) *Line 2, Yang, indicates that "good fortune will accrue from firm correctness." The reason is that it occupies a central position.*

This Yang line occupies a central position and forms a harmonious relationship with its correlate (Line 5). Its subject is not only strong but also sensible and disposed to follow a middle course. If he remains firm and correct, he will meet with good fortune.

Line 3, Yang:

(a) *The small, mean man uses strong force. The superior man does otherwise. Persistence will lead to evil. A ram butts against a fence and its horns get entangled.*

(b) *"The small, mean man uses strong force." The superior man does not do so.*

Line 3, at the top of the lower trigram, usually signifies a state of transition. Here, it is Yang and does not occupy a central position, but does form a harmonious relationship with its correlate (Line 6, Yin). All this indicates strength plus outside support. If its subject is a superior man, he will not use the strong force inherent in his position. If its subject is a small, mean man, he will use the strong force and find himself in danger, like a ram butting a wooden fence and getting its horns entangled.

The lower trigram is Ch'ien (a superior man), but if Line 3 is transformed into a Yin line, the lower trigram will become Tui, (a "small, mean man"). Hence the images of "superior man" and "mean man" in the Text. Tui also signifies sheep, and as the line is Yang, this suggests a ram.

Line 4, Yang:

(a) *Good fortune will accrue from firm correctness, and repentance will disappear. The fence breaks apart and there is no entanglement anymore. The force involved is like that exerted by the axle of a large wagon.*

(b) *"The fence breaks apart and there is no entanglement anymore." This shows it is important to go ahead.*

This Yang line is at the base of the upper trigram, Chen (strong motion), and also lies below two Yin lines. Its subject has immense strength and power: there is nothing to obstruct his upward course. In such a situation, any forward move will be propitious. However, its position in the hexagram also represents a state of transition, so its subject should not attempt to advance, but should remain firmly on his present course. This is an unfavorable situation in which to advance.

Line 5, Yin:

(a) "*A sheep strays from the herd onto a path in the rice field. No occasion for repentance.*

(b) "*A sheep strays from the herd onto a path in the rice field.*" *This shows its place is not suitable to it.*

This is a Yin line incorrectly placed, and its subject, who is easily led, is in an uncomfortable position and apt to go astray ("a sheep strays from the herd"). However, Line 5 occupies a central position, indicating that its subject favors a middle course and will return to it without regret when he realizes his error.

Line 6, Yin:

(a) *A ram butts against a fence, unable to back out and unable to act as it wishes. Nothing will be advantageous in any way. Fortitude may lead to good fortune.*

(b) "*Unable to back out and unable to act as it wishes.*" *This is because it does not exercise precaution.* "*Fortitude may lead to good fortune.*" *This means that the error will not last long.*

Being at the top of the trigram Chen (motion), Line 6 signifies a person who has a strong urge to move ahead. However, it is risky and impossible for him to do so ("ram butts against a fence") because, as indicated by the position of the line, he already stands at the extreme end and any forward move would mean a move into the unknown. But, Line 6 forms a harmonious relationship with its correlate (Line 3), and so he has a helpful partner to warn and restrain him. If the subject of Line 6 listens to good advice and firmly follows the correct path, he will escape peril and meet with good fortune.

The TSIN Hexagram
(Symbol of Advancement)

35th  晉

THE LOWER TRIGRAM is K'un (earth), and the upper is Li (sun). Together they suggest the sun rising over the earth. Hence the idea of advancement or progress.

KING WEN'S JUDGMENT ON THE HEXAGRAM:

The hexagram indicates a person who, because he has promoted the welfare of the people, is made a prince by the king, given numerous horses, and received in audience three times in one day.

The subject of this hexagram is an able minister on whom great honors are heaped by his ruler. The lower trigram is K'un (kingdom) and the upper trigram is Li (light). Together, they signify light or glory spreading throughout the kingdom.

CONFUCIUS' EXPLANATION OF KING WEN'S JUDGMENT:

Tsin, name of the hexagram, means advancement or progress.
Light appears on the earth. The meek adheres to the great light. The weak moves upward from below. Hence the "person who, because he has promoted the welfare of the people, is made a prince by the king, given numerous horses, and received in audience three times in one day."

The three Yin lines (able ministers) have been moving gradually upward and finally reach the center of the hexagram (Line 5, the ruler or the royal court). This suggests that they are rewarded by the king for their good works.

SYMBOLIC SIGNIFICANCE OF THE HEXAGRAM AS NOTED BY CONFUCIUS:

The idea behind Tsin is derived from light appearing over the earth. The superior man is inspired thereby to brighten his illustrious virtues.

The upper trigram, Li (sun or light), and the lower trigram, K'un (the earth), suggest the sun rising over the earth and shining in all its glory. The superior man is inspired to develop his own character, so that its light might help enlighten both himself and his fellow men.

DUKE OF CHOU'S EXPLANATION OF THE LINES (a) AND CONFUCIUS' COMMENT THEREON (b):

Line 1, Yin:

(a) *One tries to advance but is frustrated. A firm and correct posture will lead to good fortune. One's sincerity is not yet manifest. Liberality will dispel error.*

(b) *"One tries to advance but is frustrated." This is because he follows the correct path alone. "Liberality will dispel error." This means that he is not yet commissioned to any task.*

This Yin line, placed at the bottom of the hexagram, represents a young man who seeks advancement but is not yet trusted by the people. So he is careful to perform his tasks diligently and is eager to follow the correct path, even if he must do so alone. However, since Line 1 occupies a position neither central nor correct (Yin in a Yang place), its subject has difficulty remaining on the correct course and his advancement is frustrated. On the other hand, Line 1 has a harmonious relationship with its correlate (Line 4, Yang), so if its subject persists firmly in this course and is just in all his dealings with others, he may well receive the help and support he needs to advance and may find himself entrusted with some great task.

Line 2, Yin:

(a) *One tries to advance but manifests sorrow. Firm correctness will lead to good fortune. He will receive bountiful favors from his grandmother.*

(b) *"He will receive bountiful favors." This is because he occupies a correct and central position.*

This line fails to form a harmonious relationship with its correlate (Line 5, the ruler). The subject of Line 2 has cause to be unhappy, for he wants to advance, but the situation is not favorable. However, since he occupies a position both central and correct (Yin in a Yin place), if he remains firmly in a middle course, he will be rewarded ("receive bountiful favors") by his grandmother (Line 5, the ruler). (Since Yin represents the female, Line 3 represents the mother and Line 5 the grandmother.)

Line 3, Yin:

(a) *One enjoys confidence on the part of the people. Repentance will disappear.*

(b) *"People show confidence in him," because he aims high in his actions.*

This Yin line resides at the top of the trigram K'un (the people) and represents a leader with lofty aims who is well supported by the people (the two Yin lines below) because they all want to move upward. Even if they fail to achieve all their goals, they are reasonable people (Yin) and will experience no regret.

Line 4, Yang:

(a) *One moves forward like a big mouse. Persistence will result in peril.*

(b) *"A big mouse. Persistence will result in peril." This is because his position is improper and does not suit him.*

Line 4 occupies a position neither central nor correct (Yang in a Yin place). This situation does not suit his ability or skills and is unsuited to undertaking any major action. The subject of Line 4, therefore, is both unhappy and uncomfortable with his lot. Since Line 4 is at the top of the lower interior trigram, Ken (Lines 2, 3, 4), which signifies stoppage or cessation, its subject should cease all attempts at forward movement. The top Yang line of the

Ken trigram denotes a big mouse or rat. So its subject is said to be as timid as "a big mouse" about undertaking any forward move. If he persists in this behavior, he will encounter evil.

Line 5, Yin:

(a) *Repentance has disappeared. There should be no concern about loss or gain. It is propitious to go ahead with one's plans. There is nothing that will not be advantageous.*

(b) *"There should be no concern about loss or gain." This means that advancement will end in great rejoicing.*

This Yin line lies in a central position, signifying a wise, gentle ruler who is free from wild ambition and follows a middle course. As he is not disturbed or restrained by considerations of gain or loss, his plans can be carried out to advantage. He is free to do what he feels is right, which leads to great success and rejoicing.

Line 6, Yang:

(a) *One advances with horns. These are only used to chastise the townspeople. Alertness to peril will lead to good fortune and no blame. Persistence in the usual course will cause regret.*

(b) *"They are only used to chastise the townspeople." This shows that the light of his guiding principle has not yet become manifest.*

This is a Yang line at the extreme top of the hexagram, signifying a strong leader who wishes to advance through the use of his might, like a bull "advancing with its horns." However, his effort is directed not against an outside enemy, but against the intransigent elements among his own people, who need to be chastised because they are acting in an unenlightened and harmful manner. The situation is perilous but may end well if properly handled.

The MING YI Hexagram
(Symbol of Darkened Light)

36th  明夷

THE LOWER TRIGRAM, Li, signifies light, and the upper trigram, K'un, signifies the earth. Together they signify light hidden beneath the earth. Hence the idea of darkened light.

KING WEN'S JUDGMENT ON THE HEXAGRAM:

The hexagram indicates that advantage favors fortitude and firm correctness.

One with the strength of character to remain firmly on the right path, no matter how dark the situation, creates his own advantage.

CONFUCIUS' EXPLANATION OF KING WEN'S JUDGMENT:

Light has gone inside the earth. This is the meaning of Ming Yi, name of the hexagram.

To be inwardly cultured and enlightened while outwardly meek and submissive is the way to face a great calamity. King Wen once practiced it.

"Advantage favors fortitude and firm correctness." This means dimming one's inward light. Ability to rectify one's aim remains while afflicted with inward distress. Count Chi once practiced it.

When King Wen was imprisoned by the last emperor of the Shang dynasty, he remained obedient. Although he did not let this cause him to deviate from the right path, he submitted to the emperor's command, keeping his own opinions and thoughts to himself ("dimming one's inward light").

272

Count Chi or, as the Chinese call him, Chi Tzu, was an uncle of the last emperor of the Shang dynasty. Count Chi feigned madness in order to escape persecution by his nephew, the emperor. In Confucius' opinion, he preserved his inner rectitude by concealing his intelligence.

SYMBOLIC SIGNIFICANCE OF THE HEXAGRAM AS NOTED BY CONFUCIUS:

The idea behind Ming Yi is derived from light having gone inside the earth. The superior man is inspired thereby to approach the people with his inward light or intelligence concealed in gloom.

Light beneath the earth clearly indicates dimness or darkness. In the realm of human life, it signifies a situation in which the superior men are out of power, while those of petty, mean character are in the ascendant. Under the circumstances, the superior men consider it prudent to conceal their true thoughts and character, mingling humbly with others and waiting for a more favorable time to arrive (according to the Law of Cyclic Reversion).

DUKE OF CHOU'S EXPLANATION OF THE LINES (a) AND CONFUCIUS' COMMENT THEREON (b):

Line 1, Yang:

(a) *As the light dims, one acts like a flying bird suddenly drooping its wings. The superior man is determined to depart for another place. He may go without food for three days in a row. He has some place to go, but people there will give him some displeasing words.*

(b) *"The superior man is determined to depart for another place." It accords with reason that he is not concerned about food.*

This is a Yang line in a Yang place, lying at the bottom of the hexagram, far below the earth (the upper trigram). It signifies a strong, able man who finds himself in unfavorable circumstances ("the light dims"). Therefore, he stops attempting to advance ("a flying bird suddenly drooping its wings"). He is determined to leave the dimness for the light and join his partner (Line 4), with whom he forms a harmonious relationship. His determination is such that he is willing to go without food for three days and risk unfavorable criticism.

The Li trigram also signifies a pheasant. Hence the image of a flying bird.

Line 2, Yin:

(a) *As the light dims, one is wounded in the left thigh. He meets with good fortune, for he finds succor from a strong horse.*

(b) *The "good fortune" indicated in Line 2, Yin, lies in docile obedience to rule.*

If the hexagram is viewed as a symbol for the human body, Line 2 represents the thigh. Its subject has been wounded in the thigh by the dark forces but, since he occupies a position both correct (Yin in a Yin place) and central, he is a sensible man who obeys the dictates of reason. As it is difficult to walk with a wounded thigh, he finds a strong ally ("a strong horse") to help support him. This is good fortune indeed.

If Line 2 is transformed into a Yang line, the lower trigram becomes Ch'ien, which signifies a good (strong) horse.

Line 3, Yang:

(a) *As the light dims, one is taking arms against a southern region and captures its principal leader. He should not attempt any quick remedy of the situation.*

(b) *The objective of "taking arms against a southern region" is to accomplish a great task.*

This line is Yang in a Yang place and forms a harmonious relationship with its correlate (Line 6). Line 3 is also surrounded by weak (Yin) lines, denoting a man who is not only strong and active but who also occupies a favorable position from which to advance. He is therefore well placed to successfully undertake great tasks ("taking arms against a southern region"). However, he should not expect quick results, for the dark forces are still numerous, as indicated by the three Yin lines in the upper trigram. On the other hand, if he is willing to exercise patience, he is sure to achieve success.

According to the *Shuo Kua*, the Li trigram also signifies "south" and "armor." Hence the image of taking arms against the south.

Line 4, Yin:

(a) *One goes, as it were, into the left side of the belly and finds the heart of the darkened light. He then makes his exit through the door of the courtyard.*

(b) *"One goes into the left side of the belly." This means that one satisfies the notion in mind.*

This line is Yin in a Yin place and forms a harmonious relationship with its correlate (Line 1). Its subject is a gentle, subtle person faced by dark forces (the Yin lines above). He does not intend to battle these forces, but rather wishes to discover their secret intent ("finds the heart"). Forewarned by this knowledge, he departs openly but quietly ("through the door of the courtyard").

Line 4 is at the base of the upper trigram, K'un, which also signifies "belly" and "dark region." Its subject is supposed to go into the dark region symbolized by the belly.

Line 5, Yin:

(a) *The darkened light in the case of Count Chi. Advantageous to be firm and correct.*

(b) *"The firm correctness of Count Chi" shows that light cannot be put off.*

Line 5 is Yin in a Yang place and fails to form a harmonious relationship with its correlate (Line 2). It does, however, occupy an important central position, indicating its subject to be a virtuous ruler. Thus, even when he finds himself in adverse circumstances, he maintains his inner rectitude ("light cannot be put off") and faithfully follows a middle course.

Count Chi was a great statesman who was banished by his nephew, the emperor. However, he preserved his integrity and inner rectitude even in the face of this adversity.

Line 6, Yin:

(a) *The light is not bright, but dim. One first ascends to the sky, then falls on the earth.*

(b) *"One first ascends to the sky." His intention is to spread light throughout the four quarters of the state. "One then falls on the earth." This is because he fails to follow the proper rules.*

This line is at the extreme end of the hexagram and so is farthest from the light (the lower Li trigram). On the other hand, it is the top line of the upper trigram, K'un (the earth), symbolizing a ruler who is on top of the world. In such a lofty position, he may wish to shed light on those below and dispel the gloom. However, in attempting to do so, he violates the rules of government. As he is already at the top and cannot go any higher, he slips and plunges from the heights into the darkness which his misrule has brought about.

The CHIA REN Hexagram
(Symbol of Family)

37th  家人

THE UPPER INTERIOR TRIGRAM, Li (Lines 3, 4, 5), represents the second daughter, and the lower interior trigram, K'an (Lines 2, 3, 4), represents the second son. Together they signify a husband and wife in the home or their children. Further, the top Yang line resembles a roof, and the bottom Yang line resembles the floor, suggesting a house or home. Hence the idea of a family.

KING WEN'S JUDGMENT ON THE HEXAGRAM:

The hexagram indicates advantage for a woman who is firm and correct.

The Judgment stresses the advantage that remaining firmly on the correct course possesses for one of a Yin nature or in a Yin position (symbolically a woman).

CONFUCIUS' EXPLANATION OF KING WEN'S JUDGMENT:

The hexagram shows that woman has her correct place in the interior and man has his correct place in the exterior. The correct positions of man and woman correspond to the great principle of righteousness shown by heaven and earth.

Family, denoted by the hexagram, has in it a strict ruler. This refers to the parents.

Let the father be what a father ought to be, and the son a son, the elder brother an elder brother, the younger brother a younger brother, the husband a husband, and the wife a wife. Let them be as they respectively ought to be, and the family will be on the correct course. When families are set on the correct course, then the world will rest on a firm foundation.

Line 2 is Yin (female) and occupies a Yin place; its correlate (Line 5) is Yang (male) and occupies a Yang place. The two lines also form a harmonious relationship, representing a husband and wife. Further, Line 2, Yin, is in the lower trigram (the earth) and Line 5, Yang, is in the upper trigram (heaven). Consequently, husband and wife are said to be in correspondence with the principles of heaven and earth.

Parents must be strict in ruling the family and guide it along the correct path, and each member of a family should know his or her own status and diligently fulfill the duties proper to it. Confucius implies that a well-regulated family produces good citizens, and good citizens produce a good society; consequently the world will enjoy peace ("will rest on a firm foundation").

SYMBOLIC SIGNIFICANCE OF THE HEXAGRAM AS NOTED BY CONFUCIUS:

The idea behind Chia Ren is derived from wind (upper trigram) issuing from fire (lower trigram). The superior man is inspired thereby to see to it that his speech has a solid basis and his conduct is steady and consistent.

A steady, constant wind issues from a fire that has a "solid basis" of fuel. Seeing this, the superior man realizes that if he desires to produce a stable and well-integrated family (or group), his own words and deeds must have a sound moral basis.

DUKE OF CHOU'S EXPLANATION OF THE LINES (a) AND CONFUCIUS' COMMENT THEREON (b):

Line 1, Yang:

(a) *One takes precautions when having a family. There will be no occasion for repentance.*

(b) *"One takes precautions when having a family." This shows that his aspiration has not yet changed.*

This is a Yang line in a Yang place, indicating that its subject is a strong, intelligent person. Since it lies at the beginning of the hexagram, it also suggests the beginning of a family or a newly established home, a time when all members aspire to make the situation a good and happy one. To do this, they must plan carefully and try to foresee all the possible difficulties they may encounter, taking steps to prevent or minimize them. This will preclude accident or disaster.

Line 2, Yin:

(a) *The wife does not act as she wishes. Her duty is the preparation of food for the family. To be firm and correct will lead to good fortune.*

(b) *The "good fortune" indicate in Line 2, Yin, stems from obedience rooted in submissiveness.*

Being Yin and the second line of the hexagram Li, Line 2 signifies a very gentle, receptive person placed in a subordinate position (symbolically a wife). Because it occupies a position both central and correct, its subject is a responsible person who considers it her duty to carry out the obligations and responsibilities of her position ("preparation of food") no matter what her own desires or wishes. This can only lead to good fortune.

Line 3, Yang:

(a) *Members of a household appear stern and serious. Repentance and a sense of peril will lead to good fortune. When women and children are frivolous and garrulous, eventually there will be occasion for regret.*

(b) *"Members of a household appear stern and serious." This shows that the proper way has not been lost. "Women and children are frivolous and garrulous." This shows that the integrity of the family is missing.*

Line 3 is Yang in a Yang place, suggesting a stern and serious atmosphere in the family. This is because trouble threatens, possibly due to the indiscretion of a family member. However, a sincere desire to reform and to act more responsibly in the future will lead to good fortune.

In other words, for any association (family) to be successful, its members must act discreetly and responsibly at all times. In a person whose own life is deeply bound up with that of others, the wrong word or act at the wrong time will reflect adversely, not only on himself, but upon those around him.

This line, at the extreme end of the lower trigram, Li (light), suggests that the light is in a marginal state and about to vanish, a "stern and serious" situation.

Line 4, Yin:

(a) *She is increasing the wealth of the family. Good fortune will come on a grand scale.*

(b) *"She is increasing the wealth of the family and good fortune will come on a grand scale." The reason is that she is submissive while in her correct and proper place.*

This line is Yin in a Yin place and lies at the beginning of the Sun trigram (submissiveness and docility), suggesting a gentle and very intelligent person (symbolically a woman) occupying an intermediate but responsible position. Though her place is not a lofty one, her contribution is enormous, for through careful management she increases the family's wealth and maintains a harmonious atmosphere. For a family to be blessed with such a member is good fortune indeed.

The Sun trigram also signifies "wealth" and "eldest daughter." Hence the image of a woman who can increase the wealth of the family.

Line 5, Yang:

(a) *A king exerts his influence in shaping a good family. Do not worry. There will be good fortune.*

(b) *"A king exerts his influence in shaping a good family." This is because their relations are actuated by mutual love.*

Here, Line 5 (the ruler) is Yang and occupies a position both central and correct, suggesting a good king (or in this case, a husband). In addition, it forms a harmonious relationship with its correlate (Line 2, Yin), which also occupies a position both central and correct. Together they signify that the husband (Line 5) occupies his correct place (according to ancient tradition, outside the home, the exterior), while the wife (Line 2) occupies her correct place (traditionally, inside the home, the interior). The subject of

Line 5 wants to exert a good influence on his family (or associates), and as there is mutual love between the parents, as indicated by their harmonious relationship, his efforts are well received by the others. This can only bring good fortune.

Line 6, Yang:

(a) *One shows sincerity and appears awe-inspiring. There will be good fortune eventually.*

(b) *"The good fortune of an awe-inspiring appearance" is what may be said of self-examination and self-control.*

Being at the top of the hexagram signifying family, this Yang line symbolizes the head of a household who has done much to foster his family's security and happiness. But Line 6 occupies a position neither central nor correct (Yang in a Yin place) and fails to form a harmonious relationship with its correlate (Line 3). Its subject, therefore, is ill-placed and without any close support. However, he sincerely wishes to work for the welfare of his family (or group), and although he faces considerable difficulty in doing so, his commitment and dedication to improving his own performance can only lead to success.

The K'UEI Hexagram
(Symbol of Separation)

38th 暌

THE LOWER TRIGRAM, Tui, represents marsh water, and the upper trigram, Li, represents fire. Water tends to flow downward, while fire tends to flame up. Each moves in an opposite direction from the other. Hence the idea of separation or disunion.

KING WEN'S JUDGMENT ON THE HEXAGRAM:

The hexagram indicates good fortune in attending to small tasks.
In times of disunion, the central authority or consensus necessary to the successful undertaking of any great task does not exist. In such a situation, the superior man knows the wisest course is to turn his efforts to the cultivation of small matters, nurturing seeds that may later lead to reconciliation and union, when (according to the Law of Cyclic Reversion) the current period has run its course. This will lead to good fortune.

CONFUCIUS' EXPLANATION OF KING WEN'S JUDGMENT:

The hexagram shows fire moving upward, while water in the marsh moves downward. Two daughters live in the same house, but their aspirations do not run along the same line.
Pleasure adheres to what is brilliant. The weak advances to act above, occupies a central position, and corresponds favorably with the strong. That's why there is good fortune in attending to small tasks.
Heaven and earth are apart, but their task is similar. Man and

woman are apart, but their aspirations mutually correspond. The ten thousand things are apart, but there is similarity in their doings.

Great indeed is the timely application of separation denoted by the hexagram.

Confucius notes two ways in which the K'uei Hexagram represents the idea of separation: In addition to water and fire, the lower trigram, Tui, also represents the first daughter, and the upper trigram, Li, also represents the second daughter. Like all sisters, though they begin with the same nature ("live in the same house"), they grow up and become two separate individuals who desire different lives and husbands ("their aspirations do not run along the same line").

Tui and Li have yet another meaning, which suggests the solution or key to action in a time of disunion: Among their many other symbolisms, Tui may be taken to represent pleasure, and Li may be taken to represent brilliance. This suggests that there is pleasure in doing things brilliantly ("Pleasure adheres to what is brilliant"), even "small tasks."

Then Line 5 (the ruler), though weak (Yin), occupies a central place and forms a harmonious relationship with its correlate (Line 2), signifying a gentle ruler or a mild, unifying force which can bring dissident elements into some sort of cooperation and indicating good fortune in attending to small matters. In time of disunion, only small successes are possible, but they will lead to the greater reconciliation necessary for greater successes.

SYMBOLIC SIGNIFICANCE OF THE HEXAGRAM AS NOTED BY CONFUCIUS:

The idea behind K'uei is derived from fire above the marsh. The superior man is inspired thereby to preserve his individuality while following the common trend.

Fire and water move in opposite directions and do not get along well together. In the same way, the superior man learns to preserve and maintain his inner integrity ("individuality"), even when mixing with others in the daily routines of life.

DUKE OF CHOU'S EXPLANATION OF THE LINES (a) AND CONFUCIUS' COMMENT THEREON (b):

Line 1, Yang:

(a) *Repentance disappears. A horse has been lost. Do not try to find it. It will come back of its own accord. See the bad man. No error.*

(b) *"See the bad man." The purpose is to dispel ill feelings.*

This Yang line in a Yang place suggests a dynamic personality who (because Line 1 represents the beginning of movement in the situation symbolized by the hexagram) wants to advance and attach himself to the subject of its correlate (Line 4).

However, he has doubts and regrets, for he forms an antagonistic relationship with the subject of Line 4 and tends to perceive the other as "a bad man." He is advised to go and meet him, if only to avoid or dispel ill feelings. If the subject of Line 1 will only forget his doubts, just as he would a runaway horse that he knows will return, his meeting with the subject of Line 4 will prove auspicious.

Line 4 occupies the center of the upper interior trigram, K'an (Lines 3, 4, 5), which also signifies "horse" and "thief." Hence the images in the text.

Line 2, Yang:

(a) *One meets one's master in a lane. No error.*

(b) *"One meets one's master in a lane." The meaning is that one has not lost the proper course.*

This Yang line occupies a position incorrect but central. In addition, it forms a harmonious relationship with its correlate (Line 5, the ruler), which also occupies a central position, denoting a leader or royal court. The subjects of both lines are therefore wise and reasonable people who get along well, since they both favor the middle course and avoid extremes. In a time of social disunion and disintegration, they cannot openly meet at court; so they meet elsewhere to exchange ideas ("in a lane"). Because he does not let events separate him from his supporter, the subject of Line 2 is still on the right path and has committed no error.

Line 3, Yin:

(a) *A carriage is pulled back. Its ox is tied up. Its occupant has his forehead pricked and his nose cut off. No good beginning. A good end.*

(b) *"The carriage is pulled back." This is because the position is inappropriate. "No good beginning. A good end." This is due to the meeting with the strong.*

This line occupies a very unfavorable position which is neither central nor correct (Yin in a Yang place). Moreover, it forms the boundary between the two component trigrams, where opposition to union is the strongest. However, because Line 3 forms a harmonious relationship with its correlate (Line 6, Yang), its subject wishes to advance and meet this stronger partner. Since his position is an inauspicious one from which to advance, the subject of Line 3 finds his way blocked by another strong (Yang) man, the subject of Line 4, who pushes him back and rebukes him ("his nose is cut off"). Although this is not a good beginning, the subject of Line 6, who is the most powerful of the three, uses his influence to overcome the obstacles and bring the partners together. This is the "good end."

The upper interior trigram, K'an (Lines 3, 4, 5), denotes a wagon in trouble, and the lower interior trigram, Li (Lines 2, 3, 4), denotes a cow. This suggests the image of a carriage being "pulled back" and "its ox tied up."

Line 4, Yang:

(a) *A lonely and alienated man meets a strong fellow. They are sincere toward each other. The situation is somewhat perilous, but there will be no error.*

(b) *"They are sincere toward each other. There will be no error." This means their aims have been fulfilled.*

Line 4 occupies a position neither central nor correct (Yang in a Yin place) and fails to form a harmonious relationship with its correlate (Line 1) which, being Yang, signifies a strong man. In addition, Line 4 lies in the center of the upper interior trigram, K'an (peril or danger). Naturally, its subject feels lonely and alienated. Although he and the subject of Line 1 are usually antagonistic toward each other, in his present helpless situation he is willing to meet the "strong fellow." Since they share the same nature, they sympathize with and understand each other. They come to an agreement, and both their purposes are fulfilled.

Line 5, Yin:

(a) *Repentance disappears. One is in close touch with one's kinsman, so close as to seem to be biting into each other's skin. If one moves ahead, what error can there be?*

(b) *"One is in close touch with one's kinsman, so close as to seem to be biting into each other's skin." This means that any forward move will result in rejoicing.*

Here, Line 5 (the ruler) is Yin in a Yang place and is hemmed in by two strong lines. Its subject may at first have some regrets or misgivings over his position. However, the line occupies a central position and forms a harmonious relationship with its correlate (Line 2), which also occupies a central position. This suggests that the subjects of the two lines are close relatives ("kinsman"), and when they meet they hug each other hard ("so close as to seem to be biting into each other's skin"). Thus allied, they cooperate to help and support each other. Such ventures can only result in success.

Line 6, Yang:

(a) *One is alone and alienated. He seems to see a pig carrying a heap of mud and a wagon loaded with ghosts. At first he bends his bow, but later he unbends it. What he sees is not a highwayman but a relative. If he goes forward and encounters rain, there will be good fortune.*

(b) *"The good fortune of encountering rain" means that his doubts have disappeared.*

This line occupies the pinnacle of the trigram and therefore is in an uncomfortable and precarious position. Since its subject is at the extreme of the hexagram, he feels lonely and apart from people. However, he finds a partner ("relative") in his correlate (Line 3) with whom he forms a harmonious relationship. Although his alienated position causes him to misperceive ("seems to see a pig carrying a heap of mud and a wagon loaded with ghosts"), and he even misunderstands the friendly advance of the subject of Line 3 ("sees . . . a highwayman"), his good sense enables him to recover and put aside his doubts and suspicions.

According to the *Shuo Kua*, the upper interior trigram, K'an (Lines 3, 4, 5), stands for several things, including rain, wheel, bow, and wagon. Hence the images in the Text.

The CHIEN Hexagram
(Symbol of Difficulty)

39th  蹇

THE UPPER TRIGRAM, K'an, stands for a deep cavern or danger; the lower trigram, Ken, stands for mountain or standstill. Together they suggests the act of coming to a halt in the face of an obstruction or danger. Hence the idea of difficulty.

KING WEN'S JUDGMENT ON THE HEXAGRAM:

The hexagram indicates that advantage favors the southwest and does not favor the northeast. It is advantageous to see the great man. Firm correctness will be conducive to good fortune.

According to the *Shuo Kua,* the K'an trigram represents water and is identified with the north, and the Ken trigram represents mountain and is identified with the northeast. This indicates deep water or difficult terrain in the north and northeast. Faced with such a situation, the course of wisdom lies in turning resolutely away from the present course and seeking easier terrain (symbolically, the opposite direction, southwest).

Line 5 (the ruler) occupies an ideal position. Not only does it lie in the sphere of heaven (the top two lines), but it also occupies a central as well as correct place and finds a harmonious correlate in Line 2. Thus the subject of Line 5 may rightly be called a great man whose help or counsel can be of benefit in a time of difficulty.

CONFUCIUS' EXPLANATION OF KING WEN'S JUDGMENT:

Chien, name of the hexagram, means difficulty and danger ahead. To stop when in sight of danger is wise indeed.

The hexagram indicates that "advantage favors the southwest." This means that going there will hit upon the middle course. "It does not favor the northeast." This means that the course thereto has exhausted its possibilities. "It is advantageous to see the great man." This means that the forward move will be successful. "The good fortune of being firm and correct" while in the proper places means rectification of the state. Great indeed is the timely application of the hexagram denoting difficulty.

Confucius considers it a sign of great wisdom to cease one's course when it threatens to lead into difficulty or peril. Since advantage lies in turning away from the original course and pursuing a different or opposing task ("advantage favors the southwest"), to do so is not a sign of weakness, but of wisdom ("the middle course"). As Line 5 (the ruler) forms a harmonious relationship with its correlate (Line 2), which occupies the center of the lower trigram, it is advantageous for those below to seek assistance from the "great man." In addition, with the exception of Line 1, all the remaining lines of the hexagram occupy their correct positions (Yin line in a Yin place, Yang line in a Yang place), suggesting the importance of remaining firmly on the correct course in times of difficulty. Ultimately such action can overcome any obstacle and save the group or situation ("rectification of the state"). Those who know the proper response to difficulty are fortunate.

SYMBOLIC SIGNIFICANCE OF THE HEXAGRAM AS NOTED BY CONFUCIUS:

The idea behind Chien is derived from water over the mountain. The superior man is inspired thereby to practice self-examination and cultivate virtue.

Water has cut a deep chasm or cavern at the top of a mountain, creating difficult and dangerous terrain that can only be crossed by those possessed of caution and endurance. Thus the superior man learns to strengthen his own character and watch himself for any signs of weakness, so that he may be fully prepared when times of difficulty come.

DUKE OF CHOU'S EXPLANATION OF THE LINES (a) AND CONFUCIUS' COMMENT THEREON (b):

Line 1, Yin:

(a) *Going forward will meet with difficulty. Coming back will gain merit.*

(b) *"Going forward will meet with difficulty. Coming back will gain merit." This means that one should wait and see.*

This line occupies a position neither central nor correct (Yin in a Yang place) and also fails to form a harmonious relationship with its correlate (Line 4). The subject of this line is a man placed in unfavorable circumstances who lacks outside help or support. Since Line 1 is the first line of the hexagram, its subject is only at the beginning of his adventure or course. To initiate any project while occupying such an unfavorable position can only lead to difficulty. Instead, the wisest course is to study the situation carefully, and wait for (according to the Law of Cyclic Reversion) a more favorable time to advance.

Line 2, Yin:

(a) *The king's minister buffets wave after wave of difficulty, and this not for his own sake.*

(b) *"The king's minister buffets wave after wave of difficulty." In the end there will be no resentment.*

Line 2 is Yin in a Yin place and occupies a central position. It also forms a harmonious relationship with its correlate (Line 5, the ruler). This indicates a wise and loyal minister who is trusted by his king. When difficulty threatens, the subject of Line 2 unselfishly bears the brunt of it, tackling the most difficult problems himself. This earns his ruler's good will ("no resentment").

Line 3, Yang:

(a) *One goes forward with difficulty and comes back to his neighbor.*

(b) *"One goes forward with difficulty and comes back to his neighbor." This is because people in the inner circle are pleased with him.*

Line 3 is Yang in a Yang place. Its subject is an active, intelligent person with a strong desire to act and advance. However, difficulty or danger (the upper trigram, K'an) lies in his path. So the subject of Line 3 retraces his steps and turns to his weaker neighbor (Line 2, Yin), with whom he forms a harmonious relationship. His neighbor, who occupies a central position ("inner circle"), is delighted to benefit from his strength and ability.

Line 4, Yin:

(a) *One goes forward with difficulty and comes back to join his associate.*

(b) *"One goes forward with difficulty and comes back to join his associate." This is because his associate's position is solid.*

This Yin line in a Yin place indicates a receptive gentleness. Since it does not occupy a central position, its subject is not favorably placed for action. In addition, he can expect no aid or support from his correlate (Line 1), for they fail to form a harmonious relationship. In the face of these difficulties, the subject of Line 4 must realize that he is not strong enough to continue advancing. Instead, he must stand still and turn back to join his stronger associate, the subject of Line 3 (Yang), with whom he forms a harmonious relationship.

Line 5, Yang:

(a) *One meets with tremendous difficulty. Friends are coming.*

(b) *"One meets with tremendous difficulty. Friends are coming." This is because one occupies a central position and possesses integrity.*

Here, Line 5 (the ruler) is Yang and occupies the center of the upper trigram, K'an (danger), indicating a great king placed in grave difficulty. However, Line 5 occupies a position both central and correct (Yang in a Yang place) and forms a harmonious relationship with Line 2 (the minister). Its subject, therefore, is a wise ruler whose wise policies have earned him many loyal friends and supporters who assist him in dispelling difficulties and dangers.

Lines 2, 3, 4, all occupying their correct places, indicate that their subjects are trustworthy people who willingly rally to help the ruler overcome his difficulties.

Line 6, Yin:

(a) *One goes forward with difficulty and comes back to his strong partner. Good fortune. Advantageous to see the great man.*

(b) *"One goes forward with difficulty and comes back to his strong partner." This shows he aims at the interior. "Advantageous to see the great man." This is in order to adhere to the nobility.*

Line 6 is a Yin line at the extreme top of the hexagram; its subject is a weak person who has nowhere to go. Since further advancement would mean danger and difficulty, he sets his aim inward toward the center ("aims at the interior") and though his position is higher, joins forces with the ruler (Line 5, Yang). If instead, the subject of Line 6 goes ahead and tries to overcome the danger and difficulty confronting him, he will surely meet with failure and frustration, for to advance beyond the extreme point which Line 6 occupies is tantamount to venturing into the unknown.

The CHIEH Hexagram
(Symbol of Liberation)

40th 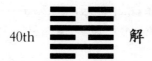 解

THE LOWER TRIGRAM , K'an, stands for water and rain, and the upper trigram, Chen, stands for thunder and motion. Thunder and rain both signify general relief and liberation, such as the clearance of heat and pressure in the atmosphere. Hence the idea of liberation.

KING WEN'S JUDGMENT ON THE HEXAGRAM:

The hexagram indicates that advantage favors the southwest. If nothing needs to be done, it will be good fortune to restore the former situation. If some move needs to be made, good fortune requires that it be given early attention.

At the time King Wen made this Judgment he was contemplating liberating the people from the tyranny of the last emperor of the Shang dynasty. Now liberation nearly always involves military operations. Line 1 (Yin) of the hexagram represents the start of military movement. If it moves upward to meet its strong and harmonious correlate (Line 4, Yang) and takes its place (changes into Yin), the upper trigram becomes K'un, and K'un (according to King Wen's arrangement of the Eight Trigrams) lies in the southwest and signifies people ("advantage favors the southwest"). Here the people under tyrannical oppression may be won over and easily pacified, restoring the region to its original peaceful condition ("the former situation"). On the other hand, if further military operations are necessary, they should be launched as soon as possible, for the best attack is always the quickest one, leaving the enemy no time for preparations or to deceive and coerce the people.

CONFUCIUS' EXPLANATION OF KING WEN'S JUDGMENT:

The hexagram shows that danger accompanies movement. Movement leading to liberation from danger: this is the meaning of the hexagram.

"The hexagram indicates that advantage favors the southwest." This means that the advance will win the support of the people. "It will be good fortune to restore the former situation." This means that the middle way has been obtained. "If some move needs to be made, good fortune requires that it be given early attention." This means that advancement will be crowned with success.

When heaven and earth undergo liberation, thunder and rain will come into action. When thunder and rain come into action, the pods and buds of the fruit trees, herbs, and plants will burst open.

Great indeed is the significance of time indicated in the hexagram.

The upper trigram, Chen, signifies motion, and the lower trigram, K'an, signifies danger. Together they suggest that there is always danger in movement. However, as Chen lies above and K'an below, movement also leads to, or has led to, the surmounting of, or liberation from, danger.

Confucius also implies that in a wider sense the phenomena of liberation ("thunder and rain") are vital to the universal process of renewal and rebirth in nature, the individual, and society. The importance of a period of liberation cannot be overestimated.

SYMBOLIC SIGNIFICANCE OF THE HEXAGRAM AS NOTED BY CONFUCIUS:

The idea behind Chieh is derived from thunder and rain coming into action. The superior man is inspired thereby to pardon misdemeanors and remit penalties.

Thunder and rain signify the liberation and release of pent-up pressure, bringing relief to all creatures. In the same way, the superior man releases social pressures and resentments by pardoning light crimes and reducing punishments. In terms of the individual, we can become psychologically liberated by forgiving the transgressions of ourselves and others.

DUKE OF CHOU'S EXPLANATION OF THE LINES (a) AND CONFUCIUS' COMMENT THEREON (b):

Line 1, Yin:
(a) *There will be no error.*
(b) *When there is harmonious correlation between the strong and the weak, there ought to be no error.*

This is a Yin line at the bottom of the hexagram, indicating a weak person in a low place. Such a man is in no position to act on his own when attempting to bring about liberation. Instead, he works to assist a stronger partner, the subject of Line 4 (his correlate), with whom he forms a harmonious relationship.

Line 2, Yang:
(a) *One captures three foxes while hunting and gets a yellow arrow. Firm correctness will lead to good fortune.*
(b) *"The good fortune of being firm and correct" indicated in Line 2, Yang, lies in the fact that the middle course has been obtained.*

Line 2 (the minister) is Yang and occupies a central position. In addition, it forms a harmonious relationship with its correlate (Line 5, the ruler). Its subject is a wise minister who actively pursues the middle course and helps the ruler (Line 5, his correlate) to liberate himself from corrupt forces ("One captures three foxes while hunting").

Yellow, since it is the color of the rich soil of the Yellow River, is considered the correct color in China. Arrows symbolize uprightness. Thus, a yellow arrow symbolizes the firm correctness with which the minister chastises the criminal elements ("three foxes"). Though he is more severe in dealing with miscreants than the subject of Line 1, he is justified by the situation, and this leads to good fortune.

The lower interior trigram, Li (Lines 2, 3, 4), signifies, among other things, weapons and soldiers. Hence the images of "hunting" and "arrow."

Line 3, Yin:

(a) *One is shouldering a burden, yet rides in a carriage. He tempts the robbers to come. Persistence will cause resentment.*

(b) *"One is shouldering a burden, yet rides in a carriage." This is something to be ashamed of. "He tempts the robbers to come." Who but himself is to be blamed?*

This Yin line occupies a position neither central nor correct. In addition, it resides at the top extreme of the lower trigram, K'an (danger), suggesting a dangerous fellow of weak character who is dissatisfied with his lot and adopts radical or unethical methods to satisfy his desires. Symbolically, he carries the burden of his ill-gotten gains, which is so heavy that he cannot walk beneath it and has to ride in a carriage. Such an ostentatious sight will naturally tempt others of his kind to robbery.

In the same sense, the greed and ill-gotten wealth of corrupt officials encourage others to commit crimes for their own gain. This must be ended if liberation is to occur.

Line 4, Yang:

(a) *One gives relief to his toes. Friends will come and show their sincerity.*

(b) *"One gives relief to his toes." This means he has not yet occupied his proper place.*

Since Line 4 (the minister) occupies a position neither central nor correct, its subject needs outside aid and support if he is to help the ruler bring about liberation. In addition, this line forms a harmonious relationship with its correlate (Line 1), which represents the toes or feet. "To give relief to the toes" is a preliminary to walking, indicating that the subject of Line 4 wants to mobilize the resources of his more lowly placed partner in the service of the ruler. Because they are in harmony on this matter, if they come together in mutual sincerity, good fortune will prevail.

Line 5, Yin:

(a) *The superior man wants only liberation. Good fortune. His sincerity will affect the small, mean men.*

(b) *"The superior man wants liberation." This means the small, mean men will go away.*

Here, Line 5 (the ruler) is Yin and occupies a central position. Its subject is a wise ruler ("the superior man") who is so sincere in his attempt to liberate the people from the influence of evil or corrupt elements ("the small, mean men") that he causes them to retire.

Line 6, Yin:

(a) *A duke shoots at a hawk from the top of a high wall and hits it. There is nothing not advantageous.*

(b) *"A duke shoots at a hawk." This has the effect of dispersing the rebellious elements.*

Due to this line's position, just above Line 5, it represents a high official close to the ruler ("a duke"). He is using his high position to dispel those of small, mean character who occupy positions of power ("shoots at a hawk from the top of a high wall"). This is indeed good fortune.

The SUN Hexagram
(Symbol of Decrease)

41st  損

HERE, THE LOWER TRIGRAM, Tui, looks like a Ch'ien trigram whose third line has been displaced by a Yin line; the upper trigram, Ken, looks like a K'un trigram whose third line has been displaced by a Yang line. Since the action runs from the bottom to the top, the symbolism of this hexagram signifies that the people below have decreased their possessions in order to benefit those above. In political terms, this is illustrated by the example of people paying taxes to their government.

KING WEN'S JUDGMENT ON THE HEXAGRAM:

The hexagram indicates that decrease conjoined with sincerity will be conducive to great good fortune. No error. Desirable to stay firm and correct. Advantageous to move forward. What is the use of sincerity? Two baskets of food may be used as offerings to the gods or ancestral spirits.

The Judgment stresses the importance of sincerely sharing with those who have less. No matter how much or little one is able to give, if one shares with a sincere heart, it is sufficient ("two baskets of food may be used"). Such an act can only lead to good fortune.

CONFUCIUS' EXPLANATION OF KING WEN'S JUDGMENT:

The hexagram suggests the decrease of what is below and the increase of what is above. The course is from below upwards.

"The hexagram indicates that decrease conjoined with sincerity will be conducive to great good fortune. No error. Desirable to stay firm and correct. Advantageous to move forward. What is the use of sincerity? Two baskets of food may be used as offerings to the gods or ancestral spirits." The two baskets of food should be offered in the proper time. The decrease of the strong to increase the weak also should be in the proper time. Decrease and increase, as well as fullness and emptiness, should proceed in accordance with the time.

The Ch'ien trigram represents the Yang forces at their point of furthest manifestation (three Yang lines), and the K'un trigram represents the Yin forces at the point of their furthest manifestation (three Yin lines). To continue to manifest would bring disaster, so the stronger exchanges its top line for the top line of the weakest, thereby forming the Sun Hexagram. All things decrease and increase in turn, and wise is he who understands the significance of the time of decrease.

SYMBOLIC SIGNIFICANCE OF THE HEXAGRAM AS NOTED BY CONFUCIUS:

The idea behind Sun is derived from marsh (lower trigram) below the mountain (upper trigram). The superior man is inspired thereby to curb his anger and to suppress his desires.

The upper trigram is Ken (mountain), and the lower trigram is Tui (marsh). Together they suggest a mountain pressing down on the marsh below. In observing this phenomenon, the superior man discovers the wisdom of repressing (decreasing) his lower self in order to strengthen his higher self.

DUKE OF CHOU'S EXPLANATION OF THE LINES (a) AND CONFUCIUS' COMMENT THEREON (b):

Line 1, Yang:
(a) *One stops work and hastens away. No error. He should deliberate carefully the decrease of his wealth.*
(b) *"One stops work and hastens away." It is considered important to harmonize aspirations.*

This line is Yang in a Yang place and forms a harmonious relationship with its correlate (Line 4). The subject of Line 1 is a strong, dynamic person who is eager to advance and join his partner (Line 4), so that they may work to further their mutual aspirations. However, he should first consider carefully to what extent he can reasonably decrease his own resources without damaging his own aspirations.

Line 2, Yang:

(a) *Advantageous to be firm and correct. Inauspicious to embark on any venture. Increase others' wealth without decreasing one's own.*

(b) *The "advantage of being firm and correct" indicated in Line 2, Yang, is due to one's aspirations being based on one's central position.*

This line occupies a position central but incorrect (Yang in a Yin place). Normally, its subject would advance to meet his partner (Line 5, the ruler), with whom he forms a harmonious relationship. However, although he is sincere, his position hampers his ability to act effectively. In such a situation, to advance is unwise. The subject of this line can best help others by remaining in his central position and discharging his own duties to the fullest extent of his abilities.

Line 3, Yin:

(a) *When three persons walk together, one will be missing. One walking alone will find a friend.*

(b) *One person walking alone is all right. "When three persons walk together," suspicions will arise.*

Confucius seems to imply that when three persons (a group) put their heads together in an attempt to lead a movement, differences of opinion are bound to arise, leading to suspicion of one another's motives.

The Sun Hexagram is supposedly derived from the T'ai Hexagram, in which the upper trigram, K'un, contains three Yin lines, and the lower trigram, Ch'ien, contains three Yang lines. The three Yang lines represent "three companions who walk together." One of them (the third line) wanders to the top of the K'un trigram ("one will be missing"), decreasing their number.

Here, he finds a friend who is willing to exchange places with him, forming the present hexagram. As Yang can signify wealth and Yin signify poverty, those below (the lower trigram) are said to have given up wealth to those above (the upper trigram).

Line 4, Yin:

(a) *One alleviates his illness through the joyful help quickly sought from a friend. No error.*

(b) *"One alleviates his illness." This nevertheless is something to be joyful about.*

This line is Yin in a Yin place. In terms of the symbolism of the hexagram as a whole, its subject is a weak person whose situation is that of a man who has contracted an illness (obstacle). However, Line 4 forms a harmonious relationship with its correlate (Line 1), so its subject receives prompt and willing aid from his more lowly partner. Since Line 1 lies in the lower trigram, and Line 4 lies in the upper, the high is again said to receive aid from the low.

Line 5, Yin:

(a) *"One gains ten pairs of tortoise shells from certain people and is not allowed to refuse them. There will be great good fortune.*

(b) *The "great good fortune" indicated in Line 5, Yin, is the blessing from the Supreme Being.*

Here, Line 5 (the ruler) occupies a central position and forms a harmonious relationship with its correlate (Line 2). This indicates a wise and humble ruler who follows a middle course and in so doing enjoys support from the people. He often receives gifts of appreciation from those whom his good works have benefited ("ten pairs of tortoise shells"). It would be ungracious to refuse to accept anything given with such sincerity. One who has earned such gratitude from mankind can also expect the blessings of heaven.

In ancient China, tortoise shells were used as money. Hence the image "ten pairs of tortoise shells ... great good fortune."

Line 6, Yang:

(a) *One gains without causing loss to others. No error. Firm correctness will be conducive to good fortune. Advantageous to advance. Submissive support will be obtained from people devoid of clannishness.*

(b) *"One gains without causing loss to others." This means one's aspirations are being realized in great measure.*

This Yang line lies at the top of the Sun Hexagram (decrease of the low in order to benefit the high) and forms a harmonious relationship with its correlate (Line 3). The subject of Line 6, the last line of the hexagram, is one who has already received great benefits. Those below can best benefit him by preserving their own resources ("one gains without causing loss"). Although it is usually dangerous to advance from such a position (the extreme, beyond which lies only the unknown), the subject of Line 6 receives loyal support from those below, without regard to any partisan feelings. By moving ahead slowly and making certain he stays on the right course, he can fulfill his deepest desires and benefit all the people.

The YI Hexagram

(Symbol of Increase)

42nd  益

THERE ARE TWO symbolic meanings in this hexagram: First, the upper trigram, Sun, stands for wind, and the lower, Chen, stands for thunder. When wind and thunder work together, there is a great increase in the power of the atmosphere. Second, the upper trigram, Sun, and the lower trigram, Chen, look like a Ch'ien trigram (three Yang lines) and a K'un trigram (three Yin lines) which have exchanged a line with each other. Together they signify that those above have decreased their own possessions (a strong Yang line) in order to increase or benefit those below. Considering the social oppression under which King Wen and his people lived during his youth, he probably had in mind the appropriation of government funds to promote the welfare of the people.

KING WEN'S JUDGMENT ON THE HEXAGRAM:

The hexagram indicates that it is propitious to go ahead with plans and to cross the great stream.

A time of increase is almost always propitious for the advancement of significant public programs ("cross the great stream").

CONFUCIUS' EXPLANATION OF KING WEN'S JUDGMENT:

The hexagram suggests that decreasing the high to increase the low will result in boundless gladness on the part of the people. The course moving from the top downward shines with great brilliance.

"It is propitious to go ahead with plans." This means that rejoicing stems from central and correct positions. "It is propitious to cross the great stream." The nature of wood will then become manifest.

The hexagram shows movement coupled with docility. Its daily progress is without limit. What heaven distributes and earth produces is so vast a benefit as to be boundless. The way of all increase or benefit proceeds in accordance with the time.

When an enlightened government undertakes measures for the welfare of the people, it receives their wholehearted support.

The second paragraph refers to Lines 2 and 5 (the minister and the ruler), which are well-placed to act as harmonious correlates because both occupy positions correct as well as central. The upper trigram, Sun, also stands for wood, which can be employed to build boats ("the nature of wood will then become manifest"). Since boats can be used "to cross the great stream," this suggests success in the undertaking of great ventures.

Here, the Sun trigram (docility), which represents Yin, is placed above the Chen trigram (motion), which represents Yang. This suggests the strong placing themselves below or cooperating with the weak. It is such interaction between the Yang and the Yin that results in the unceasing creation of the ten thousand things. As the creative process is governed by the Law of Cyclic Reversion, it proceeds in accordance with the progress of time.

SYMBOLIC SIGNIFICANCE OF THE HEXAGRAM AS NOTED BY CONFUCIUS:

The idea behind Yi is derived from wind and thunder. The superior man is inspired thereby to change to what is good when he sees it and to correct his mistakes when he makes any.

Just as wind and thunder provide a dramatic contrast for each other's awe-inspiring manifestations, so good and evil provide a dramatic contrast for each other. To the superior man, these contrasts reveal the wisdom of avoiding evil and cultivating good, symbolically cleansing his lower nature and increasing his higher nature.

DUKE OF CHOU'S EXPLANATION OF THE LINES (a) AND CONFUCIUS' COMMENT THEREON (b):

Line 1, Yang:

(a) *Advantage favors the undertaking of great tasks. There will be great good fortune and no error.*

(b) *"There will be great good fortune and no error." A lowly person is not supposed to deal with important tasks.*

This line is Yang in a Yang place and occupies the bottom of the hexagram, signifying a strong, able young man at the beginning of his career. Those who occupy such lowly positions are not normally entrusted with important responsibilities ("great tasks"); however, it is advantageous to do so in this situation, for the subject of Line 1 is wise enough to appreciate this great honor and will try his very best to prove himself equal to the trust. That such an earnest endeavor will prove successful is shown by the augury that there is "great good fortune and no error."

Line 2, Yin:

(a) *One gains ten pairs of tortoise shells from certain people and is not allowed to refuse them. To remain firm and correct constantly will lead to good fortune. The king may use it as an offering to God and meet with good fortune.*

(b) *"One gains from certain people." His gain comes from the outside.*

Line 2 is Yin in a Yin place and forms a harmonious relationship with its correlate (Line 5, the ruler). Its subject is a virtuous, humble minister whose hard work and loyalty draw rewards "from the outside" (probably the king). It would be ungracious to refuse them. Such good fortune or the able virtues which caused it may be dedicated to the service ("offering") of the country or God.

Line 3, Yin:

(a) *One is benefited by experiencing unfortunate circumstances. There will be no error. He is sincere and follows the middle course. He will report to the public with a jade emblem showing his sincerity.*

(b) *"One is benefited by experiencing unfortunate circumstances."* *Such circumstances are inherent in his position.*

This Yin line occupies a highly unfavorable position which is neither central nor correct. In addition, since it lies at the top of the lower trigram and just beneath the upper trigram, its subject finds himself embroiled in a time of transition, with all the difficulty and adjustment this entails. However, as Line 3 occupies a central position within the hexagram, its subject follows a middle path, and even in difficult circumstances his actions do him credit. Thus he receives a favorable response from his correlate (Line 6), with whom he forms a harmonious relationship ("One is benefited by experiencing unfortunate circumstances"). Such a person's sincerity and honesty are evident to everyone when he accounts to the public for the discharge of his trusts.

Line 4, Yin:

(a) *One follows a middle course. His report to the public draws confidence and support. He can be trusted with advantage even in such an important matter as the removal of the capital.*

(b) *"One's report to the public draws confidence and support."* *This is because his purpose is to render benefits.*

Line 4 (the minister) is Yin in a Yin place, and its subject serves the ruler (Line 5). Since the line also occupies a central position in the entire hexagram and forms a harmonious relationship with its correlate (Line 1), the minister is a wise and loyal man, one who follows a middle course when dispensing benefits to help those below. Consequently, he enjoys widespread popular support. No matter how important the task, the king can rely on the subject of Line 4 to act as a trustworthy aide (even to supervising "the removal of the capital").

Line 5, Yang:

(a) *One sincerely wants to render benefits. Needless to ask. There will be great good fortune. Benefits from "my" (his) virtues will be sincerely acknowledged.*

(b) *"One sincerely wants to render benefits." There is no need to ask about the matter. "Benefits from his virtues will be acknowledged." This means his aims have been amply fulfilled.*

Line 5 (the ruler) is Yang and occupies a position both central and correct. It also forms a harmonious relationship with its correlate (Line 2). The subject of Line 5, therefore, is a wise and benevolent ruler desiring to benefit those below, a man who occupies an ideal position from which to fulfill his aspirations. Such a man acts without any thought of recompense. Nevertheless, the people are sincerely grateful to him for all the benefits his measures have brought them.

Line 6, Yang:

(a) *One can receive benefit from nobody. He gets some blows. His mind does not follow any steadfast rule. There will be evil.*

(b) *"One can receive benefit from nobody." This is because he is prejudiced and selfish. "He gets some blows." Such attack comes from strangers.*

This Yang line is at the top of the Yi Hexagram ("decreasing the high to increase the low"), and its subject is one who has amassed great resources which he should sacrifice for the benefit of the people below. However, Line 6 occupies a position neither central nor correct (Yang in a Yin place). In addition, it occupies the extreme end of the hexagram, which suggests that the subject is given to radical and impulsive action ("His mind does not follow any steadfast rule"). This is not an advantageous way in which to act, and consequently, no one approves or rewards his behavior. He may even draw punishment or retaliation upon himself ("gets some blows").

The KUAI Hexagram
(Symbol of Removal)

43rd  夬

As MOVEMENT IN A hexagram is usually toward the top, in Kuai the Yang forces (the first five lines) are said to be gathering momentum in their onward course and are resolutely trying to oust the Yin line at the top, which represents an evil character in an extreme or top position. Hence the idea of removal.

KING WEN'S JUDGMENT ON THE HEXAGRAM:

The hexagram indicates a thorough exposition of a hidden evil at the royal court with a sincere appeal for redress of a perilous situation. Announcement should be made in one's own district to the effect that it is not advantageous to use armed force right away. It is advantageous to go ahead with present plans.

This hexagram represents a situation in which a corrupt or inept person has garnered great influence and power. Although many people might be tempted to use force at such a time, the good Yang forces are strong enough to try other alternatives. There are a number of such remedies set forth in the Kuai Hexagram: one is to publicly and thoroughly expose the evil; another is to forestall evil activities by remaining vigilantly on guard against them; yet another is to influence the more tractable by setting a good example.

The upper trigram, Tui, stands for mouth. Hence the idea of public exposition.

CONFUCIUS' EXPLANATION OF KING WEN'S JUDGMENT:

Kuai, name of the hexagram, means "to burst open," or the crushing of the weak by the strong. Vigor goes hand in hand with pleasure, and crushing is linked with harmony.

"A thorough exposition of a hidden evil at the royal court." This is because one weak line rides on five Yang ones. "A sincere appeal for redress of a perilous situation." This serves to bring the peril to light. "Announcement should be made in one's own district to the effect that it is not advantageous to use armed force right away." This means that resort to arms should be the last preference. "It is advantageous to go ahead with present plans." This means that the strong forces will grow and the matter will be brought to an end.

"To burst open," or remove an obstacle, in this case means the removal of weak or evil men (the Yin line) whose efforts are blocking the reforms contemplated by the good, strong forces (the five Yang lines).

The lower trigram is Ch'ien (vigor), and the upper trigram is Tui (pleasure). Since the movement in this hexagram is toward the top, motion here results in pleasure. This indicates that the attempt to remove evil elements will create no dissension and will result in general harmony.

SYMBOLIC SIGNIFICANCE OF THE HEXAGRAM AS NOTED BY CONFUCIUS:

The idea behind Kuai is derived from marsh water (upper trigram) rising toward the sky (lower trigram). The superior man is inspired thereby to dispense wealth to the people below him and to shy away from clinging to what he has amassed.

Water vapor rises into the sky when evaporation occurs and is redistributed below as rain, which nourishes the soil. In the same way, water in a high marsh can be diverted downward for the irrigation of lowlands in agricultural production. The image of a marsh in the sky therefore symbolizes the widespread dispersion of benefits from the high to the low. Thus the superior man is led to see the wisdom of sharing his bounty with others rather than letting it all accumulate uselessly for his own extravagance.

DUKE OF CHOU'S EXPLANATION OF THE LINES (a) AND CONFUCIUS' COMMENT THEREON (b):

Line 1, Yang:

(a) *One with strong toes moves forward but does not win. This is an error.*

(b) *Unable to win and yet going forward is an error.*

The line is Yang in a Yang place, indicating a strong young man who is eager to advance. Since Line 1 represents the toes or feet, he moves his "strong toes" forward. However, the line does not occupy a central position and fails to form a harmonious relationship with its correlate (Line 4). Consequently, the subject of Line 1 finds himself in unfavorable circumstances and without the support of others. As the line is placed at the beginning of the hexagram, its subject is inexperienced and as yet not well prepared for life, so when he ventures to remove the culprit (Line 6) from office, he fails. The error of inexperience is regrettable. A wiser man would know that one should never attack so highly placed a person unless there is a strong chance of victory.

Line 2, Yang:

(a) *One is on the alert and shouts out warnings. Late at night there may be armed hostilities. There is no need to worry.*

(b) *"There may be armed hostilities late at night. There is no need to worry." This is because the middle course has been obtained.*

Line 2 is Yang and occupies a central position, suggesting an active person who exercises caution and follows the middle course. Although he, like the subject of Line 1, desires the removal of the evil influence (Line 6), he is wise enough to realize he is not yet ready to attack, and so bides his time, preparing for the unavoidable conflict. He alerts his associates to the situation ("shouts out warnings") and remains alert, so that when the moment to act comes (even "late at night"), he is ready to take advantage of the situation ("no need to worry"). This is a good example of following the middle course, which always avoids reckless or radical measures.

Line 3, Yang:

(a) *One advances with a determined look (lit., with strong cheekbones). There will be evil. The superior man is very, very firm in his resolution. He will walk alone, ready to face the rain and get wet. Some people may show signs of anger. But there will be no error.*

(b) *"The superior man is very, very firm in his resolution." This means that eventually there will be no error.*

The position of this line is correct but not central. What is worse, Line 3 forms a harmonious relationship with its correlate (Line 6), whose subject is the culprit the subjects of the five Yang lines are trying to remove. The subject of Line 3, therefore, is a strong and able person and one who occupies an unfavorable position but is determined to do the right thing and oust the subject of Line 6, whatever the risk. But due to his relationship with the subject of Line 6, he stands on slippery ground and incurs suspicion and even anger on the part of his associates. In such a situation, the superior man shows his true character and walks alone, if necessary, into danger ("faces the rain") to perform his duty.

Line 4, Yang:

(a) *One walks with uncertain steps and great difficulty, as if the skin of his buttocks has been peeled off. If he walks slowly, like a lamb being led along, he will be free from regret. But he does not listen to advice.*

(b) *"He walks with uncertain steps and great difficulty." This is because his position is inappropriate to him. "He does not listen to advice." This shows that he can hear but cannot understand.*

Here, Line 4 is Yang and occupies a position neither central nor correct. In addition, being above the lower trigram and at the beginning of the upper one, it represents a period of transition. This suggests that the subject of Line 4 is a strong-willed person given to extreme and perverse behavior who finds himself constantly forced to make new adjustments to his changing situation. Such a man ignores the advice of others, and responds by making reckless moves. If he will restrain himself and listen to the guidance of others ("walk slowly, like a lamb"), he will find himself on the right path and escape error. However, he either does not listen to advice or fails to understand it, and he impulsively attempts to act prematurely against the evil person at the top of the hexagram (Line 6). This can only lead to disaster.

Line 4 is within the upper trigram, Tui, which stands for lamb and mouth. Hence such images as "led like a lamb" and "advice."

Line 5, Yang:

(a) *Noisome grass must be uprooted with unflagging resolution. Action in accord with the middle way may dispel error.*

(b) *"Action in accord with the middle way may dispel error." This means that as yet the light of the middle way has not become manifest.*

Since Line 5 (the ruler) is Yang, it signifies a wise and able king. Moreover, the line occupies a central position in the hexagram, which indicates that he has the authority and ability to remove the evil person ("noisome grass") above. The fact that the line occupies a position both central and correct (Yang in a Yang place) indicates that its subject prefers to steer a middle course through the difficulties of life and so is sure to achieve his goal. However, as the Yin (evil) line still remains above, he has not yet succeeded ("light of the middle way has not become manifest").

Line 6, Yin:

(a) *One has no one to appeal to for help. Eventually evil will befall him.*

(b) *"The evil of having no one to appeal to for help" means that in the end he will not prosper.*

Line 6 is Yin in a Yin place and lies at the top end of the hexagram. In terms of the Kuai Hexagram, its subject is a sinister, wicked person at the end of his rope. His evil deeds have antagonized all, and when the five Yang lines act to remove him from his position, nobody will give him help. Only misfortune is in store for such a man.

The KOU Hexagram

(Symbol of Contact)

44th  姤

IN THE KOU HEXAGRAM, the only Yin line (Line 1) occupies the beginning of the hexagram, indicating the sudden reappearance of or sudden contact with the evil Yin forces after a long absence. This situation is the opposite of that in the preceding Kuai Hexagram, in which the five Yang lines are virtuously overthrowing the evil Yin line at the top. The lower trigram, Sun, stands for wind, and the upper, Ch'ien, stands for sky. When wind blows through the sky, it touches everything that is exposed to it. Hence the idea of contact.

KING WEN'S JUDGMENT ON THE HEXAGRAM:

The hexagram indicates a stout, strong woman and the inadvisability of marrying her.

Since movement in a hexagram is toward the top, the appearance of a Yin line at the beginning of the hexagram (Line 1) signifies the growing strength of the darkness, or an evil, corrupt influence which is bound to grow unless checked in time. No matter how strong such a force grows, it is not wise to associate with it. The Yin force also represents the feminine, which gives us the image of "a stout, strong woman."

CONFUCIUS' EXPLANATION OF KING WEN'S JUDGMENT:

Kou, name of the hexagram, means meeting, the meeting of the weak with the strong.

313

"It is inadvisable to marry a stout, strong woman." The reason is that it is impossible to live with such a woman for long.

Heaven and earth meet, and things of every description all make their appearance.

When the strong fall into central and correct places, the world will move along a grand course.

Great indeed is the significance of contact indicated in the hexagram.

Although the weak (earth) and the strong (heaven) are of different natures, their meeting produces the ten thousand things. Lines 2 and 5 are strong (Yang) and occupy positions that are central and correct, indicating that even with the reappearance of the weak (Yin) forces below, all will be well ("move along a grand course").

Wise is he who understands the significance of the time of contact.

SYMBOLIC SIGNIFICANCE OF THE HEXAGRAM AS NOTED BY CONFUCIUS:

The idea behind Kou is derived from wind (lower trigram) blowing in the sky (upper trigram). The ruler is inspired thereby to promulgate his decrees and ordinances.

Wind blowing in the sky makes contact with all things, cleansing the atmosphere. Through observing this phenomenon, the wise ruler learns to make contact with his people and clarify the social atmosphere by promulgating "decrees and ordinances" which sweep it clear of impurities and bring about peace and order.

DUKE OF CHOU'S EXPLANATION OF THE LINES (a) AND CONFUCIUS' COMMENT THEREON (b):

Line 1, Yin:
(a) *Bound to a metal bar. Good fortune requires firm correctness. Advancement will encounter evil. A lean pig heartily jumps about.*
(b) *"Bound to a metal bar." The onward course of the weak has to be checked, or to check itself.*

Line 1 is not merely the only Yin line in the hexagram, it also occupies a position neither central nor correct. In addition, it lies at the bottom of the hexagram, below five Yang lines. Therefore, its subject finds himself in a poor position from which to advance. If he attempts to move forward and make contact, he will be frustrated and will be like a "lean pig" who jumps blindly about. If, on the other hand, he remains firmly in his place ("bound to a metal bar"), pursuing his own duties with firm correctness, he will find the good fortune he is seeking.

Line 2, Yang:

(a) *There is a fish in the bag. No error. Not advantageous to the guests.*

(b) *"There is a fish in the bag." It accords with reason not to vex the guests.*

Line 2 is Yang and occupies a central position, suggesting a strong, intelligent man who is well-placed if he wishes to act. He is the first official with whom the evil subject of Line 1 comes in contact and seeks to influence. However, with his strength and wisdom, the subject of Line 2 simply detains the culprit as easily as putting "fish in a bag" before he can influence the guests (the other Yang lines).

Line 3, Yang:

(a) *One walks with uncertain steps and great difficulty as if the skin of his buttocks has been peeled off. The situation is perilous, but there will be no great error.*

(b) *"One walks with uncertain steps and great difficulty." The reason is that he is not properly guided in his walk.*

This line occupies a position correct (Yang in a Yang place) but not central and fails to form a harmonious relationship with its correlate (Line 6). Its subject is strong and wants to act, but finds himself in unfavorable circumstances. So he wavers and cannot make up his mind on the proper course to follow ("walks with uncertain steps"). Normally, the subject of a Yin line will form a harmonious relationship with a Yang line subject and guide him into a proper path. However, the only Yin line in this hexagram is Line 1 (the culprit), who would only try to mislead him. In this case, another strong Yang line (Line 2) blocks the way, so despite their compatibility, the subject of Line 1 cannot contact and influence him to any serious extent ("no great error").

Line 4, Yang:

(a) *There are no fish in the bag. Evil will ensue.*

(b) *"The evil of having no fish in the bag" is due to keeping the people at a considerable distance.*

This line lies in a transitional stage of the hexagram and occupies a position neither central nor correct (Yang in a Yin place). Its subject occupies an awkward or inappropriate place and must adapt himself to a new and unfavorable situation. As Line 4 forms a harmonious relationship with Line 1 (its correlate), its subject may want to get hold of or contact the culprit (Line 1). However, the latter has already been detained by the strong subject of Line 2 (Yang), who is nearer to Line 1. This is because Line 2 is near Line 1, while Line 4 is far from it, like a minister who is far from the people. So the subject of Line 4 fails to catch any fish, just as a minister who lacks popular support will fail to carry out his plans.

Line 5, Yang:

(a) *A medlar tree overshadows the melons. Hide the light under a bushel, and blessings will descend from heaven.*

(b) *"Hide the light under a bushel" as indicated in Line 5, Yang. This is because of the central and correct position. "Blessings will descend from heaven." This means that one's purpose has not ignored the decrees of heaven.*

As indicated by the fact that it occupies a position both central and correct, this line represents a wise, able, active ruler who is large-hearted enough to appreciate and protect the good qualities in all things, like a big tree whose widespread branches shelter the melons below. In doing so, he follows the middle course, as is the will of heaven. This means certain success ("Blessings will descend from heaven.").

Line 6, Yang:

(a) *Meeting in a difficult place (lit., on the horn). There will be resentment but no error.*

(b) *"Meeting in a difficult place" means exhaustion and resentment at the top.*

The position of this line is far from favorable, since it is neither central nor correct (Yang in a Yin place). It also lies at the extreme end of the hexagram ("on the horn"). Its subject is a hard worker who has exhausted his resources and is ready to retire from the world. He is also farthest from the sinister subject of Line 1, so the latter can only meet him with difficulty, can only touch his "horn." In other words, the contact is so slight as to be negligible. Thus there is no error but only some resentment.

The TS'UI Hexagram
(Symbol of Assembly)

45th  萃

THE UPPER TRIGRAM, Tui, stands for marsh water, and the lower, K'un, stands for the earth. Water sinking down into the earth fertilizes it and makes possible the abundant growth ("assembly") of plants and trees. Hence the idea of assembly or gathering together. In the human realm, this hexagram signifies the gathering together of wise and able people.

KING WEN'S JUDGMENT ON THE HEXAGRAM:

The hexagram indicates prosperity and success. The king goes to his ancestral temple. Advantage to see the great man means prosperity and success. It is advantageous to be firm and correct. Good fortune favors the use of large beasts as sacrifices. Advancement will be propitious.

The Judgment shows that assembly or congregation for religious worship (or the gathering together of those involved in an undertaking to dedicate their effort to a higher power) led by the king is an effective means of strengthening the unity of the people.

Line 5 (the ruler) occupies an ideal position, with a harmonious correlate in Line 2, and both lines are central and correct. Hence the image of "king" or "great man." In addition, the lower trigram is K'un (masses of people), and the upper is Tui (pleasure). This suggests that the people are happy as a result of seeing the great man ("prosperity and success'"). The K'un trigram (Yin, receptive) also stands for cow. Hence the image of "large beasts as sacrifices," possibly indicating the importance of loyal, hardworking people to the success of any endeavor.

CONFUCIUS' EXPLANATION OF KING WEN'S JUDGMENT:

Ts'ui, name of the hexagram, means gathering together. Obedience goes hand in hand with pleasure. The strong occupies the central place and receives favorable response. Thus arises the notion of gathering together.

"The king goes to his ancestral temple." This is for the purpose of presenting filial offerings. "Advantage to see the great man means prosperity and success." This means that the gathering together is based on what is correct. "Good fortune favors the use of large beasts as sacrifices. Advancement will be propitious." This means obedience to the will of heaven.

Observe what has been gathered together, and the innate disposition of heaven and earth, as well as of the ten thousand things, can be seen.

In this hexagram, obedience (the lower trigram, K'un) is said to go hand in hand with pleasure (the upper trigram, Tui). Since Line 5 is Yang and occupies an ideal central position, it suggests that when those of a dynamic nature assume the leadership of large endeavors and those of a receptive nature follow, the result is successful and produces gratifying results. To achieve this happy union, people must first come together. When people with a common goal gather ("assemble") for a good purpose ("what is correct"), they are assured of success ("advancement will be propitious") because such an undertaking is in accord with the will of heaven.

Things of a like nature associate with others of their kind. By studying what has gathered together, the superior man apprehends the innate nature of each thing and discovers the will of heaven.

SYMBOLIC SIGNIFICANCE OF THE HEXAGRAM AS NOTED BY CONFUCIUS:

The idea behind Ts'ui is derived from marsh water above the earth. The superior man is inspired thereby to sharpen the weapons of war as a precaution against unforeseen emergences.

Marsh water above the earth represents a source of potential benefit if it can be controlled for irrigation and cultivation. Otherwise, it is wasted or becomes a source of peril, such as a flood. The superior man realizes that the same thing is true when a large mass of people gathers together. If their energies are channeled and directed toward a productive end, the results are of benefit to everyone. However, if such an assembly gets out of control, the result can be dangerous and destructive. The superior man prepares for both eventualities when assembling people for an undertaking, in order to forestall difficulty before it arises.

DUKE OF CHOU'S EXPLANATION OF THE LINES (a) AND CONFUCIUS' COMMENT THEREON (b):

Line 1, Yin:
(a) *One's desire for union does not eventuate and causes disorder in his association with people. If only he raises a cry, there will be smiles after a shake of hands. No need to worry. Advancement will be free from error.*

(b) *"It causes disorder in his association with people." This shows his mind is confused.*

This Yin line occupies a position neither central nor correct and lies at the beginning of the hexagram. It denotes a weak person in an unfavorable and unsuitable situation who is making his first attempt at social intercourse. Naturally, he does not handle himself well and his efforts end in failure ("disorder in his association"). Fortunately, Line 1 finds a strong supporter in Line 4 (Yang, the correlate), with which it forms a harmonious relationship. If the subject of Line 1 will only cease to approach the situation heedlessly and ask for guidance ("raise a cry"), his partner will gladly come forward to help.

Line 2, Yin:

(a) *One is being guided along. There will be good fortune but no error. Sincerity will make even small offerings acceptable in spring worship.*

(b) *"One is being guided along. There will be good fortune but no error." This means that his central position has not changed.*

This Yin line occupies a position both central and correct and forms a harmonious relationship with its correlate (Line 5, the ruler). The subject of Line 2, like his superior, is a wise and gentle person who works under a great leader and follows the middle course. Because of their common philosophy, he has the good fortune of being personally guided and watched over by his superior (Line 5). Although the subject of Line 2 occupies a relatively low position, even his efforts are valuable contributions to the beginning of an undertaking ("small offerings acceptable in spring worship").

Line 3, Yin:

(a) *One seems to be sighing for companionship, but no advantage is in sight. Advancement will meet with no error, only a little regret.*

(b) *"Advancement will meet with no error." This is because his superior partner is humble and obliging.*

Line 3 is Yin and occupies a position neither central nor correct. In addition, it fails to form a harmonious relationship with its correlate (Line 6, Yin). Its subject, therefore, is a weak person given to extremes who finds hismelf in an unfavorable position and lacks any close associates ("sighing for companionship"). However, Line 3 lies at the base of the upper interior trigram, Sun (Lines 3, 4, 5), which signifies penetration or movement. Thus its subject is likely to make some reckless move in attempting to alleviate his situation. However, his correlate (Line 6), toward whom he is moving, is also a gentle and reasonable person (Yin) and will take no offense ("no error").

The upper trigram, Tui, also stands for "mouth," which creates the idea of "sighing."

Line 4, Yang:

(a) *Great good fortune will dispel error or blame.*

(b) *"Great good fortune will dispel error or blame." This is because his position is inappropriate.*

Line 4 (the minister) is Yang and occupies a position neither central nor correct. Its subject is a strong person who lacks confidence in his position and feels inadequate to properly discharge his responsibilities. He may also have difficulty getting along with the ruler (Line 5, Yang), who is equally strong-willed. Therefore, he must prove his worth and do a superior job if he is to gain merit in his superior's eyes.

Line 5, Yang:

(a) *One is in a position to promote union. No error. His sincerity may not command confidence, but his perennially grand and firm virtues will cause the disappearance of repentance.*

(b) *"One is in a position to promote union." This shows that the light of his intent has not yet become manifest.*

This Yang line is ideally situated, since it is both central and correct and forms a harmonious relationship with its correlate (Line 2). Its subject is a wise and powerful king who has the ability to bring about the unification of his nation. However, his benign intentions have not yet become widely known and his sincerity has not yet communicated itself to the people. This situation will be rectified soon, for he steers a correct course and acts in a responsible manner. When this becomes evident, those below will gladly assemble to help fulfill his worthy goals.

Line 6, Yin:

(a) *One is sighing and shedding tears. No error.*

(b) *"One is sighing and shedding tears." This shows that he does not rest comfortably in his high position.*

This Yin line rests at the top of the hexagram and fails to form a harmonious relationship with its correlate (Line 3). Its subject, therefore, is a weak person in an isolated position whose career has come to an end. He has no further prospects in sight and feels the weakness of his situation ("sighing and shedding tears"). However, he is not a bad person: his desire to associate (assemble) with others is sincere and may bear some fruit. Even if it does not, there is no blame in his desire for fellowship ("no error").

Line 6 is the last line of the upper trigram Tui, which signifies mouth. Hence the image of "sighing."

The SHENG Hexagram

(Symbol of Ascension)

46th 升

THE UPPER TRIGRAM, K'un, represents the earth, and the lower, Sun, represents trees. A tree grows upward from roots beneath the earth until it spreads its leaves toward the heavens. Hence the idea of ascension or rising.

KING WEN'S JUDGMENT ON THE HEXAGRAM:

The hexagram indicates great prosperity and success. It is useful to see the great man. No need to worry. Ventures in the south will meet with good fortune.

The Jugdment suggests the rising of able and talented elements (the two Yang lines) under the wise rule of a great man. Since Line 2 is Yang, it denotes a man of intelligence who possesses a dynamic character and is eager to act or advance. As this line occupies a central position, he is favorably placed to advance. Line 2 forms a harmonious correlation with Line 5 (the ruler), which is Yin and occupies a central position, indicating a gentle ruler. Such a leader will appreciate the abilities possessed by the subject of Line 2 and aid him in his advancement.

In China, the south is a warm and flourishing region. Hence the image of "ventures in the south meeting with good fortune."

CONFUCIUS' EXPLANATION OF KING WEN'S JUDGMENT:

The weak rises in accord with the circumstances of the time.

Docility (lower trigram) is linked with submissiveness (upper trigram). The strong occupies a central place and receives favorable response. Hence great prosperity and success.

"It is useful to see the great man. No need to worry." This means there will be great rejoicing. "Ventures in the south will meet with good fortune." This means one's aspirations will be fulfilled.

Line 5 (the ruler) is Yin and occupies a central but incorrect position (Yin in a Yang place). It also lies in the center of a K'un trigram (submissiveness). Its subject, therefore, is a gentle and meek ruler in harmony with his circumstances who has risen to the place of honor. Line 2 is Yang (strong) but lies in the center of a Sun trigram (docility), signifying an able but docile person. Line 5 and Line 2 form a harmonious relationship, indicating that the ruler is responsive to the wise plans humbly advanced by the subject of Line 2, possibly a minister. This can only lead to good fortune.

The two component trigrams, K'un and Sun, also suggest that those below are docile when those above are responsive to their needs. In this situation, those of good character (Line 2) can advance because they are in harmony with the aims of the ruler. This can only bring success and prosperity.

SYMBOLIC SIGNIFICANCE OF THE HEXAGRAM AS NOTED BY CONFUCIUS:

The idea behind Sheng is derived from wood, or trees growing up from the midst of the earth. The superior man is inspired thereby to follow the course of virtue and to accumulate the small in order to form the lofty and great.

Trees begin beneath the earth as seeds that send up sprouts to break free of the ground, growing stronger and taller until they finally form hard, stout trunks. In observing this phenomenon, the superior man learns that if his career is to grow, he must start from small beginnings and can only develop through patience and perseverence. Thus he will achieve some small success each day, and these small successes will accumulate into a lofty series of accomplishments.

DUKE OF CHOU'S EXPLANATION OF THE LINES (a)
AND CONFUCIUS' COMMENT THEREON (b):

Line 1, Yin:

(a) *One rises with approval. There will be great good fortune.*

(b) *"The great good fortune of rising with approval" means that one's aspirations harmonize with those of people above.*

Being Yin and the first line of the lower trigram, Sun, which stands for "tree," Line 2 represents tender roots under the earth. The second two lines of the trigram represent a stem. The roots, obtaining nourishment from the soil, send up shoots above the earth which, nourished by sunlight, continue to grow higher and higher. Just as a tree requires nourishment in order to flourish and grow, so men of good character require the assistance and appreciation of those above if they are to reach a position in which they can be of the greatest service.

Line 2, Yang:

(a) *Sincerity renders even small offerings acceptable in the spring worship. There will be no error.*

(b) *The "sincerity" indicated in Line 2, Yang, means that there will be rejoicing.*

This Yang line, like its correlate (Line 5, the ruler), with which it forms a harmonious relationship, occupies a central position in its trigram. The subject of Line 2, like his superior, is a sincere and able man, well placed to act, who steadfastly pursues the middle course; his sincerity makes even one occupying his lowly position a valuable partner from the very beginning of their association ("even small offerings acceptable in the spring worship").

Line 3, Yang:

(a) *One rises as if going into an empty district.*

(b) *"One rises as if going into an empty district." This shows that one has no misgivings about anything.*

Line 3 is Yang in a Yang place and forms a harmonious relationship with its correlate (Line 6). Its subject is an active and able person who moves eagerly forward to meet his more highly placed partner. The fact that only Yin lines lie before him suggests that there are only minor obstacles in his way ("an empty district").

The upper trigram, K'un (territory), lies just bove Line 3, which is Yin and signifies hollowness. Hence the image of an "empty district."

Line 4, Yin:

(a) *One is entrusted by the king with the task of presenting offerings at Mount Ch'i. Good fortune. No error.*

(b) *"One is entrusted by the king with the task of presenting offerings at Mount Ch'i." This is a matter of convenience.*

Line 4 (the minister) is Yin in a Yin place, denoting a gentle, loyal person who is close to the king (Line 5). Since he has proved himself worthy, he enjoys the favor and confidence of his ruler, and so the subject of Line 4 is the natural person to be entrusted with great tasks ("offerings at Mount Ch'i").

Mount Ch'i, usually called Ch'i Shan in Chinese history and literature, was a famous mountain and the birthplace of King Wen. The presentation of offerings there was considered a very important task.

Line 5, Yin:

(a) *One's firm correctness results in good fortune. He rises steadily, step by step.*

(b) *"One's firm correctness results in good fortune. He rises steadily, step by step." This shows that his aspirations are being realized on a grand scale.*

Line 5 (the ruler) is Yin and occupies a central place. It also forms a harmonious relationship with its correlate (Line 2, Yang). Its subject is a wise, benevolent ruler who has firmly followed a middle course ("step by step") and so enjoys the support and respect of both his ministers and the people. Such a leader is in an ideal position to carry out his plans and see them realized on a grand scale, resulting in good fortune for all.

Line 6, Yin:

(a) *One rises as if with eyes closed. Advantage will come from a ceaseless maintenance of a firm and correct posture.*

(b) *"One rises as if with eyes closed" while in a high position. This means he will suffer from privation and poverty.*

This is a Yin line in a Yin place and occupies the top extreme of the hexagram. Its subject is a weak person who has reached the summit of his ambition and has nowhere else to go. In such a position, his only hope is to proceed firmly and deliberately on a correct course, avoiding any extreme actions. Otherwise, he will simply consume his resources in a vain attempt to advance ("suffer from privation and poverty").

The K'UN Hexagram

(Symbol of Disablement)

47th  困

THE UPPER TRIGRAM, Tui, signifies a marsh, and the lower trigram, K'an, signifies a cavern. Together they represent marsh water flowing down into a cavern, a process that in time will leave the marsh dry and useless. The Chinese word for this hexagram further reinforces this image. It is the image of a tree confined within an enclosure which prevents it from growing and expanding. Hence the idea of disablement or a restricted condition.

KING WEN'S JUDGMENT ON THE HEXAGRAM:

The hexagram indicates prosperity and success. The great man with firm correctness will meet with good fortune and no error. But speeches will command no credence.

The Judgment means that men of noble character can conquer adversity and change it into prosperity, but those of mean character can only grumble and talk vainly of what they might have done ("speeches will command no credence").

Since both Lines 2 and 5 are Yang and occupy central positions, they represent great men who survive adversity or disablement.

CONFUCIUS' EXPLANATION OF KING WEN'S JUDGMENT:

The hexagram shows that the strong are being eclipsed. Danger is attended with pleasure. Is it not the case that only the great men can, while in straitened circumstances, manage not to lose those attributes that are conducive to prosperity and success? "The great man with

328

firm correctness will meet with good fortune." This is because the strong occupy central places. "Speeches will command no credence." This means that lofty talks lead to exhaustion.

In this hexagram, the three Yang lines (2, 4, 5) are each obstructed by a Yin line. This suggests a situation in which the strong are being disabled or placed in straitened conditions ("eclipsed") by the weak.

The component trigrams Tui (pleasure) and K'an (danger) suggest that danger is faced with ease and self-composure and does not lead to ill fortune. This is done by men of noble character who firmly follow the middle path and do not allow danger or disablement to rob them of success and prosperity. These noble men are denoted by Lines 2 and 5, both of which are Yang (strong) and occupy central positions.

The fact that deeds are of more worth than "lofty talk" is indicated by the third and last line of the upper trigram, Tui (mouth), which lies at the extreme end of the hexagram. This gives us the image of "speeches commanding no credence."

SYMBOLIC SIGNIFICANCE OF THE HEXAGRAM AS NOTED BY CONFUCIUS:

The idea behind K'un is derived from a marsh devoid of water. The superior man is inspired thereby to lay down his life for the accomplishment of his aims.

When the waters of a marsh are allowed to flow unchecked into caverns below, the marsh becomes dry and useless. Similarly, a man in straitened circumstances may see his wealth and resources diminishing day by day. The superior man will strive to his utmost to prevent straitened circumstances from disabling him and impairing his ability to carry out his aspirations.

DUKE OF CHOU'S EXPLANATION OF THE LINES (a) AND CONFUCIUS' COMMENT THEREON (b):

Line 1, Yin:
(a) *One has his buttocks entangled in the stump of a tree. He has entered a dark valley. For three years he cannot see the light.*

(b) *"He has entered a dark valley." This shows he is benighted and unenlightened.*

Line 1 occupies a position neither central nor correct (Yin in a Yang place). Its subject is a young man placed in unfavorable circumstances from which to advance. However, since Line 1 correlates harmoniously with Line 4, its subject is attracted to his higher-placed associate and wishes to go forth and meet him. But his desires are frustrated by the strong man (Line 2, Yang) who blocks his way and disables him ("his buttocks entangled in the stump of a tree"). In such a position, the young man should not count on seeing his partner for a long time.

The first line of the hexagram, which usually represents toes or feet, here represents the buttocks, as the subject of line 1 is said to have his buttocks caught fast. Line 1 is also at the bottom of the lower trigram, K'an, which stands for danger and cavern. Hence the images of "buttocks" and "dark valleys."

Line 2, Yang:

(a) *One feels embarrassed before wine and fine food. Red decorations for official robes will come his way. Advantageous for him to present offerings and worship, but not to embark on any ventures. There will be no error.*

(b) *"One feels embarrassed before wine and fine food." This means there is joy in the center of his heart.*

This line is Yang and occupies a central position, but fails to form a harmonious relationship with its correlate (Line 5, the ruler). The subject of Line 2 is a dynamic personality who encounters difficulty (disablement) in carrying out his benevolent plans because his superior lacks sympathetic understanding. Thus, even when he receives royal favor ("red decorations"), he is confused and embarrassed, for he does not know the motive, and this disables him. For without royal approval, action can only lead to disaster. The course of wisdom lies in remaining in his current position and rededicating his efforts, either through prayer or meditation ("offerings and worship"). This brings inward joy and satisfaction.

Line 3, Yin:

(a) *One gets caught under the rocks and is resting on the thorns.*

He enters his house and fails to see his wife. Evil omen.

(b) *"He is resting on the thorns." This means he is against the strong.*

This line occupies a position neither central nor correct (Yin in a Yang place) and fails to form a harmonious relationship with its correlate (Line 6). What is worse, it is a Yin line placed between three strong Yang lines (two above and one below), which block or disable its progress. The two above represent rocks, and the one below represents thorns. The subject of Line 3, therefore, is as helpless as if he were "caught under the rocks and resting on the thorns." The upper trigram, Tui, signifies a young girl or wife, and the lower, K'an, signifies a lad or husband. Since Lines 3 and 6 are not in harmonious correlation, husband and wife cannot meet ("fails to see his wife"). Lacking support in such a difficult situation, to advance will mean disaster ("Evil omen").

Line 4, Yang:

(a) *One moves very slowly but gets caught in a metal carriage. There will be regret, but he will have a good end.*

(b) *"He moves very slowly." This shows that his heart turns toward what is below. Though in an improper position, he has a comrade.*

Line 4 (the minister) is Yang and forms a harmonious relationship with its correlate (Line 1). However, it occupies a position neither central nor correct. Its subject is an able minister who is active in the service of the ruler (Line 5), but Line 5 is also Yang, so there is little mutual attraction between them. So the subject of Line 4 turns his heart downward or inward toward his congenial partner (Line 1). As minister, he can afford to ride in "a metal carriage," but he gets caught in it and is disabled. Symbolically, he encounters some obstruction, possibly from the strong man below (Line 2, Yang) who stands between them. Since the subject of Line 4 is also a man of strong character as well as a minister, he eventually overcomes the obstruction and allows himself to join with the subject of Line 1 ("a good end").

The lower trigram, K'an, signifies wheels, giving us the image of a "metal carriage."

Line 5, Yang:

(a) *There is one with his nose and feet cut off. He is embarrassed by an official wearing a robe with red decorations, but he appears serene and satisfied. He considers it advantageous for him to present offerings and worship.*

(b) *"One with his nose and feet cut off."* This means his aim has not been realized. *"He appears serene and satisfied."* This is because he is sincere and upright. *"Advantageous for him to present offerings and worship."* This means he will receive blessings.

Line 5 (the ruler) is Yang, occupying a position both central and correct, and denoting a strong, active ruler who pursues the middle course. However, Line 5 lies in the center of the upper trigram, Tui (destruction), and forms an antagonistic relationship with its correlate (Line 2), which lies in the center of the lower trigram, K'an (blood). As Line 2 is Yang, it represents a strong official ("wearing a robe with red decorations"), and their inability to harmonize makes it difficult for the ruler to implement his commands ("his nose and feet cut off"). Although disabled in this way, the subject of Line 5 remains firmly on the correct course and does not let the situation cause him to lose his composure ("appears serene and satisfied"). Instead, he offers sincere prayers ("offerings and worship") in the hope that in time he will achieve success and overcome the adverse circumstances surrounding him.

Line 6, Yin:

(a) *One gets entangled in the wild creepers and shakes as if about to fall down. He tells himself to be careful in his motions to avoid regret. Repentance will bring good fortune to his efforts.*

(b) *"One gets entangled in the wild creepers."* This shows his course is not yet proper. *"Motions will lead to regret and he becomes repentant."* This is propitious conduct.

This line is Yin in a Yin place and lies at the extreme top of the hexagram. Its subject is a very weak person in a high position who can advance no farther and may even be in danger of falling from his present place. He cannot cope with his plight and feels trapped by the situation ("entangled in the wild creepers"). To advance farther would mean disaster ("Motions will lead to regret"). However, he learns from the experience and resolves to reform himself ("becomes repentant"). This new sobriety leads to correct action, and he frees himself from his straitened condition.

The CHING Hexagram
(Symbol of a Well)

48th  井

THE UPPER TRIGRAM, K'an, here stands for water, and the lower, Sun, stands for entrance or penetration. Together they suggest a vessel which has penetrated below the surface of the water in order to draw it out. Hence the idea of a well.

KING WEN'S JUDGMENT ON THE HEXAGRAM:

The hexagram indicates a well. In changing a district, its well is not changed. The well neither decreases nor increases its amount of water. People come and go and draw from it. On approaching the edge of the well, before the rope is fully pulled out, the earthen bucket may get broken. This is misfortune.

The Judgment stresses the permanent usefulness of a well, which remains the same no matter what the changes of fortune around it or how often its resources are drawn upon. Just as a district depends on a well for its existence and growth, so the existence and growth of an institution or society depend on sound moral principles. A society may change, but certain basic principles are not to be changed. Just as a bucket can be broken before it lifts the water to a useful level, so one's virtue can be lost or neglected before reaching fruition.

CONFUCIUS' EXPLANATION OF KING WEN'S JUDGMENT:

The hexagram suggests penetrating into the water and drawing it up, and indicates a well. A well yields nourishment and will not become exhausted.

333

"In changing a district, its well is not changed." This is because the strong occupy central positions. "On approaching the edge of the well, before the rope is fully pulled out." This means nothing has been achieved. "The earthen bucket may get broken." That's why there is misfortune.

Water in a well is like virtue in a man. Just as water in a well should be a constant source of nourishment for the body, virtue in a man should constantly nourish his spirit.

Lines 2 and 5 are Yang and both occupy a central position, suggesting men of strong moral character who firmly pursue virtue and follow the middle path. They will not deviate from it whatever changes there may be in their surrounding circumstances, ("the well is not changed").

In drawing water from a well, one should carefully pull up the rope together with the bucket. If one is careless, the "bucket may get broken" before the rope is fully pulled up. Similarly, a man should pursue virtue diligently. If he neglects it, he will achieve nothing, and his life work may be wrecked within an ace of fulfilment. This is indeed misfortune.

SYMBOLIC SIGNIFICANCE OF THE HEXAGRAM AS NOTED BY CONFUCIUS:

The idea behind Ching is derived from tree (lower trigram) with water (upper trigram) above it. The superior man is inspired thereby to encourage the people to work hard and exhort them to practice mutual assistance.

The lower trigram, Sun, stands for tree, and the upper, K'an, stands for water. Together they suggest the roots of a tree that have penetrated deep into the earth and are drawing up water to nourish the trunk and branches. Similarly, a man lets down a bucket into a well and draws up water for cooking and other purposes. By observing these phenomena, the superior man realizes the wisdom of encouraging cooperation among the people and utilizing their intelligence and industry for a high and worthy purpose which will benefit everyone ("mutual assistance").

DUKE OF CHOU'S EXPLANATION OF THE LINES (a) AND CONFUCIUS' COMMENT THEREON (b):

Line 1, Yin:
(a) *A well with muddy, undrinkable water. It is an old well where no birds come.*
(b) *"A well with muddy, undrinkable water." This is because it is low. "It is an old well where no birds come." This means time has discarded its usefulness.*

This line at the bottom of the Ching Hexagram represents the bottom of a well in which the water is muddy and undrinkable. In the human realm, it represents the lowest dregs of society or corrupt officials and politicians, those who are of no use to anyone. These worthless elements are abhorred and abandoned by decent people ("no birds come") and in time will be cast into oblivion ("discarded"). The line may also represent an outmoded idea or institution that is no longer useful.

Line 2, Yang:
(a) *A well whose water flows away through a hole to where the shrimps are. It is like a leaky bucket from which the water flows away.*
(b) *"A well whose water flows away through a hole to where the shrimps are." This indicates one who has no helpful associate.*

This is a Yang line occupying a central position and suggesting a good well whose water is sweet and pure. However, Line 2 is incorrectly placed and fails to form a harmonious relationship with its correlate (Line 5, the ruler). So, due to its awkward position ("leaking bucket"), the well's water is not drawn up for human use but flows away uselessly to feed shrimps instead. In human terms, this represents a wise and able man who fails to obtain favor with his ruler and whose talents and abilities are wasted in the wrong direction.

Line 3, Yang:
(a) *A well already dug out but unused. This fills people's heart with pity, for water could be drawn up for use. If there had been an enlightened king, he could have enjoyed the blessing with the people.*

(b) *"A well already dug out but unused." Passersby feel pity for it. Yearning for "an enlightened king" indicates the desire to receive blessings from him.*

Line 3 occupies a correct position (Yang in a Yang place) and forms a harmonious relationship with its correlate (Line 6). In terms of its position in the hexagram, this line denotes a well which has been dug out and has clear water in it. However, because Line 3 does not occupy a central position, the well is passed by and remains unused. In human society, this line (like Line 2) represents a wise and able man whose talents go to waste because they are not recognized ("unused") by the ruler (Line 5, Yang), with whom the subject of Line 3 futilely desires to form a harmonious relationship. "Passersby feel pity" for him, and all yearn for a more enlightened ruler who will make use of such able men and act to promote the general welfare ("desire to receive blessings from him").

Line 4, Yin:

(a) *A well whose brick wall is being laid out. No error.*

(b) *"A well whose brick wall is being laid out. No error." This means the need for repairing the well has been met.*

In this hexagram the Yang lines represent water, and the Yin lines represent the well itself. Here, Line 4 is Yin in a Yin place, signifying a good well, but one with little or no water in it. This is because the inlets on its wall (the Yin lines) are not in good condition and are being repaired. Since Line 4 (the minister) occupies a position at the top of the lower interior trigram (Lines 2, 3, 4), signifying a time of transition, its subject is a minister who has been awkwardly placed and does not feel adequate to his position. Therefore, he has been working to strengthen himself intellectually and physically, so that he will be fully prepared when he is called upon to act.

Line 5, Yang:

(a) *A well contains clear, cool water ready for drinking.*

(b) *"Clear, cool water ready for drinking." This stems from its central and correct position.*

Here, Line 5 occupies a position both central and correct, signifying a good well with clear water which is pleasant to the taste. In human terms, it symbolizes a wise and benevolent ruler who pursues a middle course. His good government is a fount of blessings which the people may constantly draw upon.

Line 6, Yin:

(a) *A well completed and uncovered. Sincerity shows itself, and there will be great good fortune.*

(b) *"Great good fortune" in a high place. It means grand accomplishment.*

This Yin line is at the top of the hexagram and resembles an open mouth, signifying not only the final completion of a well, but also that it is "uncovered" and open for use by all those who need its water.

Since Line 6 is Yin in a Yin place, it also signifies sincerity and faithfulness, indicating that the well will continue to supply water, no matter how often people draw from it. In the human world, this line denotes an able man of humble character who is dedicated to the service of those below him and who, no matter what their need, is always ready to offer his assistance and guidance. This is "great good fortune" to the people. He thus achieves his highest aspirations ("grand accomplishment").

The KO Hexagram
(Symbol of Reform)

49th 革

THE UPPER TRIGRAM, Tui, here represents marsh water, and the lower, Li, represents fire. Water poured from above can extinguish fire, and fire placed below water can boil it away. Thus, each transforms the other. Hence the idea of reform.

KING WEN'S JUDGMENT ON THE HEXAGRAM:

The hexagram indicates that reform should be made when the time for it is ripe; then it will inspire confidence. There will be great prosperity and success. Advantageous to be firm and correct. Repentance will disappear.

Everything has its proper time, even reform. No matter how desperate the need, if corrections or improvements are made prematurely or before those involved perceive their value, they will be neither accepted nor supported. In time of reform, staying firmly on the correct path will lead to success and bring good fortune to all.

CONFUCIUS' EXPLANATION OF KING WEN'S JUDGMENT:

The hexagram shows that water and fire are mutually destructive. Two daughters live in the same home, but their aspirations are at variance. This is the reason for reform, name of the hexagram.

"Reform should be made when the time for it is ripe; then it will inspire confidence." When reform leads to trust, pleasure will stem from cultural enlightenment, and correctness will underlie great

prosperity and success. When reform is made in the appropriate manner, repentance will disappear.

Heaven and earth undergo reform, and the four seasons come into being. T'ang and Wu reformed the mandate in accordance with the will of heaven and in response to the wishes of men. Great indeed is the time element of reform indicated in the hexagram.

Fire and water are mutually destructive. However, when under proper control, they can be of great benefit: fire to boil water and water to extinguish fire. Line 2 is the second line of the lower trigram, Li, denoting the second daughter, and Line 6 is the third line of the upper trigram, Tui, denoting the third or youngest daughter. Here, the elder daughter finds herself placed below her younger sister, which leads to much unhappiness and conflict between them. If the situation were reformed and both regained their proper places, mutual harmony and benefit would result.

The second paragraph interprets the two component trigrams in another sense. The lower trigram, Li, also means enlightenment, and the upper trigram, Tui, also signifies pleasure or satisfaction. Taken together, they suggest that enlightenment ("reform") leads to pleasure.

Just as the four seasons follow and complement each other (each reforming the excesses of its predecessor), human institutions succeed and reform each other. When such a time arrives, to institute reform is of benefit to all ("the will of heaven"). T'ang, the first emperor of the Shang dynasty, successfully led a revolt against the preceding Hsia dynasty. Wu was the first emperor of the Chou dynasty and he successfully led a revolt against the preceding Shang dynasty. These revolts are considered to have been successful because all perceived their necessity when they were undertaken.

SYMBOLIC SIGNIFICANCE OF THE HEXAGRAM AS NOTED BY CONFUCIUS:

The idea behind Ko is derived from fire (Li) inside the marsh (Tui). The superior man is inspired thereby to regulate the calendar and define the seasons clearly.

Fire or heat in the marsh suggests a drought. Observing this phenomenon, the superior man realizes the necessity of planning ahead so that that he can prepare for times of both rain and sunshine ("regulate the calendar and define the seasons").

DUKE OF CHOU'S EXPLANATION OF THE LINES (a) AND CONFUCIUS' COMMENT THEREON (b):

Line 1, Yang:

(a) *One is held fast with the hide of a yellow ox.*

(b) *"One is held fast with the hide of a yellow ox." This shows that he cannot take any action.*

This line is Yang and occupies the beginning of the hexagram, denoting an energetic young man who wants to initiate some reform. However, Line 1 occupies a position which, though correct (Yang in a Yang place), is not central. Although its subject may have the necessary talents to institute reforms, he is not advantageously placed to do so ("held fast with the hide of a yellow ox"). Consequently, he should not initiate any move unless he can obtain support from his close associate (Line 2), the centrally placed ruler of the trigram with whom he forms a harmonious relationship.

"Yellow ox" refers to Line 2, which is Yin. Three Yin lines make up the K'un trigram, which stands for both ox and yellow color. Hence the image, "hide of a yellow ox."

Line 2, Yin:

(a) *When the time is ripe, reform must be made. Ventures will meet with good fortune. There will be no error.*

(b) *"When the time is ripe, reform must be made." This means that actions taken will be praiseworthy.*

Both Line 2 and its correlate (Line 5, the ruler), with which it forms a harmonious relationship, occupy positions both central and correct. This indicates that both the king and his minister follow a middle course; so when reform is necessary, the two men are able to act together in smooth cooperation. Their efforts will be crowned with success ("actions taken will be praiseworthy").

Line 3, Yang:

(a) *Ventures will meet with misfortune; persistence will be perilous. Reform should receive careful deliberation three times before it will inspire trust.*

(b) *"Reform should receive careful deliberation three times." Then whither shall it turn?*

Here, Line 3 is Yang in a Yang place and occupies the top of the lower trigram, Li. Its subject is a wise and active man who is eager to help institute reforms. However, as his position is not central, he is unfavorably placed to act and will only encounter disaster if he insists on making any forward move ("ventures meet with misfortune"). Instead, he should take care to consult others three times (there are three other Yang lines, or wise men) before formulating his plans ("careful deliberation"). Only in this way will his efforts have a solid enough foundation to gain popular support ("inspire trust").

The upper trigram, Tui, especially its Line 6, represents an open mouth. Line 6 also forms a harmonious relationship with Line 3 (its correlate), suggesting the image of "consultation."

Line 4, Yang:

(a) *Repentance will disappear. If there is sincerity underlying the change of the legal order, there will be good fortune.*

(b) *"The good fortune of changing the legal order" shows that one's aim is sincere.*

Line 4 (the minister) is Yang, denoting a strong, able person occupying a position of trust who wishes to institute much-needed reforms. Line 5 (the ruler) is also Yang, indicating a leader possessed of equal strength and wisdom. Although their ideas and aspirations are similar, they are both strong figures who fail to form a harmonious relationship and tend to clash with each other. If the subject of Line 4 wishes to gain his superior's trust and cooperation, he must first prove his sincerity. When he has done so, he will receive all the support he needs for his reforms.

Line 5, Yang:

(a) *A great man carries out his reforms like a tiger changing its stripes. They will inspire trust even before divination is resorted to.*

341

(b) *"A great man carries out his reforms like a tiger changing its stripes." This shows the brilliance of his cultural attainment.*

Here, Line 5 (the ruler) is ideally placed, since both it and its correlate (Line 2), with whom it forms a harmonious relationship, occupy positions that are central and correct. This indicates that the subject of Line 5 is a great king or leader ("great man"), advantageously placed to act, whose plans for reform receive sympathetic support from those below. Such a man's achievements are bound to be brilliant.

Line 6, Yin:

(a) *A superior man carries out his reforms like a leopard changing its spots. The small, mean man will change his heart (lit., face). Ventures will be unfortunate. Good fortune requires staying in a firm and correct course.*

(b) *"A superior man carries out his reforms like a leopard changing its spots." This shows the exuberance of his cultural attainment. "The small, mean man changes his heart." This shows his submissive obedience to the king.*

Since it lies at the extreme top of the hexagram, this line represents a statesman or superior man whose talents and abilities have helped his ruler bring needed reforms to a successful conclusion. Inspired by his example, even those of petty character ("small, mean men") change their attitudes and obey the king (Line 5). Since Line 6 has reached the limit of the hexagram, it represents a situation in which all necessary reforms have been carried out and no further reforms are needed. In such circumstaces, the superior man knows that the correct course lies in consolidating his gains, for any further efforts will be excessive and inadvisable ("ventures will be unfortunate").

The TING Hexagram
(Symbol of a Caldron)

50th  鼎

THE STRUCTURE OF THIS hexagram is said to resemble that of a caldron. Line 1 (Yin) lies at the bottom, representing the legs; Lines
2, 3, and 4 (Yang) represent the body; and Line 5 (Yin) represents
the two side rings called "ears." Line 6 (Yang), at the top, represents the handle linked to these two "ears."

The meaning of this hexagram is closely related to that of the
preceding hexagram, Ko, for cooking things in a caldron requires
both fire and water and results in a process of transformation.

KING WEN'S JUDGMENT ON THE HEXAGRAM:

*The hexagram indicates great good fortune as well as prosperity
and success.*

Things that are cooked in a caldron are transformed from a raw
state to a wholesome one that provides nourishment to people.
This is good fortune indeed.

CONFUCIUS' EXPLANATION OF KING WEN'S JUDGMENT:

*The hexagram is a symbol for a caldron. Wood submitted to fire
suggests the process of cooking. The sages cook food as offerings to
God and give banquets to feed the wise and worthy.*

*Submissiveness goes hand in hand with sharp eyes and keen ears.
The weak advances and acts while in a high place. It obtains the central position and receives favorable response from the strong. Hence
great prosperity and success.*

343

The upper trigram is Li (fire), and the lower trigram is Sun (wood). In terms of the symbolism of the hexagram as a whole, this suggests fire flaming up from wood and heating the bottom of a caldron, which brings its contents to a boil and cooks them to provide nourishment.

To Confucius, food is not merely to be enjoyed but serves a twofold higher purpose: (1) as offerings to God; and (2) to entertain the worthies so that they can contribute their wisdom to social reform.

The lower trigram, Sun, signifies willingness to learn and reform oneself ("submissiveness"), and the upper trigram, Li, signifies intelligence ("sharp eyes and keen ears"). Together they suggest that education can transform ignorance into intelligence. Lines 1 and 5 are the only two Yin lines in the hexagram. They represent the same person in two stages of evolution. Line 1, Yin, at the bottom of the hexagram, represents a weak and lowly person; but through education and self-reform, he "obtains the central position" in Line 5, signifying a ruler or chief executive. Furthermore, Line 5 forms a harmonious relationship with its correlate (Line 2, Yang), indicating strong, valuable support. All this is good fortune indeed.

SYMBOLIC SIGNIFICANCE OF THE HEXAGRAM AS NOTED BY CONFUCIUS:

The idea behind Ting is derived from wood with fire over it. The superior man is inspired thereby to rectify his position and concentrate his attention on the will of heaven.

The "ting" is a three-legged caldron used for cooking. Wood with fire over it signifies that wood is being burned for cooking purposes. During cooking, the substances in the caldron undergo transformation and are made useful. From this, the superior man learns the wisdom of concentrating his efforts on the things that help perfect and develop his character until at last he becomes as correct and dignified as a ting. Such a man's actions and reforms are sure to be in accord with "the will of heaven."

DUKE OF CHOU'S EXPLANATION OF THE LINES (a) AND CONFUCIUS' COMMENT THEREON (b):

Line 1, Yin:

(a) A caldron is upset with upturned toes. Advantageous for pouring out what is unwholesome. One takes a concubine because of her son. No error.

(b) "A Caldron is upset with upturned toes." Not all has been spoilt. "Advantageous for pouring out what is unwholesome." This means adhesion to the nobility.

Line 1, at the bottom of the hexagram, represents the toes. Here it is Yin and unfavorably situated, since it occupies a position neither central nor correct. This suggests weak toes or feet which cannot firmly support a caldron and so cause it to overturn. However, Line 1 forms a harmonious relationship with its Yang correlate (Line 4). If the subject of Line 1 ignores the example of those who obey their lower impulses and follows the example of his strong and worthy friend ("adhesion to nobility"), he will achieve success. Then he will be like a caldron whose bad ingredients have been poured out ("what is unwholesome") but whose good ones have been retained. Because of his efforts, his friend is willing to ignore his lowly origins, the way a man might overlook the incorrect position of a concubine and dwell instead on the prospect of having a son with her.

Line 2, Yang:

(a) A caldron has solid things in it. "My associate shows ill will, but it will not affect me." There will be good fortune.

(b) "A caldron has solid things in it." One has to be careful as to whither he tends. "My associate shows ill will." In the end there will be no resentment.

This line is Yang, which suggests that the caldron contains something substantial and good to eat. The fact that it occupies a central position indicates that its subject possesses a sound character or sense of balance and so is invulnerable to or unaffected by the bad influence of his close associate (Line 1). Instead, the subject of Line 2 is attracted to and receives the support of the subject of Line 5 (the ruler), with whom he forms a harmonious relationship. This leads to good fortune, though it may bring ill will from the subject of Line 1. But under the circumstances, this is of no importance ("will not affect me").

Line 3, Yang:

(a) *A caldron with its ears removed. It cannot be moved. The delicious meat of the pheasant is not eaten. When rain falls, repentance will disappear. Eventually there will be good fortune.*

(b) *"A caldron with its ears removed." It has lost its meaning.*

This Yang line occupies a position correct but not central, indicating that its subject is a strong-minded man who is inclined to go to extremes and make rash moves. Since Line 3 forms an antagonistic relationship with its correlate (Line 6), its subject wants to advance and reform the other or remove him from his place. As Line 5 (the ruler) is Yin in a central position, it represents a gentle, kind-hearted person who denies the subject of Line 3 permission to attack the subject of Line 6. The subject of Line 3 is not satisfied and rashly wishes to disregard or get by the ruler. Symbolically, he wants to remove the ears of the caldron. In so doing, he renders the caldron practically useless, wasting the other's wisdom and ability ("the delicious meat of the pheasant"). His wise ruler reaches down and brings him into subjection, causing him to repent sincerely. Reconciliation is thus effected, just as rain is formed when Yin and Yang are in harmony. Further, the subject of Line 3 learns how unwise it is to attempt reform rashly, without carefully weighing the prospects and consequences.

If Line 3 is transformed into Yin, the lower interior trigram (Lines 2, 3, 4) becomes Li, which stands for pheasant, providing the image of "the meat of the pheasant."

Line 4, Yang:

(a) *A caldron with broken legs spills the food intended for the duke. One's face reddens with shame. Evil is in store for him.*

(b) *"Spilling the food intended for the duke." Can one be worthy of trust?*

Just as Line 1 represents the toes, Line 4 represents the legs. Here, the Line is strong and solid (Yang), and since it lies at the upper limit of the hexagram, suggests a caldron filled to the brim with food. Consequently, the caldron's legs break under the weight, upsetting its contents, which are spilled out and wasted.

Line 4 also represents a minister or assistant; the subject of this line is a strong, able individual. However, the line occupies a position neither central nor correct (Yang in a Yin place), denoting a minister under pressure who finds himself in unfavorable circumstances from which to act. He finally breaks down under the heavy burden of attempting to fulfill his duties, and his real talents are wasted ("spilling the food"). This causes him great shame and embarrassment.

Line 5, Yin:

(a) *A caldron with yellow ears linked into metal rings. Advantageous to be firm and correct.*

(b) *"A caldron with yellow ears." One has sterling virtues at heart.*

Line 5 (the ruler) is Yin, occupies a central position, and forms a harmonious relationship with its correlate (Line 2). Its subject is a kind and gentle ruler who follows a middle course ("sterling virtues") and receives the loyalty of his officials. His situation is like a caldron which not only has yellow ears but metal rings linked to them. This makes the caldron easily movable and increases its usefulness.

Line 5 represents the ears or hinges of the caldron. As it is a Yin line in the center of the upper trigram, it suggests the center of the earth, which is yellow in color. Hence the image of "yellow ears." According to Confucius, this denotes sterling virtues at heart. If Line 5 is transformed into Yang, the upper trigram becomes Ch'ien, which signifies gold or metal. Hence the image of "metal rings."

Line 6, Yang:

(a) *A caldron with jade rings. Great good fortune. Nothing not advantageous.*

(b) *"Jade rings" in the top place means that the strong and the weak have made proper mutual adjustment.*

This Yang line not only lies at the extreme top of the hexagram but also at the top of the upper trigram, Li (fire). This suggests that the food in the caldron has been thoroughly cooked and is ready to be eaten. The idea is reinforced by the fact that the caldron has "jade rings." Since jade is hard by nature but soft and mild in appearance, this suggests that the ingredients in the caldron (and the subject or group it represents) are harmoniously mixed ("have made proper . . . adjustment").

The CHEN Hexagram
(Symbol of Quaking)

51st  震

THE FIRST LINE AT the bottom of the trigram is Yang and lies beneath two Yin lines. This indicates a strong, dynamic force moving up from under the earth and about to burst through its surface (Line 2). Since this hexagram is composed of two Chen trigrams (thunder doubled), it also suggests peal after peal of thunder or a series of violent quakes.

KING WEN'S JUDGMENT ON THE HEXAGRAM:

The hexagram indicates prosperity and success. A crash of thunder comes. One first feels horrified, then laughs and talks with glee. The crash spreads terror for a hundred li (one-third of a mile) around. One does not forget the wine and the fork for worship.

Thunder can clear a long-stagnant or oppressive atmosphere. Similarly, a violent shock or quake may strike terror into the hearts of men. But it can also make them more sane and sober afterward, and grateful to God for their deliverance and continued prosperity. In the social realm, the situation may be likened to a political *coup d'état* or revolution which clarifies a long-standing political confusion.

CONFUCIUS' EXPLANATION OF KING WEN'S JUDGMENT:

The hexagram indicates prosperity and success.
"A crash of thunder comes. One first feels horrified." This means that horror may bring happiness. "One then laughs and talks with glee." This means that afterward there will be rules to abide by.

"The crash spreads terror for a hundred li around." This means that it terrifies people far and near. "One does not forget the wine and the fork for worship." He can go out to preside over the worship at the ancestral temples and at the shrines of the farm gods.

After being reminded of their mortality by a quake or storm, the wise thankfully recall the many blessings they receive from their Creator ("worship at the ancestral temples") and resolve more firmly to tread the right path.

SYMBOLIC SIGNIFICANCE OF THE HEXAGRAM AS NOTED BY CONFUCIUS:

The idea behind Chen is derived from thunder upon thunder. The superior man is inspired thereby to practice self-discipline and self-examination with fearfulness.

Peal upon peal of crashing thunder strikes terror into people's hearts and evokes thoughts of God's wrath, punishments, and trials. In such a situation, many panic and grow fearful, but the superior man realizes the need to practice self-discipline and not allow his emotions to rule him. He is merely reminded to rectify and strengthen his character, that he may make his conduct pleasing to both God and man.

DUKE OF CHOU'S EXPLANATION OF THE LINES (a) AND CONFUCIUS' COMMENT THEREON (b):

Line 1, Yang:

(a) "A crash of thunder comes. One first feels horrified, then *laughs and talks with glee." There will be good fortune.*

(b) *"A crash of thunder comes. One first feels horrified." This means that horror may bring happiness. "One then laughs and talks with glee." This means that afterward there will be rules to abide by.*

Line 1 signifies the underground beneath the earth. Since it is Yang in a Yang place, it denotes a situation in which a powerful force that is gathering unseen or under the earth will soon break forth over the land, releasing the oppressive atmospheric pressure in a clap of thunder. This naturally makes people fearful, but also shows them the wisdom of taking precautions if they are to dispel present and future dangers ("afterward there will be rules to abide by"). Then they feel safe and happy. Thus fear leads to happiness, prudence, and better rules for living.

Symbolically, Line 1 indicates good fortune, for it is Yang and its onward course encounters opposition from only two Yin lines.

Line 2, Yin:

(a) *A crash of thunder comes, threatening peril. People do not mind losing their valuables in order to go up into the high hills. They need not seek what they have lost. They will regain it in seven days.*

(b) *"A crash of thunder comes, threatening peril." This is indicated by the line riding on a strong one.*

If Line 1 represents the underground where the thunder is gathering, then Line 2 represents the surface of the earth, or the point where the impact is mightiest. It is no wonder that those who live there feel a strong sense of peril and seek refuge in the mountains in such a hurry that they leave their valuables behind.

Seven is a spiritual number, symbolically constituting a cycle at the end of which a new cycle will begin and things will return to their former state. This gives us the image of "regaining it in seven days."

Line 3, Yin:

(a) *A crash or violent quake drives people to distraction. Action taken during the quake will dispel trouble.*

(b) *"A violent quake drives people to distraction." This is indicated in the inappropriate position of the line.*

This Yin line occupies a position neither central nor correct and fails to form a harmonious relationship with its correlate (Line 6). What is worse, Line 3 lies at the top of one trigram and just below another. This symbolizes the contact point between two violent quakes or disruptions, a situation so terrifying as to drive most people mad ("distraction"). However, if they can retain or recover their presence of mind and take proper measures, they can deliver themselves from danger.

Line 4, Yang:

(a) *The violence of the quake is absorbed in the mire.*

(b) *"The violence of the quake is absorbed in the mire."* This shows that the light has not become manifest.

This Yang line is sandwiched between two Yin lines above and two below it. This suggests a situation in which both the thunder and the lightning that causes it are buried deep in the earth and are unable to manifest themselves.

Line 5, Yin:

(a) *A violent quake occurs, periling people whether coming or going. One must deliberate carefully so as not to neglect the tasks in mind.*

(b) *"A violent quake occurs, periling people whether coming or going."* It is dangerous to act. Tasks done at the center will be far from any mishap.*

Here, Line 5 (the ruler) is Yin below another Yin line, and its correlate (Line 2) is also Yin. In addition, it is mounted upon a Yang or strong line ("a violent quake"). All this indicates that its subject is a weak person in an unfavorable position from which to move ("periling people whether coming or going"). On the other hand, Line 5 occupies a central position, denoting a gentle, sensible ruler who is disposed to follow a middle course. If he considers the implications of his position carefully, he will realize that it is unwise to advance.

Line 6, Yin:

(a) *Violent quakes fill people's hearts with anxiety and make them look wildly around. Any venture will end in evil. If people are cautious when the quake reaches their neighbor and before it reaches them, they will be free from error. There will be some unpleasant words from relatives.*

(b) *"Violent quakes fill people's hearts with anxiety."* This shows that the middle way has not been found. *"Free from error, though in an evil situation."* This means that one heeds the warning from the danger in the neighborhood.

Being at the extreme top of the hexagram, this line indicates that the quakes have been going on for a prolonged period of time. People feel greatly dismayed and do not know what to do. If they attempt to initiate any great task at such a time, they will surely meet with evil. However, if they had taken precautions at the proper time, they would have nullified its ill effects. ("Free from error, though in an evil situation.") Those who do not take such precautions need not expect support in times of danger ("unpleasant words from relatives"). As Lao Tzu says in his *Tao Teh Ching* (Chapter 64): "Act before any trouble starts. Enforce order before disorder arises."

The KEN Hexagram
(Symbol of Rest, Obstacle)

52nd   艮

THIS HEXAGRAM IS composed of the Ken trigram (mountain) doubled, signifying one mountain joining another in a range of mountains. Mountains present a restful picture, but also constitute obstacles to movement or progress.

KING WEN'S JUDGMENT ON THE HEXAGRAM:

One resting on his back is unaware of his body and walking in his courtyard, does not see any person. There will be no error.

The spine of a mountain range resembles the human spine, or backbone. The backbone usually represents principle or moral integrity. A man who habitually stands on principle and follows the correct course develops the strength of will necessary to subjugate or transcend his lower self, or petty ego. Such a man cannot be tempted to deviate from the right path and is not led astray by his sensual appetites and passions ("unaware of his body"). Similarly, he is not influenced by personalities. Instead, he obeys the dictates of his reason and pursues a middle course.

CONFUCIUS' EXPLANATION OF KING WEN'S JUDGMENT:

The hexagram Ken means to rest or stop. Stop when it is time to stop. Act when it is time to act. Neither motion nor quiescence misses its timeliness. This is a bright and enlightened way.

To stop where there should be stopping is to stop at the proper place. The upper and the lower respond hostilely to each other. So they have nothing to do with each other. Hence one "is unaware of his body (or self) and walking in his courtyard, does not see any person. There will be no error."

To advance when the time is auspicious for advancement and to stop when the time is auspicious for stopping is the way of the superior man.

In the Ken Hexagram all the lines of the lower trigram (Lines 1, 2, 3) fail to form harmonious relationships with their correlates in the upper trigram (Lines 4, 5, 6). Since the elements of the two trigrams are not able to reach an accord ("the upper and the lower respond hostilely to each other"), they stop and rest, choosing the path of wisdom and going their separate ways ("have nothing to do with each other").

SYMBOLIC SIGNIFICANCE OF THE HEXAGRAM AS NOTED BY CONFUCIUS:

The idea behind Ken is derived from mountain joining mountain. The superior man is inspired thereby not to let his thoughts go beyond his proper status.

The hexagram represents a range of mountains, each of which remains in a fixed position, as if enjoying its own being, and does not interfere with its neighbors. From this the superior man learns the wisdom of acting in accordance with his own status in life and of keeping his own actions within that scope.

DUKE OF CHOU'S EXPLANATION OF THE LINES (a) AND CONFUCIUS' COMMENT THEREON (b):

Line 1, Yin:

(a) *One rests his toes. No error. Advantageous to be ever firm and correct.*

(b) *"One rests his toes." This shows that one has not missed the correct course.*

Here Line 1, which lies at the bottom and represents the toes, is Yin or weak, signifying a young, inexperienced person who has just entered society. Since the line occupies a position neither central nor correct (Yin in a Yang place), its subject is very unfavorably placed to advance or act. In such a situation the path of wisdom ("correct course") is to remain firmly in one's place ("rests his toes") and, in accordance with the Law of Cyclic Reversion, prepare himself for a more auspicious time to act.

Line 2, Yin:

(a) *One rests the calves of his legs. He is unable to rescue him whom he follows. He feels unhappy at heart.*

(b) *"He is unable to rescue him whom he follows." This means there is no turning back to listen.*

This Yin line occupies a position both central and correct, indicating that its subject is a wise and gentle person who is well placed to act. He wants to offer assistance to his troubled associate (Line 3), whom he is following, but is unable to do so because the other pays him no heed ("no turning back to listen"). This causes the subject of Line 2 grievous anguish ("unhappy at heart"), so he abandons his efforts ("rests the calves of his legs").

Just as Line 1 represents the toes, Line 2 represents the calves, suggesting the image, "rests the calves of his legs."

Line 3, Yang:

(a) *One rests his waist, with the ribs showing beneath the skin. The perilous condition makes his heart seem burning.*

(b) *"One rests his waist." This is because danger inflames his heart.*

This Yang line occupies a position not central but correct and fails to form a harmonious relationship with its correlate (Line 6). Its subject is a man of dynamic character who finds himself in unfavorable circumstances ("One rests his waist, with the ribs showing beneath the skin"). Such a man is apt to make rash and impulsive moves ("danger inflames his heart").

Line 3 represents the waist, creating the images of "waist" and "rib."

Line 4, Yin:

(a) *One keeps his trunk at rest. No error.*

(b) *"One keeps his trunk at rest." This is to poise his body in a quiescent state.*

This Yin line occupies a position correct but not central, and so its subject is not favorably placed to act. However, he is a gentle, reasonable person who is wise enough to remain in his present position, preserving his energy and vitality for a more favorable time.

Line 5, Yin:

(a) *One rests the sides of his mouth. His speech will be in proper order. Repentance will disappear.*

(b) *"One rests the sides of his mouth." This shows correct behavior in a central position.*

Here, Line 5 (the ruler) occupies a position central but not correct. Its subject is a gentle, cultured person who follows a middle course ("correct behavior") and prefers to be both cautious and judicious in speech ("rests the sides of his mouth"). Such a man will have no cause for repentance.

Line 6, Yang:

(a) *Solemn rest. Good fortune.*

(b) *The "good fortune of solemn rest" means that in the end one will attain goodness and magnanimity.*

Lying at the top of the Ken Hexagram (rest), this Yang line signifies the sound rest of the whole person, which leads to the recuperation of physical, mental, and spiritual health.

The CHIEN Hexagram

(Symbol of Gradual Progression)

53rd  漸

THE UPPER TRIGRAM, Sun, stands for trees, and the lower, Ken, stands for mountain. Trees on a mountain must grow slowly from tender shoots if they are to reach a great height. Hence the idea of gradual progression.

KING WEN'S JUDGMENT ON THE HEXAGRAM:

The hexagram indicates the good fortune of a girl getting married. Advantageous to be firm and chaste.

In traditional China, marriage was not consummated in a day or even a week. It was a gradual process involving five preliminary steps and lasting a fairly long time. A marriage begun carefully in this manner was always considered good fortune ("Advantageous to be firm and chaste").

CONFUCIUS' EXPLANATION OF KING WEN'S JUDGMENT:

The advancement indicated in the hexagram Chien is the good fortune of a girl getting married.

Advancement into the proper places shows that going ahead will meet with success. Advancement based on what is correct could be a means to rectify the state.

In regard to place, the strong has obtained a central one.

Rest going hand in hand with docile penetration bespeaks inexhuastible motion.

Lines 2, 3, 4, and 5 occupy their correct places, while Lines 2 and 5 occupy the two central positions of the hexagram. This means four of the six lines are favorably placed for advancment. Since Line 2 is Yin (female) and forms a harmonious relationship with its Yang correlate (Line 5), their advancement is symbolized by "the good fortune of a girl getting married." This idea is reinforced by the position of Line 5 ("the strong has obtained a central one [place]").

The lower trigram is Ken (mountain), and the upper trigram is Sun (trees or gradual progress), signifying something that remains in one place, putting down deep roots, and then begins a gradual progression toward its goals which cannot be stopped by any obstacle in its path ("inexhaustible motion").

This paragraph also suggests the situation of a man who advances from a lesser position to fill one for which he is more properly suited. When such advancement is based on real ability and not greed or egotism, it benefits the group or nation involved.

SYMBOLIC SIGNIFICANCE OF THE HEXAGRAM AS NOTED BY CONFUCIUS:

The idea behind Chien is derived from trees on the mountain. The superior man is inspired thereby to abide by his exemplary virtues in order to promote the moral excellence of the people.

Trees on a mountain do not shoot up instantly, but grow gradually and surely from small seeds. Similarly, the moral tone or character of a society does not develop instantly, but must be fostered gradually through the patient cultivation of virtue by its members, especially its leaders. The superior man considers it wise to act in accordance with this principle.

DUKE OF CHOU'S EXPLANATION OF THE LINES (a) AND CONFUCIUS' COMMENT THEREON (b):

Line 1, Yin:
(a) A *bevy of wild geese gradually approach the shore. A humble young man faces peril and incurs criticism. There will be no error.*

(b) *"The peril of a humble young man"* indicates that according to reason there should be no error.

This Yin line, being the first in the hexagram, represents the beach or shore of a tract of land. Migratory geese will first approach this landmark and then proceed gradually inland.

Line 1 also represents a young man beginning his career. Here, it occupies a position neither central nor correct (Yin in a Yang place) and fails to form a harmonious relationship with its correlate (Line 4). All this indicates a humble young man in adverse circumstances ("faces peril"), one who lacks strong support. Since this peril does not stem from any mistake on his part but is caused only by the adverse circumstances surrounding his position, if he remains humble and proceeds cautiously and gradually, he will remain free from error or blame.

Line 2, Yin:

(a) *The geese are gradually approaching the huge rocks, where they eat and drink harmoniously and happily. Good fortune.*

(b) *"Eat and drink harmoniously and happily."* This shows that they are not merely gratifying their hunger.

If Line 1 is the shore of a beach, this line represents the rocky promontories of the beach. Having arrived there, the geese (or group) have made some headway in their movement, and they eat and drink heartily. They do so not merely to satisfy their hunger and thirst but because they are gregarious creatures who enjoy one another's company.

Line 2 forms a harmonious relationship with its correlate (Line 5). Hence the images of "eating and drinking harmoniously and happily" and "not merely gratifying their hunger."

Line 3, Yang:

(a) *The geese are gradually approaching the plain land. A husband sets out on an expedition and will not return. A pregnant wife will have a stillborn babe. Evil omen. Advantageous in resisting robbers.*

(b) *"A husband sets out on an expedition and will not return."* This is because he has alienated himself from his companions. *"A pregnant wife will have a stillborn babe."* This is because she has missed her proper path. *"Advantageous in resisting robbers."* This means that the opportunity should be taken for mutual protection.

If Line 2 represents the rocky ridge beyond the beach, then Line 3 represents the mainland, which the geese have reached through the gradual progress of their flight.

Line 3 is Yang, occupies a position correct but not central, and fails to form a harmonious relationship with its correlate (Line 6). Its subject is a strong, active person who is eager to advance despite the fact that he is not in a favorable position to do so. Such a man is prone to make rash, dangerous moves: once he has set out on a course ("expedition") he will not consider returning to his original position, no matter how unwise his venture proves to be. The fact that Line 3 fails to form a harmonious relationship with its correlate (Line 6) and rests at the top of the lower trigram, separated from the two Yin lines below, indicates that in pursuing his dangerous behavior, the subject alienates himself from his companions (wife and babe).

If the subject of the line is a woman or one in a subordinate position, she will also be a headstrong character, apt to act on the spur of the moment. Such a person is likely to deviate from the proper path and will not enjoy the blessings of birth and motherhood.

Headstrong or self-assertive people usually meet with trouble and disappointment. However, they may be useful when banding together for mutual protection against the evil forces in society ("robbers").

The lower interior trigram, K'an (Lines 2, 3, 4), signifies robbers. The upper interior trigram, Li (Lines 3, 4, 5), signifies second daughter and large belly; hence the images of "robbers" and "pregnant wife."

Line 4, Yin:

(a) *The geese are gradually going up the trees and may land on the flat branches. No error.*

(b) *"They may land on the flat branches." This is because their obedience goes hand in hand with docile penetration.*

Line 4 represents the branches of the trees or a refuge which the geese have now reached in the gradual progression of their flight. The line is also located at the top of the lower interior trigram, K'an (danger), indicating that the geese may encounter difficulty unless they can find a secure refuge like "flat branches" for their webbed feet. However, as Line 4 is Yin, occupies its correct position, and lies at the bottom of the upper trigram, Sun (docility), these geese are gentle, receptive creatures who can cooperate smoothly with others. Thus they are likely to find the refuge they need.

Line 5, Yang:

(a) *The geese are gradually going up a hill. A wife has not been pregnant for three years. In the end nothing can prevent her marital union. There will be good fortune.*

(b) *"The good fortune of the eventual marital union" means that desires are gratified.*

Here, Line 5 represents the hills which the geese have reached in the gradual progresison of their flight. Both this line and its correlate (Line 2), with whom it forms a harmonious relationship, occupy positions central as well as correct. Since the subject of Line 5 is Yang (male or active), and the subject of Line 2 is Yin (female or receptive), they make an ideal team ("marital union") to work together successfully in accomplishing their goals ("desires are gratified").

The upper trigram, Sun, denotes first daughter, and the lower, Ken, denotes third son, creating the image of "marital relations."

Line 6, Yang:

(a) *The geese are gradually going up a high hill. Their feathers can be used as ornaments. Good fortune.*

(b) *"The good fortune of their feathers being used as ornaments" means they cannot be thrown into confusion.*

Line 6, at the top of the hexagram, represents a high hill or secure place of refuge to which their flight has finally brought the geese. They are orderly creatures, as is clearly shown in their step-by-step progression from the beach to the "high hill." This characteristic seems to be symbolized by their feathers, which are so orderly and beautiful they can be used as ornaments. Neither the geese nor their feathers can be "thrown into confusion." Their orderliness is considered a sign of good fortune.

The KUEI MEI Hexagram

(Symbol of a Maiden's Marriage)

54th  歸妹

THE THIRD LINE OF the lower Tui trigram is Yin, denoting the youngest daughter or a young maiden. The first line of the upper Chen trigram is Yang, denoting the eldest son or a young man. Placed in proximity like this they suggest a young couple in a close relationship. Hence the idea of a maiden's marriage.

KING WEN'S JUDGMENT ON THE HEXAGRAM:

The hexagram indicates that ventures will end in misfortune and cannot be advantageous in any way.

This Judgment is based on the unfavorable positions of Lines 3 and 4. As they are both incorrect and not central, they symbolize an incompatible young couple who fail to form a proper relationship. Such a situation can only augur ill for their marriage ("ventures will end in misfortune").

CONFUCIUS' EXPLANATION OF KING WEN'S JUDGMENT:

The marriage of a young maiden signifies the grand righteousness (Ta Yi) of heaven and earth. If heaven and earth do not have intercourse, the ten thousand things will not arise and flourish. A young maiden's marrige signifies the end and the beginning of mankind.

Pleasure goes hand in hand with motion. It is a young maiden getting married.

"Ventures will end in misfortune." This is because the positions are incorrect. "Ventures cannot be advantageous in any way." This is because the weak mount on the strong.

Just as heaven and earth must have intercourse or nothing would exist, so human beings must engage in it if the species is to be perpetuated. Thus, the institution of marriage is a vital one ("the end and the beginning of mankind").

The lower trigram, Tui, signifies joy or pleasure, and the upper, Chen, signifies motion. In terms of the symbolism of the hexagram as a whole, this suggests the joy a young woman feels when she approaches marriage.

Not only are Lines 3 and 4 unfavorably placed, but in both component trigrams the strong Yang lines are overriden by the weak Yin lines, which inhibit their effectiveness ("the weak mount on the strong"). This precludes any successful action or venture.

SYMBOLIC SIGNIFICANCE OF THE HEXAGRAM AS NOTED BY CONFUCIUS:

The idea behind Kuei Mei is derived from thunder (upper trigram) over the marsh (lower trigram). The superior man is inspired thereby to beware of possible faults so as to follow the course to its ultimate end.

Thunder claps above cause the marsh below to quake and agitate its water, just as the difficulties involved in marriage may similarly agitate the hearts of a young couple and cause them to fall into error. Thus, the superior man learns to anticipate and prevent possible faults, both in himself and the other party, when undertaking an intimate union or marriage. In this way he avoids possible pitfalls and carries the union to a happy end.

DUKE OF CHOU'S EXPLANATION OF THE LINES (a) AND CONFUCIUS' COMMENT THEREON (b):

Line 1, Yang:
(a) A younger sister is married off as a secondary wife. Lame but able to walk. Ventures will be propitious.

(b) *"A younger sister is married off as a secondary wife." This is a matter of usual practice. "Lame but able to walk. Propitious." This signifies orderly relations.*

Since this line lies at the base of the hexagram, it represents the younger sister (as the older sister is denoted by Line 4) to be married to a man as his secondary wife. Since Line 1 is Yang, its subject, though in a relatively inferior status ("lame"), nevertheless performs her duties well ("but able to walk"). This leads to good fortune ("Ventures will be propitious").

In ancient China, two sisters sometimes married the same man, the elder sister as the principal wife and the younger sister as the secondary one. As a form of polygamy practiced at the time, this was considered common sense, since two sisters ought to be able to get along more harmoniously as co-wives than two women who are strangers to each other. Hence the image, "younger sister is married off as a secondary wife."

Line 2, Yang:

(a) *One has a squint eye, yet is able to see. Advantageous for an obscure person to be firm and correct.*

(b) *"Advantageous for an obscure person to be firm and correct." This means that he has not changed his normal course.*

Line 2 occupies an incorrect position, and this limits its subject, who is like a man with defective vision ("One has a squint eye"). However, in spite of this difficulty, if he possesses the strength of character to remain firmly on the correct course, the situation will probably work out to his advantage. Fortunately, Line 2 is Yang and occupies a central position, suggesting an able and upright person who follows a middle course. Because the line lies in the center of the hexagram signifying marsh, its subject's talents are apt to be hidden from view or overlooked ("an obscure person").

Line 3, Yin:

(a) *A younger sister is married off as a low concubine. She returns home and then is married off as a secondary wife.*

(b) *"A younger sister is married off as a low concubine." This is improper.*

Line 3 occupies a position neither central nor correct (Yin in a Yang place) and fails to form a harmonious relationship with its correlate (Line 6). Since the line is at the top of the lower trigram, its central opening signifies mouth, eating, and talking. As Tui denotes the youngest daughter, its subject is a lonely girl or Yin person living an improper or dissolute life. She was at first to be married to a man as his concubine, but due to her behavior this was thought improper, and so she later became his secondary wife.

Line 4, Yang:

(a) *A younger sister's wedding date is postponed. The time will come for the belated marriage.*

(b) *The purpose of "postponing the wedding date" is to wait and see before taking action.*

This Yang line is in the upper trigram, signifying a maiden of high character. She is of marriageable age, and the wedding date has been set. However, Line 4 is unfavorably placed, does not form a harmonious relationship with its correlate (Line 1), and also lies in the center of the upper interior trigram, K'an (Lines 3, 4, 5), which signifies danger. Its subject, therefore, feels doubtful of her prospects, and so she prefers to postpone the wedding. This does not mean that she does not wish to get married, but only that she wants to consider the matter more carefully. When the right time comes, she will not hesitate.

Line 5, Yin:

(a) *When Emperor Yi's younger sister got married, the sleeves of her wedding gown were not so good as those of her younger sister who accompanied her as the secondary wife. The moon was about full. Good fortune.*

(b) *"When Emperor Yi's younger sister got married, the sleeves of her wedding gown were not so good as those of the secondary wife's." This was because her position was in the center and she acted in a noble and magnanimous manner.*

Line 5 (the ruler) is Yin, indicating the ruler's sister or Yin associate. The fact that it occupies a central position indicates that she is a modest, humble young person who follows a middle course. When the elder of the two younger sisters of Emperor Yi, founder of the Shang dynasty, was married, she did not vie with her youngest sister in the ornamentation of the gowns they wore on their wedding day. She was like the moon which does not become full but leaves a portion of itself in darkness. Such humility can only result in good fortune.

Line 6, Yin:

(a) *A maiden holds up a basket which has no substantial content. A scholar slaughters a sheep which has no blood. Nothing whatsoever will be advantageous.*

(b) *"The absence of substantial content" indicated in Line 6, Yin, shows that she is holding up an empty basket.*

This line is Yin in a Yin place and lies at the top extreme of the hexagram, denoting a weak woman (or Yin person) in an extremely unstable position ("an empty basket"). She also fails to form a harmonious relationship with her logical partner (Line 3, the correlate), so that marriage, even if possible, would prove disastrous ("sheep which has no blood").

The lower trigram, Tui, denotes sheep and the upper interior trigram, K'an, denotes blood. Hence the image, "a sheep has no blood."

The FENG Hexagram
(Symbol of Abundance)

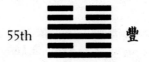

55th 豐

THE UPPER TRIGRAM, Chen, represents thunder, and the lower, Li, represents light or lightning. The interplay of thunder and lightning produces an impression of boundless energy. They also interact to create rain, which causes nature to produce her bounty. Hence the idea of abundance.

KING WEN'S JUDGMENT ON THE HEXAGRAM:

The hexagram indicates prosperity and success. If the king finds himself in the condition indicated therein, he need not worry. He should be like the sun at noonday.

When the king or leader has reached the pinnacle of power and prosperity, his knowledge of the Law of Cyclic Reversion may cause him to worry about the period of decline that will inevitably follow. However, rather than waste his time on such thought, he should continue to work for the welfare of the people and, like the sun at noontide, shower blessings upon the earth.

CONFUCIUS' EXPLANATION OF KING WEN'S JUDGMENT:

Feng, name of the hexagram, means great in quantity or extent. Action is based on enlightenment. Hence the meaning of the hexagram.

"If the king finds himself in the condition indicated in the hexagram." This means he should maintain his greatness. "He need not

worry. He should be like the sun at noonday." This means he should shed light on the world.

At noonday the sun begins to decline. When full, the moon begins to wane. Heaven and earth are now full, now empty, waxing and waning in accord with the time. How much more so should be the case with men! How much more so should be the case with the gods and demons.

Thunder (Chen) is sound in motion, and lightning (Li) suggests enlightenment. Enlightened action leads to success and therefore abundant wealth or power. However, after attaining great fortune or abundance, a leader should not rest on his laurels, but instead should continue working as hard as ever ("maintain his greatness") to benefit and enlighten the people ("shed light on the world"). At the moment of greatest abundance, decline sets in; at the moment of greatest emptiness, things begin to flourish again. The superior man places himself in accord with the times, accepting both abundance and the vicissitudes of fortune with equanimity.

SYMBOLIC SIGNIFICANCE OF THE HEXAGRAM AS NOTED BY CONFUCIUS:

The idea behind Feng is derived from thunder and lightning coming on together. The superior man is inspired thereby to decide criminal cases and mete out proper punishments.

The interplay of thunder and lightning fills the atmosphere, signifying fullness or abundance. In addition, lightning also illuminates the earth, while thunder strikes terror in the human heart. Observing this phenomenon, the superior man learns the wisdom of bringing light or intelligence to bear in resolving disputes ("decide criminal cases"), thus striking terror into the hearts of evildoers ("mete out proper punishments").

DUKE OF CHOU'S EXPLANATION OF THE LINES (a) AND CONFUCIUS' COMMENT THEREON (b):

Line 1, Yang:
(a) One encounters one's partner. Even for the full period of ten days there will be no regret. Going ahead will be given credit.

(b) *"Even for the full period of ten days, there will be no regret."* *This means that there will be calamity if the period is exceeded.*

Line 1 and its correlate (Line 4) are Yang. Normally, when correlates are of the same nature, they form an antagonistic relationship. However, here Line 1 begins the lower trigram (lightning), while Line 4 begins the upper trigram (thunder). Just as the interplay of thunder and lightning cooperates in beginning the process of abundance by creating rain, so the subjects of the two lines are said to cooperate in bringing about the time of abundance symbolized by the Feng Hexagram. Thus, the subjects of Line 1 and 4 are said to be mutually helpful and their meetings advantageous and profitable to themselves and their subjects, whose welfare they help to ensure. However, this meeting should last no more than ten days (as a whole number, ten symbolizes a complete cycle). If prolonged it will pass the point of optimum benefit and some setback is sure to occur, just as after noonday the sun begins to decline.

Line 2, Yin:

(a) *There is a profusion of curtains and screens. At noonday the Northern Star is visible. Advancement will arouse suspicion and hatred. If one is sincere at heart and able to show his sincerity, there will be good fortune.*

(b) *"If one is sincere at heart and able to show his sincerity."* This means that one's purpose is revealed through faith.

The position of Line 2 (Yin in a Yin place) denotes a person who is not very bright. If such a person advances to see his correlate (Line 5, the ruler), with whom he fails to form a harmonious relationship, his motives will only be misunderstood ("arouse suspicion and hatred"). However, since the line occupies a position both central and correct, its subject is a sincere, humble person who follows a middle course. Although the situation is difficult and not without danger, if the subject of Line 2 remains sincere, his good intentions will become apparent ("one's purpose is revealed") and he will meet with good fortune.

The Li trigram signifies light (the two Yang lines), and this Yin line at the center signifies darkness. Hence the image of "curtains and screens" which keep out the light and cause the darkness.

Line 3, Yang:

(a) *There is a profusion of thick banners. At noonday, the Mo star is visible. One's right arm is broken. There will be no error.*

(b) *"There is a profusion of thick banners." This shows incapability to attempt big tasks. "One's right arm is broken." This means that to the end one is of no use.*

This Yang line at the top of the Li trigram signifies light, but light that is obscured, for its correlate (Line 6) is weak (Yin) and therefore like "thick banners" which keep out the light. This symbolism is further reinforced by the fact that the Mo star is much smaller in magnitude than the Northern Star and harder to see.

Line 3 lies at the bottom of the upper interior trigram, Tui (Lines 3, 4, 5), which signifies breakage. If this line is transformed into a Yin line, the lower interior trigram becomes Ken (Lines 2, 3, 4), which signifies hand. This suggests the idea of significant impairment ("broken"). A person with a broken arm is certainly incapable of undertaking any great task alone. Fortunately, Line 3 forms a harmonious relationship with its correlate (Line 6), indicating that its subject will obtain the sympathy and support of others and thus have no reason for regret ("no error").

Line 4, Yang:

(a) *There is a profusion of curtains and screens. At noonday the Northern Star is visible. One encounters his counterpart. There will be good fortune.*

(b) *"There is a profusion of curtains and screens." This is because the position is incorrect. "At noonday the Northern Star is visible." This shows there is gloom but no light. "One encounters his counterpart." This indicates propitious action.*

This Yang line belongs to the upper trigram and so is above and beyond the lower trigram, which signifies the source of light. In addition, its position is neither central nor correct (Yang in a Yin place), casting it further into gloom or darkness. Its subject is like a man in a room with "a profusion of curtains and screens" which keep out the light. However, as Line 4 and its correlate, Line 1, are Yang, their subjects are mutually sympathetic and cooperative and their encounter leads to good fortune.

Line 5, Yin:

(a) *Illustrious people are coming. There will be great rejoicing and acclamation. Good fortune.*

(b) *"The good fortune" indicated in Line 5, Yin, means great rejoicing.*

Line 5 (the ruler) is Yin and occupies a central position, indicating a kind, gentle leader who follows a middle course. Such a man draws illustrious and talented people to come and serve under him. This, of course, brings good fortune and the acclaim of all ("great rejoicing").

Line 6, Yin:

(a) *The house is large and lofty. The home is heavily sheltered with curtains and screens. Peeping through the door, one sees nobody inside. For three years nobody is seen therein. Evil omen.*

(b) *"The house is large and lofty." This suggests that the curved corners of the roof seem to soar to heaven. "Peeping through the door, one sees nobody inside." This shows that the homeowner conceals himself.*

This line is Yin in a Yin place, indicating deep darkness. It lies farthest of all the lines from the source of light (the lower trigram, Li). This suggests darkness intensified. The subject of Line 6 is like one in the middle of a dark house, where the light is kept out by heavy "curtains and screens." The interior is so dark that nobody is visible from the outside. All this indicates that outward grandeur is a cover for inward weakness.

The LU Hexagram
(Symbol of a Traveller)

56th 旅

THE UPPER TRIGRAM IS Li (fire), and the lower is Ken (mountain). Fire burning on a mountain spreads to other areas. Ken also signifies an inn or hotel, and the upper trigram, Li, also signifies fitful and increasing movement, suggesting those whose journeys have brought them together. Hence the idea of a traveller.

KING WEN'S JUDGMENT ON THE HEXAGRAM:

The hexagram indicates minor success and prosperity. Good fortune for the traveller who is firm and correct.

Travel is filled with difficulty, danger, and the possibility of going astray. This is not an advantageous situation in which to attempt any great task. Those who wish good fortune in such circumstances must follow a firm and correct course.

CONFUCIUS' EXPLANATION OF KING WEN'S JUDGMENT:

"The hexagram indicates minor success and prosperity." The weak obtains a central place on the outside and is submissive to the strong. Repose goes hand in hand with adherence to intelligence. This is why "minor success and prosperity. Good fortune for the traveller who is firm and correct."

Great indeed is the timely signficance indicated in the Lu Hexagram.

Line 5 (the ruler) is Yin, occupying a central place in the upper trigram (on the outside) and below a strong, Yang line (Line 6). Its subject, therefore, is a gentle person who has obtained an important position and who listens to the advice of his more intelligent associate ("the weak . . . is submissive to the strong"). Since the lower trigram, Ken, represents rest, and the upper trigram, Li, represents brilliance, repose is said to go hand in hand with adherence to intelligence. In other words, rest or serenity is the result of wise foresight and planning. Even in a difficult situation, such preparation will bring some success and prevent ill fortune.

SYMBOLIC SIGNIFICANCE OF THE HEXAGRAM AS NOTED BY CONFUCIUS:

The idea behind Lu is derived from fire over the mountain. The superior man is inspired thereby to be judicious and cautious in applying punishments and to avoid protracting any litigation.

Fire burning on the top of a mountain, where the wind never ceases blowing, moves rapidly, while the mountain below suggests an image of stillness and calmness. In observing this phenomenon, the superior man discovers the wisdom of settling disputes rapidly ("avoid protracting any litigation") and taking care to proceed cautiously and fairly in meting out penalties and punishments.

DUKE OF CHOU'S EXPLANATION OF THE LINES (a) AND CONFUCIUS' COMMENT THEREON (b):

Line 1, Yin:
(a) *A mean and stingy traveller draws calamity to himself.*
(b) *"A mean and stingy traveller." This means that calamity will arise from the exhaustion of good will.*

This line occupies a position at the beginning of the hexagram neither central nor correct (Yin in a Yang place). This indicates that the subject is an inexperienced traveller who does not know how to behave himself properly and is apt to make wrong moves or assume wrong attitudes. Such a man exhausts the good will of others, and when disaster ensues ("calamity"), he can find no one to assist him.

Line 2, Yin:

(a) *A traveller finds his lodging in an inn. He has money in his pocket and is provided with a trustworthy young servant.*

(b) *"He is provided with a trustworthy young servant." This means that to the end there will be no resentment.*

Line 2 is Yin in a Yin place and occupies a position both central and correct, signifying a person who is kind and gentle and who follows a middle course. Unlike the subject of Line 1, the subject of Line 2 can enjoy himself and cause no resentment, as he gets along nicely with all those he meets.

Line 3, Yang:

(a) *A traveller finds his inn on fire and loses his young servant. Persistence will mean evil or peril.*

(b) *"A traveller finds his inn on fire." This is a sad case. As a traveller, he is rather headstrong toward his servant. It accords with reason that he should lose him.*

Line 3 is Yang in a Yang place, occupies a position correct but not central, and fails to form a harmonious relationship with its correlate (Line 6). The subject of the line is a strong, active person who does not occupy an advantageous position from which to act and who receives no support from others. Such a man is prone to take rash and violent steps, worsening the situation (symbolically, causing the inn to catch fire) and alienating even his most loyal supporters ("loses his young servant"). If he persists in this kind of conduct, he will surely land himself in a sorry plight ("Persistence will mean evil").

Line 4, Yang:

(a) *A traveller has reached his destination. He has the resources to protect himself but his heart is not at ease.*

(b) *"A traveller has reached his destination." This means he has not yet obtained a resting place. "He has the resources to protect himself." This suggests that his heart is not at ease.*

This line is Yang and occupies a position neither central nor correct. In addition, it represents a stage of transition, involving new adjustments. Its subject, therefore, is a strong man, eager to act, who finds himself in changing circumstances and is perplexed as to what course he should follow. Such a traveller is bound to be uncertain about his final goal or lodgings, even after he has reached his destination ("not yet obtained a resting place"). Although he can take care of himself, his heart knows no ease.

Line 5, Yin:

(a) *One shoots a pheasant and loses one arrow. Eventually he will receive acclaim and get a commission.*

(b) *"Eventually he will receive acclaim and get a commission." This means that he will attain a high position.*

Here, Line 5 (the ruler) is Yin and occupies a central position, indicating an enlightened person who possesses considerable skill and can unerringly accomplish whatever tasks he undertakes, just as a skillful marksman can shoot down a pheasant with a single arrow. Such a man's actions can only bring him credit ("acclaim") and advancement ("a high position"). The upper trigram, Li, stands for pheasant. Hence the image of "shooting a pheasant."

Line 6, Yang:

(a) *The nest of a bird is on fire. A traveller first laughs and then howls. He loses an ox in the field. There will be evil.*

(b) *When a traveller assumes a high-and-mighty attitude, it serves him right to get burned. "He loses his ox in the field." This means that to the end he does not hear of his own faults.*

This Yang line occupies a position neither central nor correct and also forms an antagonistic relationship with its correlate (Line 3). Furthermore, it lies at the extreme top of the hexagram, indicating that further travel is impossible. The subject of Line 6, therefore, represents a strong-willed, self-righteous person who habitually ignores the advice and warnings of others ("does not hear of his own faults"). When such a man finds himself in highly unfavorable circumstances, his short temper and extreme behavior antagonize all those he meets. When travelling, he enjoys himself at first ("laughs"), but then meets with trouble ("loses his ox"), and begins to complain ("howl"). Such a man is like a bird whose nest is on fire.

The SUN Hexagram
(Symbol of Gentle Penetration)

57th  巽

THE SUN TRIGRAM SIGNIFIES docility or submissiveness, symbolized by the Yin line lying below two Yang lines. The Sun Hexagram represents docility doubled, or gentleness. The Sun trigram also signifies wind, as its first and lowest line is said to resemble a hole through which the wind enters. Hence the idea of gentle penetration.

KING WEN'S JUDGMENT ON THE HEXAGRAM:

The hexagram indicates minor success and prosperity, advantage in moving forward, and advantage in seeing the great man.

In the Sun Hexagram, the weak (Yin line) is said to follow the two Yang lines above it. This suggests the wisdom of the weak in cooperating with those who are more intelligent or more advantageously placed to act than they are. This idea is reinforced by the fact that both Lines 2 and 5 are Yang and occupy central positions, denoting active, able leaders whose aid or advice would be of positive benefit ("advantage in seeing the great man"). The Yin lines below the Yang lines represent weak forces, so even though they are well led, only minor success is possible.

CONFUCIUS' EXPLANATION OF KING WEN'S JUDGMENT:

The trigram Sun is doubled to show the explanation of commands through patient repetition.

The strong has gently penetrated to a central and correct place and is carrying out his will. The weak are all submissive to the strong; hence, "minor success and prosperity, advantage in moving forward and advantage in seeing the great man."

The doubled Sun trigram (docility) suggests that ideas or commands are being repeated gently until they have time to penetrate the minds of the people.

Lines 2 and 5 are both Yang and occupy central positions, and so are said to be ideally placed to advance and realize their aspirations. Line 5 (the ruler) is particularly well-placed because it is Yang and occupies a correct as well as a central position, signifying a great leader who works for the benefit of all. He has reached his present important position gradually and without conflict or disrupting others (gentle penetration). Because of this, his subordinates all cooperate to help him carry out his plans. This idea is reinforced by the fact that both Yin lines (Lines 1 and 4) are placed below two Yang lines, suggesting receptive subjects who are obedient to the able leaders above ("The weak are all submissive to the strong"). When there is this kind of smooth cooperation between high and low or strong and weak, great things can be accomplished.

SYMBOLIC SIGNIFICANCE OF THE HEXAGRAM AS NOTED BY CONFUCIUS:

The idea behind Sun is derived from puff of wind following puff of wind. The superior man is inspired thereby to repeat his commands and conduct his affairs.

Wind penetrates everywhere. It also tends to shake and agitate things. Its effect is particularly strong and far-reaching when it continues, puff after puff, for a long time. The superior man therefore feels that he should be like the wind and make repeated and continual efforts to explain and clarify his commands or teachings to the people. This will allow them to understand the significance of his teachings, and he will thus be able to conduct his affairs smoothly and efficiently.

DUKE OF CHOU'S EXPLANATION OF THE LINES (a)
AND CONFUCIUS' COMMENT THEREON (b):

Line 1, Yin:

(a) *One hesitates to advance or retreat. It is advantageous to be firm and correct like a military man.*

(b) *"One hesitates to advance or retreat." This shows a mind in doubt. "It is advantageous to be firm and correct like a military man." This means that one's mind should be well-ordered.*

This Yin line occupies a position neither central nor correct and fails to form a harmonious relationship with its correlate (Line 4). The subject of Line 1 is a weak, inexperienced person who receives no outside help or support. He cannot make up his mind whether to go forward or back off ("One hesitates to advance or retreat") and is filled with misgivings. If such a man wishes to advance or achieve success, he must manifest the fortitude to keep himself firmly on the correct path ("like a military man").

Line 2, Yang:

(a) *A fellow cowers under the bed. Fortune-tellers and sorceresses are employed as if in a hurry. Good fortune. No error.*

(b) *"The good fortune of acting as if in a hurry" is due to the attainment of a central position.*

This line is Yang and occupies a central position, suggesting a strong-willed but sensible person who follows a middle course. He uses gentle penetration rather than violent means in handling the fellow (Line 1) who cowers under the bed. He employs fortune-tellers and sorceresses to persuade the fellow to come out and behave properly. This is the correct tack to take ("No error") and will lead to good fortune.

Line 3, Yang:

(a) *Gentle penetration is frequently repeated. There will be resentment.*

(b) *"The resentment from frequent repetition of gentle penetration" is due to exhaustion of good will.*

Although this is a Yang line in a Yang place, it does not occupy a central position and fails to form a harmonious relationship with its correlate (Line 6).

Its subject is a strong-willed person, unfavorably placed, who tends to go to extremes and so can count on no one to help him in a difficult situation. Such a man cannot carry out his plans smoothly, and when the inevitable difficulties arise, his impatience leads him to constantly repeat his desires and commands. In repeating what he imagines are attempts at gentle penetration, he wears out the good will of others and arouses resentment instead of cooperation.

Line 4, Yin:

(a) *Regret disappears. One gets three kinds of game in hunting.*

(b) *"One gets three kinds of game in hunting." This indicates that some success has been achieved.*

Line 4 (the minister) is Yin in a Yin place, denoting a gentle, loyal person who forms a harmonious relationship with and enjoys the confidence of his ruler (Line 5). Such a man will create no occasion for regret; on the contrary, he will receive many favors from his ruler for his meritorious services ("three kinds of game in hunting").

The line is in the center of the upper interior trigram, Li (lines 3, 4, 5), which signifies hunting and fishing.

Line 5, Yang:

(a) *Good fortune will stem from firm correctness. Regret will vanish. Nothing not disadvantageous. No good beginning but a good end. Notice given three days in advance and reviewed three days afterward will lead to good fortune.*

(b) *"The good fortune" indicated in Line 5, Yang, is due to its central and correct position.*

Here, Line 5 (the ruler) is Yang and occupies a position both central and correct. This signifies a wise and active leader who firmly follows the middle course and is well-placed for carrying out his noble plans. He is patient and cautious, though prone to action, and careful to plan and review all his efforts in order to detect and correct any error and maximize his chance for success ("Notice given three days in advance and reviewed three days afterward"). For such a man, every move will prove propitious, and even a bad beginning will lead to a good end.

If the subjects of the Yin lines wish to report to their superiors (the Yang lines), they must each progress through three positions in order to reach the top of the respective trigrams (the superior). Hence the image of "three days" in the Text.

Line 6, Yang:

(a) *A fellow cowers under the bed. He has lost his resources for self-protection. Persistence will lead to evil.*

(b) *"A fellow cowers under the bed." This shows that one at the top is at the end of his ropes. "He has lost his resources for self-protection." This is the very cause of his evil situation.*

Lying at the extreme top of the Sun Hexagram (gentle penetration), this Yang line denotes a person who combines gentleness and humility to such an extreme as to seem to have lost his self-respect and self-confidence ("A fellow cowers under the bed"). Since he cannot be entrusted with any important work or even a decent job at which to earn his living ("at the end of his ropes"), such a person is apt to cause resentment and be unable to get along well with people. He may well find himself in reduced circumstances ("lost his resources for self-protection").

The TUI Hexagram
(Symbol of Joy, Satisfaction)

58th  兑

THE TUI TRIGRAM signifies satisfaction and pleasure. Here in the Tui Hexagram, it signifies satisfaction and pleasure doubled or in a continuous stream. Hence the idea of joy. In any trigram, the bottom line (Line 1) represents the interior, the middle line (Line 2) represents the center, and the top line (Line 3) represents the exterior. In the Tui trigram Lines 1 and 2 are Yang (strong, dynamic), and Line 3 is Yin (docile, patient). The whole trigram denotes something that is strong and dynamic inside or at its center and docile and patient on the outside. The symbolism of the hexagram as a whole suggests that a man who can live in harmony with others while holding firm to his own values is sure to produce joy.

KING WEN'S JUDGMENT ON THE HEXAGRAM:

The hexagram indicates success and prosperity and advantage in being firm and correct.

The Tui trigram shows the Yang (strong) lines moving upward toward a Yin (weak) line, so their upward course is bound to be smooth and successful. Two such trigrams, one above the other, accentuate the favorable condition and consequently constitute a clear sign of success and prosperity.

CONFUCIUS' EXPLANATION OF KING WEN'S JUDGMENT:

The hexagram means joy.

Strength at the center is conjoined with weakness or docility out-side. Joy is based on being firm and correct. Hence comes submis-sion to the will of heaven and response to the aspirations of men. Having joy before them, the people will forget their weariness. In at-tacking difficulties with joy, the people will forget they may die. Great indeed is joy in its effects. The people are persuaded by it.

Here, both trigrams symbolize docility and gentleness on the outside and strength on the inside or at the center. Those who can cooperate with their fellows and bow gracefully to the dictates of fate ("submission to the will of heaven and response to the aspi-rations of men"), while maintaining their own inner nature, are bound to know satisfaction and joy. Such joy, in turn, inspires men to greater efforts, causing them to lose themselves in their work ("The people are persuaded by it" and "forget they may die") so that they tackle even the most difficult tasks willingly.

SYMBOLIC SIGNIFICANCE OF THE HEXAGRAM AS NOTED BY CONFUCIUS:

The idea behind Tui is derived from marsh (either trigram) adher-ing to marsh. The superior man is inspired thereby to engage with friends in discussion and actual practice.

The Tui trigram also represents a marsh, and placed together with another Tui trigram, symbolizes the interflow of water be-tween two connected marshes. In human terms this symbolizes the interchange of knowledge and property in a country or group. In addition, Tui also signifies the mouth, and to the superior man this suggests dinner with friends and social conversation. He there-fore feels that he should engage in discussion with friends and in the practice of various arts.

DUKE OF CHOU'S EXPLANATION OF THE LINES (a) AND CONFUCIUS' COMMENT THEREON (b):

Line 1, Yang:
(a) *There is joy of harmony. Good fortune.*
(b) *"The good fortune stemming from joy of harmony"* means *conduct as yet untainted with doubt.*

383

This Yang line occupies a position which is not central but correct. It does not form a harmonious relationship with its correlate (Line 4), or with its associate (Line 2). Its subject is an independent, self-sufficient person who possesses great strength of character. Such a person is seldom influenced by the actions or opinions of others and so remains free from doubt. Because he is in harmony with himself, he finds himself in harmony with others.

Line 2, Yang:

(a) *There is joy of sincerity. Good fortune. Regret vanishes.*

(b) *"The good fortune stemming from joy of sincerity" rests on faith in one's aspirations.*

This strong Yang line occupies a central position, but its influence is weakened by its Yin neighbor (Line 3). However, the subject of Line 2 is a sincere man who follows a middle course. So although he may feel some regret in his relations with his neighbor or associate (Line 3), such regret will disappear, as he will remain sincere and pleasant toward people as well as faithful to his aspirations.

Line 3, Yin:

(a) *One comes to stir up joy. There will be evil.*

(b) *"The evil of one coming to stir up joy" is due to incorrectness of position.*

Line 3 lies at the top of a Tui trigram and usually denotes mouth, which symbolizes eating, drinking, and talking. These are not bad things in themselves; however, Line 3 is Yin and occupies a position neither central nor correct, suggesting that its subject is a dissolute person given to excessive eating, drinking, and gossiping who wants to influence others to abandon the correct course and join him in the pursuit of pleasure ("evil of one coming to stir up joy"). To follow his example will only lead to disaster ("There will be evil").

Line 4, Yang:

(a) *One considers what would be his joy and feels unrest at heart. He comes very near harm's way, but there will be gladness for him.*

(b) *"The gladness" indicated in Line 4, Yang, means that there will be rejoicing.*

This Yang line is neither central nor correct in position and does not form a harmonious relationship with its correlate (Line 1). Furthermore, it is close to Line 5, which is Yang and denotes a strong ruler. The subject of Line 4, therefore, is an able and active minister who does not feel comfortable or secure in his position and has few or no friends to rely upon. He is considering what would bring joy and satisfaction to him: whether to render loyal service to the king (Line 5), or to live a life of pleasure like his dissolute neighbor (Line 3). He almost succumbs to the inducements of this dissolute fellow, but he finally decides to serve the king. This is a wise decision and ultimately leads to success ("rejoicing" and "gladness").

Line 5, Yang:

(a) *One places his trust in sharpers. There will be peril.*

(b) *"One places his trust in sharpers." This is due to one's correct and proper position.*

Line 5 (the ruler) is Yang and occupies a position both central and correct, signifying a great king or ruler who follows a middle course. However, he finds himself in the realm of a dangerous and wicked neighbor (Line 6) who may be taking advantage of his good nature to gain his confidence and lead him astray ("places his trust in sharpers"). Such a situation is fraught with difficulty and danger ("There will be peril"). However, the subject of Line 5 remains sincere and correct throughout and wards off the other's sinister designs in the end.

Line 6, Yin:

(a) *One finds pleasure in attracting others to pleasure.*

(b) *"The pleasure of attracting others to pleasure" indicated in Line 6, Yin, shows that one has not yet seen the light.*

This line is Yin in a Yin place, indicating darkness and evil influence. It is also at the extreme top of the Tui Hexagram, which denotes the mouth. It therefore signifies a very benighted and dissolute man who seduces people into sensual excesses and a wanton life. Such a person surely cannot be regarded as having seen the light of truth and wisdom.

The HUAN Hexagram
(Symbol of Dispersion)

59th 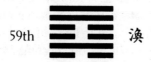 渙

THE UPPER TRIGRAM, Sun, signifies wind, and the lower, K'an, signifies water. Wind blowing over water drives the waves before it. Hence the idea of dispersion.

KING WEN'S JUDGMENT ON THE HEXAGRAM:

The hexagram indicates success and prosperity. A king goes to his ancestral temple. There will be advantage in crossing the great stream and in being firm and correct.

In time of dispersion, it is still possible to prevent division and strengthen union by recalling to all those involved their common purpose (symbolically, gathering the people together in their "ancestral temple" to reaffirm their sense of community by reminding them that they all sprang from the same source). To heal a deteriorating or disintegrating order requires a strong character ("advantage . . . in being firm and correct") and a willingness to take risks ("crossing the great stream"). An extraordinary situation requires an extraordinary remedy.

CONFUCIUS' EXPLANATION OF KING WEN'S JUDGMENT:

"The hexagram indicates success and prosperity." The strong come and do not expire. The weak gets its proper place on the outside and is of the same mind as its superiors.

"The king goes to his ancestral temple." This shows that the king is sincere at heart.

"There will be advantage in crossing the great stream." This means there will be success in riding on a wooden vessel.

The two Yang lines in the upper trigram (Lines 5 and 6) signify strength in great measure and are said to have come down from the outside or above. Since Line 4 is Yin in a Yin place, its subject is a receptive, obedient person whose aims are in harmony ("of the same mind") with those of his superiors (Lines 5 and 6). In carrying out their plans, he finds himself elevated to a higher position, one more suited to his talents ("proper place"). Such mutual cooperation among those in authority and those below (the strong and the weak) can only lead to success.

Line 5 (the ruler) is Yang and occupies a position central as well as correct, denoting a sincere and able king who knows how to re-unite the people during a time of dispersion ("goes to his ancestral temple"). This is a difficult task, but as he receives the support of those below, he is sure to succeed ("advantage in crossing the great stream").

The upper trigram is Sun (wood and wind); the lower, K'an (water). Wood can be made into a boat which, driven by the wind, can easily move across the water. Hence the image of "advantage in crossing the great stream."

SYMBOLIC SIGNIFICANCE OF THE HEXAGRAM AS NOTED BY CONFUCIUS:

The idea behind Huan is derived from wind blowing over water. The ancient kings were inspired thereby to present offerings to God and establish temples.

Wind blowing over water agitates and disperses it. In the same way, the buffeting of fate agitates and disperses the people of a nation or group, scattering them in various directions. In ancient China, the kings took care to present offerings to God and to establish temples for ancestor-worship, for through services at these temples, the people were reminded that they all came from the same forebears and so should unite together in good fellowship to perpetuate their nation.

DUKE OF CHOU'S EXPLANATION OF THE LINES (a) AND CONFUCIUS' COMMENT THEREON (b):

Line 1, Yin:

(a) *One saves himself with the aid of a strong horse. Good fortune.*

(b) *"The good fortune," indicated in Line 1, Yin, stems from docility and obedience.*

This Yin line occupies a place that is neither central nor correct and does not form a harmonious relationship with its correlate (Line 4). Furthermore, it is at the bottom not only of the entire hexagram, but also of the lower trigram, K'an, which signifies danger. All this suggests that its subject is a weak, inexperienced person who finds himself in a difficult and dangerous situation but receives no help from his friends or relatives. However, he is fortunate in having a strong associate (Line 2) who is willing to help him out of his woeful predicament ("aid of a strong horse"). He has this good luck because he is, as indicated by the Yin nature and low place of Line 1, a gentle and humble person.

The lower trigram, K'an, also signifies "strong horse." Hence the image in the Text.

Line 2, Yang:

(a) *One rushes to seize an opportunity during the time of dispersion. Regret will disappear.*

(b) *"One rushes to seize an opportunity during the time of dispersion." This means gratification of the heart's desire.*

This Yang line occupies a central position, denoting a strong, sensible man who knows how to cope with any given situation. Although he is surrounded by adverse circumstances in which nothing seems to come together, he is prepared to "seize an opportunity" when he sees it, thereby getting out of harm's way ("gratification of the heart's desire"). This leads to happiness and the disappearance of regret.

Line 3, Yin:

(a) *One disperses considerations of self. There will be no regret.*

(b) *"One disperses considerations of self." This shows that his mind is oriented outward.*

Line 3 is Yin and occupies a position neither central nor correct. Naturally, its subject is dissatisfied with the situation in which he finds himself. However, Line 3 forms a harmonious relationship with its strong correlate (Line 6, Yang), and so he turns his attention upward ("outward") and tries to cooperate with his more highly placed associate. Since Line 3 lies at the top of the lower trigram, K'an (danger), its subject may encounter some difficulty. On the other hand, if his aim is noble and unselfish ("disperses considerations of self"), he will have no reason for regret.

Line 4, Yin:

(a) *One disperses the crowd of partisans. There will be great good fortune. Scattered elements are gathered together like a mound: this is something beyond the thought of ordinary people.*

(b) *"The great good fortune of dispersing the crowd of partisans" indicates enlightenment and greatness.*

Here, Line 4 (the minister) is Yin in a Yin place and forms a harmonious relationship with its close associate (Line 5, the ruler), denoting a loyal, obedient assistant who gets along well with his superior. However, Line 4 fails to form a harmonious relationship with its correlate (Line 1), and the minister is said to be antagonistic to those of low character ("partisans"). He willingly devotes himself to dispersing them in the service of the king. Thus he achieves what ordinary people considered impossible: the unification of the scattered patriotic elements of the state into a cohesive mass ("gathered together like a mound"). This makes his enlightenment and greatness manifest to all and leads to good fortune.

Line 5, Yang:

(a) *A king issues great proclamations like drops of sweat diffusing from his body. While doing so, he is securely seated on the throne. There will be no error.*

(b) *"A king is securely seated on his throne." This is because his position is correct.*

Line 5 (the ruler) is Yang and occupies a position both central and correct, signifying a strong king or leader with the wisdom to follow the middle path. However, the line fails to form a harmonious relationship with its strong correlate (Line 2, Yang), which indicates that the king is facing important opposition or a crisis of state. However, he remains firmly on the correct course, institutes various projects, and changes his policies to resolve the situation ("great proclamations"). This proves successful and his position remains secure. Such a man is like a sick person who recovers after a profuse perspiration which disperses his fever.

Line 6, Yang:

(a) *One disperses or wipes off his bloodstains and departs for a distant land. There will be no error.*

(b) *"One disperses his bloodstains." This is in order to keep far out of harm's way.*

This Yang line occupies an incorrect position and also lies at the extreme top of the hexagram. In addition, if Line 6 is changed to Yin, the whole hexagram becomes K'an (danger), which is symbolized by blood. The line's subject, therefore, is a strong man who has gone through some peril, such as a bloody duel, and does not feel at ease in his present situation and so is ready to go elsewhere to seek more favorable circumstances. Symbolically, he is said to dispel danger by wiping "off his bloodstains," after which he leaves for a distant land to avoid further peril ("keep far out of harm's way").

The CHIEH Hexagram
(Symbol of Limitation)

60th  節

THE UPPER TRIGRAM, K'an, stands for water, and the lower, Tui, stands for marsh. Water flows down into the marsh, but the capacity of the marsh is limited: the water must be regulated and controlled or flooding will occur. Hence the idea of limitation.

KING WEN'S JUDGMENT ON THE HEXAGRAM:

The hexagram indicates success and prosperity. Harsh regulations cannot persist.

The Judgment cautions against severe regulation or limitation of anything, especially of people by their government or those placed above them. Harsh regulation leads to oppression, and oppression never produces success and prosperity. Such a situation cannot endure long without creating resentment and opposition.

CONFUCIUS' EXPLANATION OF KING WEN'S JUDGMENT:

"The hexagram indicates success and prosperity." The strong and the weak are equal in number and the strong obtain the central places.

"Harsh regulations cannot persist." Because the course tends toward the extreme.

The risking of dangers is accompanied by joy. Regulation is handled by authorities in their proper places. Smooth progress is based on what is central and correct.

Heaven and earth move in periodic phases, and the four seasons come into being. Regulation by means of methods and measures will not be detrimental to wealth nor harmful to the people.

The upper trigram, K'an, is considered strong (Yang) in nature, and the lower trigram, Tui, is considered weak (Yin) in nature. In the hexagram "the strong and the weak [lines] are equal in number," or balanced. This balance of Yin and Yang represents the harmony of nature which always results in prosperity and success. Further, the central and commanding position of each component trigram is occupied by a Yang line, which suggests its subject is someone strong and brilliant who is effectively placed to get things done. This is surely a happy augury of prosperity and success.

Courses that tend toward extremes, such as excessive limitation or regulation, are unbalanced and can only result in disaster, for they have lost the essential harmony of nature.

K'an also stands for risk; Tui for joy. In terms of the hexagram as a whole, this suggests that in times of limitation, taking risks will lead to success and joy. Since Line 5 (the ruler) occupies a position both central and correct, it denotes a wise ruler who follows a middle course and so avoids extremes in his regulations, balancing them so that they are neither too harsh nor too lax. Thus his endeavors run smoothly, for he engenders no opposition and enjoys the support of all.

SYMBOLIC SIGNIFICANCE OF THE HEXAGRAM AS NOTED BY CONFUCIUS:

The idea behind Chieh is derived from water (upper trigram) above the marsh (lower trigram). The superior man is inspired thereby to devise methods of calculation and measurement and discuss virtuous conduct.

A marsh can contain a large volume of water, but if it is allowed to fill up unchecked, it will exceed its capacity and overflow. Similarly, the superior man realizes that unrestrained freedom of the people can overflow into anarchy and license and so requires regulation if it is not to become destructive. He studies his fellow men carefully ("calculation and measurement") in order to determine what regulations are needed to prevent destructive behavior ("virtuous conduct").

DUKE OF CHOU'S EXPLANATION OF THE LINES (a) AND CONFUCIUS' COMMENT THEREON (b):

Line 1, Yang:

(a) *One does not go outside the courtyard of his house. There will be no error.*

(b) *"One does not go outside the courtyard of his house." This shows knowledge of whether there will be smooth progress or obstruction.*

Being a Yang line at the base of the trigram Tui, this line represents the bottom of a marsh, where water accumulates because it has no outlet. The subject of Line 1, therefore, is a man facing an obstruction that pens up or limits his efforts. Consequently he makes no forward move ("does not go outside"), but awaits the arrival of a more favorable occasion (according to the Law of Cyclic Reversion).

If Line 1 is transformed, the hexagram becomes K'an (danger) and its subject is said to have a strong sense of impending danger; consequently, he prefers to remain at home.

Line 2, Yang:

(a) *One does not go outside the little courtyard in front of his room. There will be evil.*

(b) *"The evil of not going outside the little courtyard in front of his room" shows that one misses the right time for action entirely.*

This Yang line in the middle of the Tui trigram denotes greatness or fullness. Since the first two lines of any hexagram also represent the earth, Line 2 shows that the water in the marsh is increasing, rising toward the surface of the earth. This is a sign of great danger: this line's subject should take prompt action if he is to avod destruction. However, he ignores this warning sign and fails to take action at the right time ("evil of not going outside"). This can only result in disaster ("There will be evil").

Line 3, Yin:

(a) *One fails to effect any regulation and then sighs and laments. No blame.*

(b) *"The lamentation of failing to effect any regulation." Who should be blamed for it?*

This Yin line occupies a position neither central nor correct and fails to form a harmonious relationship with its correlate (Line 6). Its subject is a weak, helpless person who finds himself in unfavorable circumstances. He does not take any precautions to regulate the rising water in the marsh and then laments his fate when the water overflows and disaster ensues. However, he is wise enough to learn from his experience, for his regret is sincere, and he acts to remedy the situation. Thus he frees himself from error and incurs no blame.

The lower trigram, Tui, especially Line 3, signifies mouth. Hence the image of "sighs and laments."

Line 4, Yin:

(a) *One handles regulations with ease. There will be success and prosperity.*

(b) *"The success and prosperity of handling regulations with ease" lies in submissively obeying or following the course of one's superiors.*

Here, Line 4 (the minister) is Yin in a Yin place and also forms a harmonious relationship with its correlate (Line 1). Its subject is an obedient, loyal person in a position of trust who supports the policies and actions of the king or leader (Line 5); and a man who at the same time receives the support and enthusiasm of the people. He can be entrusted to administer and devise laws and regulations that can satisfy the needs of the people. This can only lead to success and prosperity.

Line 5, Yang:

(a) *One handles regulations with a sweet disposition. There will be good fortune. Moving forward will meet with acclaim.*

(b) *"The good fortune of handling regulations with a sweet disposition" stems from the occupation of a central position.*

Line 5 (the ruler) is Yang and occupies a position both central and correct, denoting a wise and great king who is well situated to enact his wise laws and who follows a middle course. As the line fails to form a harmonious relationship with its correlate (Line 2), the king may be facing opposition and trouble. However, he deals with the situation justly and with good will ("with a sweet disposition"). This gains him credit with all concerned ("Moving forward will meet with acclaim") and will lead to good fortune.

Line 6, Yin:

(a) *Harsh regulations, if persistent, will lead to evil. Regret will disappear.*

(b) *"The evil of persistent harsh regulations" shows that the course tends toward the extreme, that is, to be radical.*

This line is Yin in a Yin place, suggesting both sinister influence and darkness. It also lies at the extreme top of the hexagram Chieh (regulation), indicating regulation that has reached its extreme limit of severity. If such a situation is allowed to remain unchanged, only evil will result; but if the subject of Line 6 possesses the wisdom to change, all occasion for regret will disappear. For the evil is inherent in the circumstances and not the result of personal folly.

The CHUNG FU Hexagram
(Symbol of Inner Sincerity)

61st  中孚

LINES 2 AND 5 ARE Yang lines occupying central positions and signifying the strong of heart. In addition, Lines 3 and 4 are Yin and lie at the center of the hexagram, symbolizing a heart empty of or free from passions such as pride, prejudice, and greed. Hence the idea of inner sincerity.

KING WEN'S JUDGMENT ON THE HEXAGRAM:

The hexagram indicates good fortune for swine and fish. Advantageous to cross the great stream. Advantageous to be firm and correct.

The Judgment stresses that the power of genuine inner sincerity can affect and influence the most intractable of individuals ("good fortune"), even those who are as dumb as pigs and fish. It implies that one with a sincere heart who follows the correct course can undertake even the most difficult tasks ("cross the great stream") successfully. For genuine sincerity, like love, conquers all.

CONFUCIUS' EXPLANATION OF KING WEN'S JUDGMENT:

This hexagram shows that the weak are in the interior, while the strong obtain the central places. Joy going hand in hand with gentle penetration makes sincerity effective in transforming the state.

"Good fortune for swine and fish." This shows that faith can affect even swine and fish. "Advantageous to cross the great stream."

This signifies riding in an empty wooden boat.

"Inner sincerity favors the advantage of being firm and correct."
This indicates submissive response to the will of heaven.

The lower trigram, Tui, represents joy or pleasure, and the upper, Sun, represents gentle penetration. A slow and patient effort ("gentle penetration") to please people will in time capture their hearts, which is an important critical factor in effecting reforms ("transforming the state").

The upper trigram, Sun, also stands for wood, and the lower trigram, Tui, can stand for marsh water. Wood over water suggests a wooden boat. Hence the image of crossing "the great stream."

One who sincerely wishes to remain firmly on a correct course follows the will of heaven.

SYMBOLIC SIGNIFICANCE OF THE HEXAGRAM
AS NOTED BY CONFUCIUS:

The idea behind Chung Fu is derived from wind (upper trigram) blowing over the marsh. The superior man is inspired thereby to discuss litigation and delay the death penalty.

The wind (Sun) fills the atmosphere above the marsh (Tui) and comes in contact with things. From this, the superior man learns to fill his heart with sincerity and humility, reaching out to justly resolve all conflicts or misunderstandings ("discuss litigation") and to postpone or remit any harsh measures ("delay the death penalty").

DUKE OF CHOU'S EXPLANATION OF THE LINES (a)
AND CONFUCIUS' COMMENT THEREON (b):

Line 1, Yang:

(a) *One enjoys the good fortune of repose. If distracted by other things, he will have no composure.*

(b) *"The good fortune of repose," indicated in Line 1, Yang, shows that his aim has not changed.*

Since this line is Yang in a Yang place and lies at the beginning of the Chung Fu hexagram (inner sincerity), its subject is a healthy young man whose pure heart and inner sincerity bring him good fortune. However, if he allows himself to become unduly obsessed by sensual pleasures or temporal cares ("distracted by other things"), his good fortune will desert him ("have no composure"). Only if he maintains the repose of his own conscience over the lure of desire can he avoid the temptations of the world.

Line 2, Yang:

(a) A *crane cries in a shady place, and its young one utters response. "I have some good wine." "I will share it with you."*

(b) *"Its young one utters response." The response represents the desire at the core of the heart.*

This Yang line occupies a central position, denoting a strong and just man whose inner sincerity affects his fellowmen and draws them to him. Just as a crane cries to its young and receives a response, so the subject of Line 1 reaches out to his more lowly associate (Line 1) and receives a favorable response. Symbolically, they share wine in mutual understanding and good will.

The lower trigram, Tui, denotes mouth. Hence the image of "crying out." Line 2 is below two Yin lines. Hence the image of "a shady place."

Line 3, Yin:

(a) *One faces hostile confrontation. He now beats the drum, now stops; now he weeps, now sings.*

(b) *"He now beats the drum, now stops." This shows that he is in an inappropriate position.*

This line is Yin and forms a harmonious relationship with its correlate (Line 6). Normally, the subjects of the two lines would experience mutual attraction and cooperate with each other. However, Line 3 occupies a position that is neither central nor correct, indicating that its subject is not comfortable in his situation and is also likely to be unstable and erratic ("now he weeps, now sings").

In addition, as the third line of the Tui trigram signifies mouth and pleasure, the subject of Line 3 is said to be a lover of pleasure whose sincerity and character may be weakend by his sensual desires. Consequently, his relationship with his partner (Line 6) cannot be consistent and friendly.

Lines 3 and 6 also occupy the top (most distant) lines of their respective trigrams, which suggests that their subjects are rash, intemperate individuals who tend to go to extremes. Hence the image of their "hostile confrontation."

Line 4, Yin:

(a) *The moon is almost full. A horse runs away from its fellow in the team. There will be no error.*

(b) *"A horse runs away from its fellow in the team." This means that one quits one's partisans and moves to a higher place.*

Line 4 (the minister) is Yin in a Yin place, denoting an obedient and loyal minister. The line also forms a harmonious relationship with its correlate (Line 1), indicating sympathetic partisans. A moon almost full is a sign of humility or a loyal minister, because it dims a portion of its light. His desire to serve the ruler (Line 5) is so sincere that he even breaks with his comrades in order to go to the royal court ("A horse runs away from its fellow"). This will prove to be the wisest course.

Line 5, Yang:

(a) *One has that sincerity which draws people together. There will be no error.*

(b) *"One has that sincerity which draws people together." This is because one's position is correct and proper.*

Here, Line 5 (the ruler) is Yang and occupies a position both central and correct. Its subject is a great and benevolent king or leader who follows the middle course and whose genuine sincerity and good will draw people together willingly and unite them behind him.

Line 6, Yang:

(a) *A rooster crows so loudly that the crowing seems to reach high heaven. Persistence will lead to evil.*

(b) *"A rooster crows so loudly that the crowing seems to reach high heaven." How can such a thing last long?*

This Yang line occupies a position neither central nor correct and lies at the extreme top of the hexagram. It denotes a vain, strong-willed person puffed up with pride and given to loud boasts ("crowing seems to reach high heaven"). Such a man is utterly lacking in sincerity or humility and when he finds himself in unfavorable circumstances, will discover that his behavior will only make matters worse ("Persistence will lead to evil").

The upper trigram, Sun, signifies a chicken and the lower, Tui, signifies mouth. Hence the image of "a rooster crowing."

The HSIAO KUO Hexagram
(Symbol of Excessive Smallness)

62nd  小過

YANG REPRESENTS WHAT is great, and Yin represents what is small.
The Hsiao Kuo Hexagram has four Yin lines and only two Yang
lines. Hence the idea of excessive smallness or an excess of the
small.

KING WEN'S JUDGMENT ON THE HEXAGRAM:

*The hexagram indicates success and prosperity. There is advantage
to be firm and correct. Small excess could be good with minor matters, not with great matters. The lingering notes of a soaring bird
favor not the upside but the downside. Great good fortune.*

The Hsiao Kuo Hexagram represents a situation in which the
weak or evil elements (the Yin lines) displace or predominate over
the strong or good elements (the Yang lines). Such a time does not
favor the undertaking of great tasks, and the superior man turns
to the cultivation of small things, waiting (according to the Law
of Cyclic Reversion) for a more favorable time to act. This idea is
further reinforced by the fact that the structure of the hexagram
resembles a bird: the two central Yang lines represent the body of
the bird, and the Yin lines on both sides represent the wings. As
a bird soars toward the heavens, the beauty of its notes is left below; so lesser tasks ("the downside") are said to be favored over
greater ones ("the upside").

CONFUCIUS' EXPLANATION OF KING WEN'S JUDGMENT:

The hexagram shows that excess of the small will lead to success and prosperity.

Excess based on firm correctness means action in accord with the times.

The weak obtain the central places. That's why there is good fortune in small matters.

The strong miss their proper places and are not in the center. That's why great tasks should not be undertaken.

There is the symbol of a soaring bird. "The lingering notes of a soaring bird favor not the upside but the downside. Great good fortune." This is because going up is against the natural trend, whereas coming down follows the natural trend.

The first paragraph suggests that the way to success and prosperity is through the intensive cultivation of small matters ("excess of the small"), and even then only when practiced by one who possesses the strength of character to remain firmly on the correct path and avoid the temptations of excess.

Lines 2 and 5 are Yin (small tasks) and each occupies a central position, which always indicates favorable placement for action. Lines 3 and 4 are Yang (great tasks) and neither occupies a central position, which always indicates unfavorable placement for action. All this suggests that circumstances are favorable for small tasks and unfavorable for great ones.

Although aspiration is laudable, there are times when it is impracticable. All tasks must be undertaken in a way that is in accord with the trend of the times.

SYMBOLIC SIGNIFICANCE OF THE HEXAGRAM AS NOTED BY CONFUCIUS:

The idea behind Hsiao Kuo is derived from thunder (upper trigram) above the mountain (lower trigram). The superior man is inspired thereby to be excessively respectful in conduct, excessively sad in mourning, and excessively frugal in expenditure.

Thunder breaks forth from under the earth with a terrific force and noise; but when it encounters the obstruction of a mountain, its force is absorbed and weakened and its noise becomes faint or a small excess. Observing this phenomenon, the superior man learns the wisdom of determining which matters may safely be carried to extremes and which may not. Thus he chooses to be excessively respectful rather than excessively haughty, excessively somber rather than excessively ostentatious in mourning, and excessively frugal rather than excessively extravagant.

DUKE OF CHOU'S EXPLANATION OF THE LINES (a) AND CONFUCIUS' COMMENT THEREON (b):

Line 1, Yin:

(a) *A bird soars high and incurs evil.*

(b) *"A bird soars high and incurs evil." This is something that cannot be helped.*

This Yin line occupies a position neither central nor correct and lies at the beginning of the hexagram. This shows that its subject is a weak young man, just starting out in life, who finds himself in unfavorable circumstances. He should content himself with his lot and make no move to advance. However, he allows himself to be dissatsified with his lot and attempts to soar like a bird and so meets with failure and misfortune. He has no one to blame but himself.

If Line 1 is transformed into Yang, it will make the lower trigram Li, which signifies a pheasant. Hence the image of "a bird soaring."

Line 2, Yin:

(a) *One bypasses his grandfather and meets his grandmother.*

(b) *"He does not go to the king." This means that the minister should not be bypassed.*

Line 2 is supposed to denote a person with a father (Line 3), a grandfather (Line 4), and a grandmother (Line 5). Since this line is naturally attracted to its correlate (Line 5), the subject of Line 2 is said to bypass his grandfather and meet his grandmother. Line

2 also denotes a minor official and fails to form a harmonious relationship with its correlate (Line 5, the ruler). Under such circumstances, it is unwise for him to seek royal favors ("does not go to the king"). However, Line 2 does form a harmonious relationship with the king's chief minister (Line 4), and so its subject deems it better to seek help at the lower level ("the minister should not be bypassed"). Because Line 2 is Yin and occupies a central position, its subject is a modest person who humbly follows a middle course. He is wise enough not to seek royal favor for the moment and so commits no error.

Line 3, Yang:

(a) *One does not make an extra effort to defend himself. Consequently, someone may do him injury. There will be evil.*

(b) *"Consequently, someone may do him injury." What can be done against such evil?*

Line 3 is Yang in a Yang place but does not occupy a central position, signifying a headstrong person who is dissatisfied with his place and tends to go to extremes. Such a man scorns prudence and fails to take precautions to protect himself. Naturally, he encounters misfortune ("There will be evil").

The line is at the base of the upper interior trigram, Tui (Lines 3, 4, 5), which denotes breakage or destruction. Hence the idea of "injury."

Line 4, Yang:

(a) *No error. One does not make an extra effort to cope with a situation. Moving forward will be perilous and must be guarded against. Do not persist in an ever-firm course.*

(b) *"One does not make an extra effort to cope with a situation." This is because one's position is not appropriate. "Moving forward will be perilous and must be guarded against." This means that to the end the forward move cannot make any headway.*

This Yang line occupies a position neither central nor correct, denoting a strong man, highly disposed to act, who is surrounded by unfavorable circumstances. Therefore, any forward move he makes is bound to meet with failure. He can only avoid error or blame if he gives up his ambitions ("an ever-firm course") and avoids making any forward move; he should stay low or aim at the downside.

Line 5, Yin:

(a) *Dense clouds spread from one's western border, but there is no rain. The duke shoots and gets a bird in a cave.*

(b) *"Dense clouds but no rain." The clouds have already risen high.*

Here, Line 5 (the ruler) is Yin and occupies a central position, indicating a sensible man of moderate ambition who faithfully follows the middle way. However, this line fails to form a harmonious relationship with its correlate (Line 2) and so he does not receive much support from those below. Although he is an able leader, the present situation makes it difficult for him to accomplish much. Therefore, he should not set his aim too high. Instead, he should prefer the downside to the upside, and confine his success to small matters. Symbolically, he should shoot at a bird in a cave rather than one in the sky. If his ambitions are too high, they cannot be realized, just as clouds rising high will vanish in the upper atmosphere and cannot dissolve as rain.

Line 6, Yin:

(a) *One does not cope with a situation reasonably, but in excess of his capacity. A bird flies away from its nest. There will be evil. This is what may be called disaster or self-inflicted injury.*

(b) *"One does not cope with a situation reasonably, but in excess of his capacity." This already shows arrogance.*

This is a Yin line in a Yin place and lies at the extreme top of the hexagram. Its subject is not a bright or able man, yet he is haughty and arrogant. He does not stop to consider his resources before acting and often attempts great tasks which are far beyond his capacities. He is like a bird which leaves its nest and soars into the unknown. This can only lead to disaster.

The CHI CHI Hexagram
(Symbol of Successful Fulfillment)

63rd  既濟

In the Chi Chi Hexagram, every line occupies its correct place (Yin lines in Yin places, Yang lines in Yang places) and forms a harmonious relationship with its correlate (Lines 1 and 4, 2 and 5, 3 and 6). Every element in the entire hexagram is therefore said to be in its ideal position. In other words, perfection has been attained. Hence the idea of successful fulfillment.

Water (the upper trigram, K'an) sinks down, and fire (the lower trigram, Li) flames up. When water is placed over fire, they cooperate to cook food. Thus they are said to successfully fulfill their purpose.

KING WEN'S JUDGMENT ON THE HEXAGRAM:

The hexagram indicates success and prosperity in minor matters. There is advantage in being firm and correct. At the beginning, good fortune; in the end, confusion.

According to the Law of Cyclic Reversion, any extreme is followed by and brings about its opposite, just as the heat of summer is followed by the cold of winter and winter by summer again. The pinnacle of success represented by the fulfillment of any goal or action cannot be sustained forever and must inevitably be followed by diminishment ("in the end, confusion"). Therefore, one should, after attaining success, take care to remain firmly on the correct course, preserving and consolidating one's gains, so that they may remain on a high level for as long as possible. Any move to advance should be made only on a small scale.

CONFUCIUS' EXPLANATION OF KING WEN'S JUDGMENT:

"The hexagram indicates success and prosperity"; that is to say, in minor matters.

"There is advantage in being firm and correct." This is because the strong and the weak are in their correct places and occupy their proper positions.

"At the beginning, good fortune." This means the weak has obtained the central place.

"Eventual end is followed by confusion." This shows the course has exhausted its possibilities.

In a time of successful fulfillment, so much has been accomplished that only minor successes are still possible. All the lines occupy their correct places, suggesting the wisdom of remaining firmly on a correct course, no matter what the temptations.

Although Line 2 is weak (Yin), it occupies a central position and finds a harmonious correlate in the ruler (Line 5), advantages that suggest the beginning of good fortune.

Line 6 is also Yin and occupies the top extreme of the hexagram, suggesting a situation that has run its course, resulting in disorganization ("confusion").

SYMBOLIC SIGNIFICANCE OF THE HEXAGRAM AS NOTED BY CONFUCIUS:

The idea behind Chi Chi is derived from water over fire. The superior man is inspired thereby to anticipate troubles and try to prevent them.

Fire and water in association fulfill a number of very important functions: when they cooperate, they create nourishment by cooking food; when antagonistic, water can extinguish a destructive fire, and fire can dry out and warm something wet and cold. Observing these phenomena, the superior man learns that advantages may be followed by disadvantages, and that there is wisdom in anticipating difficulties and trying to plan for their prevention.

DUKE OF CHOU'S EXPLANATION OF THE LINES *(a)* AND CONFUCIUS' COMMENT THEREON *(b)*:

Line 1, Yang:

(a) *The wheels are pulled back. A tail gets immersed in water. There will be no error.*

(b) *"The wheels are pulled back." This shows that there ought to be no error.*

The first line of this hexagram represents a young man who is at the beginning of his career and should prepare carefully before acting. However, here, Line 1 is also Yang in a Yang place and fails to occupy a central position, indicating a strong-willed young man in unfavorable circumstances, eager to advance, who is prone to go to extremes. He should be prudent and remain in his present position ("wheels are pulled back"), making careful preparation before moving ahead. If he is rash enough to try, he is sure to meet with misfortune ("A tail gets immersed in water").

Line 2, Yin:

(a) *A housewife has lost the back curtain of her carriage. She need not seek it. She will recover it in seven days.*

(b) *"She will recover it in seven days." This is due to her middle course.*

Line 2 is Yin and occupies a position both central and correct. Its subject is a humble, modest person who follows a middle course, but hesitates to advance due to a gentle disposition. Since Yin is traditionally associated with the female, he is compared to a woman who "has lost the back curtain of her carriage." She can advance, but the loss deters her from doing so. In traditional China, a woman had to be sheltered from sight when appearing outdoors. Thus, the loss of a curtain meant turning back for a replacement unless one could be found nearby.

Seven has always been considered an important number in the world's spiritual traditions: symbolically, the completion of a cycle when triumphant and a return to the original condition, to begin over again. Hence the image, "recover it in seven days."

As the second line of the lower trigram, Li, this line denotes a second daughter. Hence the image of "a housewife."

Line 3, Yang:

(a) *Kao Tsung led a punitive campaign against the barbarian region. It took three years to subdue the enemy. Mean people should not be employed.*

(b) *"It took three years to subdue the enemy." This indicates weariness.*

This line is Yang in a Yang place and forms a harmonious relationship with its correlate (Line 6). In addition, it lies on the border or frontier between two trigrams whose contact symbolizes fulfillment. This indicates that its subject is a dynamic personality who enjoys friendly support and has already achieved some important success. However, this success was not without cost, because Line 3 fails to occupy a central place, which suggests that its position is being subverted by those of mean character. His success, therefore, is likened to that of Kao Tsung, a noted emperor of the Shang dynasty, who subdued the barbarian region after a wearying campaign of three years and was opposed by corrupt politicians in his own court.

Line 4, Yin:

(a) *Rags are available to plug possible leaks. One should be on the alert the whole day.*

(b) *"One should be on the alert the whole day." This shows that one is in doubt about something.*

Line 4 (the minister) is Yin in a Yin place and forms a harmonious relationship with its correlate (Line 1), signifying an obedient person who is loyal to his ruler (Line 5) and enjoys popular support. However, the line is placed at the bottom of one trigram and just above another, indicating a stage of transition during which new developments threaten the success its subject has already achieved. Fortunately, the minister is a conscientious and loyal person who is wise enough to take precautions against possible future difficulties ("plug possible leaks") and unforeseen circumstances.

Line 5, Yang:

(a) *The eastern neighbor's sacrifice of a slaughtered ox is not as good as the meager spring sacrifice offered by the western neighbor. The latter will receive the actual blessing.*

(b) *"The eastern neighbor's sacrifice of a slaughtered ox is not as good as the timely sacrifice offered by the western neighbor. The latter will receive the actual blessing."* This indicates that immense good fortune is approaching.

Line 5 (the ruler) is Yang and occupies a position both central and correct. In addition, it forms a harmonious relationship with its correlate (Line 2), so its subject is a wise and able ruler who is well liked by the people. As the entire hexagram symbolizes perfection and fulfillment, Line 5 may well represent the peak of success, just as Line 6 represents the anticlimax. Remembering the law of Cyclic Reversion, that after perfect success there will be a setback, the ruler is wise enough to realize that he should be satisfied with minor success instead of continuing to embark upon great ventures. As indicated in his central position, he is a man of sincerity and reverence, so great good fortune is in store for him.

Line 6, Yin:

(a) *One's head is immersed in water. There will be grave evil.*

(b) *"One's head is immersed in water."* How can this last long?

This line is Yin in a Yin place and lies at the extreme top of the hexagram. Its subject is a weak and ignorant man, prone to go to extremes, who has passed the peak of his success. Such a man will naturally get himself into serious difficulty and does not know what to do next (his "head is immersed in water"). This is the "eventual confusion" mentioned in King Wen's Judgment.

The WEI CHI Hexagram
(Symbol of Incomplete Fulfillment)

64th  未濟

FIRE FLAMES UP; water flows downward. Here, fire (the upper trigram, Li) is set above water (the lower trigram, K'an). The meaning of the hexagram is the opposite of that of the preceding Chi Chi Hexagram, in which fire is set below water and the two are said to meet in beneficial cooperation, successfully fulfilling their purposes in boiling water for the preparation of food.

In the Wei Chi Hexagram, fire is set above water, and since the two move in opposite directions, they do not meet or have not yet met to cooperate and successfully fulfill their purpose. Hence the idea of incomplete fulfillment or prefulfillment.

KING WEN'S JUDGMENT ON THE HEXAGRAM:

The hexagram indicates success and prosperity. A little fox has almost crossed a stream, when its tail gets immersed in the water. There cannot possibly be any advantage.

Incomplete fulfillment is not necessarily an evil, but may be an intermediate stage toward successful fulfillment. Therefore, a time of incomplete fulfillment is not an ill omen, but an auspicious one. However, success and prosperity must be prepared for carefully. They cannot be rushed or hastened. To try to force one's way through a time of incomplete fulfillment can only end ingloriously ("its tail gets immersed in the water").

Foxes have heavy tails which become heavier when wet and so constitute a source of danger to a little fox, suggesting the image of "a tail immersed in the water" working to his disadvantage.

411

CONFUCIUS' EXPLANATION OF KING WEN'S JUDGMENT:

"The hexagram indicates success and prosperity." This is because the weak has obtained the central place.

"A little fox has almost crossed a stream." This shows it has not yet emerged from the midst of danger. *"Its tail gets immersed in the water. There cannot possibly be any advantage."* This means it has not pursued its purpose to the end. Though the strong and the weak are not in their proper places, they are harmoniously correlated.

Line 5 is weak (Yin) and occupies a central place, signifying a wise and gentle ruler, a queen (or Yin person) who follows a middle course. Such a ruler will surely find the successful fulfillment of her aspirations ("success and prosperity").

"A little fox" who "has almost crossed a stream" aptly symbolizes incomplete fulfillment or prefulfillment. That there is still some difficulty to overcome is suggested by the fact that all three Yang lines ("the strong") and all three Yin lines ("the weak") fail to occupy their correct places. However, the fact that every line finds a harmonious correlate indicates that cooperation offers a potential way to avoid difficulty and ensure good fortune.

SYMBOLIC SIGNIFICANCE OF THE HEXAGRAM AS NOTED BY CONFUCIUS:

The idea behind Wei Chi is derived from fire over water. The superior man is inspired thereby to discriminate between good and evil among things so that everything will be in its proper place.

Fire and water moving away from each other do not meet and fulfill their purposes. To the superior man this suggests the wisdom of determining the nature of things, so that each may be assigned the correct place to fulfill its purposes. It also suggests good and evil, which move in opposite directions, and the necessity for discriminating between them, so that they too can be consigned to their proper places.

DUKE OF CHOU'S EXPLANATION OF THE LINES (a) AND CONFUCIUS' COMMENT THEREON (b):

Line 1, Yin:

(a) *A tail gets immersed in water. There will be regret.*

(b) *"A tail gets immersed in water." This indicates crass ignorance.*

This is a Yin line at the beginning of a hexagram and occupies a position neither central nor correct. Its subject is a weak, inexperienced person who is just starting out in life and finds himself in an unfavorable situation from which to advance. Under such circumstances, for him to attempt to fulfill his ambitions would be the peak of ignorance and would only lead to peril ("a tail immersed in water").

Line 2, Yang:

(a) *Its wheels are pulled back. Firm correctness will lead to good fortune.*

(b) *"The good fortune stemming from firm correctness," indicated in Line 2, Yang, is due to correct action from a central position.*

Line 2 is Yang and occupies the central position of the lower trigram, K'an (danger). Its subject is a wise and sensible person who follows a middle course; so when he finds himself in the midst of danger, he refrains from unnecessary risks, like a chariot driver pulling back the wheels from some obstacle. Such a wise and cautious course can only lead to the successful fulfillment of his goal.

Line 3, Yin:

(a) *The situation is not yet favorable for any fulfillment. Ventures will incur evil. There will be advantage in crossing the great stream.*

(b) *"The situation is not yet favorable for any fulfillment. Ventures will incur evil." This is because the position is not a proper one.*

This line is Yin and occupies a position neither central nor correct. In addition, it rests at the top of the lower trigram, K'an (danger). Its subject is a weak person who finds himself faced with adversity and sees no hope in sight. Such a situation is not an advantageous one from which to fulfill his goals. If he ventures forward, misery will be his lot.

(The Chinese word for "not" seems to have been omitted in the third sentence in (a), here translated as "There will be advantage in crossing the great stream." As it now stands, it is in conflict with the preceding sentence.)

Line 4, Yang:

(a) *There will be good fortune in being firm and correct. Regret will disappear. If one rouses himself to lead a punitive campaign against the barbarian region, in three years he will receive rewards from a great country.*

(b) *"There will be good fortune in being firm and correct. Regret will disappear." This means one's aspirations are being realized.*

Line 4 (the minister) lies just outside the lower trigram, K'an, which signifies danger ("the barbarian region"). In addition, it occupies a position neither central nor correct (Yang in a Yin place), indicating an unfavorable situation from which to advance or take action. However, Line 4 is Yang and forms a harmonious relationship with its correlate (Line 1), and so its subject is a strong minister who enjoys the support of those below. Though the task may be an arduous one ("three years"), if he proceeds carefully, remaining on the correct course, he will be able to overcome or dispel danger ("rouses himself to lead a punitive campaign"). This may involve considerable hardship and time; but if he firmly follows the correct course, he will successfully fulfill his aspirations and meet with the good fortune he deserves.

Line 5, Yin:

(a) *Firm correctness will lead to good fortune. There will be no regret. The light of the superior man shines forth with sincerity. Good fortune.*

(b) *"The light of the superior man." Its diffusion is conducive to good fortune.*

Here, Line 5 (the ruler) is Yin, occupies a central position, and forms a harmonious relationship with its correlate (Line 2). In addition, it lies in the middle of the trigram Li (light). Its subject is a gentle, enlightened king or ruler ("the superior man") whose sincerity and benevolence have earned him the loyalty and support of the people. In other words, he has diffused his light upon them.

Naturally, such a man enjoys good fortune and the successful fulfillment of his goals. He will have no cause for regret.

Line 6, Yang:

(a) *One drinks wine with sincere regard for his capacity. There will be no error. One gets his head immersed in water. His sincerity has been transgressed.*

(b) *One drinks wine and becomes sodden-headed. This indeed shows ignorance of restraint.*

This Yang line, lying at the extreme top of the hexagram, suggests that the time of incomplete fulfillment or failure is on the wane, and that (according to the Law of Cyclic Reversion) the time of fulfillment is at hand. The line's subject, therefore, is in an optimistic mood and celebrates ("drinks wine") this change in the tide of events. As long as he is wise enough to avoid excess ("regard for his capacity") he will avoid error. However, if he does not possess self-restraint and becomes "sodden-headed," his lack of sincerity and character will be revealed. If one is overly joyful and careless when the prospect of success is approaching, he may miss his goal within an ace of fulfillment.

PREFACE
1. John Blofeld, tr., *I-Ching* (New York: Dutton, 1968) (paper), p. 17.
2. James Legge, tr., *The Yi King*, included in *The Sacred Books of the East*, Vol. XVI (Oxford: The Clarendon Press, 1899), p. 59.
3. Ibid., p. 43.
4. Ibid., p. 42.
5. Blofeld, op. cit., p. 25.
6. Ibid., p. 90.
7. Ibid., p. 127.
8. Wei Tat, *An Exposition of the I-Ching* (Hong Kong, 1977), pp. 247–264, 511–518.
9. Legge, op. cit., pp. xiii–xiv, 2, 8.

PART I
CHAPTER 1
1. *Ta Chuan (Great Treatise)*, Sect. II, Chapt. 2.
2. Ibid., Sect. I, Chapt. 11.
3. James Legge, tr., *The Yi King*, pp. 12–13.
4. *Ta Chuan*, Sect. I, Chapt. 11.
5. *Shu Ching (Book of History)*, Book V, Chapt. 22, cited in Legge, op. cit., p. 14.
6. *Lun Yu (Confucian Analects)*, Book IX, Chapt. 8.
7. Legge, op. cit., p. 15.
8. Richard Wilhelm and Cary F. Baynes, tr., *The I-Ching* (Princeton: Princeton Univ. Press, 1971), pp. 309–310.
9. Wei Tat, *An Exposition of the I-Ching*, pp. 29–33.
10. Paul Carus, *Chinese Philosophy* (Chicago: Open Court Pub. Co., 1896), p. 18.
11. Wei, op. cit., pp. 58–59.
12. Legge, op. cit., p. 18.
13. Ibid., p. 33.
14. *Shuo Kua Chuan (Treatise on Remarks about Trigrams)*, Chapt. 10.

CHAPTER 2
1. Wei Tat, *An Exposition of the I-Ching*, pp. 51–54.
2. James Legge, tr., *The Yi King*, p. xviii.
3. *Shuo Kua Chuan (Treatise on Remarks about Trigrams)*, Chapt. 2.
4. Legge, op. cit., p. 424.

5. Ibid., p. 14.
6. Wei, op. cit., p. 50.
7. Ibid., p. 46.
8. Legge, op. cit., p. 37.
9. Ibid., p. 13.

CHAPTER 3

1. *Ta Chuan (Great Treatise)*, Sect. I, Chapt. 11.
2. James Legge, tr., *Shu Ching (Book of History)*, Book IV, Chapt. 11.
3. James Legge, tr., *The Yi King*, p. 36.
4. Ibid., p. 21.
5. Wei Tat, *An Exposition of the I-Ching*, pp. 68–69.
6. Legge, op. cit., p. 21.
7. Ibid., p. 22.

CHAPTER 4

1. James Legge, tr., *The Yi King*, p. 8.
2. Ibid., pp. 29–30.
3. *Lun Yu, (Confucian Analects)*, Book VII, Chapt. 17.
4. Legge, op. cit., p. 30.
5. Ibid., p. 29.
6. Ibid., p. 32.
7. Ibid., p. 43.
8. Richard Wilhelm and Cary F. Baynes, tr., *The I-Ching*, pp. lvi, 297.
9. Legge, op. cit., p. 47.
10. Ibid., p. 47.
11. G. P. Fedotov, ed., *A Treasury of Russian Spirituality* (New York: Harper & Row, 1965), p. 447.
12. Legge, op. cit., p. 1.
13. *Lun Yu*, Book VII, Chapt. 18.
14. Ibid., Book II, Chapt. 4.
15. "Biography of Confucius," *Shih Chi* (Historical Records).
16. *Lun Yu*, Book XI, Chapt. 8.
17. Ibid., Book XIII, Chapt. 22.
18. Ibid., Book III, Chapt. 14.
19. *Li Chi (Records of Rites and Ceremonies)*, Book XXIII, Chapt. 1.
20. *Lun Yu*, Book VIII, Chapt. 20.
21. Ibid., Book VIII, Chapt. 11.
22. Ibid., Book VII, Chapt. 5.
23. Legge, op. cit., p. 55.
24. Wei Tat, *An Exposition of the I-Ching*, pp. 87–88.

CHAPTER 5

1. *Ta Chuan (Great Treatise)*, Sect. I, Chapt. 11.
2. Henry Wei, *The Guiding Light of Lao Tzu* (Wheaton: Theosophical Publishing House, 1982), pp. 81–84.
3. *Ta Chuan*, Sect. II, Chapt. 4.
4. Wei Tat, *An Exposition of the I-Ching*, pp. xxx, 152, 167, 177, 191, 208, 218.
5. *Shuo Kua Chuan (Treatise on Remarks about Trigrams)*, Chapt. 2.
6. Richard Wilhelm and Cary F. Baynes, tr., *The I-Ching*, p. liv.
7. *Ta Chuan*, Sect. I, Chapt. 3.
8. Ibid., Sect. II, Chapt. 5.

CHAPTER 6

1. *Ta Chuan (Great Treatise)*, Sect. I, Chapt. 11.
2. James Legge, tr., *Shu Ching (Book of History)*, Chapt. 2.
3. *Ta Chuan*, Sect. I, Chapt. 11.
4. *Chung Yung (The Golden Mean)*, Book VIII, Chapt. 24.
5. *Ta Chuan*, Sect. I, Chapt. 10.
6. Ibid., Sect. I, Chapt. 2.
7. Ibid., Sect. I, Chapt. 10.
8. Richard Wilhelm and Cary F. Baynes, tr., *The I-Ching*, pp. xxviii ff.
9. Wei Tat, *An Exposition of the I-Ching*, pp. 49 ff.

About the Author

Born and brought up in China, Henry Wei is an honor graduate of Lingnan University, Canton, where he studied Western and Chinese literature. Afterward, he came to the United States to study international relations at the University of Chicago, where he received his M.A. and Ph.D. degrees. He wrote his doctoral dissertation on *The Sino-Japanese Hostilities and International Law* (distributed on microfilm by the University).

Since leaving Chicago, he has lectured extensively and done considerable research in Chinese history and culture. In addition to a number of monographs, he has had two major works published: one in the field of international relations, *China and Soviet Russia*; the other on Chinese philosophy, *The Guiding Light of Lao Tzu*.

Dr. Wei considers the *I-Ching* the most wonderful and mysterious book he has ever read, and regards this translation and commentary as his major literary achievement. Though well advanced in years, Dr. Wei is still intellectually active and continues his research in Chinese philosophy.